Poverty Alleviation and Targeted Measures

Sangui Wang

Poverty Alleviation and Targeted Measures

Theory and Practice

中国财经出版传媒集团
经济科学出版社
Economic Science Press

Springer

Sangui Wang
School of Agriculture and Rural
Development
Renmin University of China
Beijing, China

Translated by
Xiaowei Chen
Department of English, School of Foreign
Languages
Fuzhou University
Fuzhou, China

ISBN 978-981-96-1492-9 ISBN 978-981-96-1493-6 (eBook)
https://doi.org/10.1007/978-981-96-1493-6

Jointly published with Economic Science Press
The print edition is not for sale in the Chinese Mainland. Customers from the Chinese Mainland please order the print book from Economic Science Press.
ISBN of the Co-Publisher's edition: 978-7-5218-1891-8

This Springer imprint is published by the registered company Springer Nature Singapore Pte Ltd.
The registered company address is: 152 Beach Road, #21-01/04 Gateway East, Singapore 189721, Singapore

Preface

In 2011, the Chinese government formulated the Outline for Development-Driven Poverty Alleviation in Rural Areas (2011–2020), stipulating the overall goal that "Through 2020, poor people living in rural areas will be assured of adequate food and clothing, and their access to compulsory education, basic medical services and safe housing will be guaranteed. Their per capita net income will increase at a higher rate than the national average, with indicators in major areas of basic public services approaching the national average, in an attempt to narrow the gap of development." In November 2013, the CPC General Secretary Xi Jinping put forward the idea of "targeted poverty alleviation" as the basic strategy for the final battle against poverty at the present stage during his inspection tour of western Hunan Province.

In November 2015, the CPC Central Committee and the State Council made Decision on Winning the Battle Against Extreme Poverty; and in 2017 the 19th CPC National Congress set poverty alleviation as one of the critical battles for building a moderately prosperous society in all respects. To lift poor people out of poverty with targeted efforts has become a major strategic task that the whole Party and people must accomplish through 2020, which is also the key to a society of moderate prosperity for all. The recent years have seen governments at all levels joining hands with market and social organizations, under a mechanism of defined responsibilities with the central government making overarching plans, provincial authorities taking overall responsibility, and city and county authorities overseeing implementation, to participate in the hard work of poverty alleviation, which has scored notable achievements.

This book is an attempt to have a systematic review of China's epic-like practice of poverty alleviation, which has been the most extensive in human history. First, it starts with an overview of the background of poverty alleviation to give a general account of why China launched the must-win battle against extreme poverty, especially the significance of eliminating absolute poverty through 2020. Second, there is a systematic analysis of organizational and policy systems crucial to poverty reduction, a presentation about how the practice has been carried out, particularly what a vital role the Chinese system has been playing in this great endeavor. At the same time, good practices will be introduced to explain how policies of targeted poverty alleviation are implemented in the tough battle to help readers better understand the precise philosophy of poverty alleviation and targeted measures. Third, the outcomes of China's efforts against poverty are closely looked at from different dimensions, presenting to readers not only China's substantial achievements in poverty reduction, but also consequent positive impacts on various aspects of economy and society so that there may be better public awareness and more support for the nation-wide battle. Fourth, it focuses on how to strive towards rural revitalization after the victory over extreme poverty and what may happen during the process. The relative poverty will be discussed together with possible solutions.

Professor Wang Sangui, Director of China Anti-Poverty Research Institute, Renmin University of China, co-authored the book with his team members, including Hu Jun, Zhou Yuanxiang, Feng Zixi, Sun Junna, Zeng Xiaoxi, Bai Zengbo, Jin Xiaojie and Ma Lan. Professor Wang has committed himself to poverty studies for more than 30 years, with findings such as the mechanism of poverty and development approaches in severely impoverished areas, China's extensive poverty reduction efforts, driving forces and institutional factors, and systematic analysis of CPC General Secretary Xi Jinping's thoughts and practices on targeted poverty alleviation. He is also known for his prospective studies on strategies of urban-rural integration to end poverty in China.

All constructive criticisms and suggestions are welcome.

Beijing, China
October 2020

Sangui Wang

Contents

Chapter 1
Winning the Battle Against Extreme Poverty to Achieve Moderate Prosperity for All

China is the world's largest developing country. Since the start of the reform and opening up in 1978, the Communist Party of China (CPC) and Chinese government have attached great importance to development-driven poverty alleviation. From the introduction of household contract responsibility system in 1978, the setting up of top-down leading groups to alleviate poverty at all levels to the releasing of the National Seven-Year Poverty Alleviation Program (1994–2000) and The Outline for Development-Driven Poverty Alleviation in Rural Areas for two ten-year periods, one from 2001 to 2010 and the other from 2011 to 2020, the Chinese government has been committed to the great endeavor step by step in the three aspects of institutional building, organizational support and development planning. With remarkable achievements, China has made notable contributions to the mission of poverty eradication and offered China's vision and approaches to the world.

To complete the building of a moderately prosperous society in all respects and achieve the First Centenary Goal through 2020 is a solemn commitment made by the Communist Party of China to the Chinese people. A key task and defining indicator in attaining the goal is lifting all rural poor out of poverty by the existing standard, with all poor counties being removed of the label, and eliminating overall regional poverty. To this end, we must make greater efforts, take more effective measures and mobilize all resources to overcome difficulties and win the battle, with the final goal to ensure that poor areas and impoverished people will enter the moderately prosperous society together with the rest of the country.

1.1 Backdrop of the Battle Against Extreme Poverty

Poverty is a constant concern and a common challenge to the economic and social development of all countries in the world. As a major issue and immense task faced by all mankind, lifting more people out of poverty has always been the goal of all

S. Wang, *Poverty Alleviation and Targeted Measures*,
https://doi.org/10.1007/978-981-96-1493-6_1

countries and governments. The adoption of the United Nations (UN) Millennium Declaration in 2000 and the 2030 Agenda for Sustainable Development in 2015 has provided an overall development framework for countries around the world, with clear targets and timeframes, as well as guidelines for the progress in accelerating global poverty alleviation and improving basic public services and the environment.

As the largest developing country in the world, China has a large population base, taking up a large proportion in that of the world, with a large absolute number of people living in poverty. This means that China's poverty alleviation outcomes will have a lasting and far-reaching impact on the international poverty reduction situation and scenario. Since the formulation of the Millennium Development Goals (MDGs), China has been committed to poverty alleviation while adhering to reform and economic development. Its anti-poverty policies have been constantly adjusted in response to the changing situation. By 2015 when the MDGs was due, China had largely fulfilled the goals, doing far better than the rest of the world and making an impressive contribution to global poverty reduction. Carrying on an ambitious post-2015 development agenda, China has made historic progress in poverty reduction under the guidance of Xi Jinping's theory concerned, which has given a strong boost to the global anti-poverty endeavor. However, the remaining people of extreme poverty in some impoverished regions in China means that the battle is a tough one to win. The goal of completing the building of a society of moderate prosperity for all is around the corner, with tight schedule and heavy tasks. We must make strenuous efforts to win the final battle against poverty to ensure that all the people in China join hands for a well-off society in an all-round way.

1.1.1 Global Goals to Eradicate Poverty in All Its Forms

At the UN General Assembly held in September 2000, 191 member states unanimously agreed and adopted a plan of action to halve global poverty by 2015 (based on the level of 1990). At the UN Millennium Summit, 189 countries signed the UN Millennium Declaration, making it a momentum goal with official commitment. Framing a wide-ranging vision, the Declaration formulated a blueprint of human development, containing the MDGs with poverty reduction as the major concern. It stated that "We will spare no effort to free our fellow men, women and children from the abject and dehumanizing conditions of extreme poverty, to which more than a billion of them are currently subjected. We are committed to making the right to development a reality for everyone and to freeing the entire human race from want." And it resolved further that "To halve, by the year 2015, the proportion of the world's people whose income is less than one dollar a day and the proportion of people who suffer from hunger and, by the same date, to halve the proportion of people who are unable to reach or to afford safe drinking water."[1]

[1] https://www.un.org/en/development/desa/population/migration/generalassembly/docs/globalcompact/A_RES_55_2.pdf.

2015 was the deadline for achieving the UN Millennium Development Goals. Over the past 15 years, significant progress had been made in the global implementation of the MDGs, which lifted hundreds of millions of people out of poverty to have achieved or nearly achieved the goals of poverty reduction and child mortality. The number of people living in extreme poverty on less than US $1.25 per day fell from 1.9 billion in 1990 to 836 million in 2015, and the extreme poverty rate dropped from nearly 50 to 14% in the same period. However, in spite of all these achievements and the fact that the general goals of MDGs were met, the world was facing profound economic and political changes and new global challenges such as population expansion, shortage of resources, environmental degradation and worsening social inequality. There was an urgent need for the international community to review and redefine the concept of sustainable development, in order to build a new global governance framework and to promote the fundamental transformation of the development onto a sustainable and resilient path.

In September 2015, the UN Sustainable Development Summit was held at the UN Headquarters in New York, with an aim to encourage the international community to continue extensive cooperation in response to the new situation and challenges of human development after the expiration of the MDGs. The 193 member states reached a consensus at the historic event and signed The 2030 Agenda for Sustainable Development, a transformative plan for people and the planet, which includes a set of 17 Sustainable Development Goals (SDGs) and 169 targets to end poverty, fight inequality and injustice, and tackle climate changes through 2030. It is stipulated in the Agenda that "We resolve, between now and 2030, to end poverty and hunger everywhere; to combat inequalities within and among countries; to build peaceful, just and inclusive societies; to protect human rights and promote gender equality and the empowerment of women and girls; and to ensure the lasting protection of the planet and its natural resources. We resolve also to create conditions for sustainable, inclusive and sustained economic growth, shared prosperity and decent work for all, taking into account different levels of national development and capacities." These goals are in line with the requirement of people in both developed and developing countries and the agenda promises that "As we embark on this collective journey, we pledge that no one will be left behind." Among all goals, the one that comes first is to "end poverty and hunger, in all their forms and dimensions, and to ensure that all human beings can fulfill their potential in dignity and equality and in a healthy environment".[2]

The 2030 Agenda for Sustainable Development has established a timeline for achieving the goal of eradicating poverty and hunger in all their forms and dimensions globally, setting targets for mankind to combat extreme poverty. Under the guidance of these sustainable development targets, China has been determined to take its responsibility, making every effort and pooling the wisdom of all its people to lift the poor out of poverty as soon as possible to meet the targets and make its contribution to the global goal of poverty eradication, even though this may mean an immensely

[2] The United Nations [1].

tough challenge given the fact that China is the largest developing country in the world, with a large number of people living in poverty.

1.1.2 Inherent Requirements for China to Build a Moderately Prosperous Society in All Respects

A "moderately prosperous society" or a "well-off society" is the description of an ideal society by ancient Chinese thinkers, showing the pursuit of the general public for an ideal life of affluence and prosperity. The expression "moderate prosperity" (xiaokang), meaning basically "being comfortably off", first appeared in *The Book of Songs* of the Western Zhou Dynasty some 3000 years ago, indicating people's aspiration for a better life. In ancient traditional Chinese culture, Confucianism regarded this as an ideal social model next to "great harmony", a society with clean government and social stability in which people lived and worked in peace and contentment. The Communist Party of China has added a new meaning these days to the expression to refer to a relatively well-off life between subsistence and affluence enjoyed by ordinary people, and regarded it as a phased target of the socialist modernization drive.

Deng Xiaoping, during his meeting with then Japanese Prime Minister Masayoshi Ohira on December 6, 1979, proposed that a well-off society is a new concept of the "Chinese path to modernization." Since then, this thought had been tried out, enriched and developed in the practice of socialist modernization with Chinese characteristics under Deng's leadership. He also proposed a three-step strategic plan on this basis. In 2002, the 16th CPC National Congress set the goal of building a moderately prosperous society in an all-round way through 2020, and defined the specific targets to achieve this in terms of economic, political and cultural progress and sustainable development. In 2007, the 17th CPC National Congress put forward new plans for quickening the step of building a moderately prosperous society in all respects. Based on these efforts, the 18th CPC National Congress in 2012 devised a master blueprint for completing the building of such society through 2020. The attaining of this goal would mark the realization of the first of the Two Centenary Goals[3] of national rejuvenation and was a solemn commitment made by the Communist Party of China to the Chinese people. Completing the great endeavor as scheduled has borne heavily on the fulfillment of the dream of the great rejuvenation of the Chinese nation.

[3] The Two Centenary Goals are to complete the building of a moderately prosperous society in all respects by the time the Communist Party of China marks its centenary in 2021 and to build China into a modern socialist country that is prosperous, strong, democratic, culturally advanced, and harmonious by the time the People's Republic of China celebrates its centenary in 2049.

1.1.2.1 China's Journey Towards Development-Oriented Poverty Alleviation

Poverty has always been the most prominent "weakness" in China's economic and social development and the key to the completion of building a moderately prosperous society in all respects. When visiting needy people in Fuping, Hebei Province, President Xi Jinping talked about the dialectical relationship between achieving the First Centenary Goal and ensuring the people a relatively affluent life in poor areas, pointing out that "With regard to building a society of moderate prosperity for all, the hardest and most arduous tasks lie in the rural areas and the poverty-stricken regions in particular. We cannot say we have realized such a society if the rural areas, especially the backward parts of the countryside, are left behind."[4]

Eliminating poverty, improving people's livelihood and achieving common prosperity step by step are the essential requirements of socialism and an important mission and unswerving goal of the CPC. Before its 18th National Congress in 2012, the CPC had led Chinese people to carry out a planned, extensive and organized government-guided poverty alleviation and development campaign for more than 30 years. Since the start of the reform and opening up, China has accelerated its economic growth, reform and development-oriented poverty alleviation. Adhering to the combination of inclusive and preferential policies, China's anti-poverty and development action has gone through four major stages, each with its distinct characteristics and targeted policies.

The first stage was from 1978 to 1985. This phase featured regional actions to end poverty, when the CPC's work focus shifted to economic development. There was an extensive introduction on a trial basis of the rural household contract responsibility system, which had greatly liberated productive forces and raised labor productivity. This gave impetus to the improvement of the rural income in general and brought about a gratifying outcome. The number of rural people living in poverty decreased from 250 million in 1978 to 125 million in 1985,[5] and the incidence of poverty dropped from 33.7% to 14.8%.

The second stage was from 1986 to 1993. In view of the unbalanced regional development, China started a nationwide reform in which the poverty eradication and development campaign focused on the identification of poverty-stricken counties. On May 16, 1986, the State Council established the Leading Group for Economic Development in Poverty-stricken Areas (renamed in 1993 as the Leading Group for Poverty Elimination and Development), marking the beginning of the establishment of special poverty alleviation institutions to carry out the anti-poverty mission in a planned and organized way. In addition, 331 poor counties were designated for state assistance based on their level of poverty, and a new model of county-based poverty eradication was defined, with a large amount of resources to help reduce poverty.

[4] Institute for Party History and Literature of the CPC Central Committee [2].

[5] In 1985, China's rural poverty standard was RMB206 per capital net income of rural residents.

Thanks to these efforts, the number of rural poor people had decreased from 125 to 70 million,[6] and the poverty incidence dropped by nearly half from 14.8% to 7.7%.

The third stage covered the period from 1994 to 2000. The State Council launched The National Seven-Year Poverty Alleviation Program (1994–2000), China's first ever national poverty elimination program with definite goals, targets, measures and deadlines. It was committed to ensuring that "the basic needs of 80 million impoverished rural residents would be met in the seven years." The number of key counties on the state's poverty alleviation work list was increased to 592 during this period, with continued efforts to carry out county-based poverty alleviation and improve the policy of government-sponsored projects. The impoverished population in rural areas had been reduced to 32.09 million by the end of 2000, and the incidence of poverty down to 3.4%.[7]

The fourth stage was from 2001 to 2012. The State Council issued The Outline for Development-Driven Poverty Alleviation in Rural Areas (2001–2010), with major adjustments to priorities and targets. Upon accurate identification, 148,000 poor villages were selected as targets, and the campaign was launched on the village basis. Thanks to the efforts made during this period, poverty reduction and development continued to make progress. However, due to the substantial raise in poverty standards in rural areas, the number of rural poor rose to 98.99 million by the end of 2012, with a headcount ratio of 10.2%.[8]

1.1.2.2 Strategies of Targeted Poverty Alleviation and Elimination

Over the past 30 years, thanks to the concerted efforts from the CPC leadership and all sectors of society, China has made great achievements in poverty reduction. Agricultural and rural reforms have been further promoted. Widespread poverty in rural areas has been tackled with by efforts of overall elimination of absolute poverty. Disposable income of rural residents has continued to rise and their living standards have been greatly improved towards a more affluent and balanced life. According to the current rural poverty standards, the number of needy people in rural areas dropped from 770 million at the end of 1978 to 98.99 million at the end of 2012, and the incidence of poverty dropped from 97.5 to 10.2%. China reduced the largest number of people living in poverty in the world and was the first country to complete the United Nations Millennium Development Goals.

However, with the changes of the overall macroeconomic environment, especially the new normal of economic development and the widening of income distribution inequality, the rural poverty alleviation campaign focusing on regional development

---

[6] China's rural poverty standard in 1994 was adjusted to RMB440 per capita net income of rural residents.

[7] China's rural poverty standard in 2000 was adjusted to RMB625 per capita net income of rural residents.

[8] The adjusted poverty standard in 2011 was RMB2300 per capita net income of rural residents (at fixed prices of 2010), up 81% from RMB1274 in 2010. According to the new rural poverty standard, the number of rural poor increased to 165 million at the end of 2010.

had deviated from the target with unsatisfactory outcomes. China's poverty reduction efforts were still facing tough challenges. There were still nearly 100 million poor rural people in China and most lived in extreme poverty in remote old revolutionary bases, ethnic minority areas, border or ecologically fragile areas, where the natural conditions were harsh and the cost for poverty reduction higher which made it more difficult to get them out of poverty. In terms of group distribution, the remaining needy population mainly consisted of the disabled, the elderly, the chronically ill and other kinds of jobless people who, in their incapacity to help themselves, were unable to get out of poverty by their own efforts, as well as those who did not receive much education and lacked in basic skills. In terms of the development environment, the economic situation was more complicated, with greater downward pressure and the bigger divergence of regional economic development, posing new challenges to narrowing the development gap between poor areas and other parts of the country. Things had been getting worse because of the weak county-level financial resources, major infrastructure bottlenecks, insufficient supply of basic public services and stagnant industrial development with simple structure in poor areas. The tighter environmental constraints had also ruled out the extensive resource development model. There were limited chances of employment for the poor which made it difficult to transfer employment and increase their incomes.

To address these tough issues of extreme poverty when the benefits brought about by economic development were diminishing, the possible way out was to have timely adjustment of strategies and try out new measures to get rid of poverty. We may say that China's poverty alleviation and development campaign had entered the toughest stage of daunting challenges and obstacles.

In the face of the pressing situation, the CPC central committee, with Xi Jinping as the core, has shouldered the responsibility of building a moderately prosperous society for all since the 18th CPC National Congress. Poverty alleviation and development has been given a prominent position in the governance of the country and the realization of the first Centenary Goal. The central leadership has made the task a key part of the Five-sphere Integrated Plan development of socialism with Chinese characteristics encompassing economic, political, cultural, and the Four-pronged Comprehensive Strategy.[9] A series of major policies were rolled out for the nationwide battle against extreme poverty, with more investment made and innovative measures taken. In November 2013, on his inspection tour of Shibadong Village, Huayuan County, Xiangxi Prefecture of Hunan Province, Xi proposed for the first time the concept of "targeted poverty alleviation", stating that "We should take a realistic attitude towards poverty alleviation and adapt measures in line with local conditions. We should take targeted approaches to alleviate poverty, and guard against empty talk or setting goals beyond our reach."[10] Since then, Xi has either

[9] The Five-sphere Integrated Plan is to promote coordinated economic, political, cultural, social, and ecological advancement. The Four-pronged Comprehensive Strategy is to make comprehensive moves to finish building a moderately prosperous society in all respects, deepen reform, advance law-based governance, and strengthen Party self-governance.

[10] Xi [3].

spoken or written on many important occasions about what it means by targeted poverty alleviation and how to carry it out. In June 2015 when Xi Jinping was on another inspection tour of Guizhou, where poverty was most widespread and most severe, he met with leading members of Party committees at different levels of the province and delivered a speech. He said, "Our work should focus more on targeted poverty alleviation and elimination,"[11] making it clear that poverty relief involves targeted efforts on both alleviation and elimination and the two aspects should be closely integrated. He also talked about six elements of targeted poverty alleviation, namely: (1) institutional innovations are required to ensure that the recipients are those in need; (2) the projects are adapted to the eligible recipients; (3) the funds are effectively used; (4) appropriate measures are taken for individual households; (5) capable officials (acting as first Party secretaries) are dispatched to individual villages; and (6) poverty alleviation outcomes reach expectations. These theoretical thoughts, enriched and modified with the times, have become guidelines for targeted poverty alleviation in China's new era.

1.1.3 An All-Out Campaign Against Poverty

In October 2015, the fifth Plenary Session of the 18th CPC Central Committee was held, at which the target of "poverty elimination" was set in place of "poverty alleviation", with the aim to achieve the First Centenary Goal of building a society of moderate prosperity for all, making it clear that through 2020, all poor rural residents living below the current poverty line would be lifted out of poverty, all poor counties get rid of poverty and the overall regional poverty is eliminated as scheduled. In November 2015, the CPC Central Committee and the State Council pointed out in the Decisions on Winning the Battle against Extreme Poverty that "development-driven poverty alleviation concerns the building of a moderately prosperous society and the well-being of the people. It is of paramount importance to the consolidation of the Party's foundation for governance, China's long-term peace and stability, and its international image. Winning the battle against extreme poverty is a major approach to enable all people to share in the fruits of reform and development to achieve common prosperity. It is a defining indicator of the strength of the socialist system with Chinese characteristics, and an important way to expand domestic demand and boost economic growth under the new normal. Party committees and governments at all levels must make development-oriented poverty alleviation a major political task, enhance their sense of responsibility, mission and urgency, and effectively address problems like lack of awareness of the importance of the issue, inadequate institutional mechanisms, and superficial implementation of work measures. We should live up to our mission and our responsibilities, seize every moment to work hard, and accelerate efforts to improve this major area of weakness for the development of a

[11] Institute for Party History and Literature of the CPC Central Committee [2].

moderately prosperous society in all respects, so that no region or ethnic group will be left behind."

Guided by the central leadership, China's battle against extreme poverty was launched in full swing. Efforts and resources nationwide and Party-wide have been mobilized to ensure that all levels of Party committees and governments have clearly defined responsibilities to take on and set goals to reach. To make sure their commitments are fulfilled, written pledges are signed, and an annual report and monitoring system has been established. The State Council leading group for poverty alleviation and development should report to the CPC Central Committee and the State Council on departments and regions that fail to implement poverty reduction and make suggestions for accountability, and introduce the practice of admonition for Party and government officials in charge of provinces, autonomous regions and municipalities that fail to fulfill their annual poverty reduction tasks. At the same time, the provinces exercise supervision and accountability over cities (prefectures), counties, townships and villages, creating a dynamic mechanism in which Party secretaries at the five levels take on responsibilities for poverty elimination and the whole Party has been making joint efforts. In response to the "four key issues in poverty alleviation", concerning how to identify the people that need help (who needs help), who should do the work of poverty alleviation (who provides help), how this work should be carried out (how to help), and what standards and procedures should be adopted to remove those who have been lifted out of poverty from the poverty list, innovative and effective "Five Measures" have been taken to address them, including: (1) boosting the economy to create more jobs for the disadvantaged; (2) relocating those living under adverse natural conditions; (3) providing eco-jobs for the poor; (4) improving education in poor areas; and (5) improving social security for poverty alleviation, with effects for ensuring precision in six areas, namely identifying target groups, carefully planning projects, making good use of funds, following through with measures on a household-by-household basis, assigning first secretaries in consideration of local needs, and setting clear objectives. All these continuous efforts have opened up a promising prospect in China's anti-poverty endeavor.

Poverty eradication is a defining indicator and bottom-line task in China's moderate prosperity drive, as CPC General Secretary Xi Jinping stressed, "To complete the building of a moderately prosperous society in all respects and achieve the First Centenary Goal, lifting all rural residents out of poverty is fundamental. To achieve initial prosperity in the countryside, it is essential to raise rural living standards and particularly those of impoverished villagers. Completing the building of such a society is a solemn commitment we have made to the whole nation. It must be realized, fully and completely, and there is no bargaining of the issue. It is non-negotiable. It will never do to postpone the task and say that we can't do it yet and need a few more years when the time is due. We cannot declare that we have completed the building of a moderately prosperous society in an all-round way while at the same time there are still tens of millions of people living below the poverty line. If so, it will certainly affect our people's sense of satisfaction and the international recognition for our efforts. It will also affect the prestige of our Party among our people and the image of China within the international community. We must mobilize all the forces of the Party, the whole country and society to launch an all-out battle against extreme poverty and ensure that through 2020 all poor areas and people will join the rest of the country in leading a moderately prosperous life."[12]

In short, the transformation and upgrading of economic and social development and the strategic requirements of building a moderately prosperous society for all constitute the overall backdrop of targeted poverty alleviation. The 13th Five-Year Plan period is a decisive stage for completing the task and achieving the First Centenary Goal. It is also a decisive stage for winning the battle against extreme poverty. The advancement of the new type of industrialization and information technology, together with urbanization and agricultural modernization, in addition to the accelerated implementation of major regional development strategies, have created a sound environment and opportunities for the development of poor areas. And this is greatly supported by China's increasing overall strength which has laid a solid foundation of material for winning the battle. The CPC Central Committee and the State Council have formulated and introduced a series of major policies and measures, providing a strong political and institutional guarantee for mobilizing the whole country to win the battle. All regions, departments and sectors of society have joined hands to take active actions. Officials and people in poor areas, with a strong desire to get rid of poverty for a better development, have been motivated by great internal impetus and vitality. Targeted Poverty alleviation has become the consensus and concerted action of the whole Party and society.

1.2 Goals of Targeted Poverty Eradication

Xi Jinping stressed in his report delivered at the 19th National Congress of the Communist Party of China in 2017: "Winning the battle against poverty and seeing that poor people and poor areas will enter the moderately prosperous society together with the rest of the country is a solemn promise made by our Party."[13] Goals are the basis for the formulation and implementation of a mechanism of strategic policies and measures, and the goal of China's targeted poverty alleviation is to eradicate absolute poverty.

In as early as 2011, the Outline for Development-Driven Poverty Alleviation in Rural Areas (2011–2020), issued by the CPC Central Committee and the State Council, set the goals as follows: "Through 2020, the rural poor will be assured of adequate food and clothing, and guaranteed access to compulsory education, basic medical services and safe housing.[14] The per capita net income of rural residents in poor areas will increase by more than the national average, and the indicators in major areas of basic public services are close to the national average, so as to narrow the widening development gap". Specific targets were set for improving infrastructure

[12] Party Literature Research Office of the CPC Central Committee [4].

[13] Xi [5].

[14] "Two Assurances and Three Guarantees" for short.

construction and basic public services in poor areas through 2020, which included: (1) The farmland infrastructure construction will be significantly improved, and a characteristic pillar industry system will be taking shape. (2) Supplies of safe drinking water will be secured and tap water coverage increased for rural residents, with comprehensive solutions to the shortage of electric power. (3) Asphalt (cement) roads will be built where conditions permit, and roads in all villages will be paved. (4) Every village will be provided with buses and hard roads with better services and capabilities to prevent and combat disasters. (5) The living conditions of people in poor areas will be significantly improved, with basically universal preschool education, better-quality compulsory education and universal senior secondary education ensured. Efforts will also be made to speed up the development of distance continuing education and community education. (6) People in poor areas will have more equal access to public health and basic medical services, and they will be fully covered by the new rural social endowment insurance system. (7) Radio and television are available to every household, and all villages have basic broadband access. Libraries and cultural centers will be established in each key county on the state's poverty alleviation work list, with comprehensive cultural stations in towns and townships, and venues for cultural activities in administrative villages.

In November 2015, the CPC Central Committee and the State Council issued the Decisions on Winning the Battle against Extreme Poverty, which set a higher overall goal for poverty alleviation. In addition to the previous requirements, it was also required that "the per capita disposable income of rural residents in poor areas increases by more than the national average, and indexes in major areas of basic public services approach the national average, to ensure that the rural population will be lifted out of poverty as defined by the existing standard, and poor counties removed from the poverty list and impoverishment over entire regions eliminated through 2020".

In December 2016, the State Council issued the Plan on Targeted Poverty Alleviation during the 13th Five-Year Plan Period (hereinafter referred to as "the Plan"), which again emphasized the overall goal of poverty alleviation: "Through the year 2020, the rural poor will be assured of adequate food and clothing, and guaranteed access to compulsory education, basic medical services and safe housing. The per capita disposable income of poor villagers will more than double that of 2010, with an increase rate higher than the national average, and indicators in major areas of basic public services close to the national average. All rural residents living below the current poverty line are lifted out of poverty, all poor counties get rid of poverty, and overall regional poverty is eliminated."

The targets were explained in detail in the Plan: Firstly, the registered rural poor households would be lifted out of poverty to ensure that they have a stable source of income, and their per capita disposable income steadily exceeds the national poverty line, with "two assurances and three guarantees". Secondly, there would be orderly exit from the registers. These are villages where infrastructure, basic public service facilities and living environment have been significantly improved, together with better primary farmland and irrigation and water conservancy facilities, as well as fledging local industries, a growing collective economy, and an enhanced community management capacity. Thirdly, all poor counties would be removed from the poverty list. These are counties with significantly improved infrastructure and enhanced capacity and quality of basic public services in transportation, education and medical care, as well as a fully covered social security system, growing economy, better ecological environment, and an enhanced capacity for sustainable development.

At the 19th CPC National Congress held in October 2017, targeted poverty alleviation was announced as one of the three critical battles (the other two being forestalling and defusing major risks and the prevention and control of pollution) that the CPC vowed to win. In June 2018, the CPC Central Committee and the State Council issued the Guidelines on the Three-Year Action Plan to Win the Battle against Extreme Poverty, setting specific aims, defining approaches and detailed measures in response to new forms of poverty. "Through the year 2020, we will consolidate our poverty-elimination achievements by 'Five Measures', namely, (1) boosting the economy to create more jobs for the disadvantaged; (2) relocating those living under adverse natural conditions; (3) providing eco-jobs for the poor; (4) improving education in poor areas; and (5) improving social security for poverty alleviation. These measures should be taken in light of the specific conditions of impoverished areas and their populations to ensure that the rural poor is lifted out of poverty with elimination of absolute poverty, that all poverty-stricken counties are removed from the list and that overall regional poverty is addressed. Through that time, the per capita disposable income of rural residents in poor areas will increase by more than the national average, and the indicators in major areas of basic public services are close to the country's average. Specifically, these include: townships and villages in impoverished areas with the right conditions are accessible by paved roads. All poor villagers have access to electric power, as well as safe housing and drinking water, with the basic requirements for a clean living environment. There will be effective solutions to the problem of school-age children dropping out of school due to financial difficulties. All poor people will be covered by rural social endowment insurance system, basic medical insurance, critical disease insurance and subsistence allowances. The environment for development in contiguous destitute areas, old revolutionary base areas, areas with large ethnic minority populations, and border areas will be significantly improved, and extremely impoverished areas are lifted out of poverty on schedule."

In general, the goal of anti-poverty campaign in China started from the rural poverty alleviation standards, which indicate the multi-dimensions of poverty measurement and the stability of poverty elimination. Being lifted out of poverty does not just mean the improvement of the working and living conditions, but also the improvement of public services in education, medical care, housing and culture, as well as the achievement of extensive economic and social goals in poverty-stricken areas. By ending extreme poverty and improving all aspects, needy people may be helped to keep up with China's prosperity drive for its entire people. This is of long-term significance which promises stability. The Plan has divided the overall goal into 10 specific targets (see Table 1.1).

It is shown that in addition to the growth rate of the per capita disposable income of the impoverished in poor villages, counties and areas mentioned in the overall

Table 1.1 Major indicators of development in poverty-stricken areas and alleviation of impoverished people during the 13th Five-Year Plan period

Indicators	2015	2020	Attributes	Data sources
Registered poor population (ten thousand)	5630[a]	Freed from poverty	Mandatory	Poverty Alleviation Office of the State Council
Registered poor villages (ten thousand)	12.8	0	Mandatory	Poverty Alleviation Office of the State Council
Number of poor counties	832[b]	0	Mandatory	Poverty Alleviation Office of the State Council
Relocation of poor people from inhospitable areas (ten thousand)	–	981	Mandatory	National Development and Reform Commission, Poverty Alleviation Office of the State Council
Growth rate of per capita disposable income of villagers in poor areas (%)	11.7	Annual growth rate higher than the national average	Anticipatory	National Bureau of Statistics
Rural centralized water supply rate in poor areas (%)	75	≥ 83	Anticipatory	Ministry of Water Resources
Renovation rate of dilapidated houses for registered poor households (%)	–	Nearly 100	Mandatory	Ministry of Housing and Urban-Rural Development Poverty Alleviation Office of the State Council
Completion rate of compulsory education in poverty-stricken counties (%)	90	93	Anticipatory	Ministry of Education
Number of registered poor households falling into or returning to poverty due to illness (ten thousand)	838.5	Basically solved	Anticipatory	National Health and Family Planning Commission
Collective economic annual income of registered poor villages (ten thousand)	2	≥ 5	Anticipatory	Poverty Alleviation Office of the State Council

Note [a] According to a sample survey by the National Bureau of Statistics, 55.75 million people lived in poverty in rural areas by the end of 2015. Based on the identification of the Development-Oriented Poverty Alleviation Information System of Poverty Alleviation Office of the State Council, by the end of 2015, 56.3 million rural people had been registered as poor. In accordance with the requirements of targeted poverty alleviation and elimination, a poverty exit mechanism was introduced to deregister those who had emerged from poverty. The number of impoverished people used in the Plan is verified by the information system

[b] In addition, six counties and one city in Aksu Prefecture of Xinjiang Uygur Autonomous Region have access to the preferential treatment

Source The Plan on Targeted Poverty Alleviation during the 13th Five-Year Plan period

goal, the priority has been placed on "two assurances and three guarantees", with more detailed indicators such as the rate of centralized water supply in rural areas, of renovation of dilapidated houses, of completion of compulsory education in poor counties, and the number of poor households returning to poverty due to critical illness. At the same time, considering that the relocation of poor people from inhospitable areas was the toughest project in winning the battle against extreme poverty and that the collective economic growth was vital in improving the production and living conditions of poor villages, the annual income targets for people to be relocated and for the collective economy of registered poor villages were set up.[15] These targets have been key indicators for the subsistence and development of the poor population, and played an important role in guiding the efforts to win the battle as scheduled and complete the building of a moderately prosperous society in all respects.

On the whole, China's poverty alleviation goal features three distinct features. Firstly, it is a basic indicator. At the Conference on Poverty Alleviation and Development by the CPC Central Committee, Xi Jinping made the point that "lifting all rural poor out of poverty is a defining indicator of completing the building of a moderately prosperous society in all respects and realizing the First Centenary Goal."[16] Therefore, poverty alleviation is the bottom-line goal indicating the success of the great endeavor. It is a hard task that must be accomplished, Secondly, no poor area or poor person should be left behind. Looking back at China's efforts to eradicate poverty, the poor were not completely lifted out of poverty when The National Seven-Year Poverty Alleviation Program was due in 2000 and the Outline for Development-Driven Poverty Alleviation in Rural Areas for the first ten-year period from 2001 to 2010 ended. Historically, poor counties had experienced three adjustments, and the total number had not been reduced. The goal is to lift all poor people and counties out of poverty, and no one is left behind. Thirdly, lifting poor people in the rural areas out of poverty must be achieved as scheduled. Xi Jinping, on behalf of the CPC, made a solemn promise to the Chinese people and the world, emphasizing the need to mobilize the morale and resources of the whole Party, the whole country, and the whole society to win the battle against extreme poverty. This is a tough battle with no route of retreat, and poverty mush be fully eliminated.

In accordance with the targets set by the central government, efforts have been made to neither lower standards nor blindly raise them to unrealistic expectations. Bringing the battle to a successful end will deliver at least three implications: First of all, it means that China's rural poor will enter the moderately prosperous society together with the rest of the country. Secondly, the issue of absolute poverty in China will be addressed with record solutions. Finally, China will achieve the poverty reduction targets set in the UN 2030 Agenda for Sustainable Development 10 years ahead of schedule and continue to lead in the world's poverty reduction endeavor.

[15] Dong and An [6].

[16] Party Literature Research Office of the CPC Central Committee [4].

1.3 Theoretical and Practical Implications

Eliminating poverty and improving people's livelihood has been an important mission of the CPC in the governance of China. Since the founding of the People's Republic of China in 1949, the CPC and government have led the people of the whole nation in self-reliance by hard work and waged war against poverty. The impoverishment and backwardness have been fundamentally improved.

In the mid-1980s, China began its nation-wide poverty alleviation and development campaign. Thanks to years of unremitting efforts, the number of rural poor was greatly reduced and their living and production standards improved. Since the 18th CPC National Congress, the Central Committee with Xi Jinping as its core has attached great importance to development-driven poverty alleviation, giving it a prominent position in the country's governance, and made significant progress and achievements. After more than 30 years of hard work, from initial efforts on a trial basis to a nationwide practice and to this last battle to eliminate extreme poverty, China has found a development-driven path with Chinese characteristics in line with local conditions and by drawing on good practices of other countries, which is of great theoretical and practical value.

1.3.1 Theoretical Value

Since the targeted campaign against extreme poverty was launched, the CPC General Secretary Xi Jinping has assumed leadership, made plans, and directed the battle in person. He called on the whole Party and nation to regard poverty alleviation as the top priority of social and economic development and a key task and defining indicator of the establishment of a moderately prosperous society. Meticulous efforts and effective measures have been required to boost the drive. Putting poverty eradication at the top of his work agenda and devoted much of his energy to it, Xi has presented a series of important ideas and proposals, and made some major policy decisions, which have reflected his insight and approaches on poverty alleviation. These observations and viewpoints are the inheritance, innovation and development of Marxist theory for poverty alleviation, as well as the enrichment and improvement of the thought on poverty alleviation and development with Chinese characteristics. As major components of Xi Jinping Thought on Socialism with Chinese Characteristics for a New Era, they have provided a realistic basis for a decisive victory in building a moderately prosperous society with a high value of the times.

1.3.1.1 Inheritance, Innovation and Development of Marxist Anti-poverty Theory

Marxist theory of poverty and poverty alleviation grew from its exposure of bourgeois exploitation of the proletariat. The theory holds that the root of the long-term poverty of the proletariat is the capitalist employment system and the unpaid private appropriation of surplus value by capitalists, and that the fundamental way to eradicate poverty and repression and finally to realize communism is to do away with the capitalist character and abolish the system of exploitation. Based on a critique of the reality of the bourgeois oppression of the proletariat in Europe at his times, Marx brought forward his poverty and anti-poverty theory.

With profound and rich implications, this theory is insightful and thought-provoking. In Marx's eyes, to achieve the emancipation of the poor, capitalism should be overthrown through revolutionary movements to finally achieve the wealth for all. Frederick Engels shared the opinion in observing that, "Our aim is to bring about a social system that will give wholesome and rewarding labor to all, ample wealth and leisure to all, and the truest and fullest freedom to all."[17] The thought of common prosperity for the development of all individuals is a major appeal of value for Marxism. Xi Jinping's important observations and ideas on poverty alleviation have inherited the Marxist thought of prosperity for all. He points out, "The pie of China's economic development continues to grow in size, but inequality remains a prominent issue .... We must ensure that development is for the people, by the people, and its fruits shared by the people. We must make more effective institutional arrangements to ensure that all our people move steadily toward common prosperity. Under no circumstances should there be a situation in which the rich reap enormous benefits while the poor eat the dregs."[18] As an old Chinese saying goes, "To govern the country well, social justice must be ensured and then the country will be at peace." To step up assistance to people in need and win the battle against extreme poverty is a vital measure to implement the vision of shared development and address issues of social equity and justice.

Marxist theory not only emphasizes common prosperity, but also the social ideal of "all-round development of individuals", which believes that every member of the society should be able to develop comprehensively and give full play to all his abilities and capacities. The universal development of the individual ensures people's basic needs—food and clothing—and also brings them a better life. The Five-sphere Integrated Plan, the "Four-pronged Comprehensive" Strategy and the Five Development Concepts of innovation, coordination, green development, openness and sharing put forward by Xi Jinping, as well as the transformation of the principal contradiction in the primary stage of socialism, all these reflect the importance attached to all-round human development. The theory includes all aspects of promoting liberation and comprehensive development of the individual.

[17] Marx and Engels [7], p. 570.

[18] Xi [8].

In line with China's actual conditions and on the basis of the Marxist anti-poverty goal, Xi Jinping has adhered to the socialist road of poverty alleviation and development with Chinese characteristics. The causes of poverty vary from person to person. Taking the approach of historical materialism, and based on the actual conditions of poverty in China with common prosperity as the aspiration and goal, Xi has proposed the strategy of targeted poverty alleviation and elimination, addressing the root cause with right remedies. A governance mechanism of the CPC leadership at the five levels, namely, the CPC committees of provinces, cities (prefectures), counties and townships, and the Party branches of villages taking up responsibilities of poverty elimination, has been established. Targeted efforts have been made in six areas to identify the poor accurately, arrange targeted programs, utilize capital efficiently, take household-based measures, dispatch first Party secretaries based on village conditions and achieve the set goals. Targeted measures include boosting the economy to provide more job opportunities, relocating poor people from inhospitable areas, compensating for economic losses associated with reducing ecological damage, improving education in impoverished areas, and providing subsistence allowances for those unable to shake off poverty through their own efforts alone. All these practices have been innovative approaches to the realization of Marxist anti-poverty theory.

Xi Jinping's thought on poverty alleviation and eradication has proved to be successful in solving specific problems in China by applying Marxist standpoint, views and methods in conformity with China's conditions and practices in the new era. It fits with the requirement of the times and the trend of development for mankind and is the latest theoretical achievement of the localization of Marxism. As the inheritance, innovation and development of Marxist poverty and anti-poverty theory, Xi's thought has promoted the development of Marxism in China.

1.3.1.2 Enrichment and Upgrades of Development-Driven Poverty Alleviation Theories with Chinese Characteristics

The Marxist poverty and anti-poverty theory is a major source of the Chinese theory of development-driven poverty alleviation. Under its guidance, the CPC has established a materialistic stance in approaching the issue of poverty, and a theory of poverty alleviation and development with Chinese characteristics has been taking shape in line with the reality of China's revolution, nation building and reforms.

From its very beginning, the CPC has taken eliminating poverty, improving well-being and achieving common prosperity as its mission and aspiration. In the early days of the founding of the People's Republic of China in 1949, the country was poor and backward. The first generation of the CPC central collective leadership centered by Mao Zedong, based on conditions at the time, proposed that the elimination of poverty should adhere to the leadership of the Communist Party of China and the principal role of villagers. The thought of "common prosperity" and the pursuit of equality laid a solid foundation for China's anti-poverty theory. In the initial period of the reform and opening up since 1978, the second generation of the central collective leadership headed by Deng Xiaoping advocated combining poverty alleviation with the economic development of China and particularly its rural areas, in an attempt to "encourage those regions and people that have become prosperous first to inspire others to follow their example towards common prosperity". In the 1990s, the CPC's third generation of central collective leadership with Jiang Zemin as the core formulated the theory of poverty alleviation and development, emphasizing the "five principles" of development-oriented poverty relief, priority of technological support, correct leadership, taking measures according to local conditions, and sustainable development. In the beginning of the twenty-first century, the CPC Central Committee with Hu Jintao as the general secretary proposed the scientific Outlook on Development, stressing the importance of the people-oriented approach and coordinated overall planning. Guidelines were suggested, emphasizing the principles of "investing more and reducing the burden on villagers to fully arouse their entrepreneurial initiative and increase income", and "industrial sectors helping rural development and cities supporting rural areas".

Xi Jinping's thought on poverty alleviation has adhered to and developed sound ideas on poverty eradication shaped in the history of the CPC. With the change of situations, Xi raised creative policies and the basic strategy of targeted poverty alleviation and elimination, focusing on major theoretical and practical issues concerning why poverty should be reduced, how to reduce it and how to ensure the overcomes are satisfactory, based on his rich frontline work experience and his inspection tours of many poverty-stricken areas. He stressed that emphasis should be placed on addressing questions such as who should be helped, who should help, how to help, how to evaluate whether someone has emerged from poverty and how to ensure those people stay out of poverty. He held that "We should take a realistic attitude towards poverty alleviation and adapt measures in line with local conditions. We should adopt targeted approaches to eliminate poverty and should never talk the talk and set unrealistic goals." "To cure a disease, we need to find the root of the disease. To alleviate poverty, we also need to identify the root causes before we apply the right remedies. Categorized and targeted measures should be introduced to reduce poverty based on the situation of individual households, local conditions and the causes for and types of poverty."[19]

Xi Jinping's thought on poverty alleviation covers the goals, strategic tasks, work dynamics, political guarantee and effective measures of development-driven poverty alleviation in a new era. With both the epistemological and methodological value, it further enriches and upgrades the theory of poverty alleviation and development with Chinese characteristics and is one of China's greatest theoretical innovations.

---

[19] Institute for Party History and Literature of the CPC Central Committee [2].

1.3.1.3 A Major Component of Xi Jinping Thought on Socialism with Chinese Characteristics for a New Era

At the 19th CPC National Congress convened in 2017, Xi Jinping put forward his Thought on Socialism with Chinese Characteristics for a New Era, spelling out the overall goals and tasks of upholding and developing socialism with Chinese characteristics to realize socialist modernization and national rejuvenation. On the basis of comprehensive development of a moderately prosperous society, a two-step approach should be taken to build China into a great modern socialist country that is prosperous, strong, democratic, harmonious, beautiful and culturally advanced by the middle of the century. In the first stage from 2020 to 2035, China will realize initial socialist modernization with a further 15 years of hard work on the foundation of the moderately prosperous society. In the second stage from 2035 to the middle of the twenty-first century, after another 15 years of hard work, China will be built into a great modern socialist country.[20] Xi Jinping Thought on socialism with Chinese characteristics for a new era is a complete and extensive theoretical system with distinct goals, rich inclusions and profound philosophies, featuring rich implications of the times and in-depth thinking.

To complete the building of a moderately prosperous society in all respects is the corner stone of the overarching goal of Xi Jinping's socialism with Chinese characteristics for a new era, and alleviation of extreme poverty is the most arduous task in achieving the First Centenary Goal. Winning the battle is the key task and defining indicator. Xi emphasized that, "Through the year 2020, we will complete the building of a moderately prosperous society in all respects. No single poor area or single poor ethnic group should be left behind in achieving this goal."[21] No single poor individual should be left behind in that goal either.

Xi Jinping Thought also makes clear the overarching Five-sphere Integrated Plan and the "Four-pronged Comprehensive" Strategy are given prominence. The former refers to the development of socialism with Chinese characteristics encompassing economic, political, cultural, social and eco-environmental development, with focus on building a society of moderate prosperity, realizing socialist modernization and rejuvenating the Chinese nation; while the latter, in addition to comprehensive development of a society of initial prosperity for all, consists of comprehensive deepening of reforms, comprehensive implementation of the rule of law, and comprehensive enforcement of Party discipline. These ultimate objectives and strategies have fully reflected the CPC's aspiration that "Our goal is to meet people's desire for a better life" and constituted one of the major components of Xi Jinping's development-driven poverty alleviation theory, in which economic development is the material basis, political advancement the institutional guarantee, cultural progress the internal driver, social development the source of energy, and ecological conservation is the new momentum.

---

[20] Xi [5].

[21] Institute for Party History and Literature of the CPC Central Committee [2].

1.3.1.4 Providing a Realistic Foundation for a Decisive Victory in Building a Moderately Prosperous Society in a New Era

With the advance of poverty alleviation and development endeavor, weaknesses of the traditional extensive approach at the regional level surfaced, such as lack of clear information of the specific number of the poverty base and misconducts like generalized broad-brush policies in project allocation, scattering of funds among the impoverished areas, superficial helping and counties that had emerged from poverty still keeping the label in order to continue accessing preferential treatment. These setbacks had called for more effective measures. Xi Jinping's ideas and proposals have provided guidelines and approaches in response to the changing situation, summarized as accomplishing "Targeted Efforts in Six Areas" (namely, to identify the poor accurately, arrange targeted programs, utilize capital efficiently, take household-based measures, dispatch first Party secretaries based on village conditions, and achieve the set goals); taking "Five Measures for Poverty Eradication" (including boosting the economy to provide more job opportunities, relocating poor people from inhospitable areas, compensating for economic losses associated with reducing ecological damage, improving education in impoverished areas, and providing subsistence allowances for those unable to shake off poverty through their own efforts alone), and addressing "four key issues" (namely how to identify the people that need help (who needs help), who should do the work of poverty alleviation (who provides help), how this work should be carried out (how to help), and what standards and procedures should be adopted for lift out of poverty). The leading officials of provincial level Party committees and governments in the 22 central and western provinces with demanding poverty elimination tasks are required to assume overall responsibility and sign written pledges to the central leadership, and they and their subordinates at all levels will be responsible for poverty alleviation under their jurisdiction. A well organized and dynamic mechanism of governance is established, with Party secretaries at the five administrative levels of province, city, county, township and village pressing forward with implementation and working together towards the same goal.

To address the bottlenecks hindering rural development, contiguous destitute areas where the work is particularly difficult are identified and targeted by giving differentiated guidance in light of local conditions and by focusing on key areas to ensure effective outcomes. Work in 10 major areas has been implemented to alleviate poverty, such as accessibility of poor villages to paved roads, safe drinking water, rural electric power security and renovation of dilapidated houses, in addition to development of special local industries to increase income, as well as poverty alleviation through rural tourism, education, public health and family planning, cultural development and information-based management, in an attempt to drive and promote the overall development-oriented poverty alleviation to reach the final success of the endeavor.

In his insightful thought on poverty alleviation, Xi Jinping has clarified the goal of building a moderately prosperous society in all respects and emphasized that the continuous effort of the campaign against extreme poverty on the basis of targeted poverty alleviation is an effective measure to achieve the goal. This has provided a realistic foundation for securing a decisive victory in building such a society in an all-round way in a new era.

1.3.2 *Practical Implications*

It is the goal set by the central leadership to win the battle against extreme poverty and ensure that through the year 2020 all the rural population will be lifted out of poverty as defined by the existing standard, all impoverished counties removed from the poverty list and poverty over entire regions eliminated. As one of the major components of building a society of moderate prosperity, as well as a major strategy to facilitate the sharing of the reform and development achievements for all the people towards common prosperity, the battle will offer workable approaches to improve coordinated regional development and avoid being caught by the "middle-income trap". In addition, the victory will be a guarantee for consolidating the Party's foundation for governance, promoting ethnic unity and border stability and enhancing China's international image. The strategy to eradicate poverty in a new era has offered practical implications in many aspects.

1.3.2.1 Economic Implications: Ending Absolute Poverty for Building a Moderately Prosperous Society in All Respects

Since the 18th CPC National Congress in 2012, Xi Jinping has assumed leadership, made plans and directed the endeavor against poverty in person. He called on the whole Party and nation to regard development-driven poverty alleviation a key task in realizing the First Centenary Goal and launched the targeted campaign against extreme poverty, which has exerted impacts far and wide. Decisive progress has been made, with the following economic implications.

Firstly, the number of people living in poverty has been greatly reduced. According to the current rural poverty standard, a total of 82.39 million people were lifted out of poverty from 2013 to 2018, with an average annual reduction of 13.73 million poor people, a cumulative reduction of 83.2%. The number of people living in poverty dropped to 5.51 million by the end of 2018, and the incidence of rural poverty dropped from 10.2% at the end of 2012 to 1.7% at the end of 2018. In 10 provinces, the incidence had dropped below 1.0%.[22] Secondly, the income of rural residents in poor areas has risen significantly. From 2013 to 2019, the per capita disposable income increased from RMB6079 to RMB10,371, with an average annual growth rate of 9.3%, higher than the national per capita disposable income, which narrowed the gap with the national average significantly. Thirdly, the development of poverty-stricken areas has been accelerated, with marked improvements in working and living conditions. Problems like lack of access to transport, education, medical care and safe

[22] Office of Household Surveys, National Bureau of Statistics [9].

drinking water are being addressed. The gap between basic public services in rural areas and the national average has been narrowing, with more resources allocated to poor areas. Local industries with distinctive advantages have developed rapidly, and new forms of poverty alleviation, such as tourism, photovoltaic and e-commerce projects have emerged and grown rapidly in size and strength, giving full play to the initiative of the poor and greatly enhancing their capacity for self-development.

Through 2020, absolute poverty that has plagued the Chinese nation for thousands of years will be eradicated, with the realization of the First Centenary Goal of building a moderately prosperous society for all.

1.3.2.2 Political Implications: Full and Strict Discipline Over the CPC to Strengthen the Foundation of the Party's Governance

An old Chinese saying goes, "People are the root of a country. When the root is stable, the country is safe." The Communist Party of China is of the people, by the people and for the people. Its original aspiration and goal of building socialism with Chinese characteristics is to serve the interests of the people wholeheartedly. Only when people-centered development is always kept in mind and in practice by adhering to the fundamental purpose of serving the people, benefiting the people, and ensuring that all the people live a better life, can the foundation of the Party's governance be solid and unbreakable. Xi Jinping has pointed out that "Fighting against poverty is a major issue in the governance of China and other countries. The CPC's governance in China aims to benefit the people, and only by doing so the foundation of CPC governance can remain solid."[23]

As the core of leadership in all national undertakings, the CPC is also the backbone of poverty alleviation efforts in China. Ending poverty is a visible manifestation of the fundamental position of Communist Party of China, its unchanging aspiration to wholeheartedly serve the people and seek happiness for the people, and its determination to lead all the people toward a moderately prosperous society in all respects. The implementation of the anti-poverty strategy will help the entire people share in the fruits of reform and development towards common prosperity. It will also promote the Party's engagement with the people and bring closer relationship between officials and the general public. This will be of great significance for consolidating the foundation of the Party's governance.

Comprehensive enforcement of strict self-governance over the Party is a major component of the Four-pronged Comprehensive strategy, as well as a vital guarantee for building a moderately prosperous society. An important manifestation in the effort of poverty alleviation is to enhance the primary-level officials and Party members' sense of mission, sense of responsibility, innovative spirit, and hard-working style, which is conducive to cultivating excellent front-line cadres for the country.

---

[23] Institute for Party History and Literature of the CPC Central Committee [2].

To address the question of "who should do the work of poverty alleviation", more than 3 million officials from governments at or above the county level, state-owned enterprises and institutions have participated in the rural support, and about 206,000 first Party secretaries and 700,000 members of resident work teams have been selected and dispatched to poverty-stricken villages. They have worked together with 1.974 million township officials and millions of village leaders, going all out to help poor people out of poverty and work towards a better life. The initiative of the general public to participate in poverty alleviation has been aroused, and the poor have an enhanced awareness of their principal role with a stronger sense of satisfaction. The fight against poverty has well demonstrated the political and institutional strengths of the CPC, the fundamental belief of the CPC Central Committee with Xi Jinping as its core that development is by the people and for the people, and the political commitment to the well-being of people, including needy people in impoverished areas.

For officials taking part, poverty alleviation is a test of not only their ability, but also their sense of responsibility. To encourage them to do their best in the final stages of fighting against extreme poverty, the strictest possible evaluation and supervision mechanism has been established, with the pressure of accountability to boost their motivation. At the same time, incentives have been improved by taking the performance in poverty alleviation as one of the key factors to consider in the selection and appointment of officials. Those on the front line have been inspected and identified so that officials with abilities, integrity and achievements have stood out to do even better. In this way a positive atmosphere has been created in which hard work and strong sense of responsibility are respected.[24]

Poverty alleviation is one of the best ways to train and test officials. In his speech at a seminar on poverty alleviation for destitute areas, Xi Jinping said, "Winning the battle against extreme poverty is by no means an overnight feat, nor can it be easily solved. The CPC Central Committee has not required local governments to complete the task ahead of schedule, let alone the poverty-stricken areas with complex conditions and problems. Anti-poverty plans should not be arbitrarily advanced and poverty reduction standards should not be arbitrarily lowered. Misconduct such as manipulation and falsification of data must not be allowed. The strictest possible evaluation and supervision mechanism should be established, together with the system of the annual report and oversight. There will be accountability for lax and deceptive practices, and strict monitoring of the management and utilization of capital so that misappropriation or embezzlement of the funds are resolutely corrected and dealt with. Poverty alleviation must reach those who truly need it, and poverty must be fully eliminated to win public approval. The evaluation and supervision of results should be strengthened to ensure solid and authentic outcomes that can survive the test of time and practice."[25]

---

[24] Understanding and implementing President Xi Jinping's important speech at the Central Conference on Poverty Alleviation and Development [EB/OL]. (2015-11-29). http://www.xinhuane.com/politics/2015-11/29/c_1117295719.htm.

[25] Institute for Party History and Literature of the CPC Central Committee [2].

There have been explicit provisions for officials at all levels engaged in the implementation of poverty alleviation so as to restrain and manage the awareness and practices of Party members, which is conducive to not only the implementation of poverty alleviation as scheduled, but also strict Party governance.

1.3.2.3 Social Implication: Beneficial to Social Justice and National Stability

As noted by the ancient sage Confucius, "Fair distribution of wealth and social stability are essential to a good government." The existence of poverty and the widening gap between the rich and the poor have seriously affected social equity and justice, and exacerbated social tensions, which may have a negative impact on social stability and harmony, and even endanger national security and unity.

Since the start of the reform and opening up, China has made remarkable progress in poverty relief and development, which has greatly improved working and living conditions, boosted the morale of people in poor areas and played an important role in promoting social progress, ethnic unity, and assurance of lasting peace and stability of the country. However, as Xi stressed at the 2015 Global Poverty Reduction and Development Forum, "Despite the achievements, China remains the world's biggest developing country, and to narrow the urban-rural gap is still a big challenge for us. A moderately prosperous society in all respects is for the benefit of all Chinese people, and no one should be left behind. In the next five years, we will lift more than 70 million poor people living below the current standard out of poverty. This is an important step in China's implementation of the Post-2015 Development Agenda. In order to win this battle, we will put poverty alleviation and development as one of the major components of the economic and social development planning, with more investment of funds, more preferential policies and measures for the poor in impoverished areas. We will also improve the market mechanism to make it beneficial to eradicate poverty, and encourage inclusive social and economic development, with the introduction of more targeted measures."[26] It is the commitment of officials engaged in anti-poverty endeavor at all levels in China that promises the advancement of the cause, and it is their hard work for the well-being of the people that guarantees China's peace and stability.

During the 13th Five-Year Plan period, poverty alleviation efforts focused on improving not only the working and living conditions of the poor, but also public services in education, medical care and culture. Various resources and assistance were pooled for poor areas, particularly old revolutionary base areas, areas with large ethnic minority populations, border areas, and contiguous destitute areas. The government has encouraged the market, society and other players to participate in the poverty elimination efforts, which helped inspire people's kindness and compassion to help needy people out of poverty and share the fruits of reform and development. Fighting against extreme poverty has brought about a new look to impoverished

[26] Institute for Party History and Literature of the CPC Central Committee [2].

areas and a better life to local people. The income and the opportunity inequality have been under control and widening gaps between regions and between urban and rural areas have been under control. The support and assistance from all sectors have helped promote the harmonious development of society and ease the tensions for sustainable and healthy development of national economy. It has played an important part in social progress, political stability, consolidation of border areas and unity of ethnic groups, contributing greatly to bringing peace to the country.

1.3.2.4 Cultural Implications: Conducive to Building up Self-belief Through Education and Promoting Cultural Progress in Rural Areas

Getting rid of poverty requires wisdom, and education is fundamental to developing wisdom. It is an important way to root out poverty and prevent the intergenerational transmission of poverty. Needy children must be provided the access to education, no matter how poor they are.

Xi Jinping has stressed many times that "Poverty alleviation requires the support of education. To ensure that children in poor areas receive good education is a vital task of poverty relief and development as well as an effective way to prevent intergenerational transmission of poverty."[27] As a part of paramount importance in the campaign against poverty, development of education has always been a priority, through which, poor children can receive better education and enrich themselves with the power of knowledge. In that way, they may enhance their overall quality to have the possibility to change their lives and stop the intergenerational transmission of poverty.

Chinese people believe that one must have great aspirations to achieve high and poverty cannot be eradicated without one's own will power. Poor people can get rid of poverty only with their own determination and motivation. Without that, poverty eradication in the long run cannot be assured even with the support from the government and the public. As long as there are motivation and self-belief, there is no obstacle that cannot be overcome. It is an important measure to win the battle against poverty by strengthening poverty alleviation through education and stimulating the internal driver of the rural poor. By changing the model from mainly relying on external support like a blood transfusion to a more sustained effort from self-motivation, and from providing mainly physical and financial support to education and personal development, poor people have been helped to better understand the importance of mastering expertise to end poverty with enhanced cultural quality and vocational skills. All this has enriched their mind and cultivated their aspirations and capabilities to create a better life through their own efforts.

The cultural implications of poverty alleviation are also reflected in its promotion of cultural progress in rural areas. Undesirable habits such as extravagances and lavish feasts in weddings, funerals and other major occasions have been long-standing

[27] Institute for Party History and Literature of the CPC Central Committee [2].

and deep-rooted in rural areas. The bandwagon effect and all kinds of "relationship chipping in" have been popular practices but bitter grievances in the minds of most rural people. Many families have been suffering from them and dragged back into poverty.

Guided by core socialist values, the fight against extreme poverty has taken changing the outmoded social habits and customs as a major task by developing core values and doing away with extravagance and waste in weddings and funerals as an important part of rural cultural and ethical progress. Efforts have been made to improve local customs, enhance living conditions, and enrich cultural life. New and good practices have been encouraged, and the public has been guided to get rid of stale rules and customs by advocating good and healthy ones. This has helped Party members, officials and the general public to update their ideas, eliminate and curb undesirable customs, and foster a frugal, civilized and healthy way of life, which has been widely believed in and practiced by rural people.

1.3.2.5 Ecological Implications: Helping Maintain Ecological Balance and Promote Green Development

Green mountains are as valuable as gold mountains. But gold mountains could only sustain with green mountains. This is the dialectical relationship between conservation of natural environment and development of economy. The strategy of poverty alleviation is not to exploit resources at will, but to promote ecological improvement at the same time by coordinated development. As stipulated in the Outline for Development-Driven Poverty Alleviation in Rural Areas (2011–2020), "We will speed up the development and utilization of renewable energy in poor areas, develop eco-energy projects covering small hydropower, solar energy, wind energy and biomass energy in light of local conditions. We will also promote the application of biogas, energy-saving stoves, solid formed fuels and centralized gas supply stations of straw gasification. At the same time, more work should be done to advance the improvement of water supply, kitchen, toilet, pigsty and comprehensive utilization of straw. We will raise the rate of harmless treatment of urban sewage and garbage, and intensify efforts to comprehensively improve the rural environment. We will strengthen protection and development of grassland and nature reserves, and vigorously support projects to return grazing land to grassland. Measures such as grazing ban, rest and rotation should be taken to restore natural vegetation and ecological functions." This indicates that the CPC and Chinese government have attached great importance to ecological conservation and balance in the process of targeted poverty alleviation.

In November 2015, the CPC Central Committee and the State Council proposed in Decision on Winning the Battle against Extreme Poverty that poverty alleviation should go hand in hand with ecological conservation. Measures are suggested as follows: "Major ecological projects will be carried out, such as returning farmland to forest and grassland, protecting natural forests, building shelterbelts, preventing and controlling stony and sandy desertification, protecting and restoring wetlands, comprehensively improving slope farmland, returning grazing land to grassland and improving water ecology. More support will be given to poor areas in project and funding allocation to increase the participation and benefits of the needy people.

Efforts will be made to step up ecological protection and restoration in poor areas and increase transfer payments to key ecological function zones. Together with the establishment of the national park system, new ways will be explored for using ecological funds, such as funds from ecological compensation and conservation projects to employ some of the poor local labor as ecological protection staff like forest rangers.

There will be reasonable adjustments to the quota for basic farmland in poor areas, and intensified efforts to return farmland to forest and grassland. The practice of comprehensive ecological compensation will be introduced on a trial basis in poor areas, with the improved mechanism for dynamically adjusting compensation standards for non-commercial forests, as well as subsidies and rewards policies for grassland ecological conservation to promote the establishment of a horizontal system of ecological compensation between regions."

These measures have been of great significance to accelerate the process of poverty alleviation, maintain ecological balance and promote green development in poor areas.

1.3.2.6 Implications for China as a Major Country: Helping Accelerate the World's Poverty Reduction Progress with China's Vision and Approaches

Winning the battle against extreme poverty is a great cause of great significance to the entire mankind. As the first developing country in the world to achieve the poverty reduction target set in the UN Millennium Development Goals, China's achievements have accelerated the progress of global poverty reduction and its practices have made impressive contributions to the global cause, adding a great chapter of anti-poverty efforts to the human history.

China has explored and accumulated valuable experience in poverty alleviation and development, with constantly responsive and updated institutional mechanisms with Chinese characteristics. What China has achieved through its own solutions and practices has become a milestone in the cause of global poverty reduction. China's contributions have been widely applauded by the international community. According to *China Systematic Country Diagnostic (SCD)*, a report by the World Bank Group in 2018, China has made "'historic and unprecedented achievements' in rapid economic growth and poverty decline." In his congratulatory message at the Poverty Reduction and Development Forum 2017, UN Secretary-General Antonio Guterres spoke highly of China's poverty reduction approaches, saying, "Targeted poverty reduction is the only way to help the poorest and achieve the ambitious goals of the 2030 Agenda for Sustainable Development. China has lifted hundreds of millions of people out of poverty, and its experience can serve as a useful reference for other developing countries."[28]

Chinese people believe in kindness and benevolence, valuing friendship, honesty, good faith and a sense of responsibility, with the fine cultural tradition of supporting the poor. They have been generous and happy to help others. As Xi Jinping stressed at the 2015 Global Poverty Reduction and Development Forum, "Poverty eradication is the common mission of mankind. While striving to reduce poverty at home, China has also been actively supporting and cooperating with other developing countries. Assistance within its capacity has been provided with no political strings attached to developing countries, especially the least developed countries, in poverty eradication. Over the past 60 years and more, China has offered financial support to 166 countries and international organizations with nearly RMB 400 billion and over 600,000 aid workers, among them over 700 laid down their lives for the development of other countries. On seven occasions, China has announced unconditional cancellation of interest-free government loans owed by heavily indebted poor countries and least developed countries. China has given medical assistance to 69 countries in Asia, Africa, Latin America and the Caribbean and Oceania, and has helped more than 120 developing countries in implementing the Millennium Development Goals."[29]

In addition, China has vigorously advanced the Belt and Road Initiative, so that more countries and people will benefit from international cooperation on poverty reduction. China has always stood for safeguarding world peace, promoting global development and building a community with a shared future for humanity. Facts and statistics have shown that as a responsible country, China has been an active advocate and player in the cause of global poverty reduction, and has made its own contributions to achieving the goal of eliminating poverty in all its forms.

Bibliography

1. The United Nations. (2015, September 25). *Transforming our world: The 2030 agenda for sustainable development.* http://www.un.org/zh/documents/view_doc.asp?symbol=A/RES/70/1
2. Institute for Party History and Literature of the CPC Central Committee. (2018). *Xi Jinping on poverty alleviation.* Central Party Literature Publishing House.
3. Xi, J. (2013, November 03). *Poverty alleviation: No empty talk nor setting goals beyond reach.* https://www.chinanews.com.cn/gn/2013/11-03/5457417.shtml
4. Party Literature Research Office of the CPC Central Committee. (2018). *Selected documents since the 18th CPC National Congress* (II). Central Party Literature Publishing House.
5. Xi, J. (2017, October 28). *Secure a decisive victory in building a moderately prosperous society in all respects and strive for the great success of socialism with Chinese characteristics for a new era: Report delivered at the 19th CPC National Congress.* http://cpc.people.com.cn/n1/2017/1028/c64094-29613660.html

[28] Achievements in Poverty Alleviation Drawing Attention Far and Wide [EB/OL]. (2018-09-03). http://www.gov.cn/xinwen/2018-09/03/content_5318888.htm.

[29] Institute for Party History and Literature of the CPC Central Committee [2].

6. Dong, J., & An, B. (2016, December 02). *Promoting the in-step realization of all-round prosperity for the poor in poverty-stricken areas: Understanding the six highlights of China's anti-poverty campaign during the 13th five-year plan period*. http://news.cnr.cn/native/gd/20161202/t20161202_523301510.shtml
7. Marx, K., & Engels, F. (1965). *Collected works of Marx and Engels* (Chinese ed.) (XXI). People's Publishing House.
8. Xi, J. (2016, January 01). Speech at the second meeting of the fifth plenary session of the 18th CPC Central Committee (excerpts). *Qiushi*. http://cpc.people.com.cn/n1/2016/0101/c64094-28002398.html
9. Office of Household Surveys, National Bureau of Statistics. (2019). *Monitoring report of rural poverty in China 2019* (p. 2019). China Statistics Press.
10. Hu, F. (2018). *Understanding poverty alleviation in China*. Foreign Languages Press.
11. Huang, C. (2018, September 25). Understanding the significance of winning the battle against extreme poverty. *Guangming Daily*.
12. The United Nations. (2000, September 08). *United Nations millennium declaration*. http://www.un.org/Chinese/ga/55/res/a55R2.htm
13. National Mobilization and Education Center for Poverty Alleviation. (2018). *Research on the theoretical and practical innovation of poverty alleviation*. China Agriculture Press.
14. Xi, J. (2019). Speech at the symposium on solving pressing problems in "the two assurances and three guarantees." *Qiushi, 16*, 4–12.
15. Xi, J. (2017). *Speech at the symposium on poverty alleviation in destitute areas*. People's Publishing House.
16. The State Council. (2016, December 02). *Notice on circulating the plan on targeted poverty alleviation during the 13th five-year plan period*. http://www.gov.cn/zhengce/content/2016-12/02/content_5142197.htm
17. The CPC Central Committee, the State Council. (2015, December 07). *Decisions on winning the battle against extreme poverty*. http://www.gov.cn/zhengce/2015-12/07/content_5020963.htm
18. The CPC Central Committee, the State Council. *The outline for development-driven poverty alleviation in rural areas (2011–2020)*. http://www.gov.cn/gongbao/content/2011/content_2020905.htm
19. The CPC Central Committee, the State Council. (2018, August 19). *Guidelines on the three-year action plan to win the battle against extreme poverty*. http://www.gov.cn/zhengce/2018-08/19/content_5314959.htm

Chapter 2
Organizational System of the Battle Against Extreme Poverty

Targeted poverty eradication is one of the major battles for China to secure a decisive victory in building a moderately prosperous society in all respects. A well-structured organizational setup has been a vital guarantee for winning the battle. Under the leadership of the CPC and Chinese government, and by stimulating the internal impetus of the poor population, a strong organizational system has been established with the participation of multiple players of the Party committees, governments, officials, villagers, society and market as the key components. And mobilizing the strength of all sectors to launch an all-encompassing campaign against extreme poverty is a major innovation in the building of the system, under which the mechanism for policy making, project implementation and assessment has played an important role to ensure the success of poverty alleviation.

2.1 Organization of the System

Since its 18th National Congress in 2012, the CPC Central Committee has placed a high priority on poverty alleviation as part of its endeavor to complete the building of a moderately prosperous society for all, marking that China's battle against poverty has entered the final decisive stage. At its fifth plenary session held in October 2015, the 18th CPC Central Committee redefined the "battle to alleviate poverty" as "battle to end extreme poverty", which indicated a clearer goal with a people-centered philosophy and the aspiration for common prosperity, specifically a well-off society for all.

To win the battle, a responsibility system is required. President Xi Jinping has made a series of instructions that a working mechanism should be built whereby the central leadership makes overall plans, provincial authorities take overall responsibility, city and county authorities take charge of implementation. The framework covers all poor areas and officials have been sent to villages to help needy households.

S. Wang, *Poverty Alleviation and Targeted Measures*,
https://doi.org/10.1007/978-981-96-1493-6_2

The Party secretaries at the five administrative levels of province, city, county, township and village are required to work towards the same goal to provide the political guarantee for the victory against extreme poverty.

Taking this as a major political task, the Party committees and governments at all levels are required to enhance political awareness, the sense of responsibility and initiatives at work, coordinating between higher authorities and counties at primary levels and reviewing relevant work and progress by establishing a better organization and accountability system. This has helped not only boost the sense of commitment of government departments at all levels, but also make the delegation of tasks, rights and responsibilities of different departments more clearly defined.

Adhering to the CPC's overall leadership is the political basis for winning the battle. Only the CPC can unite the people of the whole country in reaching the consensus and working together towards the same goal in poverty alleviation, so that new breakthroughs and greater achievements can be made.

Adhering to the CPC's leadership is also the organizational guarantee for winning the battle. Poverty alleviation in China is challenging, complex and difficult because it involves a large area and a large population. Without a strong organizational support, there will be no historic victory. Only by adhering to the CPC's leadership and only under the unified decision-making, deployment and command of the Party committees at all levels to create a synergy, can the difficulties be tackled head on.

Adhering to the CPC's leadership is the correct approach to win the battle. Poverty alleviation is targeted at the poor people, while serving the people is the philosophy and principle held by the CPC. Therefore, to gain the victory, we must follow the Party's absolute leadership.

Poverty alleviation in China has made the most of the strengths of China's socialist system by pooling resources to solve major problems and mobilizing the administrative forces at all levels. These have contributed to what we have achieved so far. China's poverty elimination practices have proven that the socialist system has a strong capacity for integration and mobilization. On the one hand, the strengths of the system allow it to mobilize the participation of market and social forces to realize the effective allocation of poverty alleviation resources; on the other hand, the fundamental task of socialism is to end poverty and improve people's livelihood, which makes the policy making and implementation clearly oriented.

Within the framework of China's responsibility and performance appraisal systems, governments at all levels have been motivated to pool resources and forces from all sectors for poverty eradication, ensuring that the policies of the central government can be implemented effectively at local levels. In addition, the policy of integrating government funds for rural development in poor counties has required that funds be used for projects. Under this organizational system, governments at the county level have full autonomy to select projects according to local conditions, which ensures that the policies truly reach poor households and bring them real benefits. Actually, China's great achievements in poverty alleviation have owed to the institutional strengths of socialism with Chinese characteristics.

2.1.1 Administrative System of Poverty Alleviation

China's development-driven poverty alleviation is in accordance with its administrative system which is divided into five levels, namely, the central governments and committees, provinces (autonomous regions and municipalities directly under the central government), cities (regions, autonomous prefectures and leagues), counties (districts, banners, county-level cities and executive councils) and townships (towns and neighborhoods).

Organized poverty reduction campaigns in large scale began in the 1980s. In 1986, the State Council Leading Group for Economic Development in Poor Areas was set up, which was renamed in 1993 the State Council Leading Group for Poverty Alleviation and Development (hereinafter referred to as "the State Council Leading Group"). The campaigns included the Outline for Development-Driven Poverty Alleviation in Rural Areas (2001–2010) and the Outline for Development-Driven Poverty Alleviation in Rural Areas (2011–2020). The central government has always attached importance to poverty alleviation in its overall plan for national economic and social development. Since 1997, China has established the accountability system of poor provinces (autonomous regions and municipalities), which have formulated plans and taken actions in accordance with the national blueprint.

At the same time, relying on its administrative system, the Chinese government has established a top-down poverty alleviation organization (see Fig. 2.1) and a leading group composed of relevant departments of the central government, which has been responsible for organizing, guiding, coordinating, supervising and assessing the overall work. The leading group has an office responsible for the daily work. Relevant provinces (autonomous regions, municipalities), and counties (cities, banners) have also set up corresponding sections and departments to guide and coordinate local work.

In order to address the weak primary-level governance in poverty relief, first secretaries have been dispatched to poor villages with resident work teams, who have been committed to helping poor villages and people out of poverty.

As primary-level implementers of anti-poverty policies, poor villages have usually been economically and socially underdeveloped. In line with Guidelines on Strengthening the Management of the Selection and Assignment of Resident Work Teams in Poor Villages, the county Party committees and governments have organized and coordinated different departments to select excellent officials as first Party secretaries and resident work team members based on different local conditions, giving full play to the advantages of related departments to improve the efficiency of poverty eradication. Each resident work team is supposedly made up of at least 3 people, and stay in the poor village for at least 2 years. Team members are not responsible for their previous work anymore during their residence, and their organizational Party memberships are transferred to the village. During their residence, they are responsible for five tasks: (1) helping the village Party branch and village committee to improve ways of identifying poor households and coordinate and solve conflicts that may take place in the process; (2) mobilizing more corporate and social forces

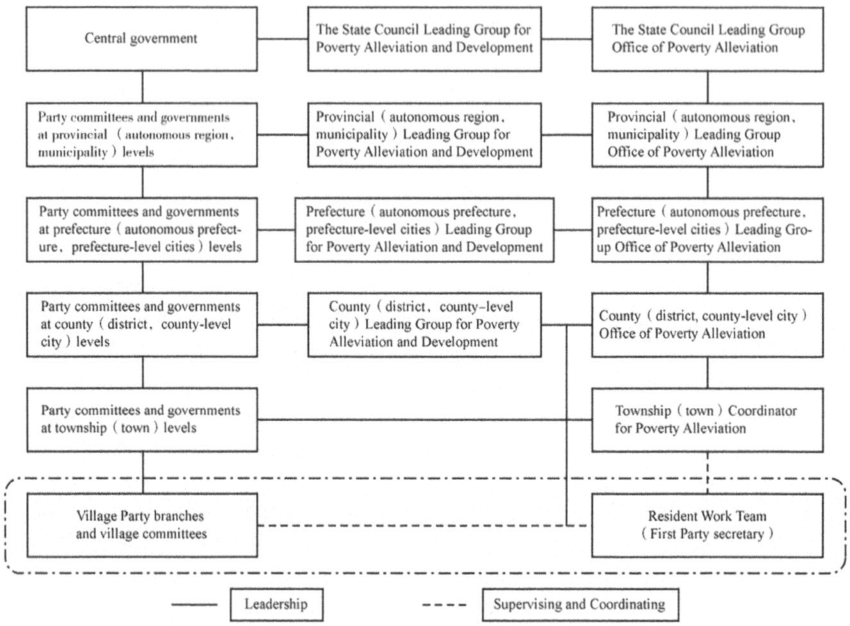

Fig. 2.1 Poverty alleviation organizations of Chinese governments at all levels

and resources for targeted poverty alleviation; (3) assisting the village committee to build an effective pairing assistance mechanism to benefit the poor households in the long run; (4) supervising the targeted poverty alleviation work at the village level to prevent fraud and corruption; (5) enhancing local officials' sense of responsibility and stimulating their internal driver in poverty alleviation for better and sustainable development. The resident work team system has greatly improved the local governance and promoted a further development of poverty alleviation.

2.1.2 Responsibility System of Poverty Alleviation

China has set up an effective working mechanism for poverty alleviation with clearly defined responsibilities, whereby the central leadership makes overall plans, provincial authorities take overall responsibility, and city and county authorities oversee implementation. Under the leadership of the CPC Central Committee with Xi Jinping as its core, governments at all levels have signed written pledges to the CPC Central Committee. During the poverty eradication campaign, Party committee secretaries and county governors have been required to remain unchanged in their posts, which has been conducive for five administrative levels of provinces, cities, counties, townships and villages to work together towards the same goal.

First of all, the central leadership and other state departments are in charge of the overall work. The CPC Central Committee and the State Council are responsible for formulating major policies and measures, improving systems and mechanisms, planning major projects and coordinating major issues of common and overall concern. The State Council Leading Group for Poverty Alleviation and Development is responsible for the overall coordination, including mechanisms for performance evaluation, restraints, supervision, inspection and exit of poor counties as well as assessing the poverty alleviation work of the provincial Party committees and governments, establishing big data platforms and improving the statistics monitoring system. Relevant central and state institutions have been taking advantages of their functions and resources to bear their responsibilities for poverty alleviation, and to formulate and implement relevant policies in accordance with requirements. The Central Commission for Discipline Inspection supervises and enforces discipline. The Supreme People's Procuratorate prevents and rectifies duty-related crimes in the field of poverty alleviation. The National Audit Office tracks and audits the implementation of policies and key projects funds.

Secondly, provincial Party committees and governments take overall responsibility for poverty alleviation within their jurisdiction and ensure the implementation of responsibilities at all levels. Major principles and policies of the CPC Central Committee and the State Council are implemented in line with local conditions. According to the poverty alleviation goal, provincial Party committees and governments should formulate the rolling and annual plans, and carry them out as scheduled.

Chief leaders of provincial Party committees and governments sign written pledges to the CPC Central Committee and report their work on a yearly basis. They are responsible for adjusting the structure of fiscal expenditure, establishing the mechanism for poverty alleviation fund growth, defining major players of investment and financing, and ensuring that the investment is commensurate with the goal. Their tasks also include coordinating the use of resources from projects such as poverty alleviation cooperation, pair-up assistance and designated poverty relief to mobilize social forces to participate; strengthening the inspection, supervision and audit of the distribution and use of funds and the management of projects, along with rectifying and solving problems of discipline violations in the process. In addition, they are also required to reinforce the management of poor counties by implementing the mechanisms of assessment, restraints and exit, ensuring the stability of the principal Party and government posts, and doing better jobs in goal setting, project release, fund allocation, organization and mobilization, as well as supervision and assessment, so as to ensure that all the poor counties and people within their jurisdiction get rid of poverty on schedule.

Thirdly, the Party committees and governments at municipal and county levels bear the responsibility as major implementers of poverty alleviation policies made by the provincial leaders. They are required to supervise the implementation, fund use and management of cross-county projects within their jurisdiction, and see to the completion of the tasks. In addition, they are responsible for making plans, optimizing the allocation of resources, guiding townships and villages to implement the registration and deregistration of poor villages and people, formulating guidance on targeted poverty alleviation in townships and villages according to local conditions and overseeing the implementation, as well as ensuring the authenticity and effectiveness of the exit of counties that have emerged from poverty from the registration list.

In this process, the governments at municipal and county levels are required to boost the motivation and creativity of the people in poverty, delivering to them genuine benefits. They are expected to make efforts to strengthen the building of primary-level Party committees by selecting the best CPC members for the posts. County level governments are responsible for setting up and updating the poverty alleviation project bank and the information disclosure system, integrating government funds for rural development as well as supervising and managing them for poverty alleviation.

Finally, the county Party secretaries and governors are responsible for accurate identification of poor population, arrangement and implementation of anti-poverty projects, use of funds and deployment of human resources. In fighting the battle against extreme poverty, Party committee secretaries and county governors have been required to remain unchanged in their posts to ensure the continuity of their work. In places where the work is particularly difficult, targeted poverty alleviation should be regarded as the top priority of social and economic development, which helps local Party committee and government leaders establish a correct view of work performance and promote the transformation of modes of growth in poor areas. According to Guidelines on Improving the Assessment of the Economic and Social Achievements of the Party and Government Leading Groups and Officials in Poor Counties, the assessment for county-level officials has been based on local conditions, with focus on the improvement of people's livelihood and social development instead of simply on the economic growth rate.

The responsibility system has helped establish and improve the accountability system, fully stimulated the sense of responsibility of leaders at all levels, which has not only ensured the implementation of major national policies, but also improved the leadership and governance at all levels, especially at the primary level. Within the responsibility system, poverty alleviation has become a major approach to rural development.

2.1.3 Forces and Resources in Poverty Alleviation

Targeted poverty eradication is a protracted battle. It is not about one area or one part of China, nor can it be completed by the government alone or the poor people on their own. Only by adhering to the leadership of the governments, mobilizing and pooling all forces and resources, can we win this tough battle in the new era.

Poverty alleviation involves many sectors such as industries, education, housing, healthcare, water conservancy, real estate development and construction. They are all encouraged to actively participate and play their roles, so that poverty alleviation could reach those who truly need it and deliver genuine outcomes.

2.1.3.1 Forces and Resources at Home

The first is the Party committees and governments of the eastern China region. They support the western China region through collaboration actions, which began in 1994 when the State Council launched The National Seven-Year Poverty Alleviation Program (1994–2000). In 1996, the CPC Central Committee and the State Council made a strategic decision about poverty alleviation cooperation between the east and the west, pairing nine developed provinces and four cities in the east with 10 impoverished regions in the west, namely, Beijing with Inner Mongolia, Tianjin with Gansu, Shanghai with Yunnan, Guangdong with Guangxi, Jiangsu with Shaanxi, Zhejiang with Sichuan, Shandong with Xinjiang, Liaoning with Qinghai, Fujian with Ningxia, and Dalian, Qingdao, Ningbo and Shenzhen jointly with Guizhou. In December 2016, the Guidelines on Further Strengthening Poverty Alleviation Cooperation between the East and the West (hereinafter referred to as "the Guidelines") was issued which adjusted the pairing relationship between the east and the west and increased assistance to destitute areas by full coverage of 30 ethnic autonomous prefectures.

At the same time, owing to great downward economic pressure, poverty relief tasks of eastern provinces were appropriately reduced. The Guidelines has strengthened the assistance to key poverty-stricken urban areas such as Yunnan, Sichuan, Gansu and Qinghai, and adjusted the assistance tasks of Liaoning, Shanghai and Tianjin. After the adjustment, nine provinces and municipalities in the east helped 14 provinces, autonomous regions and municipalities in the central and western regions, and the whole country supported Tibet and Xinjiang. 343 economically developed areas in the east have launched the Joint Efforts towards Prosperity Campaign with 573 poverty-stricken counties in the central and western regions. The adjusted pairing assistance relationship is shown in Table 2.1.

The second is the central departments and institutions. They have helped the western regions through paired-up assistance.

In 2012, China deployed a new round of paired-up assistance in poverty alleviation. A total of 310 central departments and institutions participated in the joint effort and even the military and armed police forces paired up with 63 counties, 547 townships and 2856 poor villages across the country, with full coverage of the 592 key counties on the state's poverty alleviation work list for the first time. However, with the advance of the work and the restructuring of administrative system, new problems appeared. For instance, the number of participating central departments and enterprises decreased from 310 to 300. Also, there were 22 institutions which had not yet been designated any poverty alleviation tasks. In addition, the assistance tasks for some institutions were either too light or too heavy, which made it difficult to conduct appraisals of their performance. Last but not the least, some pairings themselves needed adjustment.

Table 2.1 East-west collaboration in poverty alleviation

Eastern provinces, municipalities and cities	Western provinces, autonomous regions, municipalities and cities
Beijing	Inner Mongolia Autonomous Region; Zhangjiakou and Baoding, Hebei Province
Tianjin	Gansu Province; Chengde, Hebei Province
Dalian, Liaoning Province	Liupanshui, Guizhou Province
Shanghai	Yunnan Province; Zunyi, Guizhou Province
Jiangsu Province	Shaanxi Province; Xining and Haidong, Qinghai Province
Suzhou, Jiangsu Province	Tongren, Guizhou Province
Zhejiang Province	Sichuan Province
Hangzhou, Zhejiang Province	Miao and Tujia Autonomous Prefectures in Enshi, Hubei Province; Miao and Dong Autonomous Prefectures in Southeast Guizhou Province
Ningbo, Zhejiang Province	Yanbian Korean Autonomous Prefecture, Jilin Province; Buyi and Miao Autonomous Prefectures in Southwest Guizhou Province
Fujian Province	Ningxia Hui Autonomous Region
Fuzhou, Fujian Province	Dingxi, Gansu Province
Xiamen, Fujian Province	Linxia Hui Autonomous Prefecture, Gansu Province
Shandong Province	Chongqing
Jinan, Shandong Province	Xiangxi Tujia and Miao Autonomous Prefecture
Qingdao, Shandong Province	Anshun, Guizhou Province; Longnan, Gansu Province
Guangdong Province	Guangxi Zhuang Autonomous Region; Garze Tibetan Autonomous Prefecture, Sichuan Province
Guangzhou, Guangdong Province	Buyi and Miao Autonomous Prefectures and Bijie in Southwest Guizhou Province
Foshan, Guangdong Province	Liangshan Yi Autonomous Prefecture, Sichuan Province
Zhongshan and Dongguan, Guangdong Province	Zhaotong, Yunnan Province
Zhuhai, Guangdong Province	Nujiang Lisu Autonomous Prefecture, Yunnan Province

Source The Guidelines on Further Strengthening Poverty Alleviation Cooperation between the East and the West

Under the new situation, in August 2015, the general office of the CPC Central Committee and the State Council issued the Notice on Further Improving the Paired-Up Assistance in Poverty Alleviation, which adjusted the pairs and made it clear that the Work Committee for Departments Directly under the CPC Central Committee, State Organs Work Committee of the CPC Central Committee, the United Front Work Department of the CPC Central Committee, Ministry of Education, the People's Bank of China, the State Owned Assets Supervision and Administration Commission of the State Council, the General Political Department of the Chinese People's Liberation Army (renamed the Political Work Department of the Central Military Commission of the CPC after the reform of national defense and army in 2016) were responsible for the designated poverty alleviation work by contacting departments directly under the CPC Central Committee, state departments, the central committees of other political Parties and the All-China Federation of Industry and Commerce, institutions of higher learning, financial institutions, central enterprises, the People's Liberation Army and the armed police force.

After the adjustments, the number of central departments, institutions and enterprises participating in poverty reduction reached 320, assisting the 592 key counties on the state's poverty alleviation work list. The army and the armed police force continued to promote the work, offering paired-up assistance to more poor counties, towns and villages.

By nature, the helping organizations can be divided into seven categories as mentioned above, involving 32 departments directly under the CPC Central Committee, 78 central state departments, central committees of 9 other political parties and the All-China Federation of Industry and Commerce, 100 central enterprises, 49 colleges and universities and 19 financial institutions, according to incomplete statistics, in addition to the people's Liberation Army and the armed police forces.

Box 2.1 Central departments responsible for the paired-up assistance in poverty alleviation and their contacts

Contacts have been established respectively between central departments responsible for the paired-up assistance in poverty alleviation and those under their jurisdiction, such as Work Committee for Departments Directly under the CPC Central Committee and Organization Department of the CPC Central Committee, Publicity Department of the CPC Central Committee; State Organs Work Committee of the CPC Central Committee and Ministry of Foreign Affairs, National Development and Reform Commission and Ministry of Education; the United Front Work Department of the CPC Central Committee and central committees of other political parties and the All-China Federation of Industry and Commerce; Ministry of Education and institutions of higher learning such as Peking University, Tsinghua University and China Agricultural University; The People's Bank of China and Industrial and Commercial

Bank of China, Agricultural Bank of China and Bank of China, as well as China Banking Regulatory Commission, China Securities Regulatory Commission and China Insurance Regulatory Commission; State-owned Assets Supervision and Administration Commission of the State Council and central enterprises such as China National Nuclear Industry Corporation, China National Nuclear Industry Construction Corporation and China Aerospace Science and Technology Corporation; the Political Work Department of the Central Military Commission and People's Liberation Army and the Armed Police Force. The Organization Department of the CPC Central Committee is responsible for selecting and dispatching temporary poverty alleviation officials and first Party secretaries together with their contact departments.

Source The Plan on Targeted Poverty Alleviation during the 13th Five-Year Plan Period

The third is private enterprises, social organizations and individuals. They have taken initiative to fulfill their social responsibilities by supporting and participating in poverty alleviation efforts and using their own resources to carry out a series of aid activities for poor areas.

Since the reform and opening-up in 1978, all sectors of society have made their own contributions to poverty alleviation and development. However, there were still some problems, such as insufficient mobilization and inadequate policy support as well as unsatisfactory institutional mechanisms. In order to solve these problems, the General Office of the State Council issued the Guidelines on Further Mobilizing All Sectors of Society to Participate in Poverty Alleviation and Development in 2014, specifying the requirement to incubate diversified social sectors to join in. Measures included:

(1) Encouraging private enterprises to join in poverty alleviation. They have been called for to actively bear social responsibility to fully stimulate the vitality of the market. By giving full play to their advantages of capital, technology, market and management, they may lead to help poor villages by making investment, training skills, creating jobs and giving donations through resource development, industrial incubation, market development, village-enterprise collaboration and other forms. (2) Guiding social forces to participate in poverty alleviation. Social organizations, foundations, non-profit private businesses and other organizations have been given support to actively engage in poverty alleviation. Local governments at all levels and relevant departments are required to provide information and professional guidance to encourage them to participate in the mobilization, allocation and use of social poverty eradication resources, and build a dynamic mechanism for their participation. (3) Mobilizing individuals to help the poor people. While advocating the philosophy of "all for one and one for all", various field visits and fact-finding tours have been organized to enhance the communication among different sections of society and reach out to people in need. Efforts from the public, including people from Hong Kong, Macao and Taiwan regions, as well as Overseas Chinese, are encouraged to

participate in poverty alleviation in various forms, such as donation, voluntary service and paired-up assistance.

2.1.3.2 International Resources

International cooperation has always been an important part of China's poverty alleviation. International organizations have not only provided financial assistance, but also brought in a series of advanced concepts, models and methods which have had a far-reaching impact on China's poverty reduction practice.

Among many international organizations that have offered assistance to China, the poverty reduction projects in China implemented by the World Bank and the Asian Development Bank are representative and have played a very important role in facilitating the progress of China's extensive poverty reduction.

By the end of June 30, 2014, loans from the World Bank to China (the total loans of the International Bank for Reconstruction and Development and the International Development Association) had been about US $54 billion in 376 projects, which covered environment, transportation, urban development, rural development, energy, water resources management and human development. In 2015, the World Bank approved 13 projects with a pledged total investment of US $1.2785 billion (see Table 2.2).

Together with the World Bank, the Asian Development Bank has also played a significant role in China's poverty reduction process. Since the People's Republic of China joined the Asian Development Bank in 1986, China has received a total loan of US $29.76 billion from the bank, making it the bank's second largest borrower. In the year of 2013, ADB's loan assistance to China totaled US $1.54 billion, including 12 loan projects, involving four priority development areas, namely, agriculture and natural resources, energy, transportation, and urban and social sectors.

2.2 An All-Encompassing Campaign Against Poverty

Xi Jinping points out: "Poverty alleviation and development are the common responsibility of the whole Party and society. We should mobilize and rally the whole of society for extensive participation. Consequently, government-sponsored projects, sector-specific programs, and corporate and societal assistance must be integrated to create a synergy."[1] To implement and improve the development-driven poverty alleviation strategy, efforts should be made to further the cooperation between the government, the market and society. While emphasizing the role of the government, the enthusiasm of the market and society should be stimulated to make full use of their resources, too.

[1] Literature Research Office of the CPC Central Committee [1].

Table 2.2 Projects of World Bank in China, 2015

No.	Projects	Pledged investment (million US dollars)
1	Guilin Integrated Environment Management Project	100
2	Hebei Rural Renewable Energy Development Project	71.5
3	Sichuan-Chongqing Collaboration (Guang'an) Demonstration Area Infrastructure Development Project	100
4	Gansu Rural-Urban Integration Project	150
5	Yunnan Highway Asset Management Project	150
6	China Contaminated Site Management Project	15
7	Anhui (Huainan) Mining Area Rehabilitation Project	100
8	Xinjiang Technical and Vocational Education and Training Project	50
9	China Sustainable Cities Integrated Approach Pilot Project	2
10	Demonstration Pilot Projects of Poverty Alleviation through Industrial Development in Contiguous Poor Areas	150
11	Guizhou (Tongren) Rural Transport Project	150
12	Urumqi Urban Transport Upgrading Project (Phase II)	140
13	Tianjin Urban Transport Upgrading Project	100
14	Total	1278.5

Note What the table shows is the pledged investment amount owing to the fact that the projects are still under way and the actual amount may change with the progress
Source World Bank website, http://www.shihang.org/zh/country/China/projects/all?qterm=&lang_exact=Chinese&os=0

Various forms such as government-sponsored projects, sector-specific programs, corporate and societal assistance have been explored for the innovation of the system and mechanism to establish a unified information sharing and exchanging platform with the help of the Internet and mobile network technology and promote the overall integration of human and other resources to deliver genuine outcomes.

2.2.1 Government-Sponsored Projects

Also known as special poverty alleviation programs, they refer to that under the working mechanism whereby the central leadership makes overall plans, provincial authorities take overall responsibility, and city and county authorities oversee implementation, the central financial department arranges special poverty alleviation funds and relevant industry departments set up special projects, and delegate the tasks and quotas to governments at all levels under the overall leadership of provincial government institutions. Then local government and relevant institutions are responsible for promoting regional and individual poverty alleviation through the projects.

Government-sponsored projects usually cover a wide range, including relocation, village-based poverty alleviation, providing jobs instead of grants and poverty alleviation through industrial development, employment promotion, pilot programs for poverty alleviation and developing old revolutionary base areas.

2.2.1.1 Relocation for Poverty Alleviation

Relocating those from inhospitable areas has been a special program designed to help rural poor to shake off poverty, supported by funds allocated by the state ministries and commissions. Located in remote mountains with unfavorable natural conditions, the majority of the poverty-stricken areas in China are underdeveloped with fragile eco-environment, shortage of resources and backward infrastructure such as water supply, electricity and roads, as well as poor facilities of public services in education, medical care and culture. As a result, people living in these regions have been trapped in a vicious cycle of poverty. As their sustainable livelihoods are under threat, it is impossible for the poor to get out of poverty if they remained where they were. This has given rise to the program, which, during the 13th Five-year Plan period, had been carried out by adhering to the principle of respecting people's wishes and adopting proactive and prudent policies to integrate this initiative with the new type of urbanization.

It is required that the relocation to other more livable areas should be implemented by taking into consideration many factors, such as site selection, housing, industry and employment support for those who agree to move, in addition to community governance, environmental protection, infrastructure and public services. Decisions should be made in line with local resources, environment and population size to ensure that the resettlement sites well meet the needs of work, life and employment of the relocated people, which should be as close as possible to central villages, small towns, industrial parks and tourist attractions, so as to prevent another relocation caused by unsatisfactory site selection. The government should guide relocated people to seek employment near their relocation areas. Moreover, in line with conditions of different resettlement sites and poor areas, measures like returning farmland to forest, merger of towns and villages, and industrial restructuring have been taken to achieve sound and sustainable economic development in those areas, while improving the living conditions of the rural poor and their quality of life.

2.2.1.2 Village-Based Poverty Alleviation

This refers to a government-sponsored poverty alleviation program focusing on key villages of poverty, aiming at increasing individual income while improving local infrastructure, public services and the rural residents' living and working conditions in general, so as to facilitate an all-round economic, social and cultural progress. Governments at county, township and village levels subdivide the tasks and indicators of the program, formulate effective and responsive working plans, and implement them as scheduled. The measures have been as follows:

(1) Improving rural poor's basic well-being and rural living environment to increase their incomes. This can be done by boosting the cultivation of basic farmland and raising food self-sufficiency. In light of the principle of voluntary and steady progress, people living in extremely poor conditions have been relocated to places suitable for living and working. Multiple channels have been explored to increase their agricultural and non-agricultural income, such as developing local industries, organizing professional trainings on agriculture, setting up specialized cooperative organizations and guiding surplus poor labor forces to find jobs outside their villages. These have helped to gradually improve the overall social and economic development, and increase individual income of the rural poor in general.
(2) Under the guidance of leadership at all levels who take the responsibility of development-oriented poverty alleviation as a whole, all kinds of disposable funds related to agricultural production and people's life, together with other resources such as social donations, have been effectively integrated and allocated according to the actual needs of poor areas to support construction projects of public infrastructure services. Substantial assistance networks have been set up to help introduce social resources into villages and households to build a more prosperous socialist countryside and rural communities with Chinese characteristics.
(3) Continuous efforts have been made to improve the innovation mechanism of these newly-built villages and communities, strengthening their supervision, monitoring and management and helping poor households find new ways to raise their income and to achieve a long-term stable growth. An oversight system and network has been established to strengthen statistical monitoring of poverty alleviation, supervise and manage funds and programs for poverty eradication in villages. Rural people have been encouraged to participate in the management, inspection and appraisal of related programs to ensure their pertinence and effectiveness.

2.2.1.3 Providing Employment as a Form of Relief

Work relief means that the state allocates funds in deposit or cash to poverty areas for the implementation of infrastructure construction, so as to engage poor people to participate in the remuneration work as a source to support their families. It is a way of providing jobs instead of grants. The funds for work relief come from the central government's special poverty alleviation program. Based on fact-finding investigations to poverty-stricken areas, different construction projects have been designed in light of different local conditions to encourage local poor to actively take part in so as to achieve sustainable development by both improving infrastructure facilities of poor areas and activating the internal driver of the poor population. For instance, there could be road construction projects in places with poor communications. And protection projects on water and soil resources could be set up in areas where soil erosion is serious and water management is not satisfactory. Therefore, these programs have not only raised the income of the rural poor, but also encouraged them to rely on their own efforts rather than wait for external assistance. The programs have played a significant role in the sustainable development of local economy and society.

2.2.1.4 Poverty Alleviation Through Industrial Development

Poverty alleviation through creating new economic activity refers to developing local economy and industries with local characteristics in line with local cultural, economic, ecological and natural advantages to promote the coordinated development between individuals (households) and their region. Driven by development, poverty eradication efforts are made to activate the momentum of growth and block the causes of poverty. For instance, it is advisable to advance the development of tourism for poor areas endowed with beautiful natural environment; and for poor areas with favorable climate, it is good to promote fruit industry, cultivate high-end products and increase average output so that the operating income of the poor people can be increased in an actual way. For poor areas rich in ethnic culture, they could try out the "agriculture + cultural and creative industry" to add to the rural attraction. In addition, attention has been paid to developing local agriculture in a creative way and exploring new drivers for economy growth through the integration of agriculture and tourism and other new forms of business. For poverty-stricken areas with traditional farming industries, processing industries could be developed in line with local conditions to extend the industrial growth chain and increase the added value so that poor population can benefit from the development.

2.2.1.5 Employment Promotion for Poverty Alleviation

Employment promotion includes measures taken to create employment opportunities for people to guarantee their rights to work. These measures are: Firstly, paying attention to local labor demands while releasing timely recruitment information to guide eligible poor people to work outside their villages with transportation subsidies. Secondly, providing poor laborers with professional trainings to develop their knowledge and skills and enhance their employment capacities in response to their needs. Thirdly, capable migrant workers are encouraged to return to their hometowns to start businesses. It is true that "To achieve initial prosperity in the countryside, it is essential to raise rural living standards and particularly those of impoverished villagers." Led by these capable people with their start-ups in poor areas, more job opportunities have been created and more local people are employed who work to lift themselves out of poverty.

2.2.1.6 Pilot Programs for Poverty Alleviation

Pilot programs for poverty alleviation are termed as a series of exploratory and experimental work or programs in innovating mechanisms for development-oriented poverty alleviation and eliminating extreme poverty. These programs have helped bring new ideas on anti-poverty mechanisms and provided valuable experience as well as useful approaches and solutions to problems and difficulties in poverty alleviation for other poor areas to draw on.

2.2.1.7 Developing Old Revolutionary Base Areas

Developing old revolutionary base areas has constituted a major component in government-sponsored programs. As is stated in Guidelines on Intensifying Poverty Alleviation Efforts to Support the Development of Old Revolutionary Base Areas, this involves supporting those areas in poverty, helping people in need and focusing on the toughest problems. Major tasks in this regard have included: stepping up infrastructure development, exploring competitive resources on an active and well-coordinated basis; focusing on the advancement of industries with local characteristics and protecting the environment through effective ways. In addition, no efforts are spared to improve people's well-being and assist more poor people in finding stable jobs other than farming to ensure targeted poverty alleviation is implemented with actual outcome. Consequently, old revolutionary base areas have taken a new look with more vitality and momentum towards a more promising and innovative development.

2.2.2 Sector-Specific Programs

Poverty alleviation through sector-specific programs means the development-oriented poverty alleviation tasks undertaken and completed by China's departments of public administration (hereinafter referred to as "industrial departments"), in accordance with the statutory division of functions and poverty alleviation tasks designated by the central leadership. In 2013, China issued Guidelines on Promoting Rural Poverty Alleviation and Development through Innovative Mechanisms, which emphasized that: in response to bottleneck issues of the development of poor areas, measures should be taken by prioritizing tasks and ensuring effectiveness in line with local conditions and by clearly-defined classifications. It also stressed the significance of integrating all resources and clarifying goals and responsibilities to implement development-oriented poverty alleviation in ten priority aspects, namely, guarantees of roads to villages, safe drinking water, power supplies, renovation of dilapidated houses, revenue increase from specialty industries, rural tourism, education, healthcare, cultural development and IT application in poor villages.

Since the implementation of targeted poverty alleviation, Xi Jinping has proposed a series of new ideas and proposals and one of them is "Five Measures for Poverty Eradication", which addresses the question about "how to help" and enriches the practice of sector-specific programs to alleviate poverty. Based on the requirements of the "Two Assurances and Three Guarantees" and the "Five Measures for Poverty Eradication", the programs have covered ten key projects, namely: guarantees of safe drinking water supply, relocation of rural poor, renovation of dilapidated rural houses, more access to education, improved healthcare services, industrial development, more employment opportunities for the poor, subsistence allowances for those unable to shake off poverty through their own efforts, technological support and the development of transportation as the priority. Each project has a government department responsible for the implementation, and the practices will be introduced in detail in the third chapter of the book.

Poverty alleviation through sector-specific programs is characteristic of departments of a particular sector utilizing all its public resources to boost the development of poor areas. Including resources in finance, environment, humans, technology, culture, programs and policies, public resources could be made best use of to help implement policies and measures in respects of general planning, industrial layouts, program investment, payments transfer and preferential policies. In terms of its organization system, governments at all levels delegate responsibilities to sector departments and people in charge, so as to ensure rational divisions of tasks with clearly defined rights and responsibilities.

2.2.3 Corporate and Societal Assistance

Under the leadership of governments at all levels, the general public, social organizations, enterprises and public institutions have been fully mobilized to take the initiative to join in the effort of poverty elimination. Players from all walks of life have worked together to speed up the economic development of poverty-stricken areas, with improved living conditions and quality of life for the poor, which have complied with the goals to achieve a moderately prosperous society in all aspects with Chinese characteristics. Based on realities in China, corporate and societal assistance in poverty relief has been conducted in several forms, including paired-up assistance, East-West collaboration, and the participation of private enterprises as well as social organizations and individuals.

2.2.3.1 Paired-Up Assistance in Poverty Alleviation

This refers to the practice in which the CPC and government departments, enterprises, public institutions and social organizations are paired up with poor counties to provide assistance to the latter. It is a major component of China's poverty elimination campaign and a significant manifestation of China's political and institutional strengths.[2] It involves the participation of central and local governments. At the central level, it is the CPC and government departments, other political parties and All-China Federation of Industry and Commerce, people's organizations, state-run public institutions, sizable state-owned backbone enterprises, state-owned financial institutions, leading national institutions of research and higher learning, in addition to the People's Army and the armed police force, being partnered with the key counties on the state's poverty alleviation work list under the unified deployment of the CPC Central committee. They have provided substantial support to these counties in capital, material, technology, human resources, projects and information. At the local level, measures that have proved to be successful include: leading officials pairing up with designated poor regions, comprehensive and targeted assistance to poor villages or households in need, performance evaluations and incentives. Starting from the mid-1980s, paired-up assistance in poverty alleviation has undergone four stages: fledging period (1986–1993), growth (1994–2000), advancement (2001–2010) and improvement (since 2011).

The first stage or the fledging period began in 1986, when ten ministries and commissions, including those of science and technology, agriculture, forestry and geology, and mineral resources, each selected a region to pair up in the 18 contiguous poor areas across the country to assist the local people out of poverty. In 1987, the State Council held the first conference on paired-up assistance in poverty alleviation to introduce the practice nationwide. This was followed by the participation of other central departments, state-owned enterprises and public institutions. During this period, there were mainly five tasks in their paired-up assistance to help poverty-stricken areas. First, to publicize and implement policies of the central government on poverty-stricken areas; second, to make useful suggestions for poor people to get rid of poverty based on fact-finding tours and research; third, to offer opportunities of training for poor people to acquire practical knowledge and skills; fourth, to oversee the funds and materials allocated by the state and local governments and to solve existing problems; fifth, to select more places for introducing the practice. It shows that even from the very beginning, the State Council adopted a long-term development perspective and made corresponding requirements for paired-up assistance in poverty alleviation, evidenced by tasks above.

The second stage was that of growth. At the end of 1993, there were still 80 million rural poor people in China, with a poverty rate of 8.87%, who, without adequate food and clothing, mostly lived in the central and western parts of China. Given this situation, on April 15, 1994, the State Council issued The National Seven-Year Poverty Alleviation Program (1994–2000), which emphasized the requirement to

[2] Xi [2].

mobilize and organize all social forces to participate in poverty alleviation, and made a special point that "The CPC and government departments, enterprises and public institutions should try to be engaged in helping the poverty-stricken counties out of poverty. They should make the paired-up assistance a long-term job and see to it that their efforts generate satisfactory outcomes". As a result, the framework of paired-up assistance in poverty alleviation under the leadership of the CPC and central government was taking shape, with 120 central departments helping 330 poor counties listed by the state. On October 17, 1998, the Leading Group for Development-Oriented Poverty Alleviation of the State Council, and two central commissions jointly convened a conference on paired-up assistance in poverty elimination, and made plans in this aspect on account of institutional reform. In this second stage, 138 central departments paired up with 325 poor counties listed by the state.[3]

The main tasks at this stage covered the following three aspects: Implementing policies aiming at development-oriented poverty alleviation and providing assistance to every village, and every household; taking advantages of departments and sectors to create opportunities for local areas to give full play to their competitive resources and to ensure smooth commodity circulation channels for the development of industrialized agricultural operations; taking various forms to train and develop human resources for poor areas so that poor people are better motivated and rely more on their own efforts to get out of poverty. During this period, a total of 3498 officials from central and state departments were dispatched as members of resident work teams in poor villages; 17,400 officials paid fact-finding visits to their paired poor counties; and RMB5.427 billion was invested.[4]

The third stage was advancement. By 2000, the number of rural people living in poverty had dropped from 250 million in 1978 to 30 million. However, this remaining poor population lived in areas with harsh natural conditions, underdeveloped social environment and poor public services, and the outcome in poverty elimination seriously fell short of what had invested. To address the situation, the State Council released The Outline for Development-Driven Poverty Alleviation in Rural Areas (2001–2010) based on a review of the achievements and experience of implementing the previous Seven-year Program, and made arrangements for the following ten years. It was decided that 272 ministries, commissions, state-owned enterprises and public institutions worked together to assist 481 key poor counties. As a result of institutional reforms and the dissolution and merger of some state-owned enterprises, the number of participating departments declined, with 241 helping 440 listed poor counties, leaving 152 without assisting pairs[5] in 2010. To better advance the work, the CPC Central Committee and the State Council jointly released a notice on a new round of paired-up assistance in 2010, rearranging the work and redefining the

[3] Wen [3].

[4] Xia [4].

[5] China Committed to Full Coverage of Major Poor Regions and Counties for Development-Oriented Poverty Alleviation [EB/OL]. (2010-07-08). http://www.gov.cn/jrzg/2010-07/08/content_1648985.htm.

overall tasks and priorities. In this stage, the CPC and central departments invested a total of RMB8.487 billion and dispatched 3077 resident officials to work in poor counties, helping absorb RMB29.25 billion and creating 9432 poverty alleviation projects. Altogether 3904 talented people were brought in and 1712 advanced technologies introduced. 288 thousand poverty-stricken students were provided financial support.[6] These efforts have generated effective outcomes.

The final stage was improvement. This was a period when rural residents had basic security of food and clothing and their subsistence was guaranteed. The major problem was the deep-seated contradiction that restricted regional development, especially in contiguous areas of extreme poverty where the development gap among regions had become increasingly prominent. To address the situation, the State Council promulgated the renewed The Outline for Development-Driven Poverty Alleviation in Rural Areas (2011–2020), placing greater emphasis on paired-up assistance in poverty alleviation. In 2012, the State Council Leading Group Office of Poverty Alleviation and Development and seven other government departments jointly released a notice on a new round of paired-up assistance by central departments and ministries, and worked out a new list of cooperation partners. 310 central and state departments partnered with 592 poor counties, covering for the first time all the key counties on the state's poverty alleviation work list.

In 2015, the General Office of the CPC Central Committee and the State Council issued Decision on Winning the Battle against Extreme Poverty, stressing that the work on paired-up assistance should be improved systematically by establishing assessment and evaluation mechanisms to ensure that all departments fulfill their responsibility for poverty alleviation. Responsibility mechanism for leading departments should be improved for supervision and guidance of departments under their jurisdiction to do a better job. Since the 18th CPC National Congress in 2012, 1727 officials have been dispatched by the designated CPC and central departments to work as resident team members or first Party secretaries in poor villages, and RMB 71.37 billion have been invested to help lift 89 counties, 19,000 villages and 13 million people out of poverty. These have provided major support for winning the battle against extreme poverty.[7]

2.2.3.2 East-West Collaboration in Poverty Alleviation

This refers to the practice carried out since the start of reform and opening up of pairing the developed provinces and municipalities in the east with the impoverished regions in the west by providing financial and human resources support through transfer of industries and other forms. It aims at facilitating the collaboration between the eastern and western regions so that they could complement each other to narrow the gap and promote the development and prosperity of poor areas. Xi Jinping once stated that "We should explore new ways to promote industrial collaboration between

[6] He [5].

[7] Jiang [6].

the east and the west, so that they may complement each other with their respective strengths."[8] This has been a guideline for promoting the collaboration between the eastern and western regions and targeted assistance in poverty eradication. To tackle tough problems in the western poverty-stricken areas, it is important to both give a fuller play to the government functions and allow the market to play its decisive role in resource allocation.

To enhance industrial collaboration, it is important to take a market-oriented approach, with a good balance between supply and demand, to promote the transfer of industries from the east to the west. While driving the development of the west, the east can benefit from the cooperation to speed up its industrial development so that mutual benefit and common development can be achieved. Efforts have been made to inspire the motivation of the poverty-stricken areas in the west by utilizing the strength of the east to make up for the weakness of the west to drive its development. Consequently, the model of poverty alleviation has changed from providing external support like a blood transfusion to a more sustained effort from self-motivation.

The idea was first proposed in 1994 when The National Seven-Year Poverty Alleviation Program (1994–2000) was released, in which it was stipulated that big cities like Beijing, Tianjin and Shanghai as well as developed coastal provinces such as Guangdong, Jiangsu, Zhejiang, Shandong, Liaoning and Fujian should each pair up with one or two poverty-stricken provinces or regions in the west to boost their economy. In 1995, the fifth plenary session of the 14th Central Committee of the CPC passed decisions concerned; requiring developed coastal regions to assist 10 provinces, regions and municipalities in central and western China. In 1996, the Central Conference on Poverty Alleviation and Development stressed the requirements and made arrangements for developed coastal provinces and cities to support their poverty-afflicted counterparts in the west. This marked the official launching of the east-west anti-poverty collaboration. It has been required that the assistance should be provided to counties, and the collaboration implemented by specific enterprises and programs. Better-off and poor counties should be paired up to carry out economic cooperation as well as exchange of officials. Enterprises from the east have been encouraged to transfer their industries to poor areas in the west to jointly develop local resources by making full use of their strengths in human resources, technology, information, market, management and capital on the basis of mutual benefit. Provincial level partnership has been established to be in charge of coordinating and organizing work between the two sides.

Over the past two decades, eastern and western regions have made notable progress in fighting poverty through collaboration. Party committees and governments of relevant provinces and cities in eastern and western China have promoted the collaboration on poverty alleviation by adhering to the strategic thinking of the CPC on the development of both the coastal areas and the interior to move step by step towards common prosperity. The campaign has been carried out at various levels, with all forms and in every way to form a work system with participation of all players from the government, enterprises, social organizations and individuals. Distinctive eastern

[8] Institute for Party History and Literature of the CPC Central Committee [7].

and western cooperation models have emerged, such as Cooperation between Fujian in southeast China and Ningxia in northwest China, cooperation between Shanghai and Yunnan and cooperation between Guangdong and Guangxi. This practice has contributed significantly to poverty alleviation in China.

2.2.3.3 Corporate and Societal Assistance in Poverty Alleviation

Corporate participation in poverty alleviation started during the period of implementing The National Seven-Year Poverty Alleviation Program from 1994 to 2000. Titled "Guangcai (Glory) Program", the poverty-relief initiative of entrepreneurs did not draw much attention from governments and society because of the limited involvement of enterprises at the beginning. Since the launch of targeted poverty alleviation, private enterprises have provided a great amount of financial and materiel support together with human resources in response to the country's anti-poverty endeavor to gradually develop their efforts into mechanisms and actions for systematic participation in ending poverty.

A case in point is the well-known program of "10,000 Enterprises Helping 10,000 Villages". Initiated by All-China Federation of Industry and Commerce, the State Council Leading Group Office and China Society for Promotion of the Guangcai Program, the action had private enterprises as players to help poor counties and households by signing up cooperation or pairing-up agreements. More than 10,000 private enterprises in China were mobilized to participate in the program, with the goal of helping more than 10,000 poor villages to speed up poverty eradication in 3–5 years. By the end of December 2019, the effort had made notable progress. A total of 99,900 private enterprises were registered for the program, providing targeted help to 116,600 villages (including 65,600 registered poor villages), investing RMB 81.957 billion in rural industries and RMB 14.922 billion in public welfare. 736,600 people were provided jobs and 1.1133 million received technical training. The entrepreneurs have helped and benefited 14.3442 million registered rural poor.

As an important part in socialist modernization drive, social organizations have served as a bridge connecting social resources with poor areas and a significant leader mobilizing social forces to join hands in poverty eradication. They are one of the major players of China's all-encompassing framework against poverty. Over the years, they have played a unique role in helping establish closer ties between governments and poor people, dovetailing market and social mechanisms, and integrating resources from the government, market and society (see Table 2.3).

Societal assistance in poverty alleviation has been conducted through voluntary services and donations. People from all walks of life, including young students, skilled professionals and retirees, have worked as volunteers to do their bit in poverty alleviation by offering medical and educational assistance, cultural assistance, scientific and technological promotion, employment assistance, and entrepreneurship guidance. At the same time, by virtue of designated donations, these volunteers have made contributions in helping lift poor villages and families out of poverty.

Table 2.3 Major poverty alleviation programs of non-governmental organizations

Programs for poverty alleviation	Non-governmental organizations	Operations
Project Hope	China Youth Development Foundation	Helping build Hope schools; assisting poor students
Spring Buds Project	China Children and Teenagers' Fund	Assisting poor girl dropouts by running "Spring Buds Classes" and donating "Spring Buds Schools"
Programme of Happiness	China Population Warfare Foundation	Providing small grant, work relief, development funds for mothers from poor families
	China Family Planning Association	
	China's Population	
Angel Project	China Federation for Rural Development	Providing trainings for hospital presidents and administrators in the West China; equipping hospitals there with information management system and medical assistance facilities
Grant Program for Girls of Soong Qing Ling Foundation	China Soong Qing Ling Foundation	Assisting girl dropouts getting back to school and providing them with scholarships; setting up boarding centers and primary schools for girls
Water Cellar for Mothers Project	Chinese Women's Development Foundation	Growing from a clean water supply project for rural mothers to a comprehensive rural development program covering cellar construction, cultivation, garden planting, biogas, sanitary toilet and micro processing
Guangcai Program	All-China Federation of Industry and Commerce	Poverty alleviation through industrialization of agriculture, advantageous resources, medical and health care, intellectual development, relocation, employment, market development, public welfare donations and state assistance

(continued)

Table 2.3 (continued)

Programs for poverty alleviation	Non-governmental organizations	Operations
China Health Poverty Alleviation Project	Chinese Primary Health Care Foundation	Popularizing basic principles of primary health care to rural poor; helping poor regions to improve their medical conditions
Poverty Relief	China Charity Federation	Providing relief in eight areas including disaster relief, poverty eradication, elderly care, love outreach for orphans, volunteer teaching, student aids, caring for the disabled and medical support

Source Liu et al. [8]

2.3 Mechanisms for Policy Making, Project Implementation, Supervision and Assessment

2.3.1 Policy-Making Mechanism

The policy-making mechanism for poverty eradication has been closely related to the working mechanism. According to Decision on Winning the Battle against Extreme Poverty issued by the CPC Central Committee and the State Council, the working mechanism operates to ensure that the central leadership makes overall plans, provincial authorities take overall responsibility, and city and county authorities take charge of the implementation. In response to this requirement, the poverty alleviation policies of the central government, provinces, cities and counties have been closely related. The heads of provincial level Party committees and governments assume overall responsibility, while CPC committee secretaries at five levels of provinces, cities (prefectures), counties and townships, and the Party branches of villages are responsible for poverty alleviation under their jurisdiction. They play different roles in the making of policies. In general, from the central to the local levels, poverty alleviation policies have become more and more in detail. The central government issues general guidelines and provincial, city and county authorities formulate policies tailored to local conditions. This consistent, coordinated and complementary policy-making mechanism has effectively prevented the "one-size-fits-all" approach.

In addition, to ensure different roles from the central to local governments are brought into full play, the tasks of Party committees and governments at all levels have been clearly defined. With provincial Party committees and governments issuing policies based on the central government's guidelines, city and county authorities should work out specific implementation briefs in line with local conditions. This mechanism has ensured that government instructions are not only circulated, but also implemented in anti-poverty measures and generate expected results, so that the poor people can get real benefits. In formulating specific policies, governments at all levels have taken four major principles into consideration, namely, combining short-term and long-term effects, integrating funds and projects, seeking truth from facts with categorized and targeted measures, and maintaining policy continuity and dynamic coordination.

2.3.1.1 Principle of Combining Short-Term and Long-Term Effects

At the end of 2014, there were still 70.17 million rural people living in poverty in China. With the situation at the time, it was a pressing and heavy task to achieve the set goal of lifting more than 70 million people out of poverty through 2020. Therefore, more creative and effective measures should be taken to solve the poverty problem of the rural population.

It was in this context that the fight against extreme poverty was proposed. As an innovative measure, it was short-term and typical of the campaign style. However, poverty is a long-standing social phenomenon, and even after we eliminate absolute poverty within a short period, relative poverty will persist for some time in the future.

In light of this, policies for poverty alleviation are bound to be the combination of long-term and short-term ones. Typical short term policies have been those related to the poverty alleviation standards concerning assurances of adequate food and clothing and guarantees of access to compulsory education, basic medical services and safe housing, specifically in supply of safe drinking water, relocation, renovation of dilapidated houses, control of school dropouts of children entitled to compulsory education, and guarantee of basic medical care. All these have aimed to improve the basic living conditions for poor people in the short term.

However, poverty eradication policies should also feature a long-term mechanism. These have been reflected in policies related to poverty eradication measures, such as developing industries, boosting employment for the poor and providing micro-credit programs. These policies have emphasized and encouraged more participation and internal impetus of impoverished people. They are the most important stakeholders for targeted poverty alleviation, and fully meeting their diversified needs and expectations has been a vital prerequisite for the success of the endeavor.

Targeted poverty alleviation must foster the internal driver of the poor and build a mechanism for them to participate. They should be guided to take part in goal setting, needs assessment, project selection, implementation and monitoring, so that they can fully express their interests and demands, and change from passive recipients of assistance to active participants to improve their capability for self management and development. These are all important issues to be considered in the formulation of poverty alleviation policies.

2.3.1.2 Principle of Integrating Funds and Projects

Targeted poverty alleviation requires allocating resources based on targeted assistance to households rather than regional development. Among decision-makers in the process, the county-level government, as the one that enjoys the most convenient access to effective and comprehensive information, should be the major platform and implementer for resource integration and allocation. To ensure that poverty eradication is well targeted, the traditional way of allocating funds and projects should be changed by exploring a more optimal resource integration mechanism, and delegating the management authority to county authorities, so as to avoid inefficiency caused by overlapping funds and projects.

Before poverty alleviation, governments at all levels, under the "project-based mechanism", mainly helped poor people get rid of poverty through special projects, and the main source of funding for these projects was special government funds, which was far from sufficient to meet the actual demands. The small government funds, with the separate management of related agricultural sectors and the insufficient funds provided to individual households, have affected the outcome and efficiency of poverty alleviation.

Under this backdrop, the CPC Central Committee and the State Council have made targeted arrangements and deployment with a series of policies introduced to coordinate poverty relief funds and projects. The most representative ones are the Guidelines on Supporting Poverty-Stricken Counties to Carry out Pilot Projects of Integrating Funds for Rural Development and the Notice on Improving the Construction of County-Level Project Banks for Poverty Alleviation. The former put forward the integration scope, measures and organizational guarantee of the funds, and defined the coverage of use of funds and the supervisors. And the latter required poor counties to establish project banks for poverty eradication, pursuing targeted assistance, public participation, openness and transparency, and gradual improvement.

The policy of integrating government funds for rural development in poor counties has promoted poverty alleviation projects. Funds for agricultural development have been more efficiently used for supply to meet demand. The policy has also solved the dilemma of asymmetric information in distributing funds and projects, providing a strong institutional guarantee for poverty alleviation. The project banks have standardized the project management mechanism which adapts the funds for rural development to the practice of decentralized fund project approval authority. They have together promoted the targeted use of funds and projects.

2.3.1.3 Principle of Differentiated and Targeted Measures by Seeking Truth from Facts

There used to be 832 key counties and 14 contiguous poverty-stricken areas on the state's poverty alleviation work list, mainly distributed in 22 provinces, autonomous regions and municipalities in central and western China. Each of the counties had different features of poverty due to its location, climate and social environment. Even in the same county, different poor people may have different causes of poverty. Therefore, poverty eradication policies must be tailored for different places and households, which have been reflected in their rich variety.

For example, for impoverished labor forces, each province has introduced corresponding industrial employment policies to guide poor population to participate in industrial development and get jobs, helping them find the way out of poverty. The government has provided transportation subsidies to encourage poor laborers to go to other places to work and guided enterprises to generate jobs that match the laborers' ability in local industrial development bases and poverty alleviation workshops for those who stay in their villages. For weak labor forces, the government would guide villager committees to create more welfare jobs and use government funds or village collective revenue as welfare job wages to give them a sense of satisfaction from work; for people who are unable to work, the government would use the social security policy and maintain its continuity and stability to help lift them out of poverty. There have also been policies for poor people with previous experience of doing business who wish to get loans for a new start up, by which the government would provide them with micro-credits for poverty alleviation and subsidizes the interest rate for them to address the capital shortage. The government has introduced all these policies to create a synergy with full consideration of the causes of poverty and different regional development.

2.3.1.4 Principle of Maintaining Policy Continuity and Dynamic Coordination

China began its poverty alleviation and development in 1978. From 1978 to 2012, the policies mainly focused on regional development, as in The National Seven-Year Poverty Alleviation Program (1994–2000), The Outline for Development-Driven Poverty Alleviation in Rural Areas (2001–2010) and The Outline for Development-Driven Poverty Alleviation in Rural Areas (2011–2020). The stability and continuity of the policy has been a clear manifestation of China's institutional strengths.

In 2013, President Xi Jinping put forward the strategic proposal of targeted poverty alleviation according to the actual conditions of the time, which was the development and deepening of the previous regional poverty alleviation and development policy. The formulation of policies against extreme poverty also maintained the principle of policy continuity, such as continuing to promote the development of 14 contiguous poverty-stricken areas, pursuing the combination of targeted poverty alleviation with regional development, and ensuring that the social and economic development in poor counties would be boosted through the fight against extreme poverty. For instance, the efforts such as improving local transportation have not only enhanced regional development, but also improved the external conditions for the poor to get rid of poverty.

In addition, a coordination of various policies has also been taken into consideration. Before the launch of the battle against extreme poverty, despite the establishment of the all-encompassing poverty alleviation framework of government-sponsored projects, sector-specific programs, and corporate and societal assistance, they were generally separated from each other, with no effective coordination mechanism.

Sometimes they even conflicted with each other, which made it difficult to create joint efforts in targeted poverty alleviation.

In 2015, Decision on Winning the Battle against Extreme Poverty was issued, calling for the extensive mobilization of social forces and joint efforts to promote poverty eradication. In 2018, with Guidelines on the Three-Year Action Plan to Win the Battle against Extreme Poverty, the CPC Central Committee and the State Council stressed on further mobilizing the whole society in poverty alleviation, giving full play to both government and social resources, and building an all-encompassing framework with government-sponsored projects, sector-specific programs, and corporate and societal assistance working together and supplementing each other. In terms of specific policies, the dovetailing of the rural system of subsistence allowances with the development-driven poverty alleviation system manifested the principle of policy coordination.

2.3.2 Mechanism for Project Implementation

In mid-1990s, China started the reform of tax distribution system, which led to a series of major changes in the revenue and fund allocation system. This brought about a new form of top-down allocation of project funds, i.e., fiscal transfer payments could be flexibly handled outside the administrative system through a project system. Most of these payments could be made by higher-level operational departments by special payments or project funds that flow from top to bottom, while primary-level governments may receive payments from bottom to top through applications.[9] Poverty alleviation projects fall into this category. Higher-level governments would set up special poverty alleviation funds and encourage primary-level governments to apply for related projects. The mechanism of matching special funds and projects has ensured that local governments put poverty alleviation efforts into practice. To improve the implementation, the approval and management authority has been decentralized to counties, so that the objectives, tasks, funds, as well as rights and responsibilities would be set by county governments, with provincial and municipal governments responsible for project supervision.

Taking the overarching plan and major projects of poverty alleviation as platforms, county-level governments have been making efforts to establish a mechanism to benefit poor households. In line with different causes of poverty, they have tailored policies for different individuals and households, ensuring that these projects provide targeted assistance. A strict monitoring and evaluation mechanism has also been introduced to guarantee the delivery of satisfactory outcomes. It was emphasized that, unlike major national planning and technological projects in professional fields, these projects as carriers of various anti-poverty policies have reflected the logic and policies of governance as a whole of the state on the issue of poverty.

[9] She and Chen [9].

This special model of "governance through projects" has worked well in targeted poverty alleviation. Based on diverse methods adopted in different places in China, the management process usually includes four phases: application, review and approval, implementation and supervision, and assessment and acceptance.

2.3.2.1 Project Application

Application is the first step of the project operation and it is also the reference and source of project implementation. The policy of integrating government funds for rural development in poor counties has delegated the project approval to local governments to boost their initiative to map out and carry out plans to encourage poor areas to apply for the projects, which is conducive to creating a synergy in poverty elimination. Township governments and villages are responsible for the application, while village officials and members of resident work teams learn about specific project needs based on visits to poor households.

2.3.2.2 Project Review and Approval

After township and village governments make the application, the county leadership for poverty alleviation will review and decide whether to approve or not according to laws and regulations and local conditions. After the approval, poor counties need to make public on local official websites and major media the sources and uses of the funds and project proposals for rural development. They also need to keep villagers well informed of the projects for public supervision.

2.3.2.3 Project Implementation and Supervision

Projects are implemented by following the responsibility system, with defined responsibilities for departments and individuals in charge. The implementation of the projects and the use of funds are separated, so are the supervision of the projects and of the funds. This has helped ensure clean operation and efficiency, prevent misconducts such as embezzlement and retention of funds, and also make the supervision more independent. Project supervision mainly involves the supervision of project approval, implementation, quality and safety; while supervision of funds includes supervision of appropriation and clean use of funds.

2.3.2.4 Project Assessment and Acceptance

This is mainly carried out by the County Poverty Alleviation Office together with other departments in charge. After the completion, the implementation townships and villages will conduct self-assessment and acceptance, and then report to the county office, which, together with relevant departments, will deliver on-site spot checks according to the detailed terms of the project plan and decide the results.

2.3.3 Mechanism for Supervision and Assessment

Supervision and assessment mechanism is a characteristic and important part of the campaign against extreme poverty. It provides supervision and incentives for winning the battle against poverty and motivates local governments to promote the implementation of policies and responsibilities. In addition, it has also trained a large number of officials, community members and third-party assessors, who are valuable assets for the management of the rural areas in general.

2.3.3.1 Supervision Mechanism

A sound policy system can only be put into practice with an appropriate overseeing mechanism. Poverty elimination involves a large area and population. Therefore, a complete supervision system is highly necessary. The supervision mechanism includes three aspects: supervision by inspection, democratic supervision and public supervision.

First, supervision by inspection. In 2016, the General office of the CPC Central Committee and the General office of the State Council issued Regulations on Supervision by Inspection for Poverty Alleviation, which stressed that the work should be carried out by adhering to the basic strategy of targeted poverty alleviation and elimination, focusing on the objectives and problems by seeking truth from facts, encouraging public participation, and delegating responsibilities to different levels. Relevant areas and departments have been urged to define responsibilities, policies and measures. Complying with discipline and regulations, they have been encouraged to find solutions, improve working methods and complete tasks to ensure the victory in the battle against poverty.

The supervision has focused on the delivery of objectives and effective outcomes. The State Council Leading Group for Poverty Alleviation and Development is responsible for the overall supervision and reports to the central leadership, which provides a major reference for provincial Party committees and governments to assess their work. The Office of the Leading Group is in charge of the daily routine and the inspection team sees to the arrangement, with the team leader and staff being selected from relevant departments under the Leading Group.

The supervision includes that of comprehensive performance and of specialized areas. The former concentrates on poverty eradication in all relevant areas and departments, generally once a year, while the latter aims at the key work and is carried out from time to time as needed. The supervision involves major concerns such as the delegation of responsibilities for poverty eradication, implementation of specialized planning, major policies and measures, the poverty alleviation of people in extreme poverty, accurate registration of impoverished people and deregistration of those who have emerged out of poverty, in addition to government-sponsored projects, sector-specific programs, East-West collaboration, paired-up assistance, the implementation of key projects, and the integration of government funds for rural development in poor counties.

The inspection has been problem-oriented and focused on solving key issues. The work is carried out regularly by inspection teams set up with the approval of the central leadership, based on progress of the anti-poverty campaign. The State Council Poverty Alleviation Office is responsible for daily work. The team leader takes the responsibility, who is one of the leading officials at the provincial or ministerial level. Members of the team are selected from relevant departments and local governments as required.

The key issues to be inspected have been: malfeasance, inaction or malpractice of officials in poverty alleviation; embezzlement, misappropriation and illegal arrangement of poverty alleviation funds and projects; misconducts in poverty identification and exit, and dishonesty such as manipulation and falsification of data; violation of stable-tenure disciplinary requirements of the CPC and government leaders and the restraint mechanism of poverty-stricken counties. The inspection results and rectification suggestions would be reported to the CPC Central Committee and the State Council after examination by the Poverty Alleviation Leading Group. If there are violations of law and discipline, they would be transferred to Central Commission for Discipline Inspection or procuratorial organs.

Poverty alleviation inspection is an important form of self-supervision by the CPC, and a product of the organic combination of inner-Party supervision and public supervision. The practice helps supervise, review and promote, and it is an important measure taken by the CPC to realize self-purification, self-improvement, self-renovation and self-enhancement.

Second, democratic supervision. It is one of the important forms of democratic governance for socialism with Chinese characteristics, which refers to suggestions, opinions and criticisms from other political parties, eminent people without Party affiliation, people's groups and patriots from all walks of life participating in the CPPCC on important national and local affairs.

In October 2017, the United Front Work Department of CPC Central Committee and the State Council Poverty Alleviation Leading Group Office issued the Plan on Supporting the Central Committees of Other Political parties to Carry Out Democratic Supervision of the Fight against Poverty, pointing out that democratic supervision is an important form of other political parties assisting local CPC Party committees and governments in winning the battle against poverty. In the Plan, the central committees of the eight other political parties were designated the tasks of providing pair-up assistance respectively to the eight central and western regions with large poor populations and high incidence of poverty, namely, the Revolutionary Committee of the Chinese Kuomintang to Guizhou Province, the China Democratic League to Henan Province, the China National Democratic Construction Association to Guangxi Province, the China Association for Promoting Democracy to Hunan Province, the Chinese Peasants and Workers Democratic Party to Yunnan

Province, the China Zhi Gong Party to Sichuan Province, the Jiusan Society to Shaanxi Province, and the Taiwan Democratic Self-Government League to Gansu Province.

Democratic supervision of poverty eradication has included: identifying the impoverished people; targeted poverty alleviation; removal of counties from poverty list; performance of responsibilities of poverty alleviation; implementation of major policies and measures; and management and use of poverty alleviation funds.

Major forms of democratic supervision are: carrying out inspection and fact-finding tours; making suggestions; participating in specialized supervision and evaluation; strengthening routine contacts; and conducting publicity of policies.

Democratic supervision in poverty eradication has given full play to the advantages of other political parties in terms of experience, intelligence, talent and networking. It promotes poverty eradication in poor areas and highlights China's strengths in multi-Party cooperation system. To take the Jiusan Society as a Party participating in government affairs as an example. It is mainly composed of middle and senior intellectuals in the science and technology sector, which enjoys strengths in offering anti-poverty assistance and support through technology, education and healthcare. Their proposals have helped solve major problems and assist the CPC committees and governments to fight poverty in poor areas.

Third, public supervision. This refers to the supervision of poverty alleviation by the media, individuals and other social forces. First of all, governments and their departments at all levels have promoted open management of Party affairs and made public announcements of major policies on poverty eradication, so that people are well informed of important decisions involving their interests. In addition, the supervision of petitioning has been improved. The State Council Leading Group Office has set up the hotline "12317" for public oversight to ensure that the people have access to expressing their opinions. Last but not least, news media at all levels are required to shoulder the responsibility as "whistleblowers" in social affairs, supervising major policies, the implementation of Party rules and regulations in poverty alleviation, and exposing more misconducts that infringe on the interests of the public. The media is also required to focus on solving conflicts and making improvements, giving full play to the role of supervision by public opinions.

2.3.3.2 Assessment Mechanism

While supervision mechanism is a monitoring and incentive mechanism to boost poverty alleviation, the assessment mechanism is goal-oriented, checking and appraising whether and how well the goals have been accomplished. It assesses the outcome of anti-poverty efforts by provincial Party committees and governments and of east-west collaboration, paired-up assistance by the central departments, as well as the exit of counties from the poverty list.

Firstly, the assessment on the performances of provincial Party committees and governments. In 2016, the central leadership issued the Methods for Evaluating the

Performances of Provincial Party Committees and Governments in Poverty Alleviation and Development. The State Council Leading Group was in charge of organizing annual assessments from 2016 to 2020, which were conducted by its member departments headed by the Leading Group's office and the Department of Organization under the CPC Central Committee. The assessment involved four aspects of results of poverty reduction, precise identification of the poor population, targeted assistance, management and utilization of assistance funds, covering seven quantitative indicators and two qualitative indicators. Methods used were mainly cross-appraisal, third-party assessment and media investigations. Starting from 2017, with the approval of the CPC Central Committee and the State Council, rewards were given to provinces, autonomous regions and municipalities for excellent performances. If problems were found, there were admonitions for officials in charge; and if problems were serious, chief officials of the Party and the government would be given admonitions.

Secondly, the assessment on the east-west poverty alleviation collaboration. In August 2017, the State Council Leading Group Office issued the Methods for Evaluating the Performances of East-West Poverty Alleviation Collaboration (on Trial Basis). From 2017 to 2020, the assessments were carried out annually, by teams led by the central government, with members from the Organization Department and the United Front Work Department of the CPC Central Committee, the National Development and Reform Commission, the Ministry of Education, the National Ethnic Affairs Commission, the Ministry of Finance, the Ministry of Human Resources and Social Security, the National Health Commission, and the All-China Federation of Industry and Commerce.

The assessment on poverty relief work in the eastern and the western regions both included 6 elements: organization and leadership, human resources assistance, financial support, industrial cooperation, labor collaboration, and Joint Efforts towards Prosperity Campaign. For the eastern regions, 22 indicators were involved while for the western regions, it involved 14 indicators.

The assessment was mainly conducted by cross-appraisal. The Leading Group reported the results to the CPC Central Committee and the State Council on a yearly basis and circulated the results to related departments. The records were kept as a reference for assessing the anti-poverty performances of provincial Party committees and governments in central and western China.

Thirdly, the assessment on poverty alleviation assistance of central departments to designated areas. In August 2017, the State Council Leading Group Office issued Methods for Evaluating Poverty Alleviation Assistance of Central Departments to Designated Areas (on Trial Basis). From 2017 to 2020, the annual assessment was organized by the State Council Leading Group, and coordinated by its Office. The Organization Department of the CPC Central Committee led in supervising central departments in selecting and dispatching poverty alleviation officials and first Party secretaries in villages.

The Work Committee for Departments Directly under the CPC Central Committee, State Organs Work Committee of CPC Central Committee, the United

Front Work Department of the CPC Central Committee, the Ministry of Education, the People's Bank of China, State-Owned Assets Supervision and Administration Commission of the State Council led in assessing the designated poverty alleviation tasks of Departments directly under the CPC Central Committee, Central State Organs, Central Committees of other political Parties, the All-China Federation of Industry and Commerce, colleges and universities, financial institutions, and enterprises under the central government respectively. Political Work Department of the Central Military Commission conducted inspection and supervision of missions performed by the military and armed police forces.

The assessment involved 6 aspects with 11 indicators, covering the outcome in poverty alleviation, organization and leadership, the selection of officials, supervision and inspection, villager satisfaction, and innovation measures. Assessment by classification has been introduced, and the six leading departments for poverty alleviation carried out the work by assessing their respective contact departments by reviewing the work summary and conducting on-site inspections. The State Council Leading Group annually reported the assessment results to the CPC Central Committee and the State Council, which was also informed to the central departments and sent to the Organization Department of the CPC Central Committee to keep records.

In 2018, the three aforementioned assessments were integrated as the assessment on poverty elimination results, and were deployed under unified arrangement. The assessment on the performances of provincial Party committees and governments concentrated on responsibilities taken and implementation of policies and tasks, by ways of third-party assessment, inter-provincial cross-check and media investigations. Compared to the previous appraisals, the new approach had improvements in several aspects.

One was to streamline the process. The combined assessment approach reduced the burden of primary-level governments in responding to inspections and the pressure of report submission. The reduction in the number of counties for random inspection also relieved the pressure on poor areas. Another was to optimize methods and issues covered for the assessment. It was based on categories of poor counties, non-poor counties, and deregistered counties, with a different focus to avoid unfair judgments. Also, issues for inter-provincial cross-assessments were optimized. The appraisal no longer had the accuracy of poverty identification and exit as major concerns, which shifted the focus to assessing on responsibilities taken and implementation of policies and tasks. In addition, the third-party assessment was enhanced. Based on the assessment of accurate poverty identification and deregistration, and public satisfaction, the third-party assessment focused on salient issues and areas of weaknesses that affected the implementation of targeted policies and measures for individual households and the stability and sustainability of poverty eradication, which helped the establishment of a long-term mechanism for stable poverty eradication with more satisfactory outcomes delivered.

Fourthly, the specialized assessment on poverty exit. In November 2015, the CPC Central Committee and the State Council issued Decision on Winning the Battle Against Extreme Poverty, which required the development of strict, standardized and transparent criteria, procedures and verification methods for poverty exit of key counties. In June 2018, the Guidelines on the Three-Year Action Plan to Win the Battle Against Extreme Poverty was released, proposing to implement the criteria and procedures, and standardize the implementation of the withdrawal of counties, villages and population that had emerged out of poverty from the list. Local governments were guided to revise the assessment and evaluation indicators, removing or demoting those that exceeded the standard or tasks that were unrelated to poverty alleviation.

Removing the label of extreme poverty was based on indicators covering three aspects: (1) key indicator, i.e. the overall poverty incidence; (2) reference indicators, including false deregistration and missing registration of poverty, and the recognition of the public; (3) other issues, including poverty eradication planning, implementation of major policies and measures, improvement of infrastructure and public services, follow-up assistance plans and arrangements for consolidation and enhancement, with emphasis on the specific measures, quality and stability of poverty eradication.

In terms of the assessment approach, the removal of poverty was reviewed and decided by third parties. According to the requirements, while poor counties deregistered from 2015 to 2017 were assessed by the State Council Leading Group Office, those deregistered in 2018 and beyond were assessed by provinces, autonomous regions and municipalities. At the same time, the CPC Central Committee would make spot checks on deregistered counties.

As indicated above, the assessment on poverty alleviation results and the specialized appraisal on the exit of counties that had emerged out of poverty have been carried out by third parties, which is a major anti-poverty innovation in China. In general, the third-party assessment has functioned like a baton, a quality checker, a propeller, and a thermometer. It is a mechanism encouraging better performance instead of "nitpicking"; and it is evaluation based on truth rather than a layman's judgment of a professional. Practice in the past few years has proven that the third-party assessment is an important tool of public governance and a major component of democratic supervision in China.

Bibliography

1. Literature Research Office of the CPC Central Committee. (2018). *Selected documents since the 18th CPC National Congress (II)*. Central Party Literature Publishing House.
2. Xi, J. (2015, December 11). *Paired-up assistance in poverty alleviation from central departments, enterprises and institutions*. http://www.xinhuanet.com/politics/2015-12/11/c_1117436744.htm
3. Wen, J. (1998). Central departments should contribute more to poverty alleviation: Speech at central conference on paired-up assistance in poverty alleviation. *China's Underdeveloped Regions* (10), 7.
4. Xia, J. (2002, January 20). *For the people: 15 years of paired-up assistance in poverty alleviation from central departments*. http://text.news.sohu.com/97/52/news147705297.shtml
5. He, P. (2010, July 09). Paired-up assistance reaches to 440 poor counties. http://epaper.gmw.cn/gmrb/html/2010-07/09/nw.D110000gmrb_201000709_3-04.htm
6. Jiang, L. (2019, August 16). *Staying true to our founding mission: Achievements in paired-up assistance for poverty alleviation by CPC and central departments exhibited in Beijing*. http://www.xinhuanet.com/2019-08/16/c_1124884858.htm
7. Institute for Party History and Literature of the CPC Central Committee. (2018). *Xi Jinping on poverty alleviation*. Central Party Literature Publishing House.
8. Liu, J., et al. (2009). *Poverty reduction in rural China*. China Financial & Economic Publishing House.
9. She, X., & Chen, Y. (2011). Hierarchical operation mechanism and governance logic of project system: Sociological analysis of the case of "projects for village". *Social Sciences in China* (4), 126–148, 223.
10. Liu, Y. (2017, September 04). *Achievements of poverty alleviation and development with Chinese characteristics*. Retrieved July 20, 2020, from http://www.cpad.gov.cn/art/2017/9/4/art_56_69341.html
11. Wang, S. (2018). Large-scale poverty reduction in China over the past 40 years: Driving force and institutional foundation. *Journal of Renmin University of China, 32*(6), 1–11.
12. Gong, F. (2016, March 10). *Prioritizing the targeted arrangement of poverty alleviation projects*. Retrieved August 04, 2020, from http://edu.cssn.cn/zt/zt_xkzt/27923/123456/123/201604/t20160420_2975949.shtml
13. Han, X., & Han, G. (2020). Historical process and experience implications of paired-up assistance for poverty alleviation by central and state government departments. *Collected Papers of Historical Studies* (4), 56–64.
14. Zhao, Y., & Shi, F. (2018). Development of ideological and political work in private enterprises over the 40 years of reform and opening up. *Theory Monthly* (7), 168–176.
15. Lu, J. (2020). A new practice of poverty alleviation in China: Private business participation and its implications. *Guizhou Social Sciences, 3*, 154–160.
16. Yang, Y., & Liu, A. (2020). A literature review of researches on corporate participation in targeted poverty alleviation. *Rural Economy and Science Technology, 31*(10), 143–145.
17. Guo, J., & Bian, S. (2018). Models of corporate assistance in relocation of rural poor for targeted poverty alleviation in western China: A case study of the paired-up assistance between Evergrande Group and Dafang County. *Journal of Northwest University (Philosophy and Social Sciences Edition), 48*(6), 43–52.
18. Feng, M. (2018). Development of social organizations in Pudong: History, logic and experience. *Jiangnan Forum, 11*, 18–20.
19. Song, Z. (2019). Nine suggestions on promoting active participation of social organizations in the battle against extreme poverty. *Chinese Social Organization, 7*, 9–10.
20. Hu, Y. (2020). Guided involvement: Analysis of policy texts on social organizations' participation in poverty alleviation. *Journal of Anqing Normal University (Social Sciences Edition), 39*(1), 79–86.

21. Li, Y. (2020). New changes of corporate participation in poverty alleviation: More attention to effectiveness and sustainable development mechanism: An interview with Liu Wenkui, Vice President and Secretary General of China Foundation for poverty alleviation. *China Sustainability Tribune, 5*, 18–20.
22. Yang, A. (2014). Regional development and poverty alleviation in contiguous impoverished areas. *Journal of Jishou University (Social Sciences Edition), 35*(2), 80–87.
23. *Notes on the proposal of the central committee of the communist party of China on formulating the 13th five-year plan for national economic and social development*, November 15, 2015. Retrieved August 04, 2020, from http://theory.people.com.cn/n1/2015/1231/c83845-28001269.html
24. The State Council. (2016, September 23). *The outline for development-driven poverty alleviation in rural areas (2001–2010)*. Retrieved August 03, 2020, from http://www.gov.cn/zhengce/content/2016-09-23/content_5111138
25. Xi, J. (2015, October 16). *Working together to eradicate poverty and promote common development*. Retrieved August 03, 2020, from http://www.beijingreview.com.cn/shishi/201510/t20151016_800040417.html
26. Li, G., & Wang, Z. (2017). A functional analysis of multi-player poverty governance under the all-encompassing mechanism. *Journal of Party School of Nanjing Municipal Committee of CPC* (6), 64–69.
27. *Innovating mechanisms to encourage market players to participate in poverty alleviation and development*, October 27, 2015. Retrieved August 03, 2020, from http://www.gov.cn/xinwen/2015-10/27/content_5001438.htm
28. Huang, C., & Zhou, J. (2015). Participation of private enterprises in poverty governance driven by win-win and collaborative development. *Inner Mongolia Social Sciences, 36*(2), 144–149.
29. Li, M. (2018). Government, market and society: Order dimensions of targeted poverty alleviation. *Academics, 7*, 62–71.
30. Sun, W. (2013). Innovation of poverty alleviation modes in rural China: A perspective of new developmentalism. *Guangdong Social Sciences, 6*, 207–213.
31. Zeng, B. (2006). Literature review of studies on poverty alleviation through tourism in China. *Tourism Tribune, 2*, 89–94.
32. *The State Council on management mechanism reform of special poverty alleviation funds*, August 08, 2014. Retrieved August 03, 2020, from http://www.cpad.gov.cn/art/2014/8/8/art_46_72584.html
33. Fan, X. (2013). *Understanding common terms in poverty alleviation and development*. China Financial & Economic Publishing House.
34. General Office of the CPC Central Committee and General Office of the State Council. (2010, July 08). *Notice on further improving the work of targeted poverty alleviation*. http://www.gov.cn/jrzg/2010-07/08/content_1649275
35. Zhang, S. (2017). Improving the mechanism of targeted financial investment to win the battle against poverty. *China State Finance, 9*, 24–25.
36. Huang, J. (2018). Pooling organizational strengths to cope with extreme poverty: Understanding and implementing Xi Jinping's important ideas and proposals on winning the battle against poverty. *Qiushi, 8*, 15–16.
37. Miao, G. (2018). Three major problems to address in winning the battle against poverty. *People's Forum, 11*, 62–63.
38. Shi, T. (2017). Work hard to win: In-depth understanding and implementing Xi Jinping's speech at the symposium on poverty alleviation in impoverished areas. *Qiushi* (18), 8–10.
39. Yang, J., & Yao, J. (2018). Analysis of poverty alleviation mechanism of "government leadership with multi-player collaboration" and policy implications. *Review of Economic Research, 2916*(68), 77–82.
40. Si, L., Yin, M., & Yang, F. (2018). Breaking the paradox of double poverty alleviation with the all-encompassing campaign: Poverty alleviation policy innovations in the past 40 years of reform and opening up. *Journal of Lanzhou University (Social Sciences Edition), 46*(5), 117–127.

41. Ma, Y. (2018). Reflections and suggestions on strengthening the management of government funds for poverty alleviation: Based on the use of poverty alleviation funds in Zhangjiakou, Hengshui, Chengde and other cities and counties. *Review of Economic Research, 70*, 26–29.
42. Huang, H. (2018). Reflections and suggestions on financial support for the development of new agricultural business entities for poverty alleviation. *Wuhan Finance, 227*(11), 65–67.
43. Jiang, Z. (2018). Stability of poverty alleviation under targeted measures. *Chinese Rural Economy, 407*(11), 19–33.
44. Ma, B., & Wu, Z. (2018). Improving the governance capacity of local governments and winning the battle against poverty. *Review of Economic Research* (30), 37–39.
45. Wu, W. (2018). Leveraging the effectiveness of democratic oversight to help fight poverty. *People's Forum, 601*(20), 6–9.
46. Hou, S. (2017). Targeted performance evaluation of poverty alleviation. *Gansu Social Sciences, 2*, 251–255.
47. Wan, L., & Xue, Y. (2018). Mechanism innovation of corporate participation in poverty alleviation in ethnic poverty areas guided by "targeted poverty alleviation." *Guizhou Ethnic Studies, 39*(11), 43–49.
48. Peng, X. (2018). Winning targeted poverty alleviation campaign with the spirit of reform and innovation. *People's Forum, 602*(21), 14–15.
49. Wang, S., & Wang, C. (2018). Weaknesses and enhancement of collaboration between government and social sectors in targeted poverty alleviation. *Theoretical Exploration* (5), 74–79.
50. Hong, Y., Zhang, X., & Chen, J. (2019). Performance evaluation and poverty alleviation mechanism establishment from the perspective of public value. *Rural Economy* (2), 54–61.
51. Sun, D., & Cao, Z. (2018). Primary practice in targeted industrial poverty alleviation: Strategy selection and dual constraints: Based on fact-finding tours in county A. *Journal of Social Sciences, 460*(12), 5–15.
52. Wang, J., & Shi, Z. (2017). Overall framework and index system of poverty exit mechanism. *Reform* (1), 119–131.
53. Li, W. (2016). Xi Jinping on basic strategies of poverty alleviation and their internal logical relations. *Learning Forum, 32*(12), 35–39.
54. Yuan, L. (2018). Analysis on the practical effect, existing problems and countermeasures of poverty alleviation through employment in China. *Modern Management Science, 306*(9), 111–113.
55. General Office of the CPC Central Committee and General Office of the State Council. (2015, December 08). *Framework guidelines on several major issues concerning the improvement of audit system and supporting documents.* http://www.gov.cn/xinwen/2015-12/08/content_5021377.htm
56. General Office of the CPC Central Committee and General Office of the State Council. (2016, February 16). *Measures for effectiveness appraisal of poverty alleviation and development by provincial party committees and governments.* http://politics.people.com.cn/n1/2016/0216/c1001-28128635.html
57. Wu, X., & Zhao, P. (2015). Negotiation in targeted poverty alleviation in rural areas: Content and mechanism: Based on observations of village A in Nanbu County, Sichuan Province. *Socialism Studies* (6), 102–110.
58. Park, A., & Wang, S. (2010). Community-based development and poverty alleviation: An evaluation of China's poor village investment program. *Journal of Public Economics, 94*(9–10), 790–799.

Chapter 3
Policy System for Targeted Poverty Alleviation

Targeted poverty alleviation is a complex and systematic project involving all and every aspect of the economic and social development of poor areas and the production and life of poor people. It requires the joint participation of government departments, market players, social organizations and individuals. At the Poverty Reduction and Development Forum in 2015, President Xi Jinping stressed that "China will significantly increase input in poverty alleviation, introduce more policies and measures that will benefit poor areas and people to give full play to the strengths of the Chinese system. We will apply targeted measures to different groups of people and mobilize all social sectors, supporting and encouraging the whole society to participate in poverty alleviation in flexible and diversified forms."[1]

Since the 18th CPC National Congress, under the guidance of Xi Jinping's Theory and in accordance with the requirements of the basic strategy of targeted poverty alleviation, the CPC Central Committee and the State Council have rolled out a series of plans, policies and guidelines for the final battle against poverty. Among them, there are Guidelines on Further Mobilizing All Sectors of Society to Participate in Poverty Alleviation and Development; Decision on Winning the Battle Against Extreme Poverty; The 13th Five-Year Plan for Poverty Alleviation; and Guidelines on the Three-Year Action Plan to Win the Battle Against Extreme Poverty.

Through intensive planning, the central leadership has worked with governments at all levels to formulate a package of innovative poverty alleviation policies, which have developed to create extensive policy synergies. With constant reviews and improvements, a policy framework for poverty elimination has been built to provide a strong support for winning the anti-poverty campaign.

[1] Xi [1].

S. Wang, *Poverty Alleviation and Targeted Measures*,
https://doi.org/10.1007/978-981-96-1493-6_3

3.1 Policies of Government Funds for Poverty Alleviation

As an old saying goes, "Food and fodder should go ahead of troops and horses to win a battle." Government funding is the food and fodder for winning the battle against poverty, a strong support to ensure that the basic strategy of targeted poverty elimination is effectively implemented. Since the start of the reform and opening up, particularly since the 18th CPC National Congress, the CPC and the government have attached great importance to development-driven poverty alleviation, with increased financial support for poverty alleviation to ensure the smooth delivery of a series of effective poverty reduction measures.

President Xi Jinping has made it clear that "The input in poverty alleviation and development should match the requirements of winning the battle against extreme poverty" and "the increase of the central government's funds should reflect the requirements of stepping up development-driven poverty alleviation efforts".[2] Decision on Winning the Battle Against Extreme Poverty clearly requires that government funds play a leading role in the endeavor. New funding channels should be tapped to ensure that the government input is commensurate with the task of poverty alleviation.

3.1.1 Poverty Alleviation Funds

Government funds for poverty alleviation are funds allocated by the central government through the general public budget to support provinces (autonomous regions and municipalities directly under the Central Government) and Xinjiang Production and Construction Corps (a state-owned economic organization) for targeted poverty alleviation. The capital expenditure covers six major areas, namely, poverty alleviation and development, ethnic development, work relief, poverty alleviation for poor state-owned farms and forestry centers, agricultural development in the three western regions of Hexi Region and Dingxi Region in Gansu Province and the mountainous region in southern Ningxia Hui Autonomous Region. Efforts are made to ensure targeted use of funds to generate actual benefits for the rural poor.

Poverty alleviation funds from the central government are allocated in accordance with the factor method, which mainly covers factors such as poverty situation, policy tasks and poverty alleviation outcome. In respect of poverty situation, considerations include the size and proportion of the poor population in each province, depth of poverty, per capita net income of rural residents, local per capita financial resources and other objective indicators reflecting poverty. In terms of policy tasks, the national poverty alleviation and development policies, annual poverty alleviation tasks and the development of poor ethnic people are taken into account. As for poverty alleviation outcomes, what is to be considered are the results of the anti-poverty performance assessment, the results of the performance evaluation of the special government funds for poverty alleviation, and the outcome of the

[2] Institute of Party History and Literature of the CPC Central Committee [2].

pilot work of the overall planning and integrated use of government funds for rural development in poor counties. The use of funds has focused on the cultivation and expansion of specialty industries, the improvement of small public welfare production and living facilities, and the strengthening of the poor population's capacity for self-development and risk-resistance.[3]

Since the implementation of China's organized and planned poverty alleviation and development drive in the 1980s, the central government's poverty alleviation funds have played a supporting role and their amount has kept increasing. From 1980 to 1984, the central government set up funds to support the development of economically underdeveloped areas, which allocated RMB 2.98 billion for poverty alleviation over five years, with an average annual increase of 11.76%. From 1985 to 1993, a total of RMB 20.127 billion was earmarked to help the poor, again with an average annual increase of 11.76%. In the period between 1994 and 2000, when the National Seven-Year Poverty Alleviation Program was launched, a total of RMB53.181 billion was invested, with an average annual rise of 9.81%. During 2001–2010 when the Outline for Development-Driven Poverty Alleviation in Rural Areas was implemented for the first 10 years, a total of RMB144.034 billion of poverty alleviation funds was allocated, with an average annual growth of 9.3%. From 2011 to 2015, during the 12th Five-Year Plan period, a total of RMB189.822 billion was allocated, with an average annual growth of 14.5%.[4]

Since the 18th CPC National Congress, the central collective leadership has issued a series of policies on increasing fiscal funding for poverty alleviation and strengthening its management, with aims to guide the use of government funds. In January 2014, the General Offices of the CPC Central Committee and the State Council issued Guidelines on Promoting Rural Poverty Alleviation and Development through Innovative Mechanisms, requiring governments at all levels to gradually increase the input of fiscal funds for poverty alleviation, step up the reform of fund management, and make the use of funds more targeted and effective. Oriented to major poverty elimination programs and projects, government funds for rural development are integrated to address prominent poverty issues.[5]

In November 2015, Decision on Winning the Battle Against Extreme Poverty was issued, which pointed out that the government should step up input in poverty alleviation. The central government continued to increase transfer payments to poor areas, and the amount of funds increased significantly. General transfer payments, various special transfer payments related to rural people's livelihood, and investment from the central budget have prioritized poor areas and the poor population.

At the same time, it was required that the central public welfare lottery fund should step up support for poverty alleviation. Government funds like transfer payments for comprehensive agricultural development and rural reform should be allocated to poor villages in a certain proportion. And all the policies, programs and projects arranged

[3] *Notice on Measures for the Management of Central Government Funds for Poverty Alleviation* [EB/OL]. (2017-03-24). http://www.gov.cn/xinwen/2017-03/24/content-518043.htm [3].

[4] Hu [4].

[5] General Office of the CPC Central Committee and General Office of the State Council [5].

by various government departments to benefit rural people should give maximum priority to poor areas, villages and people.

All provinces (autonomous regions and municipalities directly under the Central Government) were required to actively adjust the structure of provincial fiscal expenditures and effectively increase funding for poverty alleviation in light of local needs. In addition, the government fund supply system should be optimized to support major poor counties by coordinating and integrating the use of government funds for rural development. Prominence should be given to poverty alleviation and targeted utilization of the funds, with strict supervision and assessment to ensure their safety and effectiveness. Malpractices such as false claims, private withholding of funds, embezzlement, and extravagance would be severely punished.[6]

In March 2017, Ministry of Finance and other ministries and commissions (offices) issued Measures for the Administration of Poverty Alleviation Funds of the Central Government, which, in line with the basic strategy of poverty alleviation, clearly stated that "The approval of poverty alleviation funds will be delegated to the county", "Poor counties could arrange the funds according to their anti-poverty needs". Meanwhile, the supervision of funds was tightened by introducing mechanisms such as performance evaluation, making the government affairs public and requiring departments concerned cooperate with audit, discipline inspection and the procuratorial authorities to do a good job in auditing and inspection so that safe, standardized and effective use of the funds could be ensured.

In September 2017, the Ministry of Finance and the Poverty Alleviation Office of the State Council jointly issued the Measures for the Performance Evaluation of Government Funds for Poverty Alleviation, defining performance evaluation indicators in terms of funds, fund allocation, fund supervision, efficiency of fund use, point addition (mechanism innovation) and subtraction (violation of rules and regulations). The results of fund performance evaluation were included in the evaluation of poverty alleviation performance of provincial Party committees and governments, and were used as one of the factors for the allocation of government poverty eradication funds.[7]

Poverty alleviation funds have been "life-saving money" for the poor. The steady growth of the government funding has played an important role in making it possible to achieve more targeted poverty alleviation by more targeted measures to address prominent problems of poor areas and poor people, so that their development can be accelerated and their basic working and living conditions be improved.

3.1.2 Integrating Government Funds for Rural Development

The central government has always attached great importance to issues related to rural people, agriculture and rural areas, to which a series of policies, measures

---

[6] The CPC Central Committee and the State Council [6].

[7] Notice on Measures for the Performance Evaluation of Government Funds for Poverty Alleviation[EB/OL]. (2017-09-19). http://www.gov.cn/xinwen/2017-09/19/content_5226116.htm [7].

and increased investment have been in place to give strong support. However, with the continuous increase of funding, problems emerged, such as segmentation, overlapping and duplication as well as mismatch of authority and responsibility, which greatly affected the efficiency of the fund use.

Since the start of the fight against extreme poverty, in order to further raise the targeted and efficient use of government funds for rural development to win the battle, the central government has paid great attention to integrating the funds. In April 2016, the State Council issued Guidelines on Supporting Pilot Programs of Integrating Government Funds for Rural Development in Poor Counties, clearly pointing out that the pilot projects should be carried out in counties in contiguous destitute areas and key counties on the state's poverty alleviation work list. The funds cover those arranged by governments at various levels for agricultural production and rural infrastructure development. At the same time, the integration of funds should be guaranteed in the following aspects:

Firstly, strengthening the financial security capacity of poor counties. With the central and provincial governments improving the structure of transfer payments, poor areas have been greatly benefited in size and proportion of general transfer payments, and their financial security capability is improved.

Secondly, increasing the preferential support for poor counties. In accordance with the requirement that the government's anti-poverty investment should be commensurate with the task of poverty alleviation, the central, provincial and municipal financial departments should, on the basis of a substantial increase in investment, give more preference to poor counties and take poverty alleviation as an important factor to consider in fund allocation.

Thirdly, empowering poor counties as major players in coordinating and integrating the use of funds. In line with the policy objectives and tasks of all departments and in accordance with local plans, a full play should be given to the advantages of county-level governments. Close to the front line of poverty alleviation and with sufficient management information, they are in a better position to distinguish priorities, identify key projects and tasks, and make overall arrangements of government funds for specific implementation.

Fourthly, innovating mechanisms for using government funds. Innovative mechanisms should be explored for poverty alleviation through industries and asset income, and by drawing on the fund-raising model in relocating people from inhospitable areas. Full play should be given to the guiding and leveraging role of government funds through effective means such as public–private partnership, government purchase of services, loans with discounted interest, and the establishment of industrial development funds. These efforts have helped leverage more financial capital and nongovernmental funds for poverty alleviation.

Fifthly, establishing an institutional system for the overall planning and integrated use of funds. Relevant departments at the central, provincial and municipal levels should timely revise and improve all rules and regulations and cancel provisions restricting the pooling, integration and use of funds. Poverty-stricken counties should formulate specific measures for the overall planning and integration of the use of government funds, and clearly define the division of labor among departments, operating procedures, use of funds and supervision measures.[8]

In February 2017, Ministry of Finance and the State Council Poverty Alleviation Office jointly issued the Notice on Pilot Programs of Integrating Government Funds for Rural Development in Poor Counties, pointing out that the pilot work should be extended to all 832 poor counties, and provinces should increase preferential support to pilot counties. In order to provide financial guarantee for the pilot work, a set proportion of government funds is allocated, and no specific projects or tasks unrelated to poverty alleviation should be designated.[9] In December of the year, the State Council issued Guidelines on Exploring the Establishment of a Long-Term Mechanism for Overall Planning and Integrating Government Funds for Rural Development, which further clarified the integration of government funds in poor counties. Specifically, efforts should be made in the following:

(1) To promote the integration of government funds within the industry. The management system should be improved to merge government funds as special funds for rural development. A management mode of "integrated funds + task list" has been introduced, which features a reasonably worked-out task list covering items to be guaranteed of financial support and the sum to be allocated.
(2) To promote the pooling of government funds among industries. Rolling fiscal and government investment plans should be worked out to play the leading role in the coordination, in an attempt to further facilitate the coordinated utilization of the funds with similar purposes in rural development and the concentrated input of funds with complementary functions and dovetailed uses.
(3) To reform and improve the management mechanisms for government funds. Efforts should be made to further delegate to primary-level governments the jurisdiction to review and approve related projects, grant local governments the right to make policy decisions and allocate funds, and improve their autonomy and flexibility in project decision making. Measures should be taken to strengthen supervision and management of government funds and prevent them from being misappropriated in the name of coordination and integration. In addition, more attention should be paid to information disclosure and improve the transparency of the use of funds.[10]

In March 2019, the Ministry of Finance and the State Council Poverty Alleviation Office jointly issued the Notice on the Pilot Work of the Integrating Government Funds for Rural Development in Poor Counties 2019, explicitly requiring that the misuse of funds in the name of integration be prohibited and the funds should not be used for items on the "negative list". Delegation of management should be in place and provisions restricting coordination and integration should be cancelled to ensure the effective increase of the proportion of substantial integration in an attempt to better use the funds to address the most urgent poverty alleviation issues.

---

[8] General Office of the State Council [8].

[9] Ministry of Finance and the State Council Poverty Alleviation Office [9].

[10] The State Council [10].

The integration of government funds in poor counties is one of the major components of the policy system for poverty alleviation. By reforming the supply mechanism of government funds for rural development, the structure of fiscal expenditure has been further optimized, which changed the past practice of "sprinkling pepper" of government funds and is conducive to pooling enough financial poverty alleviation funds for the development of anti-poverty industrial projects. It is an important part of the reform of the fiscal and taxation system, and has played a vital role of support in lifting poor counties out of poverty as scheduled.

3.2 Financial Policies for Poverty Alleviation

In development-driven poverty alleviation for rural areas, financial measures and government funding complement each other. Taken to address financing problems of poor areas and poor villagers, financial measures are important to promote the industrial development in poor areas and help poor people to get rid of poverty, while government funding is an important channel to enhance the efficiency of various funds in developing key projects to divert more capital and social assistance resources into poverty elimination. In November 2015, Xi Jinping specified at the Central Conference on Poverty Alleviation and Development that "We should take effective financial measures for poverty alleviation to accelerate the pace of rural financial reform and innovation",[11] putting forward new requirements for poverty alleviation through financial measures in the new period.

A rational allocation of financial resources and innovation of financial products and services are as important as improving financial infrastructure and optimizing financial ecological environment in boosting the development of inclusive finance and supporting the sustainable and healthy economic and social development of poor areas to lift people out of poverty. In order to do the job well, the People's Bank of China and six other government departments jointly issued the Guidelines on Providing Comprehensive Financial Services for Poverty Alleviation and Development in March 2014, pointing out that financial services in poor areas should be comprehensively improved to approach the national average through 2020. An inclusive financial system covering all people in poor areas, including vulnerable groups, should be established in an effort to give full play to the role of finance in helping rural poor get out of poverty with sustainable economic and social development in the region.[12] In November 2015, the CPC Central Committee and the State Council issued Decision on Winning the Battle Against Extreme Poverty, stressing that commercial, policy-based, developmental and cooperative financial institutions should be encouraged and guided to increase financial support for poverty alleviation and development. Policies like setting up anti-poverty further-credits programs and

[11] Literature Research Office of the CPC Central Committee [11].

[12] Guidelines on Providing Comprehensive Financial Services for Poverty Alleviation and Development [EB/OL]. (2014-04-10). http://www.gov.cn/xinwen/2014-04/10/content_2656095.htm [12].

issuing policy-based financial bonds should be introduced and practiced to help fight poverty.[13]

To comprehensively improve and upgrade financial services for poverty alleviation to enhance the accuracy and effectiveness, the People's Bank of China and six other departments jointly issued Guidelines on the Implementation of Financial Assistance for Poverty Alleviation in March 2016, defining the general requirements, objectives and key tasks of financial assistance under the new situation of targeted poverty alleviation. 22 specific measures were suggested to require that "Priority groups and key tasks in poverty alleviation should be targeted and identified, with accurate financial support meeting the needs. Emphasis should be placed on innovating and improving institutional mechanisms, policies and measures of financial services to ensure better quality and efficiency. Efforts should be made to combine targeted support with overall drive, coordinate financial policies with poverty alleviation policies, promote innovative development with risk prevention, and take the development of inclusive finance as the foundation. Every effort should be made to extend financial services in poor areas to every village and every household, and ensure that all eligible rural poor may have easy access to loans according to their needs, and every one of them in need of financial services may enjoy convenient modern financial services. Strong and effective support should be provided for winning the battle against extreme poverty and building a moderately prosperous society in all respects through 2020."[14] Under the overall deployment of the document, the China Banking Regulatory Commission, the China Securities Regulatory Commission (CSRC) and the China Insurance Regulatory Commission (CIRC) issued relevant policies respectively at the national level from the three aspects of poverty alleviation in terms of credit, insurance and capital market.

3.2.1 *Credit for Poverty Alleviation Policy*

As a rule, financial institutions are reluctant to serve the poor population and poor areas due to their weak risk tolerance, the poor quality of scarce standardized mortgageable and pledged assets, and the small amount of single loans with usually a large number, let alone the complicated formalities, high service charges and interest rates. Under the market economy, information asymmetry and agricultural weaknesses may cause high risks; while out-of-the-way geographical locations and petty amount of the loan may lead to high costs. The profit-seeking nature of capital makes it natural for financial institutions to refrain from taking the initiative to target poor areas and let capital flow there. Out of consideration of factors such as credit costs and benefits, as well as the natural preference for credit, they would not choose the rural poor as targets to extend credit. In addition, local governments have limited funds available for discount interest, interest exemption and risk compensation. All

[13] The CPC Central Committee and the State Council [6].

[14] People's Bank of China and Six Other Departments [13].

this has resulted in that financial institutions tend to invest less in the poor, and traditional finance is unwilling or finds it difficult to serve vulnerable groups like the rural poor.

3.2.1.1 Micro Loans for Poverty Alleviation

In order to alleviate poverty by taking financial measures to provide services to the poor and meet their needs through market operation, the State Council Poverty Alleviation Office worked with the Ministry of Finance, the People's Bank of China, China Banking Regulatory Commission (CBRC) and China Insurance Regulatory Commission (CIRC) to jointly issue in December 2014 Guidelines on Innovative Development of Microfinance for Poverty Alleviation, pointing out that the fundamental task of innovative development of micro loans for poverty alleviation is to stimulate the motivation of registered poor households to work out of poverty towards a better life. Efforts should be made to promote the positive interaction between anti-poverty financial policies and finance by giving full play to the role of financial institutions, with more products and forms of micro loans introduced, and by innovating financial services for poor villages to improve the financial ecology in poor areas.[15]

Micro loans for poverty alleviation are customized financial products targeted for registered poor households. In August 2017, the State Council Poverty Alleviation Office, the Ministry of Finance, the People's Bank of China, the CBRC and the CIRC jointly issued Notice on Promoting the Healthy Development of Microfinance for Poverty Alleviation. The highlights of its six policies included "Less than RMB 50,000, 3-year loan, no guarantee or mortgage, benchmark interest rate lending, financial discount and risk compensation set up at the county level".

As for prospective borrowers, only "registered poor households" are eligible and non-registered households are not to be considered. And the loan has required to be used precisely for development of production or specialty industries that may effectively help the poor to shake off poverty. They should never be permitted to be used for nonproductive expenditure such as house building, financial planning and the purchase of household appliances, and neither should the loans be packaged for government financing platforms, real estate development or infrastructure construction. All banking institutions must adhere to the two basic principles of willingness and participation of poor households in the process of exploring the use of micro loans in special and advantageous industries that may effectively drive poor households to lift themselves out of poverty. In this way, poor households may get involved in the industrial development and benefited in the long run, so that their internal motivation for poverty alleviation may be boosted.[16]

---

[15] Guidelines on Innovative Development of Microfinance for Poverty Alleviation [EB/OL]. (2014-12-15). http://www.cpad.gov.cn/art/2014/12/15/art_46_23778.html [14].

[16] China Banking Regulatory Commission and Other Central Departments [15].

Micro loans for poverty alleviation have always been accurately targeted at households registered as living under the poverty line, who are usually poor people capable of production and in need of loans but are unable to get them owing to lack of channels and approaches. Their needs for capital usually feature small amount and diversification, and the small loan policy is just responsive to the credit needs of these groups. Compared with the traditional loan policy, there is no mortgage guarantee threshold in the policy design of micro loans for poverty alleviation, which may solve the practical problem existing previously that registered poor households could not find mortgages and guarantors, and systematically overcome the "financial exclusion" of poor people by traditional loan policies. To be specific, the micro loan policy has the following advantages for poverty elimination:

First of all, they have a large amount with more fund-raising channels, which are sustainable and circulative as paid funds. Secondly, such loans can help develop the poor households' awareness of the market economy and sense of responsibility by "borrowing money to develop production and paying back when they are out of poverty", and inspire the initiative of poor households to improve their life through incentives and trust. Thirdly, poverty alleviation funds are required to be "borrowed and repaid", and the terms for the amount and the due date are stipulated, which can not only meet the demand for loans of the majority of poor households, but also reduce the risks of financial institutions. It can gradually establish a credit system for poor areas and poor households, contributing to the building of a creditworthy society. Fourthly, the change from a one-off grant to loans that can be used repeatedly can ensure the security and sustainability of poverty alleviation funds, so as to effectively supplement the insufficiency of such funds. In other words, the micro loan is also characteristic of a government policy for public welfare, and adhering to sustainability and commercial operation can help make up for the gap of financial input, limited amount and low efficiency of government funds to improve rural financial services and invigorate rural economy.

3.2.1.2 Industrial Loans for Poverty Alleviation

Industrial loans for poverty alleviation refer to the practice of taking financial measures in which the government tries to leverage more bank funds to support the development of poverty alleviation enterprises. By using government funds, poor villagers are helped to increase their stable income and realize the "all win" outcome among the government, banks, enterprises and poor households.

In line with the actual situation of each region, industrial loans for poverty alleviation can be divided into two forms, one is "poor households taking out loans for enterprises and enterprises paying back and benefiting the poor households"; and the other is enterprises being the direct borrower. Specifically, the former refers to the practice by which eligible villagers apply for the loan which is put to use by a particular enterprise, specialized cooperative or business leader in production, who are supposed to pay back the loan and the villagers may benefit either by participating in the industrial production to earn their income or getting dividends. Enterprises being direct borrowers of the loan have been selected by the government among start-ups. Loans from financial institutions are extended to those eligible ones that are capable of leading poor households out of poverty and increase income through production. On getting the loan, enterprises have to sign agreements with the government and the bank to create jobs for the poor, develop their industries or make donations. This approach of poverty alleviation through financial measures have not only effectively solved the financing difficulties of enterprises, but also ensured the stable income increase of poor villagers.

Different from the micro loan, industrial loans for poverty alleviation have enterprises as the actual users, although there may be different borrowers of the loan. The investment is mainly used for industrial development according to the actual situation of the start-ups. Being granted with the favorable financial policy, they have the responsibility of helping poor villagers out of poverty and increasing their income. Forms taken may include: helping the poor people to develop industries, providing jobs for poor households, purchasing poor households' agricultural products, making targeted donations and guaranteeing dividends. This practice has been in line with the actual situation in most rural areas of China.

Considering that poor households in some regions cannot develop industries by themselves and micro loans have fewer eligible borrowers, industrial loans are more favored by local governments, financial institutions and enterprises. This practice has overcome many problems such as high default risk for poor households and difficulty in financing for businesses. Through the design of flexible pairing mechanisms in various regions, it helps solve the practical problem that some poor households are not capable of developing industries by themselves, and strengthen the foundation of local industrial development, which can better increase the income of local poor households.

It should be noted that in extending the industrial loans, the tendency of giving priority to industrial development instead of poverty alleviation should be guarded against. Start-ups that have got the loans should not turn a blind eye to the poor, and simply giving donations or dividends cannot eliminate poverty in the long run. For poor people who have the ability to work, it is important to pay attention to their capacity building by providing them with employment and engaging them in production to ensure that they can not only obtain higher income, but also enhance the capability of sustained and stable poverty alleviation.

3.2.2 Insurance Policies for Poverty Alleviation

In order to effectively overcome the vulnerability of poor households and prevent them from falling back to poverty due to illnesses or accidents, the CIRC and the State Council Poverty Alleviation Office jointly issued Guidelines on Insurance Industry's Contribution to Poverty Alleviation in May 2016 to give full play to the unique advantages of insurance in risk guarantee and economic compensation, ensuring that poor villagers have no worries on their way out of poverty. The document specified that it is necessary to accurately meet the diversified insurance needs of the people registered as living below the poverty line by working out targeted policies, and improving supportive measures with innovative mechanisms, so that insurance institutions may function as better players in the fight against extreme poverty. It was required that through 2020, basic insurance service mechanisms be established in line with China's poverty elimination campaign, and an insurance service practice should be introduced with the coordinated participation of commercial, policy-backed and cooperative institutions. Efforts should be made to provide insurance services to villages and households and cover all eligible poor individuals with the intention. By the time the coverage of insurance in poverty-stricken areas would have been close to the national average, and the life and production of the poor would be fully guaranteed by modern insurance.[17]

In August 2017, the Ministry of Human Resources and Social Security, the Ministry of Finance and the State Council Poverty Alleviation Office jointly released Guidelines on Effective Implementation of Social Insurance for Poverty Alleviation, which proposed to give prominence to the role of existing social insurance policies, improving and implementing those on poverty alleviation with upgraded services. Supports should be given to needy groups like registered poor villagers, recipients of subsistence allowances and those living in extreme poverty and other members of society to participate in social insurance. To basically achieve full coverage of statutory population, China would gradually raise social security benefits, and help the poor insured lift themselves out of poverty with targeted measures. Meanwhile, other insured people would be prevented from falling into poverty due to old age, illness, work-related injury and unemployment, so as to contribute to winning the battle against poverty.[18]

In December 2017, the People's Bank of China worked with three other departments to jointly issue Guidelines on Financial Support for Poverty Alleviation in Poverty-Stricken Areas, proposing to develop innovative insurance products and improve the coverage of insurance in the areas. Products and services such as commercial medical supplementary insurance, disease insurance, micro insurance and rural housing insurance would be boosted, with focus on serving vulnerable groups sinking into poverty due to illness and disability. Insurance premium subsidies would be increased for registered poor households with moderate reduction of premiums for agricultural insurance. Innovative development of Agricultural product price insurance and income insurance would be encouraged to enhance the capability against agricultural risks. The aim was to achieve wide coverage of supplementary medical insurance for the poor and full coverage of policy-backed agricultural insurance in villages and towns by the end of 2020.[19]

Now the insurance industry has improve its poverty alleviation practice from providing relief to development-driven poverty alleviation and targeted measures,

[17] China Insurance Regulatory Commission and the State Council Poverty Alleviation Office [16].

[18] Ministry of Human Resources and Social Security, Ministry of Finance and State Council Poverty Alleviation Office [17].

[19] People's Bank and Three Other Departments [18].

and three sets of insurance systems with coordinated functions have been taking shape.

(1) The insurance system for poverty alleviation with agricultural insurance as its core. Based on the resource advantages and industrial characteristics of poor areas, insurance for agricultural products with distinctive advantages in light of local conditions are devolved, together with target price insurance, weather index insurance and facility agriculture insurance to prevent poor villagers from returning to poverty due to natural disasters.
(2) The life insurance system with critical illness insurance as its core. The dovetailing of basic medical insurance, critical illness insurance, commercial health insurance, medical assistance, disease emergency assistance and social charity has been strengthened, with the rise of the actual reimbursement proportion of medical expenses for the poor to prevent them from falling into or sinking back into poverty caused by illness.
(3) The credit enhancement insurance system for poverty alleviation with petty loan guarantee insurance as its core. The credit enhancement support is provided for the financing of poor households to help them obtain loans for production growth and promote the release of credit resources to boost local industries.

As poverty alleviation through industrial development reinvigorates the economy of poor areas, the role of insurance mechanism in poverty alleviation is given more and more attention. This is particular true when many regions need to use market mechanisms to consolidate their anti-poverty achievements. Actually there is much to be done for insurance to play its role in the market. Whether it is the development of the agricultural industry or the increasing demand for life and property insurance by villagers themselves, the insurance industry is required to further innovate products and services to better help the fight against extreme poverty.[20]

3.2.3 Capital Market Policies for Poverty Alleviation

In order to effectively accelerate the financing of businesses and the development of poor areas, China Securities Regulatory Commission (CSRC) issued Guidelines on Leveraging the Role of Capital Market to Serve the National Poverty Alleviation Strategy in September 2016, with policies calling for the capital market to tap its industrial advantages and contribute to poverty alleviation. Oriented to the needs of the real economy in poor areas and focusing on serving poverty alleviation through industrial development, the capital market should give substantial supports to businesses in poor areas to finance from its multi-level resources. In addition, listed companies, securities fund operating institutions and futures institutions should all be encouraged to fulfill their social responsibilities and serve the national strategy. It was required that the protection of investors in destitute areas be strengthened,

[20] Wang [19].

giving priority to local enterprises to make use of capital market resources, broaden direct financing channels, improve financing efficiency and reduce financing costs so as to unlock their development potential.[21]

The introduction of these policies in the capital market has made most of its own reality to help the listing of enterprises in poor areas and their financial development. In view of the relatively backward financial services and the lack of human resources serving the capital market, the process preparation in poor areas often lags behind under the same conditions. Therefore, priority should be given to the audit process for projects in poor areas to make up for their weaknesses in the capital market. In a sense, it has been an important measure to achieve market equity. Under poverty alleviation policies of "Immediate review and release upon approval without lowering the standards and eligibility criteria" for the capital market, some enterprises could be listed quickly through green channels as long as they are eligible, which has speeded up their own growth and enhanced the local industrial development.

3.3 Sector-Specific Policies for Poverty Alleviation

Xi Jinping points out, "Poverty alleviation and development are the common responsibility of the whole Party and society. We should mobilize and rally the entire society for extensive participation. Consequently, government-sponsored projects, sector-specific programs and corporate and societal assistance must be integrated to create a synergy."[22]

As one of the important measures of this all-encompassing campaign against poverty, sector-specific programs mainly refer to policies and projects that all related sectors perform their management functions to support the development of poor areas and people, and undertake the task of improving their development environment and the capacity of development. The sector-specific support is an important starting point for the government to lead the work. In the process, all sector departments are expected to do their best to perform management functions and focus on major issues related to the "Two Assurances and Three Guarantees". Keeping well informed, they should be problem-oriented and try to find solutions. With a strong sense of responsibility, related departments have formulated targeted policies and plans for poverty alleviation within their capacity and played their role in providing policy guidance.

---

[21] China Securities Regulatory Commission [20].

[22] Institute of Party History and Literature of the CPC Central Committee [2].

3.3.1 *Implementing Safe Water Program Led by the Ministry of Water Resources*

A Chinese saying goes, "Food is the paramount necessity of the people and water is the most essential." Access to safe drinking water is the basic need for humans to survive, and has everything to do with the health and life of the people. The CPC Central Committee and the State Council have attached great importance to the issue of safe drinking water, and regarded the protection of drinking water sources and people's access to it as the primary task.

Drinking water safety is of great significance for registered poor households to be assured of adequate food in the overall goal of "Two Assurances and Three Guarantees", and it is an important part of Central Committee's appraisal of the poverty alleviation performance of provincial Party committees and governments. Since the start of the targeted anti-poverty campaign, the overall situation of rural drinking water safety has been improved, there are however still some prominent problems to be solved in some areas. To crack the hard nut, every effort should be made to overcome the problem, especially in destitute areas.

To address the issue, the Ministry of Water Resources, the State Council Poverty Alleviation Office and the National Health Commission jointly launched the Circular on Winning the Battle against Extreme Poverty through Ensuring Water Safety in Rural Areas in August 2018, requiring the introduction of the working mechanism whereby the central leadership make overall plans, provincial authorities take overall responsibility, and city and county authorities ensure implementation in rural areas. All localities should take water safety as a targeted poverty alleviation measure and a major political task, making it part of the assessment of poverty alleviation, with clearly defined responsibilities and implementation at all levels to ensure the safety and security of drinking water in poor areas.

The document required all localities to formulate feasible plans and strengthen preliminary fact-finding work with supporting measures. Focus should be placed on solving key and difficult issues to ensure that poor villages and people have access to the safe drinking water through 2020 in accordance with Plans for Rural Drinking Water Safety Consolidation and Improvement Project during the 13th Five-Year Plan Period approved by provincial governments and the yearly county objectives and tasks. All localities could directly use the Rural Drinking Water Safety Evaluation Criteria issued by the China Water Conservancy Society as the benchmark, or combine actual conditions with the evaluation criteria to formulate their own ones with detailed rules applicable to local realities, which could be used as the basis for the accurate identification, formulation of solutions and standards by which rural drinking water safety projects were assessed and accepted. In areas with poor water sources, difficult project construction, high cost and remote and scattered population, the daily water supply per person shall not be less than 20 L, and the round-trip time to fetch water by manual power shall not exceed 20 min (which could be relaxed in pastoral areas).[23]

To ensure safe drinking water means safeguarding the fundamental interests of the overwhelming majority of the people. It has embodied the idea of "people-orientation", and is vital for winning the battle against poverty and completing the process of building a moderately prosperous society.

3.3.2 Implementing Relocation Program Led by National Development and Reform Commission

As China's economic development entered the new normal, poverty has remained the most prominent area of weakness in hindering the building of a moderately prosperous society in all respects, and the old saying "Each place has its own way of supporting its own inhabitants" just doesn't apply to some extremely impoverished places. Greater efforts should therefore be made and effective measures taken to make up for this weakness, so as to improve the wellbeing of the poor people and enable them to share the fruits of development. President Xi Jinping once said, "Relocating those living under adverse natural conditions is a necessary and complex systematic project, which is highly policy-backed and complicated. It is necessary to broaden the sources of fund raising for the relocation. We should make good planning, reasonably determine the relocation size, distinguish priorities, and clarify the relocation objectives, tasks and construction phases, so that those who cannot escape poverty locally can be relocated in a well planned and organized way."[24]

In order to win the battle against extreme poverty and ensure that all poor people will enter a well-off society with other people of the whole country through 2020, the CPC Central Committee and the State Council decided to accelerate the relocation of rural poor. In September 2016, the National Development and Reform Commission issued the Notice on the Relocation Plan for Poverty Alleviation during 13th Five-Year Plan Period, stipulating the relocation of 10 million registered poor people through 2020, who will be ensured the housing safety and the access to the basic living needs such as safe drinking water, transport, electricity and communication, as well as convenient and accessible basic public services such as education, medical care and stable income channels in order to achieve stable poverty elimination. The ecological environment of the out-migration area will be significantly improved, and the development of characteristic industry in the resettlement area will be accelerated.[25]

The document set out detailed requirements on the relocation area and people to be relocated, ways of relocation and resettlement, construction tasks, costing and

---

[23] Ministry of Water Resources, the State Council Poverty Alleviation Office and National Health Commission [21].

[24] Institute of Party History and Literature of the CPC Central Committee [2].

[25] National Development and Reform Commission [22].

financing, fund operation, relocation progress and investment arrangement, as well as development and safeguarding measures of registered poor rural residents to ensure that they could make a better living after relocation.

Since the full-fledged implementation of the anti-poverty relocation, central and local governments concerned at all levels have taken effective measures to promote the campaign with great efforts. The housing conditions of the relocated people have been significantly improved, together with their way of life and production. However, according to reports from different channels and inspections at all levels, some relocation projects have problems such as non-standard construction procedures, unsatisfactory practice of the "four regulations" (of project legal person responsibility, bidding, project supervision and contract management), inadequate supervision and management, and poor construction quality, especially housing quality, which have become major hazards posing direct threat to the safety of people's lives and property, calling for more attention and effective measures to address.

In October 2018, the National Development and Reform Commission and the State Council Poverty Alleviation Office released the Notice on Further Strengthening the Quality and Safety Management of Relocation Projects, requiring all localities to further enhance their political awareness and adhere to the people-centered development philosophy, firming their sense of responsibility and risk and regarding quality and safety as the lifeline of the relocation program. The document stressed the importance of strengthening the leadership, clarifying responsibilities, improving the supervision mechanism to strictly implement the relevant laws and regulations and mandatory technical standards of project construction. Emphasis has been placed on the inspection and investigation of project quality and safety and discipline accountability to ensure that the relocated people live in safe houses.

3.3.3 Implementing Renovation Program of Dilapidated Houses Led by the Ministry of Housing and Urban–Rural Development

Housing security is an important part of "Two Assurances and Three Guarantees" and it is vital to do it well for the poor. The renovation of dilapidated houses in rural areas is a major work in this respect. Since the start of targeted poverty alleviation, significant progress has been made, but there were still problems in the process, such as inaccurate identification of needy people, inability of house building for extremely impoverished poor households, and non-standard allocation and use of subsidies.

To further strengthen and improve the renovation of dilapidated houses in rural areas, the Ministry of Housing and Urban–Rural Development, the Ministry of Finance and the State Council Poverty Alleviation Office jointly issued the Notice on Strengthening and Improving Renovation of Dilapidated Houses for Registered Poor Households in Rural Areas in August 2017, which clearly stipulated the identification criteria and procedures. Four kinds of households would be eligible, including registered poor households, households receiving the minimum living allowances, the extremely poor that are taken care of by any of the rural institutions, and households with one or more disabled members. By increasing capital input, promoting low-cost renovation and helping to coordinate and organize the procurement and transportation of major building materials, more preferential supports have been given to help reduce their burden and ensure house safety.[26]

In November 2018, the Ministry of Housing and Urban–Rural Development and the Ministry of Finance jointly formulated A Three-Year Action Plan for Poverty Alleviation through Renovation of Dilapidated Rural Houses in order to speed up the renovation of dilapidated rural houses for registered poor households and the most vulnerable groups to ensure that they live in safe houses through 2020. The document required that all efforts be made to deliver the work, and the renovation of dilapidated rural houses for the existing 2 million registered poor households should be completed through 2020. Priority support should be given to destitute "three regions and three prefectures"[27] in their renovation of dilapidated houses. A long-term mechanism to support the effort and ensure housing security for rural poor has been under exploration.[28]

3.3.4 Implementing Education Program Led by Ministry of Education

"To end poverty, the first step is to end ignorance and illiteracy," says President Xi Jinping on several occasions. "Education is the best way to stop intergenerational transmission of poverty. National education funds should continue to prioritize towards poverty-stricken areas, towards basic education and vocational education. We should improve their education facilities, and give more care to poor young children, especially 'left-behind' children who stay in rural areas while their parents are away from home as migrant workers."[29]

Then Premier Li Keqiang also points out that to get out of poverty, it is essential to rely on education and improve the quality of the poor. We should strengthen education to help the poor. Senior high school students from poor families should be exempted from tuition and miscellaneous fees. Key colleges and universities should be open

---

[26] Ministry of Housing and Urban-Rural Development, Ministry of Finance and the State Council Poverty Alleviation Office [23].

[27] The "three regions" refer to Tibet Autonomous Region; Hotan Prefecture, Aksu Prefecture, Kashi Prefecture and Kizilsu Kirgiz Autonomous Prefecture in southern Xinjiang Uygur Autonomous Region; and Tibetan-inhabited areas in the provinces of Sichuan, Yunnan, Gansu and Qinghai. The "three prefectures" refer to the Liangshan Yi Autonomous Prefecture in Sichuan Province, the Nujiang Lisu Autonomous Prefecture in Yunnan Province, and the Linxia Hui Autonomous Prefecture in Gansu Province.—The translator's note.

[28] Ministry of Housing and Urban-Rural Development and Ministry of Finance [24].

[29] Institute of Party History and Literature of the CPC Central Committee [2].

to more poor rural students by expanding targeted enrolment plans, so that more opportunities are provided for students from needy families to receive high-quality education and develop more human resources for poor areas.

The Ministry of Education has put winning the battle of poverty alleviation through education in its action plans, and worked with other departments and education departments at primary levels to promote the work. Under its leadership, a series of plans and programs have been introduced, such as the three-year action plan for preschool education, the nutrition improvement program for rural compulsory education students, the plan for comprehensive improvement of the basic school running facilities of underdeveloped schools in rural compulsory education, the special plan for targeted enrollment in poor areas, and the living subsidy policy for rural teachers. Many policies have been formulated to clarify the road map and timetable for winning the anti-poverty battle.

In July 2013, the Ministry of Education and five other departments jointly issued Guidelines on Implementing Poverty Alleviation through Education Project, which put forward the goal of improving basic education in terms of popularity and quality, upgrading vocational education to better develop capabilities and skills that could help rural young people to get out of poverty and work towards prosperity, improving higher education to better serve regional economic and social development, and continuing education to better serve employment and entrepreneurship. Specifically, the main tasks included strengthening basic education in an all-round way, accelerating the development of modern vocational education, improving the service capacity of higher education, raising financial assistance to students and improving the application of information technology in education. It was required that China's efforts to end poverty through education cover preschool education, basic education, vocational education, special education and ethnic education. The document called for upgrading the software and hardware facilities and environment of education to improve the quality of school running, giving full play to the role of education in helping poor areas get rid of poverty.[30]

In December 2016, led by the Ministry of Education and other five departments released Plans for Poverty Alleviation through Education during the 13th Five-Year Plan Period; emphasizing that educational development in poor areas should be significantly improved through 2020. Measures were suggested to achieve the goal, such as developing preschool education, consolidating the nine-year compulsory education, teambuilding of rural teachers, support of vulnerable groups and facilitating secondary vocational education. In addition, public welfare vocational skills training should be widely carried out with further development of ordinary senior high school education. Colleges and universities should continue with priority policies to enroll more candidates from poor areas and update education and employment subsidy service together with decision-making advisory. By that time, basic education would have covered all poor population, with no children having to drop out of

[30] Guidelines on Implementing Poverty Alleviation through Education Project issued by the Ministry of Education and forwarded by the General Office of the State Council [EB/OL]. (2013-09-12). http://www.cpad.gov.cn/art/2013/9/12/art_50_23748.html [25].

school owing to financial difficulties. Everyone would have had the opportunity to lift their families out of poverty through vocational education, higher education or vocational training, and the role of education to serve regional economic and social development would be significantly enhanced.[31]

In January 2018, the Ministry of Education worked with the State Council Poverty Alleviation Office to issue the Implementation Plan for Poverty Alleviation through Education in Destitute Areas (2018–2020) in order to further focus on poverty alleviation through education in destitute areas in three years. It is required to establish accurate assistance accounts for poverty alleviation through education in the most impoverished "three areas and three prefectures" and steadily improve their basic public service of education. Universal basic education should be implemented with increased investment, projects and new measures to ensure the success of the fight against extreme poverty by means of education.[32]

3.3.5 Implementing Health Program Led by Health Commission

China's poverty alleviation effort has long been perplexed by the fact that many rural people fall back into poverty because of critical illnesses. Therefore, the health program for poverty alleviation is of great significance to ensure that the rural poor have access to basic medical and health services, promote the building of the Healthy China and lift the rural poor out of poverty through 2020. China Health Commission has integrated this goal with further healthcare reform, with focus on poverty caused by illnesses by targeting the key areas, key groups and key illnesses. Efforts have been made to coordinate and integrate resources, and effective measures taken to improve medical services to the rural poor in poor areas for the overall improvement of health of all Chinese people.

In June 2016, 15 central government departments led by the then National Health and Family Planning Commission (renamed in 2018), worked out the Guidelines on Implementing the Health Program for Poverty Alleviation, pointing out that medical security should be improved and categorized and targeted measures be adopted for the poor rural population suffering from critical and chronic diseases, and those who are hospitalized in county hospitals should receive treatment before payment. The medical and health service system in poverty-stricken areas and the paired-up assistance between Tier-3 (the highest tier) hospitals and hospitals in poor counties should be strengthened. Chronic diseases, infectious diseases, endemic disease prevention and control should be intensified, with more attention paid to maternal and child healthcare and by launching health campaigns. Through 2020, everyone in poor areas would have access to basic medical and health services and the rural poor

[31] Ministry of Education and Other Five Departments [26].

[32] Ministry of Education and the State Council Poverty Alleviation Office [27].

would receive timely and effective treatment for serious diseases, with the individual burden of medical expenses greatly reduced.

The guideline also pointed out that critical infectious and endemic diseases in poor areas would by that time be brought under effective control and basic public health indicators would be close to the national average with increased average life expectancy. Maternal mortality, infant mortality and the incidence of infectious diseases would be dropped significantly. At least one hospital in a county rated as poor would reach the service level of a Tier-2 medical institution, with significantly improved facilities, capacity and accessibility. Regional disparities in the allocation of medical and health resources and in the health conditions of the people would be further narrowed, and rural poor would be effectively prevented from being trapped in or returning to poverty because of illness.[33]

In April 2017, the Notice on "Affordable Medical Services" Action Plan in Implementing the Health Program for Poverty Alleviation was formulated by relevant departments, proposing that efforts should be made to ensure that the poor suffering from serious and chronic diseases would be treated by differentiated categories and groups, as they could expect help from serious illness insurance and chronic illness services. Government funds would cover the remaining cost of critical ailments after the relevant reimbursements. Poverty alleviation through healthcare would be further implemented by targeted individuals and diseases.[34]

3.3.6 Implementing Industrial Development Program Led by Ministry of Agriculture and Rural Affairs

An age-old Chinese saying goes, "It is better to teach a man to fish than to give him a fish." This common-sense wisdom applies well in China's poverty alleviation. Developing specialty industries has been an effective measure to improve the self-development capacity of poverty-stricken areas and their population to work out of poverty. As the most important of the five measures for poverty elimination, industrial development has aimed to lift more than 30 million people out of poverty, with the widest coverage of targeted rural poor. Actually, the outcome of all the other anti-poverty efforts through relocation, education and ecological conservation depends much on the long-term, stable employment and income growth through the development of industries.

Many poor areas are rich in natural, cultural and labor resources, with weak overall development of specialty industries, and the resource advantages have not been effectively transformed into industrial and economic advantages,. This has been

---

[33] Guidelines on Implementing the Health Program for Poverty Alleviation [EB/OL]. (2016-06-20). http://www.cpad.gov.cn/art/2016/6/20/art_1747_682.html [28].

[34] Notice on "Affordable Medical Services" Action Plan in Implementing the Health Program for Poverty Allevi-ation [EB/OL]. (2017-08-16). http://www.cpad.gov.cn/art/2017/8/16/art_1747_847.html [29].

the bottleneck to increasing the income of the rural poor and eliminating poverty. Therefore, industrial development has been of vital importance to the implementation of central government's major plan for poverty alleviation and the building of a society with moderate prosperity for all.

In May 2016, the Ministry of Agriculture worked with eight other departments to jointly issue the Guidelines on Promoting Targeted Poverty Eradication through Developing Specialty Industries in Poor Areas, proposing to promote poverty alleviation through economic activities in the following eight aspects.

(1) Selecting right specialty industries for development. Through in-depth analysis of many factors such as resources endowment, industry status, market space, environmental capacity, leadership of newly emerging business players and industry coverage, industries with local features can be selected for the betterment of poor counties.
(2) Promoting the integrated development of primary, secondary and tertiary industries. By processing special products, expanding multiple functions of the industry, efforts would be ramped up to develop leisure agriculture, rural tourism and forest tourism, with more jobs created for poor households to increase their income.
(3) Giving full play to the role of newly emerging business players. They would be given more support to develop specialty industries in poor areas to help poor households by providing them with whole industry chain services, the value-added capacity of industries and opportunities of employment.
(4) Improving the benefit coupling mechanism. Stock cooperation would be encouraged, in which members of collective economic organizations enjoy the right to share their collective profits by holding shares at a discounted price through the use of contracted rural land management rights and villagers' housing property rights. As long as the use of relevant government funds is not changed, the assets generated by such projects as facility agriculture, breeding, photovoltaic projects, hydropower and rural tourism would be quantified as convertible shares to poor villages and households if conditions permit.
(5) Enhancing industrial support. Greater efforts should be made to accelerate the development of e-commerce to facilitate the branding of specialty products and the application of research outcomes to ensure that they are progressed to viable commercial products or practical techniques. Useful information should be brought to villages and households. More support should be given to training of new types of agricultural professionals in poor areas and to entrepreneurial individuals so that they play a better role in helping and leading other villagers out of poverty.
(6) Increasing investment in poverty alleviation through industries. Government funds for rural development at different levels and of all types should prioritize specialty industries in poor areas, and guidance should be strengthened on the use of funds to develop planting and breeding.

(7) Innovating financial support mechanisms. Financial institutions have been encouraged to introduce new products and services to meet the industrial development in poor areas, and localities have been expected to explore more effective financial modes for poverty elimination.
(8) Increasing insurance support. Active development of insurance for special products should be boosted, with trial practices for price insurance. Insurance institutions have been encouraged to target poor areas to introduce insurance for special local products and guarantee insurance for small loans for poverty alleviation.

These measures have been expected to deliver the following outcomes through 2020, namely, an industrial system with distinctive features at the county level would have been taking shape, with the construction of a number of characteristic industrial bases with high participation of poor people, together with a number of product processing and service bases to drive and help poor households out of poverty. Poor towns and villages would have their own specialty industries, with the added value of the industries significantly increasing. Poor households would be expected to have good mastery of 1–2 practical skills to enhance their self-development capability.[35]

In September 2016, Ministry of Agriculture issued Guidelines on Increasing Preferential Support for Project Funds in Poor Areas to Promote Targeted Poverty Alleviation through Specialty Industries, which called for investing more project funds in agricultural infrastructure construction, agricultural technology promotion services, establishment of modern agricultural industrial system and development of new business players, agricultural disaster prevention and mitigation capacity, in addition to resources and environment protection in poor areas, to support targeted poverty alleviation through specialty industries.[36]

3.3.7 Promoting Employment Led by Ministry of Human Resources and Social Security

People often say "One employment may help lift the whole family out of poverty." Providing employment opportunities for the poor who have the ability and willingness to work is one of the effective ways to reduce poverty. Through vocational training, the employability of the rural poor can be improved to help them find jobs beyond their villages and increase their income, which will not only consolidate the achievements of poverty alleviation, but also help stimulate their internal motivation. Promoting employment of poor rural labor has been a key measure in the battle against extreme poverty.

In December 2016, the Ministry of Human Resources and Social Security, together with the Ministry of Finance and the State Council Poverty Alleviation Office, issued

[35] Ministry of Agriculture and Eight Other Departments [30].

[36] Ministry of Agriculture [31].

Guidelines on Effective Implementation of Poverty Alleviation through Employment, which focused on the targeted provision of job opportunities to rural people, aiming to help unemployed poor labors to seek stable employment by measures such as creating jobs, labor service cooperation, skills training and employment services as well as maintenance of rights and interests. A number of poor labors would be helped to secure transfer employment or stable employment. A number of children from poor families who had finished their junior or senior high school education would be helped to be enrolled by technical schools or colleges to become skill competent and job ready after graduation. All this would help drive about 10 million people to get out of poverty. To address the employment for women and empty-nesters left behind in the village, the guidelines suggested that localities should create more jobs to help them find employment locally. Channels should be expanded by encouraging businesses to create poverty-alleviation workshops and processing points in towns and villages and organizing those concerned to engage in flexible employment at home.[37]

Vocational training is a starting measure to promote the registered poor population to get employed. In October 2018, the Ministry of Human Resources and Social Security and the Poverty Alleviation Department of the State Council jointly issued the Notice on Launching Poverty Alleviation Campaign through Skills Training in Extremely Impoverished Areas, aiming to advance targeted vocational training for employment of rural poor. It was required that vocational training should be available to every poor villager with the needs, and every junior or senior high graduate from registered poor households should have access to technical education. In the efforts to boost employment and alleviate poverty through vocational training, the public service system should be established, integrating vocational guidance, classified trainings, skill assessment and employment service.[38]

3.3.8 Improving Social Security Led by Ministry of Civil Affairs

In the cause of poverty eradication, vulnerable groups like the elderly, the critically ill and the disabled are the most impoverished because they are unable to shake off poverty through their own efforts alone. By providing subsistence allowances as the "final line of defense", the Chinese government has ensured the basic livelihood of the most vulnerable people who have completely or partially lost the ability to work and cannot eradicate poverty through industries or employment.

---

[37] Ministry of Human Resources and Social Security, Ministry of Finance and the State Council Poverty Alleviation Office [32].

[38] Ministry of Human Resources and Social Security and the State Council Poverty Alleviation Office [33].

In order to eliminate poverty through 2020 for rural people living below the current poverty line, the Ministry of Civil Affairs worked with other five departments to jointly issue Guidelines on Effective Dovetailing of the Rural Subsistence Allowances Frame-work with Development-Oriented Poverty Alleviation Policies in September 2016. The document pointed out that by adhering to the basic strategy of targeted poverty alleviation and the principles of dynamic management and resource integration, all eligible people should be supported by subsistence allowances. It was advised that the framework be effectively dovetailed with poverty alleviation policies to create a synergy to lift all poor people out of poverty through 2020.

The document further clarified the relevant key tasks. The first was to coordinate relevant policies to ensure that all eligible registered poor households would have access to subsistence allowances, and all rural households living on subsistence allowances would be registered. For vulnerable groups living on subsistence allowances but not eligible to be registered, the localities should coordinate by applying relevant poverty alleviation policies.

The second was to identify those to be helped with more accuracy. It was required that the index system be improved for assessing the poverty situation of rural families receiving subsistence allowances. A comprehensive assessment should be conducted by taking family income and property as the main indicators, together with considerations of local conditions and the increasing rigid expenditures of family members due to disabilities and critical diseases.

The third was to dovetail the two standards. Where the rural subsistence allowances were lower than the national standard, the minimum guideline should be applied in accordance with the national standard. Where rural subsistence allowances have reached the national poverty alleviation standard, they could be adjusted reasonably based on a dynamic mechanism.

The fourth was to strengthen joint management. County-level civil affairs departments should provide the list of the rural families receiving subsistence allowances and vulnerable people to their poverty alleviation peers; which should timely provide the list of registered poor people and those eligible to subsistence allowances as well as the per capita income of poor families to the civil affairs departments of the same level. In this way, information could be shared for sound decision-making.[39]

3.3.9 Providing Technological Assistance Led by Ministry of Science and Technology

More sustained poverty alleviation by developing industries has been strongly supported by technologies and professionals. It is an important initiative to innovate social services in science and technology and an effective approach to enhance the relationship between Party and government officials and people. Therefore, the

[39] Ministry of Civil Affairs and Other Five Departments [34].

philosophy of development through technological innovation should be rooted in the poor areas and the rural poor to provide them with substantial support.

In April 2016, the Ministry of Science and Technology issued Guidelines on Implementing Targeted Poverty Alleviation through Science and Technology, proposing measures for poor areas, including team building of technological professionals, training new types of skilled farmers, popularizing scientific knowledge, and dispatching technology-oriented officials and specialized professionals to work for some time in those places. Supports should be given to startup businesses and platforms, developing specialty pillar industries and encouraging paired-up assistance in technology with poor areas. In this way, scientific and technological resources of the whole society could be mobilized and their leading role in innovation could be given full play in the fight against extreme poverty.

In October 2016, the Ministry of Science and Technology and six other departments jointly issued Action Plan for Poverty Alleviation through Science and Technology. It required meeting the specific demands of poor areas and poor people to give shape to a new model of innovation-driven development by 2020 through actions such as research and development, transformation of scientific results, platform construction, partnering of production factors, entrepreneurship assistance, teaching and training, and popularization of science and agriculture. As a result, the capability of primary-level sci-tech services in poor areas would be significantly enhanced, regional industries develop faster and local people's quality of science and culture be greatly improved. All these would bolster the enthusiasm for innovation and entrepreneurship, as well as the internal impetus of development so that targeted poverty alleviation could be driven by innovation to deliver effective outcomes.[40]

In July 2017, in order to mobilize sci-tech resources of the whole society to contribute to poverty alleviation, General Office of the Ministry of Science and Technology issued a document, proposing the implementation of the project of poverty alleviation through science and technology. Specifically, 100 platforms in poor areas such as sci-tech parks and business clusters to accommodate startups were to be constructed. 1000 universities, research institutes, business parks and enterprises would pair up with poor areas in offering technological assistance to 1000 projects. 10,000 technical professionals would be dispatched to 10,000 poor villages.

3.3.10 Prioritizing Transportation Led by the Ministry of Transport

There has been a popular saying in rural China, "Building roads is the first step to get prosperous." Good transportation is a prerequisite and basic condition for

[40] Ministry of Science and Technology, Ministry of Education, Chinese Academy of Sciences, Chinese Academy of Engineering, National Natural Science Foundation of China, State Administration of Science, Technology and Industry for National Defense, the State Council Poverty Alleviation Office [35].

poverty alleviation and speeding up infrastructure construction is still a primary task. President Xi Jinping points out that "The construction of transport infrastructure plays a critically leading role, particularly for some poor areas. Minor improvements in transport conditions can make great differences and open doors for poor villagers to overcome poverty and work towards prosperity". He also observes that "We should introduce mechanisms and improve policies to ensure that roads in rural areas are constructed, operated, managed and maintained in a better way. As a result, barriers in transport that hinder rural development can be gradually removed so that rural people can have better prospects of a moderately prosperous life."

In July 2016, the Ministry of Transport issued Plans for Poverty Alleviation through Transportation during the 13th Five-Year Plan Period, clearly defining eight major tasks by taking into account the actual needs of transport development in poor areas, namely, establishing transport networks that connect major roads in and outside poor areas, all villages being connected with other local villages, road safety being significantly improved, transport helping specialty industries, upgrading transport terminals and stations, promoting water transport infrastructure, increasing the efficiency of roads and the quality of transport services and comprehensively improving basic public services of transport. By 2020, such a transport network in poor areas would have been completed and villagers could enjoy safe and easy access to bus services, which would facilitate better communications and sounder economic development.[41]

In November 2017, General Office of the Ministry of Transport issued the Implementation Plan for Lifting Destitute Areas out of Poverty through Transportation, proposing to offer more support to extremely impoverished areas and have the basic poverty alleviation goals of paved roads and bus services in villages delivered through 2020 as scheduled. By strengthening the construction of transport infrastructure, enhancing transport services together with safety and security and maintenance efficiency, a strong support has been provided for severely poverty-stricken areas to achieve the goal of prosperity.[42]

In July 2018, the General Office of the Ministry of Transport issued the Three-Year Action Plan for Poverty Alleviation through Transportation (2018–2020), specifying that through 2020, towns and villages of poor areas should have access to paved roads, counties to open highways and villages to bus services, where conditions permit. Safety issues should be basically solved and the construction, operation, management and maintenance mechanisms of rural roads should be improved.[43]

---

[41] Ministry of Transport [36].

[42] General Office of Ministry of Transport [37].

[43] General Office of Ministry of Transport [38].

3.4 Policies to Encourage Market Participation

The Third Plenary Session of the 18th CPC Central Committee made it clear that we should properly handle the relationship between the government and the market, so that the market could play a decisive role in resource allocation with a better leading role of the government. The strengths of the socialist system with Chinese characteristics determine the leading role of public ownership and the dominant role of the state-owned economy which give the government strong capabilities in centralized decision-making, mobilization and coordination, so that social resources can be integrated to the maximum to address major issues. The decisive role of the market in resource allocation allows the market vitality to be fully released and the government's proactiveness and the market's effectiveness have laid a good foundation for the great achievements in poverty eradication. In the face of the toughest difficulties in the anti-poverty campaign, we must better balance the relationship between the government and the market by adhering to the interplay of market-orientation and policy support to give full play to the decisive role of the market in allocating resources.

In the all-encompassing national campaign against poverty in which government-sponsored projects, sector-specific programs and corporate and societal assistance coordinate to create a synergy, market participation plays a key role. In December 2014, General Office of the State Council issued the Guidelines on Further Mobilizing All Sectors of Society to Participate in Poverty Alleviation and Development, calling for active participation of private enterprises in the nationwide drive and encouraging them to shoulder social responsibilities and stimulate market vitality by giving full play to their advantages in capital, technology, market and management. Through resource development, industry incubation, market expansion, village-enterprise pairing up and other forms, private enterprises could participate in development-oriented poverty alleviation to help and lead poor people out of poverty by investing in poor areas, training skills, creating jobs and making donations in cash and kind.[44] The document also made specific provisions on the tasks, forms and supporting measures for enterprises to participate in poverty alleviation.

In October 2015, the All-China Federation of Industry and Commerce, the State Council Poverty Alleviation Office and China Society for Promotion of the Guangcai Program jointly launched a targeted poverty alleviation program of "10,000 Enterprises Helping 10,000 Villages". 26 private enterprises from Hebei, Hunan, Guangdong, Guangxi and Guizhou signed assistance agreements with poor villages, providing a demonstration for the comprehensive promotion of the action.[45] In January 2016, the three initiators jointly issued the Guidelines on Implementing Targeted Poverty Alleviation by the "10,000 Enterprises Helping 10,000 Villages" Program, which had private enterprises as major players to help registered poor villages by signing up cooperation or pairing-up agreements between them. Their

44 General Office of the State Council [39].

45 The CPC Central Committee and the State Council [6].

poverty alleviation efforts would be delivered through various forms including developing industries, creating jobs, public welfare donation and assistance in education, with the goal of mobilizing more than 10,000 private enterprises nationwide in 3–5 years to help more than 10,000 poor villages to speed up poverty alleviation. Their contributions would not only greatly help the fight against poverty and the building of a moderately prosperous society in all respects, but also promote the healthy development of non-public sectors of the economy and the growth of entrepreneurs.[46]

The Plan for Poverty Alleviation during the 13th Five-Year Plan Period issued by the State Council in December 2016 made further requirements on market participation. The policies focused on strengthening the responsibility of state-owned enterprises to assist the poor and encouraging central enterprises to help poor old revolutionary base areas by providing paired-up assistance in various forms such as setting up industrial funds and engaging themselves in resource development, industrial park construction and new urbanization by market-oriented operations. Enterprises of private or other ownerships would be guided and helped to participate in development-driven poverty alleviation by giving full play to the role of Federation of Industry and Commerce to contribute to the national campaign. Through the "10,000 Enterprises Helping 10,000 Villages" program, private enterprises in eastern China have been organized to help poor villages in the west. Supportive policies for leading enterprises would be improved and those that create jobs for the poor would enjoy vocational training subsidies and other employment-supporting policies and tax incentives in accordance with regulations.[47]

The synergy between the government and the market is the key to poverty eradication through reform and development. The government administration helps solve large-scale and concentrated poverty problems, but it is less professional and targeted, while the decentralized decision-making market mechanism is more professional and targeted than the government. Therefore, under the leadership of the CPC, the introduction of market mechanisms and forces to participate in poverty alleviation is an effective way to improve accuracy and efficiency and contribute to the approach of poverty alleviation under socialism with Chinese characteristics. It is conducive to enterprises themselves and the improvement of the backward industrial structure and economic development in poor areas. However, under the market economy, "resource input and target efficiency" must be considered. On the one hand, the government should appropriately hand over poverty alleviation resources to the market for operation through strict review, granting reasonable autonomy and independence to market players, and break the monopoly on the resources; on the other hand, the government should strengthen supervision by establishing performance evaluation and withdrawal mechanisms, and improving fair macro policies to guide and drive social capital to increase investment in poverty alleviation, so as to provide funds and other resources for economic and social development in poor areas.

---

[46] All-China Federation of Industry and Commerce, the State Council Poverty Alleviation Office and China Society for Promotion of the Guangcai Program [40].

[47] The State Council [41].

3.5 Policies of East–West Collaboration for Poverty Alleviation

Xi Jinping once observed, "Over the past 20 years, the CPC Central Committee has continuously increased its efforts to form a multi-level, multi-faceted and all-round framework of poverty alleviation and supporting policies, gradually reversing the trend of widening regional development disparities and making significant progress in poverty alleviation and development in poor western regions and old revolutionary base areas. When the income of urban and rural residents in the western region has increased significantly, together with remarkably improved infrastructure and greatly enhanced comprehensive strengths, the overall national and regional development strategy has been effectively implemented, and the coordination of regional development has been enhanced, creating a good prospect of complementary advantages, long-term and win–win cooperation. East–West collaboration for poverty alleviation and supporting policies must be sustained in the long run."[48] Since the 18th National Congress of the CPC, several policies have been worked out, with new requirements for East–West collaboration in poverty alleviation. New highlights have been added, with more distinctive focuses, clearer tasks, more emphasized priorities and more substantial guarantee.

In December 2014, General Office of the State Council issued Guidelines on Further Mobilizing All Sectors of Society to Participate in Poverty Alleviation and Development, pointing out that the collaboration between the eastern and western regions should be strengthened. The two regions should invigorate the coordination and contact mechanism and continue the city-to-county and department-to-department paired-up assistance. Focus should be placed on the role of the market mechanism, in accordance with the principles of complementary advantages, mutual benefit and win–win, long-term cooperation and common development. All-round poverty alleviation should be deepened through government leadership and guidance, enterprise collaboration, social support, exchange of human resources, vocational training and other forms. In this way, industrial structure would be transformed and upgraded and poor areas would pick up pace in development to lift poor villagers out of poverty. Regular contact mechanisms would be established between collaborating parties to increase assistance to poor areas. Through the two-way exchange policies of Party and government officials, professionals and technicians in the east and west, human resources would be encouraged to work in poor areas in the west.[49] The document has set on the right track poverty alleviation through East–West collaboration in the new era.

In December 2016, the State Council issued the Plan on Poverty Alleviation during the 13th Five-Year Plan Period to further clarify the main tasks of the East–West collaboration: First, to carry out multi-level collaboration for poverty alleviation.

[48] Institute of Party History and Literature of the CPC Central Committee [2].

[49] General Office of the State Council [39].

Taking the Fujian-Ningxia collaboration as a pace-setter, a targeted paired-up assistance mechanism would be established between the east and registered poor villages and households in the western region, together with the dovetailing of poverty alleviation plans to ensure that industrial cooperation, labor collaboration, human resources and financial support are accurately targeted at the eligible rural poor. Second, to expand the effective ways of anti-poverty collaboration. Focus would be placed on market mechanisms to promote the flow of talents, capital and technology from the east to poor areas and encourage the eastern regions to utilized all types of assistance funds in setting up loan guarantee funds, risk guarantee funds, loan interest funds and small and medium-sized business development funds. Competitive enterprises would be guided to branch out or start new businesses in western regions. In addition, enterprises would be encouraged to help and drive local poor people out of poverty and increase their income by quantifying shares and providing jobs. Eastern regions would be expected to offer vocational training and employment counseling services through joint construction of vocational training bases, cooperation in school running, targeted enrolment and other forms. The pairing parties were required to establish and improve the labor collaboration mechanisms in coordination by provinces and municipalities, organization by counties and townships, vocational school training, targeted arrangement and follow-up services, and improve the organization of labor exports. The exchange of Party and government officials would be carried out mainly at the county level. By swapping working posts and training venues in both regions, efforts had been ramped up to enhance the quality of officials in the western region, especially primary-level officials and entrepreneurial individuals in poor villages.[50]

In December 2016, general offices of the CPC Central Committee and of the State Council co-issued the Guidelines on Further Strengthening East–West Collaboration for Poverty Alleviation (hereinafter referred to as "the Guidelines"), adjusting the pairing relationship of East–West collaboration and between provinces. Aiming to offer more support to areas with large ethnic minority populations and extremely impoverished areas in the west by integrating Beijing, Tianjin and Hebei in the collaboration system to fully cover those areas, the Guidelines defined the tasks of the new phase, i.e. to undertake industrial and labor cooperation, to increase professional and financial support and to encourage social participation so as to improve assistance to the poor areas and people.

In addition, the Guidelines proposed some supporting measures for the east–west collaboration in poverty alleviation. These included assisting major Party committee and government leaders from both sides to pay regular visits to each other on a yearly basis, giving more guidance and support from the central departments to the collaboration and paired-up assistance, and making this work part of the national assessment of poverty elimination, with an aim to further improve the assistance mechanism to expand the collaboration to best tap comprehensive benefits.[51] In line with the Guidelines, the State Council Leading Group Office issued Measures for Evaluating East–West Collaboration in Poverty Alleviation (for Trial Implementation)

[50] The State Council [41].

[51] General Office of the CPC Central Committee and General Office of the State Council [42].

in August 2017, which reviewed the anti-poverty performance both of the eastern provinces providing assistance and their pairs in western regions by a process of "self assessment, cross reviews and overall appraisal".[52] Related Party and government departments have worked out policies and measures to support the collaboration, and primary-level departments concerned have had their implementation plans in line with local conditions.

The policy and practice of east–west collaboration and paired-up assistance in poverty alleviation have demonstrated political and institutional strengths of socialism with Chinese characteristics, as well as how China's strategy of regional development has worked in the battle against extreme poverty. As a strategic measure promoting regional cooperation for coordinated and common development, the policy is of great significance in strengthening regional cooperation, improving industrial distribution and expanding the scope for opening up to the outside world. With those who become prosperous first helping those lagging behind, efforts have been made to achieve the ultimate goal of common prosperity.

3.6 Policies of Paired-Up Assistance for Poverty Alleviation

The practice of having the CPC Central Committee and government departments, people's army and police forces, enterprises and public institutions paired up with poor counties to provide assistance to the latter is an important part of China's poverty elimination campaign. Demonstrating the political and institutional strengths of China, the paired-up poverty alleviation practice has included efforts from both central and local governments. At the central level, bodies like the CPC and government departments, other political parties and All-China Federation of Industry and Commerce, people's organizations, state-run public institutions, sizable state-owned backbone enterprises, state-owned financial institutions, leading national institutions of research and higher learning, in addition to people's army and police forces, have paired up with the key counties on the state's poverty alleviation work list under the unified deployment of the CPC Central Committee. They have provided substantial support to these counties in capital, material, technology, human resources, projects and information. At the local level, measures that have proved to be successful include: leading officials paired up with designated poor regions, comprehensive assistance, targeted assistance to needy individuals or households, performance evaluations and incentives. Since 2012 when the 18th CPC National Congress was convened, China's poverty alleviation and development work has entered the toughest stage where the new situation and tasks have brought new requirements. New arrangements for the paired-up assistance in the new period have been made through the promulgation of a series of policies.

---

[52] Measures for Evaluating East-West Collaboration in Poverty Alleviation (for Trial Implementation) [EB/OL]. (2017-08-08). http://www.cpad.gov.cn/art/2017/8/8/art_1747_861.html [43].

In December 2014, the General Office of the State Council issued Guidelines on Further Mobilizing All Sectors of Society to Participate in Poverty Alleviation and Development, which stressed the importance of deepening the paired-up assistance for poverty alleviation. Governments and institutions undertaking the assistance should give full play to their own advantages and resources through multiple channels and new ways to help coordinate and solve key problems encountered in economic and social development in designated areas, in an effort to delegate the assistance tasks to local governments in charge to ensure that measures are implemented in the counties and villages with effective outcomes. Outstanding young and middle-aged officials are selected at a regular basis to work as members of resident teams in poor villages to help lift the locals out of poverty.[53] The document has pointed out the direction for China's paired-up assistance for poverty alleviation.

To ensure that the CPC Central Committee and government departments and relevant institutions play their full role in the anti-poverty campaign and to make the paired-up assistance more efficient, a total of 9 departments, including the State Council Leading Group Office and Organization Department of the CPC Central Committee jointly issued a notice in September 2015 on further improving the paired-up assistance for poverty alleviation. The notice adjusted the paired-up relationship, and added a number of institutions previously not involved in the assistance. As a result, a total of 320 departments and institutions joined in, covering all the 592 key counties on the state's poverty alleviation work list.

The notice also proposed clearer and higher standards for every aspect of the paired-up assistance. First, a working mechanism should be established to define responsibilities for particular departments and persons in charge. Second, officials should be dispatched to work temporarily in counties or as first Party secretaries in poor villages to help in local eradication of poverty. Third, the participating departments and institutions should make the best of their own resources and strengths by fully tapping local resources and providing training courses and transfer employment to enhance the rural poor's capability to end poverty and increase income. Fourth, assistance should be continued for counties that have been removed from the poverty list. Fifth, the contact mechanism should be improved between central departments responsible for the paired-up assistance and those under their jurisdiction. Coordinated by the State Council Leading Group Office, the Work Committee for Departments Directly under the CPC Central Committee, State Organs Work Committee of the CPC Central Committee, United Front Work Department of the CPC Central Committee, Ministry of Education, the People's Bank of China, the State Owned Assets Supervision and Administration Commission of the State Council and the General Political Department of the Chinese People's Liberation Army would be responsible for the designated poverty alleviation work by contacting departments directly under the CPC Central Committee, state departments, the Central Committee of other political parties and the All-China Federation of Industry and Commerce, colleges, financial institutions, central enterprises, the People's Liberation Army and Armed Police Forces. The Organization Department of the CPC Central Committee

[53] General Office of the State Council [39].

is responsible for selecting and dispatching temporary poverty alleviation officials and first Party secretaries together with their contact departments.[54]

In March 2017, general offices of central CPC Committee and the State Council jointly released Guidelines on Further Strengthening the Paired-Up Assistance by Central Departments for Poverty Alleviation, which made institutional arrangements for the central departments and institutions to better perform the task in a new situation. The guidelines made it clear that in addition to donations in cash and kind, departments and institutions concerned should focus more on the following six tasks: namely, selecting officials to implement targeted poverty elimination; working together with local governments to explore new ways to alleviate poverty; making efforts to mobilize rural people and stimulate their motivation to get out of poverty; carrying out effective supervision to ensure officials shoulder and implement their responsibilities; paying attention to team-building at the primary level; and looking back to draw on experiences and to recognize and promote those with excellent performance.[55]

In order to stimulate the role models and spur those lagging behind and to ensure that the central departments better implement their designated responsibilities to help the poor areas, the State Council Leading Group Office issued Notice on Evaluating Paired-Up Assistance for Poverty Alleviation undertaken by Central Departments (for Trial Implementation) in August 2017. The notice specified six aspects to evaluate the departments' performance, including "outcome of the paired-up assistance, organization and leadership, selection of officials, supervision and inspection, primary-level satisfaction, and work innovation", in line with the procedures of "self assessment, cross reviews and overall appraisal" to ensure better results of the practice.[56]

Being an important part of China's poverty eradication and development with Chinese characteristics, the paired-up assistance has demonstrated the political and institutional strengths of China in the course of ending poverty. It is a vital measure to give more support to the development of the old revolutionary base areas, areas with large ethnic populations, border areas and poor regions, as well as a significant way for central Party and government departments to be closer to their primary-level counterparts, better informed of the situation of the people, better develop their officials, improve working style and maintain closer ties between the Party and the people.

Doing this well has been of great significance to ensure the accomplishment of poverty alleviation and the smooth realization of the goal of building a moderately prosperous society in all respects.

[54] Guidelines on Further Improving the Paired-Up Assistance for Poverty Alleviation [EB/OL]. (2015-09-08). http://www.cpad.gov.cn/art/2015/9/8/art_50_22397.html [44].

[55] The State Council Leading Group for Poverty Alleviation and Development [45].

[56] Ibid.

3.7 Policies of Corporate and Social Assistance for Poverty Alleviation

Poverty is often the result of complex factors, and it is a social problem in various forms, which is difficult to address only by one sector or one mechanism. Only by giving full play to various social sectors with multiple mechanisms working together, can it be better solved. Helping the poor is a traditional virtue of the Chinese nation, and achieving common prosperity is the essential requirement for the CPC to lead China's cause of socialism. Poverty alleviation in China is an all-encompassing campaign. One of China's good practices in poverty reduction is to constantly improve and give impetus to the campaign with participation of all players. Among them, social organizations function as not only critical forces driving China's socialist modernization, but as ties connecting caring enterprises and individuals with poor population. They have played important roles in encouraging social sectors to participate in the battle against poverty and have been important parts themselves in the all-encompassing anti-poverty campaign involving government-sponsored projects, sector-specific programs, and corporate and societal assistance.

Social organizations in China have been involved in poverty eradication and development for many years. Since 1994 when the State Council put forward in The National Seven-Year Poverty Alleviation Program the idea of "giving full play to the role of China Foundation for Poverty Alleviation and other non-governmental organizations", China has been emphasizing in all its poverty relief outlines that attention should be paid to the roles of social organizations. Arrangements have been made to encourage them to participate in poverty alleviation in various forms. For instance, China Foundation for Poverty Alleviation, China Youth Development Foundation, China Women's Development Foundation and China Foundation for Disabled Persons have taken an active part and launched a number of influential public anti-poverty projects like "Guangcai Program", "Project Hope", "Water Cellar for Mothers", "Nutrition Improvement for Children in Poverty-Stricken Areas" and "Action Plan for Poverty Alleviation Volunteers". Since the 18th CPC National Congress in 2012, social organizations have been optimizing their working mechanisms and practices, showing great potential for poverty alleviation. In order to better fight against poverty in the new era by further mobilizing all social sectors to participate in the endeavor and promoting the innovation in the social assistance system and mechanism, the central government has introduced relevant policies to lead and guide social organizations to engage in poverty alleviation.

In December 2014, General Office of the State Council issued Guidelines on Further Mobilizing All Sectors of Society to Participate in Poverty Alleviation and Development, which fully acknowledged the effectiveness and potential of sectors of society in poverty relief, and made it clear that social organizations are one of the major players. Specific requirements and supporting measures have been given to encourage them to participate in poverty alleviation. It was stressed that social organizations, foundations and private non-profit organizations should be encouraged to take active part in development-driven poverty eradication. To build a dynamic anti-poverty mechanism with the participation of social organizations, local governments at all levels and their departments should provide information services and professional guidance for sectors of society to carry out poverty alleviation activities and encourage them to join in the mobilization, allocation and use of social poverty relief resources.[57] The document has pointed the way for mobilizing social sectors to participate in poverty relief.

In November 2017, the State Council Leading Group Office released the Notice on Extensively Guiding and Mobilizing Social Sectors to Participate in the Battle against Poverty. It further specified major areas in need of their contributions, and advocated to encourage social sectors to take active part in poverty alleviation through industries, education, health, relocation, and voluntary work. Among them, social organizations at national and provincial levels have been encouraged to play the role of pace setters and lead other organizations at different levels to make full use of their strengths and advantages. Starting from addressing the most immediate, practical and pressing problems, they have been expected to pool social assistance resources for poor areas and people by providing public services, human resources, relief projects and assistance in decision making. With these efforts, social organizations have played a significant role in the anti-poverty campaign.[58]

Social organizations have played and are still playing an important part in poverty alleviation. Their engagement in the great endeavor is not only their major responsibility, but also a practice of their commitment to the nation, the society, the people and the industry, as well as a venue and approach to develop themselves. Corporate and societal assistance can help governments solve problems that may have been overlooked before, and inspire the government to do better through their innovative practices. The strengths of socialism with Chinese characteristics should be given full play to motivate all social organizations to join in the battle against extreme poverty. Developing a diversified mechanism for poverty relief and incorporating corporate and societal assistance into the all-encompassing anti-poverty campaign is a unique feature of the Chinese approach to poverty alleviation, as well as a major component of the theory of the all-encompassing anti-poverty campaign. It is also a practical demand and necessary choice to win the battle against extreme poverty to achieve a moderately prosperous society in an all-round way.

With the enhanced awareness of the roles of social sectors in poverty eradication and development, the Ministry of Civil Affairs, the Ministry of Finance, and the State Council Poverty Alleviation Office jointly released Guidelines on Encouraging Professionals in Social Work to Participate in Poverty Alleviation in June 2017, which defined the social workers' tasks in poverty alleviation and their agent role, with suggested forms and guidelines on assistance they may provide, including poverty relief, capacity enhancement, helping the relocated impoverished people adapt to the new environment, caring for the left-behind children in poor areas, and love outreach to special groups such as the elderly, women and children. Social work professionals are emerging forces that provide social services such as psychological counseling,

[57] General Office of the State Council [39].

[58] The State Council Leading Group of Poverty Alleviation and Development [46].

mental health care, relation adjustment and ability improvement for the poor. They can play active roles in helping the poor change attitudes, establish self-confidence in getting rid of poverty, find more ways and means to be prosperous, and improve their ability to eradicate poverty.[59]

Bibliography

1. Xi, J. (2015). *Keynote speech at 2015. Global Poverty Reduction and Development Forum* [EB/OL], October 16, 2015. http://www.xinhuanet.com//politics/2015-10/16/c_1116851045.htm
2. Institute of Party History and Literature of CPC Central Committee. (2018). *Xi Jinping on poverty alleviation*. Central Party Literature Publishing House.
3. *Notice on Measures for the Management of Central Government Funds for Poverty Alleviation* [EB/OL], March 24, 2017. http://www.gov.cn/xinwen/2017-03/24/content_518043.htm
4. Hu, J. (2016). Increasing financial investment to support poverty alleviation. *Administration Reform, 8*, 12–15.
5. General Office of the CPC Central Committee and General Office of the State Council. *Guidelines on Promoting Rural Poverty Alleviation and Development Through Innovative Mechanisms* [EB/OL]. http://www.cpad.gov.cn/art/2014/2/13/art46_12338.html
6. The CPC Central Committee and the State Council. (2015). *Decisions on Winning the Battle against Extreme Poverty* [EB/OL], December 7, 2015. http://www.gov.cn/xinwen/2015-12/07/content_5020963.htm
7. *Notice on Measures for the Performance Evaluation of Government Funds for Poverty Alleviation* [EB/OL], September 19, 2017. http://www.gov.cn/xinwen/2017-09/19/content_5226116.htm.
8. General Office of the State Council. (2016). *Guidelines on Supporting Pilot Programs of Integrating Government Funds for Rural Development in Poor Counties* [EB/OL], April 22, 2016. http://www.gov.cn/zhengce/2016-04-22/content_5066842.htm
9. Ministry of Finance and the State Council Poverty Alleviation Office. (2017). *Notice on Pilot Program of Integrating Government Funds for Rural Development in Poor Counties in 2017* [EB/OL], December 16, 2017. http://www.gov.cn/xinwen/2017-02/16/content_5168451. htm
10. The State Council. (2017). *Guidelines on Exploring the Establishment of a Long-Term Mechanism for Overall Planning and Integrating Government Funds for Rural Development* [EB/OL], December 21, 2017. http://www.gov.cn/zhengce/content/2017-12/21/content_5249187.htm
11. Literature Research Office of the CPC Central Committee. (2018). *Selected literature since the 18th CPC National Congress (II)*. Central Party Literature Publishing House.
12. *Guidelines on Providing Comprehensive Financial Services for Poverty Alleviation and Development* [EB/OL], April 10, 2014–04–10. http://www.gov.cn/xinwen/2014-04/10/content_2656095.htm
13. People's Bank of China and Six Other Departments. (2016). *Guidelines on the Implementation of Financial Assistance for Poverty Alleviation* [EB/OL], March 23, 2016. http://www.pbc.gov.cn/goutongjiaoliu/113456/113469/3037335/index.html
14. *Guidelines on Innovative Development of Microfinance for Poverty Alleviation* [EB/OL], December 15, 2014. http://www.cpad.gov.cn/art/2014/12/15/art_46_23778.html
15. China Banking Regulatory Commission and Other Central Departments. (2017). *Notice on Promoting the Healthy Development of Microfinance for Poverty Alleviation* [EB/OL], August 17, 2017. http://www.cbrc.gov.cn/chinese/home/docView/62052ABA472345E2A8C0B973A32945E2.html

[59] Ministry of Civil Affairs, Ministry of Finance and the State Council Poverty Alleviation Office [47].

16. China Insurance Regulatory Commission and the State Council Poverty Alleviation Office. (2016). *Guidelines on Insurance Industry's Contribution to Poverty Alleviation* [EB/OL], May 26, 2016. http://www.cpad.gov.cn/art/2016/5/26/art_1747_669.html
17. Ministry of Human Resources and Social Security, Ministry of Finance and State Council Poverty Alleviation Office. (2017). *Guidelines on Effective Implementation of Social Insurance for Poverty Alleviation* [EB/OL], August 8, 2017. http://www.mohrss.gov.cn/ncshbxs/NCSHBXSzhengcewenjian/201708/t20170808_275361.html
18. People's Bank and Three Other Departments. (2018). *Guidelines on Financial Support for Poverty Alleviation in Poverty-Stricken Areas* [EB/OL], January 15, 2018. http://www.cpad.gov.cn/art/2018/1/15/art_22_76781.html
19. Wang, X. (2019). *Poverty alleviation through insurance: Financial backing for the development of agriculture, rural areas and rural people* [EB/OL]. August 21, 2019. https://insurance.hexun.com/2019-08-21/198276335.html
20. China Securities Regulatory Commission. (2017). *Guidelines on Leveraging the Role of Capital Market to Serve the National Poverty Alleviation Strategy* [EB/OL], January 11, 2017. http://www.csrc.gov.cn/pub/newsite/flb/flfg/bmgf/zh/qt/201701/t20170111._309303.html
21. Ministry of Water Resources, the State Council Poverty Alleviation Office and National Health Commission. (2018). *Circular on Winning the Battle against Extreme Poverty through Ensuring Water Safety in Rural Areas* [EB/OL], August 2, 2018. http://www.mwr.gov.cn/zw/tzgg/tzgs/201808/t20180802_1044428.html
22. National Development and Reform Commission. (2017). *Notice on the Relocation Plan for Poverty Alleviation during the 13th Five-Year Plan Period* [EB/OL], April 28, 2017. http://www.cpad.gov.cn/art/2017/4/28/art_50_62482.html
23. Ministry of Housing and Urban-Rural Development, Ministry of Finance and the State Council Poverty Alleviation Office. (2017). *Notice on Strengthening and Improving Renovation of Dilapidated Houses for Registered Poor Households in Rural Areas* [EB/OL], September 6, 2017. http://www.mohurd.gov.cn/wjfb/201709/t20170906_233201.html
24. Ministry of Housing and Urban-Rural Development and Ministry of Finance. (2019). *A Three-Year Action Plan for Poverty Relief through Renovation of Dilapidated Rural Houses* [EB/OL], April 10, 2019. http://www.mohurd.gov.cn/wjfb/201904/t20190410_240136.html
25. *Guidelines on Implementing the Education Program for Poverty Alleviation* [EB/OL], September 12, 2013. http://www.cpad.gov.cn/art/2013/9/12/art_50_23748.html
26. Ministry of Education and Other Five Departments. (2016). *Plans for Poverty Alleviation through Education during the 13th Five-Year Plan Period* [EB/OL], December 29, 2016. http://www.moe.gov.cn/srcsite/A03/moe_1892/moe_630/201612/t20161229_293351.html
27. Ministry of Education and the State Council Poverty Alleviation Office. (2018). *Implementation Plan of Poverty Alleviation through Education in Destitute Areas (2018–2020)* [EB/OL], February 27, 2018. http://www.gov.cn/xinwen/2018-02/27/content_5269090.htm
28. *Guidelines on Implementing the Health Program for Poverty Alleviation* [EB/OL], June 20, 2016. http://www.cpad.gov.cn/art/2016/6/20/art_1747_682.html
29. *Notice on "Affordable Medical Services" Action Plan in Implementing the Health Program for Poverty Alleviation* [EB/OL], August 16, 2017. http://www.cpad.gov.cn/art/2017/8/16/art_1747_847.html
30. Ministry of Agriculture and Eight Other Departments. (2016). *Guidelines on Promoting Targeted Poverty Eradication through Developing Specialty Industries in Poor Areas* [EB/OL], May 27, 2016. http://www.gov.cn/xinwen/2016-05/27/content_5077245.htm
31. Ministry of Agriculture. (2017). *Guidelines on Increasing Preferential Support for Project Funds in Poor Areas to Promote Targeted Poverty Alleviation through Specialty Industries* [EB/OL], November 28, 2017. http://www.moa.gov.cn/nybgb/2016/dijiuqi/201711/t20171128_5921938.htm
32. Ministry of Human Resources and Social Security, Ministry of Finance and State Council Poverty Alleviation Office. (2016). *Guidelines on Effective Implementation of Poverty Alleviation through Employment* [EB/OL], December 8, 2016. http://www.mohrss.gov.cn/SYrlzyhshbzb/jiuye/zcwj/201612/t20161208_261480.html

33. Ministry of Human Resources and Social Security and the State Council Poverty Alleviation Office. (2018). *Notice on Launching Poverty Alleviation Campaign through Skills Training in Extremely Impoverished Areas* [EB/OL], October 10, 2018. http://www.gov.cn/xinwen/2018-10/10/content_5329307.htm
34. Ministry of Civil Affairs and Other Five Departments. (2016). *Guidelines on Effective Dovetailing of the Rural Subsistence Allowances Framework with Development-Oriented Poverty Alleviation Policies* [EB/OL], September 27, 2016. http://www.gov.cn/zhengce/content/2016-09/27/content_5112631.htm
35. Ministry of Science and Technology, Ministry of Education, Chinese Academy of Sciences, Chinese Academy of Engineering, National Natural Science Foundation, State Administration of Science, Technology and Industry for National Defense, the State Council Poverty Alleviation Office. (2016). *Action Plan for Poverty Alleviation through Science and Technology* [EB/OL], October 13, 2016. http://www.cpad.gov.cn/art/2016/10/13/art_1744_76.html
36. Ministry of Transport. (2019). *Notice on Plans for Poverty Alleviation through Transportation during the 13th Five-Year Plan Period* [EB/OL], March 29, 2019. http://xxgk.mot.gov.cn/jigou/zhghs/201903/t20190329_3182337.html
37. General Office of Ministry of Transport. (2019). *Notice on Implementation Plan for Lifting Destitute Areas out of Poverty through Transportation* [EB/OL], March 29, 2019. http://xxgk.mot.gov.cn/jigou/zhghs/201903/t20190329_3182339.html
38. General Office of Ministry of Transport. (2019). *Notice on Three-Year Action Plan for Poverty Alleviation through Transportation (2018–2020)* [EB/OL], March 29, 2019. http://xxgk.mot.gov.cn/jigou/zhghs/201903/t20190329_3182332.html
39. General Office of the State Council. (2014). *Guidelines on further mobilizing all sectors of society to participate in poverty alleviation and development* [EB/OL]. December 4, 2014. http://www.gov.cn/zhengce/content/2014-12/04/content_9289.htm
40. All-China Federation of Industry and Commerce, the State Council Poverty Alleviation Office and China Society for Promotion of the Guangcai Program. (2016). *Guidelines on Implementing Targeted Poverty Alleviation by the "10,000 Enterprises Helping 10,000 Villages" Program* [EB/OL], January 18, 2016. http://www.cpad.gov.cn/art/2016/1/18/art_1747_656.html
41. The State Council. (2016). *Plan for Poverty Alleviation During the 13th Five-Year Plan Period* [EB/OL], December 2, 2016. http://www.gov.cn/zhengce/content/2016-12/02/content_5142197.htm.
42. General Office of the CPC Central Committee and General Office of the State Council. (2016). *Guidelines on Further Strengthening East-West Collaboration for Poverty Alleviation* [EB/OL], December 7, 2016. http://www.gov.cn/zhengce/2016-12/07/content_5144678.htm
43. *Measures for Evaluating East-West Collaboration in Poverty Alleviation (for Trial Implementation)* [EB/OL], August 8, 2017. http://www.cpad.gov.cn/art/2017/8/8/art_1747_861.html
44. *Guidelines on Further Improving the Paired-Up Assistance for Poverty Alleviation* [EB/OL], September 8, 2015. http://www.cpad.gov.cn/art/2015/9/8/art_50_22397.html
45. The State Council Leading Group of Poverty Alleviation and Development. (2017). *Notice on Evaluating Paired-Up Assistance for Poverty Alleviation Undertaken by Central Departments (for Trial Implementation) issued by* [EB/OL], August 8, 2017. http://www.cpad.gov.cn/art/2017/8/8/art_1747_862.html
46. The State Council Leading Group of Poverty Alleviation and Development. (2017). *Notice on Extensively Guiding and Mobilizing Social Sectors to Participate in the Battle against Poverty* [EB/OL], December 5, 2017. http://www.cpad. gov.cn/art/2017/12/5/art_50_74541.html
47. Ministry of Civil Affairs, Ministry of Finance and the State Council Poverty Alleviation Office. (2017). *Guidelines on Encouraging Professionals in Social Work to Participate in Poverty Alleviation* [EB/OL], August 19, 2017. http://www.gov.cn/xinwen/2017-08/19/content_5218659.htm
48. Fan, X. (2013). *Understanding common terms for poverty alleviation and development*. China Financial & Economic Publishing House.

49. Office of Household Surveys of National Bureau of Statistics. (2019). *Monitoring report on rural poverty in China 2019*. China Statistics Press.
50. The State Council Poverty Alleviation Office and Seven Other Departments. (2012). *Notice on a New Round of Paired-Up Assistance by Central Departments* [EB/OL], November 13, 2012. http://www.cpad.gov.cn/art/2012/11/13/art50_23725.html
51. Hu, F. (2018). *Understanding China: Poverty alleviation*. Foreign Languages Press.
52. Li, X. (2015). On improving east-west collaboration mechanism for poverty alleviation: A case study of paired-up assistance between Fujian and Ningxia. *Journal of the Party School of CPC Yinchuan Municipal Committee, 17*(5), 48–52.
53. Lu, Y. (2017). Approaches to building an effective societal assistance mechanism for targeted poverty alleviation. *Reform, 10*, 58–61.
54. National Publicity and Education Center for Poverty Alleviation. (2018). *Innovation on poverty alleviation: Theory and practice*. China Agriculture Press.
55. National Publicity and Education Center for Poverty Alleviation. (2018). *Strategies and policies for poverty alleviation*. China Agriculture Press.
56. General Office of the CPC Central Committee and General Office of the State Council. (2010). *Notice on Further Improving Paired-Up Assistance for Poverty Alleviation* [EB/OL], July 8, 2010. http://www.gov.cn/jrzg/2010-07/08/content_1649275.htm
57. *Notice on the 2019 Pilot Implementation of Integrating Government Funds in Poor Counties* [EB/OL], March 14, 2019. http://www.gov.cn/xinwen/2019-03/14/content_5373713.htm
58. *China Strives to Achieve Full Coverage of Poverty Alleviation and Development in Major Impoverished Counties* [EB/OL], July 8, 2010. http://www.gov.cn/jrzg/2010-07/08/content_1648985.htm
59. General Office of the CPC Central Committee and General Office of the State Council. (2010). *Notice on Further Improving Paired-Up Assistance for Poverty Alleviation* [EB/OL], July 8, 2010. http//www.gov.cn/jrzg/2010-07/08/content_1649275.htm

Chapter 4
Targeted Poverty Alleviation and Elimination: Approaches and Models

"The people's aspiration for a better life is our goal." This is a promise made by Xi Jinping as the newly elected General Secretary on behalf of the Communist Party of China at the 18th CPC National Congress held in 2012. And the CPC Central Committee with Xi Jinping as its core has since then placed a high priority on poverty elimination in the governance of China and mobilized the whole Party and all sectors of society to jointly fight the battle against extreme poverty. In November 2013, on his inspection tour to Shibadong Village, Huayuan County, Hunan Province, Xi proposed for the first time the concept of targeted poverty alleviation, which has been enriched and developed over the time to become a fundamental strategy for poverty alleviation in China. In June 2015, when he addressed to a meeting of senior officials of some provinces, autonomous regions and municipalities held in Guizhou, President Xi Jinping offered a profound analysis of the general idea and basic requirements of targeted poverty alleviation and elimination.

At the Central Conference on Poverty Alleviation and Development in 2015, Xi Jinping once again elaborated on the strategy and boiled it down as accomplishing "Targeted Efforts in Six Areas" and taking "Five Measures for Poverty Eradication". Specifically, the former refers to efforts to identify the poor accurately, arrange targeted programs, utilize capital efficiently, take household-based measures, dispatch first Party secretaries based on village conditions, and achieve the set goals[1]; while the latter include: boosting the economy to provide more job opportunities, relocating poor people from inhospitable areas, compensating for economic losses associated with reducing ecological damage, improving education in impoverished areas, and providing subsistence allowances for those unable to shake off poverty through their own efforts alone. In addition, poverty alleviation through health programs and earnings from funds and assets should also be delivered. All these efforts, including accurate withdrawal, have aimed to address four key issues in poverty alleviation—who needs help, who provides help, how to help and how to be

[1] The Proposal of the CPC Central Committee on Formulating the 13th Five-Year Plan for National Economic and Social Development [N]. *People's Daily*, 2015-11-04 [1].

S. Wang, *Poverty Alleviation and Targeted Measures*,
https://doi.org/10.1007/978-981-96-1493-6_4

removed from the poverty lists.[2] For this purpose, the central government has issued a series of effective policies and measures to ensure solid and authentic outcomes that can survive the test of time and practice.

4.1 Identifying and Targeting Poor Population

Accurate identification is an essential foundation for targeted poverty alleviation and elimination, which must "reach those who truly need it and deliver genuine outcomes" by "identifying the genuinely poor" as the basic premise. To do this well, we must first know who they are and analyze the causes of their poverty. All those living in poverty will be registered and the database will be built to record detailed information about their production and living conditions, which provides the basis for the implementation of targeted policies. With these measures, the assistance can reach poor households by means of projects, funds and industries with satisfactory outcomes.

In late 2013, the CPC Central Committee and the State Council released Guidelines on Creating New Mechanisms for Promoting Rural Poverty Alleviation and Development, proposing better mechanisms to identify impoverished people in rural development. Every poor household and village should be registered to build a nationwide unified information system of poverty alleviation, following the principles of county basis, size control, hierarchical responsibility, accurate identification and dynamic management. In May 2014, the objectives, methods, steps, and work requirements for the registration of poor households and villages were planned in a series of documents jointly issued by the State Council Leading Group Office and other central departments. The rural households and people would be labeled as "poor" if their per capita net incomes in 2013 were lower than the national poverty line of RMB2736 (equivalent to the constant price of RMB2300 in 2010, the same below). However, accurately accounting the income of individual households was not easy and used to be conducted by professional organizations (e. g. statistical departments) through sampling, which was costly and beyond the capability of primary-level governments. In the absence of accurate household income information, poverty identification and registration could only rely on grassroots democratic appraisal constrained by quotas. Poor households were identified mainly based on their incomes and consumption, with consideration given to other factors such as health conditions, education, capabilities, family burden, property and interpersonal relationships.

Poverty identified at the primary level was multidimensional, and was not just considered by income and consumption. The inconsistency of indicators and methods used by statistical organizations and grassroots poverty alleviation departments in estimating and identifying the poor population inevitably led to divergences in results. Informed by investigations of typical cases and random checks conducted by the

[2] The CPC Central Committee and the State Council [2].

State Council Leading Group Office, only 50% of the poor confirmed by the democratic appraisal coincided with estimated results based on consumption and income, which implied that a significant number of rural poor were not registered for government assistance, while some households living above the poverty line were wrongly identified as the poor [3].

Accurate identification has acquired the base conditions of the poor population and the causes of poverty, fixing the problem of "who needs help". But given the fact that poverty is a dynamic process, more detailed and in-depth work should be done to ensure that the identification is authentic and the real poor people are included in the poverty registration system. Dynamic management of the poor population needs to be strengthened, with timely adjustment through follow-up checks for accuracy. A rural household would be confirmed as poor, if its annual per capita net income was lower than the national poverty line, and had yet achieved "Two Assurances and Three Guarantees" to be secured adequate food and clothing, with access to compulsory education, basic medical services and safe housing. Only by continuously enhancing the accuracy of poverty identification can targeted assistance reach the needy households.

4.1.1 Formulation of Poverty Reduction Goals

In his report to the 19th CPC National Congress in 2018, General Secretary Xi Jinping defined the current poverty alleviation goals for the year 2020 as: to ensure the poor people and poor areas enter the moderately prosperous society together with the rest of the country; lift all rural population living under current poverty line out of poverty and eliminate overall regional poverty; guarantee that the people have their basic living needs and access to compulsory education, basic medical services and safe housing; and ensure that the growth rate in rural per capita disposable income surpasses the national average growth rate and the main indicators of basic public services approach the national average.[3]

The Communist Party of China has held fast to building a moderately prosperous society in all respects and achieving common prosperity without leaving anyone behind, so that the development gains can be shared by all people. Xi Jinping once said, "In building a moderately prosperous society in all respects, the most arduous task lies in the rural areas, especially in poverty-stricken areas. This goal cannot be completed if these areas have not reached moderate prosperity."[4] The goal of development-driven poverty alleviation in the new era has reflected the CPC's fundamental position of remaining true to its original aspiration and pursuing the fundamental values of people-oriented development, which is to better realize, safeguard, and advance the fundamental interest of the overwhelming majority of the people. Xi's theory of poverty alleviation, starting from achieving common prosperity, has

[3] Xi [4].

[4] Xi [3].

worked to safeguard the fundamental interests of the majority of the people and ensure that all people share in the fruits of development. It is a manifestation of the CPC's full commitment to serving the people.

4.1.2 *Identification of the Poor Population*

Building a sound mechanism for accurate poverty identification is the realistic premise and important foundation for targeted poverty alleviation. Accurate identification aims to identify families and populations living below the poverty line and analyze the key factors that lead to their poverty.[5] In other words, this refers to the detailed and accurate classification of the rural poor. As Xi Jinping points out, officials must identify the truly poor, helping them and delivering genuine outcomes.[6] A top-down poverty identification system of "region-county-village-household" should be established for the work.

Only through accurate identification can we achieve effective results in the targeted poverty elimination campaign. It is essential to identify and register those who are genuinely poor. Accurate information should be obtained about the poor, including their family members, causes and degree of their poverty, so that targeted measures can be tailored for different households in need. The national unified standards for poverty registration have been applied in targeted poverty identification. Any household whose annual average per capita income was below the international poverty line, and had yet achieved the criteria of "Two Assurances and Three Guarantees" would be identified and registered as poor. Localities would not be permitted to raise or lower these criteria. Accurate identification has solved the problem of "who needs help", with clear information of the base number of poor people and the causes of their poverty. Informed by the results of poverty registration, multiple efforts could be made to coordinate and decide whom to help, without missing or withdrawing the real needy people.

Reasons that may affect the accuracy of poverty identification are as follows:

(1) Exclusion by size. Featuring standardized procedures, joint participation of multiple departments and a strengthened public notification system, the practice could help improve the accuracy of identification. However, the "level-by-level allocation of assigned quotas" has set the limit of the number of poor people in counties and villages and may lead to the exclusion of some poor people.
(2) Exclusion by ways of identification. The way of benefit measurement based on the democratic appraisal has been designed to address information asymmetry in poverty identification. However, the differences in perceptions of income and expenditure between the measurement methods and villagers' participation may cause inconsistent poverty standards among regions, counties and villages, and would then result in the exclusion of some poor groups.

[5] Wang and Guo [5].

[6] Institute of Party History and Literature of the CPC Central Committee [6].

(3) Exclusion by malpractices. Some grassroots officials may give unfair privileges to friends and relatives in identification, and manipulate the distribution of poverty quotas, which would generate malicious exclusion of poor groups.[7]

Therefore, the building of an accurate identification mechanism needs to focus on the following three aspects:

(1) Innovating the evaluation system. Reasonable income standards should be set up by starting from the differences in the causes and degree of poverty, in line with local conditions, different times and actual situation of different regions, instead of being limited to evaluating only the material conditions, so that a diversified, multi-level, and autonomous poverty evaluation system can be worked out.
(2) Establishing a file system for the rural poor. Officials at the primary level should work in villages and households to carry out thorough investigations for first-hand information, and to build files on poor households in line with the information received and the local evaluation system. Based on the poverty status, the registration for poor households, villages, counties, and regions should be conducted to establish a multi-dimensional file system so that the records can be tracked and referred to.
(3) Implementing a public notification system. In line with the principle of fairness and justice, a disclosure system should be established to advance primary-level democracy. Villagers may participate in the identification by reviewing the information, so that they could have their own judgment about whether or not the potential candidates meet the criteria for assistance. This is an effective way to play the supervisory role of the general rural public.[8]

4.1.3 Innovation of Poverty Alleviation Practices

Fighting against extreme poverty should not only base on what has worked in the past but also endeavor to innovate. The development of poverty alleviation in China has been a process of redoubling efforts, more accurate identification of the poor and more innovative measures and approaches. Helping the poor get rid of poverty and seeking happiness for all people is the fundamental goal of the CPC and Chinese government in promoting development. To win the battle against poverty, the departments at all levels must adopt multiple and creative measures to shake off poverty. However, the work remains tough at the final stage since we have to crack the "hardest nuts" and finish the challenging and demanding tasks within a very tight schedule. More efforts have been required to overcome the difficulties with enduring resilience and draw on valuable experience and practices to raise efficiency. Departments at all levels should work out their own strategies and measures for poverty elimination based on local conditions while drawing on good practices from other places, trying to innovate the ways and mechanisms and take multiple measures. A reward and punishment

[7] Wang et al. [7].

[8] Wang and Wang [8].

mechanism should be established to fully play the leadership of the government, and policies for rural development issued by the CPC and the central government should be popularized and implemented through all channels for greater progress in the campaign.

Effective measures should be innovated in targeted poverty alleviation, which could turn into strong driving forces and workable practices to ensure sustainable and stable achievements in the endeavor. Since the 18th CPC National Congress in 2012, guided by Xi Jinping's thought on poverty alleviation, China has continued to make innovations on the models and approaches by targeted measures. These are necessary for different localities and households, given their diverse causes of poverty, such as poor education, critical diseases, house building, and lack of labor and capital. Only by considering local realities and people's will could we prevent making just lip service or going through formalities so as to find effective ideas and approaches to reduce poverty. The projects and funds should be well arranged to fully leverage the economic role of local industries, address the root cause of poverty and work towards prosperity. The demand for innovative measures has shown that programs and funds alone are far from enough for achieving sustained and stable poverty alleviation. Categorized and targeted measures should be adopted based on the causes and types of poverty.

Innovative measures have approached from the following aspects:

First, building new villages for rural development. The primary purpose of new village construction is to upgrade living environment for the rural poor so that they would be uplifted from their original surroundings featuring poor infrastructure facilities. With the new village building as a vital carrier, the construction of rural infrastructure and the transformation of agricultural production modes can be boosted to enhance rural modernization. In the implementation, emphasis should be laid on the upgrading of rural living environment in general, particularly in infrastructure, public services, the protection of traditional villages and the renovation of dilapidated houses. Meanwhile, the rebuilt better rural environment can serve as the foundation for the development of leisure agriculture and rural tourism.

Second, developing industries. Industrial development is the key to solving the "last-mile" bottlenecks and leading poor households out of poverty by their own efforts. In order to improve performance and escape the dilemma, it is necessary to correctly assess suitable industries and develop special and leading ones on the basis of market research and available resources in line with local conditions and regional advantages. They are expected to boost employment, generate profits as soon as possible and benefit more local people. The "small workshops" production model should be phased out due to their vulnerability to resist market risks. Well-run industries should be appropriately scaled up by diversifying to create supporting industries with the specialty industry as the core, and gradually develop industrial parks for poverty alleviation to improve the chain.

Third, improving education. In addition to promoting the building of new villages and developing industries to create good external conditions for poverty reduction, it is more crucial to enhance people's capacity for self-development through education. According to Amartya Sen, the 1998 Nobel Prize winner in economics, the lack of education is the "poverty as capability deprivation," and it is a kind of poverty worse than income poverty, which may lead to the "intergenerational transmission of poverty." Thus education has been given the mission of "preventing the intergenerational transmission of poverty," and the way to achieve this has been well summed up as "ensuring all children from poor families have access to fair and quality education", which requires more financial investments to support education in poor areas. Focusing on the timetable of "moderate prosperity for all" and the goals of poverty alleviation, we should address the most pressing, critical and particular difficulties and issues of the poor people in receiving education, and ensure national education funds continue to give more support to basic education in poor areas. Meanwhile, it is necessary to facilitate the government reform of education through combining education with developing industries for poverty alleviation. The anti-poverty function of education should be enhanced through industry-education integration. Together with these measures, we should also provide jobs for poor graduates, set up incentive mechanisms to support those who return to their hometown to start businesses, and encourage poor graduates to earn their living through what they have learned. Benefiting from the cooperation between educational institutions and enterprises, the "industry + education" model can be established to improve the capacity for independent development by delivering technologies and knowledge to the poor areas.

4.2 Poverty Alleviation Through Industrial Development

At one of the group study sessions of the Political Bureau of the 19th CPC Central Committee, General Secretary Xi Jinping pointed out, "A thriving business environment is the basis for resolving all issues in rural areas. The transformation from 'production development' to 'thriving industries' has brought with it new requirements for the agricultural sector and the rural economy to adapt to changing market demands, accelerate optimization and upgrading and boost industrial integration."[9] To secure victory against poverty, we must attach great importance to economic development. As one of the most dynamic models to alleviate poverty in China, local industrial development has been a good way to provide opportunities of sustainable development for rural poor. The approach has received increasing attention since the 18th CPC National Congress held in 2012 when the "Five Measures for Poverty Elimination" was formulated by the central leadership in which economic development comes first. It has become a fundamental strategy to get rid of poverty, which can foster the internal impetus of the poor people. Without a strong catalyst for sustainable economic growth, these localities would still face problems and fail to end poverty.

According to the Plan on Poverty Alleviation during the 13th Five-Year Plan Period, farmer cooperatives and leading enterprises should be supported to play a

[9] Song [9].

principal role in the market based on local resources, and a sound mechanism should be put in place whereby the industries may give targeted aids to households and people. A number of specialty industries should be developed in each poor county to help poor townships and villages produce quality products with local characteristics. This could effectively upgrade the skills of impoverished people and steadily increase their business and property incomes.

As the primary measure for poverty reduction, local industrial development has leveraged the strengths of resources in poor areas through creative approaches, which include introducing projects and capital, developing production and local industries to employ the labor force in poor areas. It can help achieve the full flow of factors such as capital for poverty relief and labor in the market, and strengthen ties between the poor people and other market players. Additionally, the distribution of returns should prioritized poverty-stricken areas, targeting villages and households, in an attempt to realize the stable and healthy economic development and help the people out of poverty through sustainable incomes (including the incomes from wages, salary, business, property, etc.). Economic development could help poor regions find ways to help themselves. For this reason, it is necessary to comprehensively promote poverty alleviation through new economic activities. Instead of seeking short-term profits, attention should be paid to selecting a suitable industry for long-term development, enhancing brand awareness and ensuring the quality of products. Localities should also exert their advantages by integrating local culture and industrial development and adding the cultural value to their industries. China has encouraged poverty alleviation through new forms of business and new industries such as agriculture, forestry, tourism, e-commerce and technology. The financial measures, as well as the earnings from poverty alleviation funds and assets, have also been used to support the poor.

4.2.1 Poverty Alleviation Through Agriculture and Forestry Industries

Agriculture and forestry industries act as the core of poverty elimination and the key to realizing rural revitalization. In order to effectively shake off poverty, we must ensure that the poor people can obtain stable jobs and sustainable income through the development of specialty industries. In this sense, agriculture and forestry industries are major industries for poverty alleviation and major sources of income for poor populations in rural areas. By improving these industries and extending the relevant chains, we can advance the development of the agricultural industry and explore new modes in poverty relief. To be specific, a standardized system for brand quality management can be set up for industrial complexes, along with a benefits-coupling mechanism. The agricultural industry has provided inexhaustible drive in China's poverty elimination campaign. The following are some measures in agriculture and forestry industries for poverty reduction:

First, developing a leading industry with local features. As the basis for poverty eradication and the material foundation for rural revitalization, the development of specialty industries should be guided and supported to change the situation from "helping poor people" to "giving opportunities for poor people to help themselves." In selecting specialty industries, factors such as available local resources, market prospects and development potential should be taken into account to implement the practice of household-based measures for targeted poverty alleviation.

Efforts should be made to ensure that the local people can engage in these industries with their incomes increased, taking the achievement of delivering stable, long-term benefits to poor people as the starting point and the ultimate goal. Based on the ecology, geography, climate and industrial base, the specialty industries should be developed in line with targeted poverty alleviation, creating opportunities for impoverished households to participate in the development and share the gains. By implementing the action of "one industry for one village", we can boost the construction of leading industrial bases with sustainable and stable revenues in deep poverty-stricken villages by improving the overall benefits of industries to lead villagers to increase their incomes and emerge from poverty.

These industries can be generally divided into three types:

(1) The planting industry. To consolidate and improve grain production capacity, major grain-producing counties should build eco-friendly and high-standard farmland on a large scale in contiguous areas, ensuring stable and high yields of crops despite drought or excessive rain. Non-major grain-producing counties should adjust the planting structure by cultivating varieties suitable to local climate with good economic benefits and great market potential. Various planting bases featuring high participation of poor people and considerable benefit rates can be built. Besides, the characteristic planting industry with high added value can be moderately developed.
(2) The farming industry. It is essential to develop moderate standardized farming in line with local conditions, which requires efforts to strengthen the prevention and control of animal diseases, establish a sound breeding system of livestock, poultry and aquatic species, reinforce the protection and utilization of local breeds, and develop animal husbandry with local features. There should be steady development of a healthy aquaculture industry to promote the branding of ecological aquaculture products with local features.
(3) The forest industry. Keeping abreast with the national ecological conservation project, a number of specialty forest industries with both ecological and economic benefits should be developed with demonstration bases, to better help and lift the poor out of poverty. Particular importance should be attached to promoting the integrated development of industries and explore the multiple functions of agriculture, create new industries and business models, and advance the deep integration of agriculture with other industries such as tourism, culture, and healthcare for the elderly, with the aim to boost the shaping of a modern industrial system that integrates the primary, secondary and tertiary industries in rural areas. In addition, efforts should be made to accelerate the branding

strategy of agricultural products for their better development and promote the upgrading of supply and demand structure.

Second, cultivating new business players. They have been encouraged to help drive disadvantaged households out of poverty by providing them the whole industrial chain services, enhancing their employment capacity and enabling them to share more of the value-added benefits of agricultural industrial and value chains. The government has rolled out preferential policies to attract more investments and support new business entities such as specialized farmer cooperatives, leading enterprises, sizable family farms (forests) and shareholding farms (forests) in poor areas.

Enterprises have been encouraged to lead in developing the direct sale model, through various means such as planting on order, purchasing at protective prices and providing unified technical services to provide targeted assistance to poor households and help them break the bottlenecks of low farming skills, poor sales and weak capability to withstand market risks. Leading enterprises and cooperatives should be supported in developing new industries, new forms and new models of business, expand employment capacity, and offer more jobs to the rural poor. Industrial cooperatives should be upgraded to promote the establishment of demonstration bases, and ensure that each poor village has a specialized breeding cooperative and a planting cooperative, so as to better help the poor shake off poverty. And cooperative associations would be a very good practice.

Third, establishing a mechanism to couple interests. More efforts should be made towards a more intensive, organized and large-scale agricultural industry by means of land trusteeship, land transfer, contract farming, livestock care, shareholding cooperation in land management rights to shape an industrial development mechanism in which market players, village collectives and the poor households can share the benefit and become a stable partnership with closely related interest. Local enterprises are encouraged to carry out agricultural cooperation with other countries, improving their management and exporting more agricultural products.

There are several ways of profit sharing. One is government awards and subsidies as shares for profits. Such funds are used as village collective shares invested in market players specializing in rural industries. They can help drive the development of industrial bases of the poor villages and households by establishing funds for industry development and providing seedlings and facilities needed in developing industries. This could boost the creation of an all-win situation where enterprises make profits, village collectives increase income and poor households get rid of poverty. Another is resources and assets as shares for profits. Village-based shareholding cooperatives can be established by sorting out and pulling all the village funds, assets and resources to become shareholders in the cooperatives. The poor can become shareholders with their land management rights and labors; and enterprises with seedlings, fertilizers and technologies. Specialized cooperatives are encouraged to establish industrial bases in order to form interest connections, in which villagers, enterprises, specialized cooperatives and village collectives shall share out profits in fixed proportion. Still another is land transfers as shares for profits. The land management rights would be transferred by rural poor to village collectives, which would transfer them to market players, with the turnover funds used as shares. Through the re-transfer of land, a profit sharing mechanism by proportion is established, making it possible for poor villagers to increase income. The model of "guaranteed bottom-line returns plus share-based dividends" is encouraged to improve the interest coupling mechanism such as "farming on order" and "guaranteed bottom-line dividends", so that poor households may participate in and share the benefits of industrial development.

Fourth, redoubling efforts for the promotion and training of agricultural and forestry technologies. More work has been done to enhance the quality and capacity of poor households and strengthen technological assistance to poor areas, in an attempt to consolidate the basis of intellectual help and step up the development of primary-level agricultural technology application system. Targeting the technical needs of registered poor villages and people, measures should be specifically designed to suit different villages, households and people. The approach of "choices made by villagers and paid by the government" has been encouraged, giving rural poor the opportunities to independently choose what to learn. This practice has changed the assistance from generalized broad-brush policies to targeted measures based on specific conditions, helping the poor end poverty through industrial development. This kind of customized technical guidance has been provided for poor households with labor force, including showing and teaching them how to do and helping them how to earn. Paired-up assistance relationship has been established between agricultural technicians and poor households to give them access to point-to-point, face-to-face and hands-on technical services. Tailored technical support plans have been made and measures taken to offer targeted help to the rural poor.

This substantial assistance, together with the pace-setting role of entrepreneurial individuals, can stimulate internal motivation of rural residents and their enthusiasm for work. The advantages of licensed professional farmers should be given full play to help and lead the poor to work in agricultural parks, in cooperatives, and in farms by teaching technology and sharing experience with them. Paired-up assistance should be arranged between professional farmers and poor households to help improve their skills in industrial development. Building of technical support teams for poverty alleviation should be strengthened, with a three-tier technical support network consisting of county-level experts, technical services teams and resident work teams in poor villages, ensuring technical support could reach the whole area by various forms, including tour guides, technical training and consulting.

Trainings may cover the following areas: (1) Leading industries. Based on the development layout of the local industry and the wishes of poor households, training sessions to enhance the practical skills can be conducted in four leading industries, including grain, fruit, vegetables and livestock. (2) Niche industries. According to the five requirements of characteristics, bases, entities, benefits and markets, we can carry out the training on production and management techniques of edible mushrooms, small grains, seedlings and flowers, beekeeping, aquaculture and traditional Chinese herbal medicine. (3) Marketing of agricultural products. Efforts should be made to standardize production techniques, organize training sessions on marketing, brand planning, product processing and rural e-commerce to maximize the product value and benefit poor households in each industrial chain.

Fifth, adhering to the philosophy of green development. Obviously, production, life and ecology in the countryside constitute a natural organism, which we should respect and protect. Most of the poor villages are characterized by fragile ecological conditions, weak resource carrying capacity and low land output, with poor comprehensive capacity in agricultural production. A sound development of agriculture must be based on the carrying capacity of the resources and environment, and take into full consideration such factors as agricultural foundation, market demand and technical support to optimize the layout based on the above conditions and effectively turn the ecological advantages into economic advantages. This can be achieved through the following measures. The first is to boost eco-agriculture tourism. Relying on special planting or breeding industries, we should promote the development of contiguous areas by exploring their cultural resources, and guide poor villages to develop new businesses such as ecological agricultural tourism. The second is to establish a channel for the sale of green agricultural products. With the help of big data platform, cloud computing and big data technology, the product information tracking platform and quality supervision system can be established. E-commerce enterprises are encouraged to sign planting contracts with poor villagers and establish a three-tier platform comprising villages, towns and counties for the purpose of promoting the consumption of green agricultural products in poor areas and increasing villagers' incomes. The third is to advance ecological recycling agriculture, paying attention to the combination of breeding and planting to reduce pollution at source, and ensure harmless, low-emission and sustainable development. By practices such as returning straw to fields through mechanization to increase soil fertility, developing straw processing businesses, and promoting livestock production and reduce the use of chemical fertilizers, a positive interplay between green production and ecological conservation can be expected to happen.

4.2.2 Poverty Alleviation Through Tourism

As an important way to reduce poverty, the development of tourism has become one of the major channels for poverty alleviation and a booster for material and cultural progress in rural areas. By utilizing the local tourism resources, this measure could exert a great potential in the targeted poverty elimination campaign. A good development of tourism in poor areas can invigorate the integrated growth of agriculture, industry and the tertiary sector, which serves as one of the stepping stones to the building of a beautiful countryside. In face of the demanding and challenging task of poverty eradication, great efforts should be made to develop tourism by taking advantages of special local history and culture as well as rich tourist resources.

First, developing rural tourism in line with local conditions. Fact-finding tours and general surveys about tourism resources in poverty-stricken villages should be conducted to establish a list of key villages for poverty alleviation through rural tourism projects. Focusing on the impoverished villages with the potential for developing tourism, the construction of rural infrastructure should be promoted along with other projects such as developing special local products for tourists to take back home as well as the infrastructure upgrading. Attention should also be paid to designing recommended tourist routes to offer more for tourists to share and arranging training and employment for rural poor in tourism service.

Second, boosting the development of leisure agriculture. Relying on resources such as special local products and farm produce, agricultural landscapes and cultural attractions in poor areas, there can be a great development of leisure agriculture and health industries to increase poor people's income. It is necessary to upgrade relevant projects, strengthen the construction of leisure agriculture cluster villages, agricultural parks and other service facilities, and cultivate new business players. This could help promote the deep integration of agriculture, tourism and health industries, and guide and support social capital to develop leisure agriculture projects that may attract a larger number of villagers to create more benefit.

Third, developing special cultural tourism. A number of scenic spots and small towns with distinctive features should be promoted that will increase the employment and income of the poor. Projects have been carried out to protect and develop distinctive ethnic villages and towns as well as traditional and famous historic and cultural towns and villages. Local ethnic culture, revolutionary culture, rural culture and intangible cultural heritages should be fully tapped to launch rural cultural tourist events such as traditional cultural exhibitions and hands-on activities, in which the poor can participate and make profits. Creative development of tourism products and souvenirs with local characteristics is encouraged. For example, women of poor households are supported to develop family handicrafts.[10]

4.2.3 Poverty Alleviation Through E-Commerce

In the present Internet age, e-commerce is becoming a new driving force for China's economic development, as well as a new engine for poverty alleviation. During his inspection in Jinmi Village, Xiaoling Town, Zhashui County, Shaanxi Province, President Xi Jinping pointed out that e-commerce, as a new business form, could not only promote the sale of subsidiary agricultural products and help people get rid of poverty, but also boost rural revitalization. The new business form has promised bright anti-poverty prospects. For example, the "big industry of tiny wood ear mushroom" in Zhashui County was a typical case of e-commerce helping poverty alleviation. E-commerce in rural areas has been an important carrier in China's poverty alleviation through industries, and has been incorporated into the development-driven poverty alleviation work system. With the focus on registered poor villages, measures have been taken to strengthen the capability of poor households to start businesses and increase their income through e-commerce.

Poverty alleviation through e-commerce has set up a bridge to a promising future for rural areas, and it has also accelerated the poverty elimination process. To make

[10] Cf. Plan on Poverty Alleviation during the 13th Five-Year Plan Period (2016–2022).

the best of e-commerce in poverty alleviation, priorities should be given to Internet accessibility, which is vital to connecting subsidiary agricultural products to the market. This requires not only the support of IT technology, but also a smooth logistics network, more rural e-commerce outlets and the building of a bridge for farm produce from the fields to reach the dining table of the general public.

To develop poverty alleviation through e-commerce, the following practices are important:

(1) Paying attention to the cultivation of e-commerce market players. As an important carrier of targeted poverty alleviation, e-commerce in rural areas should be integrated to the development-driven poverty alleviation work system. Measures should be taken by focusing on registered poor villages to strengthen the capability of poor households to start businesses and increase income through e-commerce. Relying on local organizations, rural e-commerce market players should be fostered. Taking the advantage of the incubating and leading role of sizable e-commerce enterprises in driving business and development, technical support should be given to poor households who have the wish, as well as specialized farmer cooperatives, to open online stores. In addition, e-commerce enterprises should be encouraged to open platforms for the sale of special farm produce and agricultural products, and to tie up with cooperatives and specialized farmers for direct supply and procurement. The development of the logistics and distribution system should be accelerated by encouraging postal services and supply and marketing cooperatives to establish or upgrade service outlets in poor rural areas, and guiding businesses to branch out to rural areas to form a two-way circulation service network of agricultural products into the city and industrial products to the countryside.

(2) Improving the environment for e-commerce development. The Internet has solved the problem of connecting agricultural products with market so that some excellent products from remote rural areas are directly accessible to customers with expanded sales channels and increased sales. However, it is difficult to achieve sustainable development if the product quality is not up to the standard for brand development, or there is no targeted promotion for the market. Therefore, poverty alleviation through e-commerce needs to integrate the government, enterprises, platforms, media and other resources to create a stronger synergy. Only in this way can efforts generate real outcomes and the poor have sustainable income increase to consolidate the anti-poverty achievements. Meanwhile, efforts should be made to enhance information network sharing between departments such as traffic, trade circulation, supply and marketing cooperatives, postal services and enterprises of e-commerce and express delivery. We also need to accelerate the introduction of agricultural products quality standards and traceability systems, as well as the development and application of grading, packaging and transportation standards for e-commerce. For poor households who start a business or find a job on the e-commerce platform, local governments and enterprises concerned are encouraged to provide free online store

design, promotion services and management training, Internet subsidies and micro credit support for them.

(3) Giving priorities to human resources development. Well-planned e-commerce training for villagers should be carried out to help them improve their Internet skills, together with greater efforts to attract more young people to work and develop themselves in poor areas through assigned placements, temporary posts and volunteer services to provide more human resources support for the sound development of local e-commerce industries.

4.2.4 Poverty Alleviation Through Assets Income

This refers to assets earnings generated from the use of special government funds for poverty alleviation and rural development to invest in facility agriculture, farming, photovoltaic projects, hydropower, rural tourism and other projects, which have been converted into shares and allocated proportionately to poor villages and households, especially those who have lost the ability of work. In the Plan on Poverty Alleviation during the 13th Five-Year Plan Period (2016–2020), the State Council pointed out that in order to implement poverty alleviation through assets earnings, the government should encourage and guide poor households to become shareholders with their registered land contract management rights invested in enterprises, cooperatives, and family farms of all kinds (planting, breeding or foresting), forming a community of interests with new business players and sharing benefits together. By actively promoting the use of rural collective assets, collectively owned land and other assets and resources rights as shares, collective equity can be formed to be allocated to rural collective economic organizations. The assets income generated from the projects mentioned above using government funds or social assistance funds would be reasonably distributed by establishing and improving the income distribution mechanism and strengthening the supervision and management to ensure that shareholding poor households and rural economic collectives can share the assets earnings. More effective new ways should be adopted to pay compensation subsides for the occupation of rural collective land in developing hydropower and mineral resources. A number of projects in poor areas can be selected to carry out a pilot reform of poverty alleviation through earnings from resource development assets. Based on the trial, we are able to form replicable and feasible models and systems for other poor areas to draw on so that the fruits of resource development can be shared with the poor.

By means of "turning resources into assets, funds into shares and villagers into shareholders", the assets income mechanism has integrated natural resources and government funds for poverty alleviation, relying on business operations of enterprises, specialized farmer cooperatives, large family farms and other business entities that have the will to alleviate poverty, together with strong driving capabilities and good prospects for income increase, to help and lead poor households out of poverty by increasing their income. For example, the Cultural Tourism Development

Company of Hunan's Shimen County has adopted the land resource returns model to increase the income of the rural poor. The company invested in the construction of Longwang Cave Scenic Area, and increased the income of poor households by encouraging them to transfer and rent their unused land at a price of RMB 30 per Chinese mu per year. By now, 500 mu (about 33 hectares) of forest land has been transferred, which has significantly increased the income of villages. Another example is Hainan TianDiRen Ecological Agriculture Company, which has increased the income of poor households through earnings from resources and capital. To start with, the company introduced the model of "enterprise + village collective + households" land intensive shareholding, in which villagers organized by the village committee collectively invested the whole land in the company to be used as the company's production base. In this way, every poor household could earn a dividend of 8% of the planting output value, with a guarantee of RMB500 per Chinese mu (about 0.07 ha) per year. Then, authorized by poor households, the village committee signed an investment cooperation agreement with the company. The poor households invested their personal funds ranging from RMB30,000 to RMB50,000 in the company for 15 years. Upon expiration of the agreement, the company would return all the funds equal to the amount invested. The enterprise would bear all the risks in operation and give fixed returns to them at an average annual rate of 12%.

Featuring targeted assistance with remarkable outcomes, leading enterprises have enjoyed strengths in helping disadvantaged poor households through earnings from assets. First, it is target-oriented. The poverty alleviation through earnings from credit asset has registered poor households as its target group, which is usually not for non-registered households to participate in. Poor households can invest the small loans they have obtained in enterprises, which are responsible for repayment, and receive certain percentage of dividends every year. Informed by our research, if the enterprises were in good financial conditions, each household may get annual dividends ranging from RMB3000 to RMB4000. Second, their anti-poverty efforts have generated remarkable outcomes. Some villagers do not have the ability to work because of old age or poor health and cannot shake off poverty by engaging in agricultural and non-agricultural production. Earnings from assets have broadened their sources of income by giving them property rights or equity, which is conducive for these vulnerable groups to accumulate assets and use them to gain continuous returns.

4.2.5 Poverty Alleviation Through Technological Development

As science and technology constitute a primary productive force, they have played a significant role in improving regional economy and optimizing economic structure. Actually technological development has opened up an effective path to alleviate poverty by helping rural industrial growth. This approach includes the following measures:

First, promoting technologies to transfer to poor areas. Professionals from higher education institutions, research institutes and enterprises have been organized for technological breakthroughs to solve critical technical issues in industrial development and ecological conservation in poor areas. Focusing on the needs of the whole industrial chain, efforts have been made to develop, introduce, integrate, test and demonstrate new varieties, new technologies and new projects. Poor counties have been encouraged to build demonstration bases for the transfer of research findings, and promote the application of advanced and applicable technologies in pillar industries.

Second, enhancing the capacity of the rural poor for innovation and entrepreneurship. The sci-tech commissioner system has been implemented to cover all poor villages. This has been designed to guide and support professionals from institutions of higher learning and research institutes to provide technological services and help foster local entrepreneurial individuals so that they could develop their technical skills to lead and help other villagers shake off poverty. Programs supporting human resources in outlying poverty-stricken areas, border areas of ethnic groups, and old revolutionary base areas, as well as special programs for technicians have been conducted. By establishing, leading, and cooperating with enterprises and specialized farmer cooperatives, these programs have formed communities of shared interests among sci-tech professionals and poor households to help lift the poor out of poverty. Additionally, popularizing science in rural areas have been strengthened by providing online and offline, point-to-point and face-to-face training for the poor.

Third, strengthening the cultivation of rural innovative businesses and service platforms in poor areas. Substantial support has been given to construction of science parks to give full play to their roles in integrating modern production elements, such as technology, information, capital and management, as well as in application demonstration to drive the in-depth development of the rural poor in the model of "sci-tech parks + poor villages + poor households". In addition, universities, research institutes and local governments have been encouraged to set up institutes focusing on studies of new rural development and provide agricultural technology services to rural areas.

In addition, support should be given to the establishment of agricultural technology associations (consortia) and rural professional skill associations to push technical advances in poverty alleviation.[11]

4.2.6 *Poverty Alleviation Through Financial Measures*

Financial measures are important to support the poverty elimination campaign in poor areas, and help poor people escape poverty and increase income by the development

[11] Cf. Plan on Poverty Alleviation during the 13th Five-Year Plan Period (2016–2020).

of production. They have been taken to motivate people to help themselves instead of helping people directly. The key is to keep employment stable, so that the rural poor can have sustainable incomes. In the long run, ensuring stable and high-quality economic growth is fundamental to win the battle against extreme poverty. Compared with government assistance to eliminate poverty, financial measures would give poor areas the capacity for independent development by establishing a sound financial service system, promoting micro loans and building up risk guarantee networks. These financial measures would alleviate the shortage of capital investment that had long plagued poor villagers, create more opportunities for them to make a better living and enhance their self-development capability, so that they would bring about fundamental changes and new looks to poor areas.

4.3 Poverty Alleviation Through Employment

To win the battle against extreme poverty, it is important to promote the employment of poor people and increase their income, since an employed member may help substantially in lifting the whole family out of poverty. Creating more jobs is the most efficient and direct way to escape poverty and steady perseverance in this can effectively address the intergenerational transmission of poverty. The human resources and social security departments have regarded boosting employment to facilitate the winning of the battle against poverty as a major political task of paramount importance, going all out to help poor laborers find jobs or start businesses. The work has been centered on stabilizing the employed and creating more jobs by offering substantial services for job stabilization and providing assistance in education to increase the employment capacity of the rural poor. Transfer of employment has been very effective in industrial support and relocation for poverty alleviation, which is not only one of the important approaches, but also a crucial task in the fight against poverty [10].

Employment transfer in China has been guided by Xi Jinping Thought on socialism with Chinese characteristics in the new era, and by what was formulated at the 19th CPC National Congress. Fully aware of the importance and urgency of targeted poverty eradication, governments at all levels have taken various measures to promote the employment of poor laborers and increase their income. The effective implementation of these measures has played a vital role in winning the anti-poverty victory and the establishment of a moderately prosperous society. Efforts have been made to ensure employment for every poor rural resident who has the ability of work, and deliver employment policies with the priority given to impoverished areas, taking targeted measures to expand and stabilize employment for the poor and ensuring that at least one person in a poor household is employed.

4.3.1 Creating More Local Jobs Through Multiple Channels

Local and nearby employment to boost rural development refers to a model of poverty alleviation, in which enterprises provide jobs for rural poor labor and ensure due payment according to the work they have completed to increase their income. For this purpose, enterprises and industrial parks supported by government funds have been encouraged to give priorities to the employment of poor population, and make the employment an index to decide the amount of funds granted to them. Supports have been given to the self-employment of poor households and the development of new forms of employment such as home-based working, prompting the employment of the poor at or near their own localities. The construction of poverty alleviation platforms and the allocation of funds have been speeded up. In some places, a green channel policy has been introduced for related projects. Local governments have been encouraged to adjust poverty alleviation projects flexibly in response to changes of situation and requirements of pandemic prevention and control. Priorities have been given to projects that promote employment and increase the income of poor villagers. Meanwhile, targeted measures have been taken to mobilize poor labor to participate in these projects.

Local governments have contributed through employment models such as workshops, community factories, satellite factories and other models in line with local conditions. In addition, they have been expected to further standardize construction criteria, explore operational mechanisms, increase policy support and promote sustainable development, in order to attract prospective employers to provide more job opportunities for registered poor populations. Poor households are encouraged to participate in various projects for rural development, so that more people can get employed. Employment has also been boosted through entrepreneurship by guiding migrant workers, college graduates and veterans to start up their own businesses in poor counties and villages, and by supporting qualified personnel from enterprises and institutions to come to poor villages to start up businesses. In this way, more entrepreneurial people can be cultivated. In order to increase the employment, support should be given to the development of rural e-commerce and the construction of entrepreneurship parks in poor counties. Trainings and services of entrepreneurship policies and skills should be strengthened to tap the potential of agriculture-related employment by encouraging family farms, agricultural cooperatives, leading enterprises and other agriculture business entities to absorb more poor laborers. Home-based flexible employment should be encouraged by utilizing the traditional local culture, natural environment and industrial foundation to guide poor laborers to engage in traditional handicraft production, processing of agricultural products or supplied materials at home. Coordinated measures have been taken to develop more welfare jobs. Poor counties and townships have tried to create more jobs in road maintenance, forestry protection, grass protection and ecological management for poverty alleviation. Employment opportunities have been provided for eligible poor laborers who have difficulties finding jobs themselves.

4.3.2 Carrying Out Labor Collaboration

Labor collaboration has been regarded as a political task and put in a prominent position, which requires more cooperation with redoubled efforts to achieve expected results. The effectiveness can be guaranteed by signing the labor service agreement, which can be adjusted, supplemented and revised in light of the progress. Information on jobs suitable for impoverished laborers can be widely collected and a cross-regional and regular mechanism for job information sharing and distribution is established, with various recruitment activities organized to build a platform for poor laborers and employers.

Governments of places where the labor service is exported should work closely with their peers at places where the service is imported on information sharing and labor collaboration exchange, and fully implement the policies and measures related to the transfer employment. The former should collect accurate data about the labor of poor families and their willingness of taking jobs away from their villages; while the latter should coordinate the provision of employment information and jobs, and take various measures for employment placement. As for capacity building, poor counties could be helped to establish the human resources market and vocational training agencies with vocational mentors and trainers to enhance their abilities in public employment service and vocational training.

More work has to be done to encourage more poor laborers to participate in labor collaboration for transfer employment with better public services for them. The government of places where the labor service is imported should provide policy support to the poor who have found a stable job. For example, eligible migrant workers may enjoy local housing security and their children may have access to compulsory education and enter for senior high school and college entrance examinations. Local governments have been encouraged to allow migrant workers and their families to settle down in their places, and provide them with legal aids and other basic public services.

4.3.3 Offering Better Employment Services

An all-round, targeted and customized employment services have been provided based on the features of poor laborers to motivate them to help themselves towards prosperity. Vocational guidance has been given to them for correct ideas of employment and to stimulate their motivation and enthusiasm to work and get out of poverty through their own efforts.

More career information and employment services have been provided. Based on a clear knowledge of the actual condition and the intention, customized job placement plans have been worked out for the poor labor to find jobs with prospective employers. Besides, labor and human resources agencies have been mobilized to join in poverty alleviation by arranging organized exports of rural labor. Fully leveraging local industries and strengths in human resources, labor service brands could even be built to drive transfer employment.

4.3.4 Implementing Poverty Alleviation Through Vocational Training

It is important to improve the system of lifelong vocational training for laborers. With this in mind, differentiated skills training programs have been carried out in line with different features and employment needs of the laborers from poor households who have the wish for employment transfer, or have been transferred to employment, or are newly emerging. All kinds of training have been conducted by integrating resources of various departments in all sectors, with the service purchased by the government. Focused on skills for employment, on-the-job advancement and entrepreneurship, new models of training have been introduced, such as training of agricultural and forestry technologies, order-based training, job-specific training and "Internet plus" training. Efforts have been made to enhance the targeted vocational training for rural poor migrant workers to upgrade their skills and strengthen their on-the-job training.

Meanwhile, free vocational training programs for children from poor families, junior or senior high school graduates not going on with further studies and rural workers have continued in a more targeted and effective way. In light of their actual conditions and job intentions, large-scale vocational training and technical education have been carried out to ensure that the poor labor have access to vocational training and those who are eligible and willing could attend technical schools.

Vocational schools, training institutions and enterprises of all kinds and at all levels have been encouraged to provide vocational training, with subsidy policies well implemented and project-based training programs carried out by purchasing integrated vocational training programs from government-accredited training institutions. Great efforts have been made to recommend poor students/trainees who have received technical education and vocational training for employment, in order to achieve the goal of "an educated and trained individual who is capable of finding a job or starting a new business to help his or her family shake off poverty". In addition, a mechanism of training for specific posts has been set up to promote school-enterprise collaboration and order-based training. By integrating the employment transfer of the impoverished with the development of industrial parks and urbanization, enterprises have been guided and supported to create jobs for the rural poor.

4.3.5 *Making Efforts to Boost Employment for the Poor in Destitute Areas*

To truly prioritize employment for the poor in severely impoverished areas, special plans for clearly defined targets and tasks on a yearly basis have been worked out, including the number and channels of employment, and establishing the system of accountability. Based on collaboration and paired assistance between the eastern and the western regions, the employment potential would be tapped through efforts directed to business development, projects and other ways of fighting against poverty to create suitable jobs and more employment opportunities.

More targeted measures have been taken to address issues such as poor communications, language barriers and lack of enthusiasm to work among some poor laborers. A comprehensive range of policies and services have been introduced to improve targeted skills training to ensure that at least one person gets employed in a poor family. Provinces where conditions permit could organize poor labor and staff working in primary-level employment services to go to economically developed areas for fact-finding visits, short-term training and internship, in order to broaden horizons, change ideas and upgrade skills. The central government has stepped up efforts to coordinate with National Development and Reform Commission, Ministry of Finance and other departments to ensure that funding and project allocations prioritize the needs of severely poor areas to solve practical problems.

4.3.6 *Fostering Right Attitudes Towards Poverty Alleviation Through Employment*

In accordance with the specialized requirements for addressing issues concerning poverty alleviation, attention has been paid to fostering right attitudes to truly fulfill the responsibilities, adhere to a goal-oriented and problem-oriented approach and improve mechanisms as well as measures to guarantee that there would be effective outcomes in creating employment for the poor.

More work has been done to be well informed about the true situation of employment of the rural labor and implement dynamic management based on the information gathered from various resources. Policies concerned have been better implemented by introducing working methods with better feasibility, ensuring that eligible poor laborers and employers may enjoy the benefit of anti-poverty policies. Employment subsidies and poverty-alleviation funds from governments have been better managed and used to prevent embezzlement, waste or misappropriation. More in-depth investigations and field visits have been encouraged to help solve pressing issues in poverty-stricken areas.

4.3.7 *Creating a Better Social Atmosphere*

Efforts have been redoubled on enhancing public awareness of the importance of employment for poverty alleviation by promoting policies, measures and good practices, as well as role models and examples of entrepreneurial individuals and business start-ups, to create a good social atmosphere of getting out of poverty by self help and hard work. Social sectors and non-governmental organizations have been further mobilized to participate in poverty alleviation through employment by collecting cases of caring enterprises that have made outstanding contributions, to stimulate more people to join in and create more jobs for the rural poor.

Based on the work of local governments, Ministry of Human Resources and Social Security and the State Council Poverty Alleviation Office would soon reward some demonstration places and caring enterprises to give full play to their exemplary roles and create a better social atmosphere.

4.4 Poverty Alleviation Through Relocation

This model has to do with relocating the impoverished from inhospitable areas, which has been an important strategy to achieve both poverty alleviation and ecological conservation, as well as a fundamental way to help the rural poor shake off poverty and achieve rapid development. In some uninhabitable areas with harsh living conditions and frequent natural disasters, the cost of access to water, transportation and electricity could be so high that it would be hard for poor people to shake off poverty if they remained where they were, so the government relocated them to other areas. This has been a necessary measure as well as a complex, systematic, and challenging project, which requires strong policy support and meticulous work.

China has been at a time to secure a full victory in building a moderately prosperous society in all respects and effective measures have to be taken to address poverty among people from inhospitable areas. In this sense, relocation is not only required to improve living conditions, but also to achieve sustainable development.

As a complex issue of social building, poverty alleviation through relocation has been embedded in a political, economic, social and institutional framework. Consequently, sound and reasonable relocation policies have been worked out, including the social assistance system for poor migrants, communities where migrant people could live comfortably, further inheritance and protection of ethnic culture together with the migration policy, and enhancement of the social integration of relocated residents in the new places. With all this in mind, more public welfare jobs should be created, with priority considerations given to vulnerable groups for jobs like sanitation and gardening. Non-agricultural employment agencies should be established to effectively increase and implement job-specific trainings for relocated people, raising their employment opportunities to diversify and stabilize their sources of income.

To solve the regional problem that people from inhospitable areas cannot shake off poverty locally, there have been considerations about not only how to get rid of poverty and achieve sustainable development, but also the protection of the eco-environment. Poverty alleviation through relocation is not just the moving of rural residents and herdsmen out of over dependence on natural resources and ecological environment. It is the restoration and conservation of the natural environment in the original areas at the same time to prevent its further deterioration.

In response to the relocation plan of creating a beautiful and livable environment, resettlement areas have been required to be built into distinctive eco-friendly places in line with local conditions, combining the development of fruit economy, courtyard economy, ecological recycling agriculture and animal husbandry, small watershed governance, new village greening and farmland shelterbelt construction. The plan has given priority consideration to poor population from areas where farmland needs to be converted to forest or grassland or where grazing is not allowed, areas severely eroded by wind, desertification, water and soil, as well as natural forest protection areas. During this process, national ecological and environmental protection policies have been strictly implemented to integrate resettlement work with ecological conservation projects.

4.4.1 Identifying Who to Relocate

It is vital to reasonably determine the size and people of relocation. The main targets are the poor in destitute areas where it is difficult for them to get rid of poverty if they remained where they were. People in such areas do not have the resources to lift themselves out of poverty through current approaches, or the cost of these approaches is much higher than that of relocation.

First of all, the organization and implementation of the relocation project have been based on the identification results of the registration system for development-driven poverty alleviation, to achieve the intended purpose that registered poor people are capable of moving, living, and getting out of poverty. Under this arrangement, the total size and annual relocation tasks could be set for registered rural poor people in areas with harsh natural, living and development conditions, by referring to the annual relocation schedule approved by provincial governments.

Secondly, efforts have been made to ensure that all registered poor people who are eligible are moving out on the basis of fully respecting their wills. With effective mobilization, guidance and organization, in addition to guaranteed relocation funds, all eligible registered poor people would preferably move out together with other populations as coordinated.

Finally, there have been four types of the areas where people would have to move out. Type one: Areas that are remote and uninhabitable and can hardly develop with harsh stony mountains, severely cold climate, serious desertification and loss of soil and water. Type two: Areas that have been prohibited or restricted for development designated by the State. Type three: Areas with weak infrastructure such as transportation, water conservancy, electricity and communications, as well as underdeveloped basic public services in education and healthcare. It would be extremely demanding with high costs of construction and operation if construction projects were carried out to address these problems. Type four: Areas with serious endemic diseases and frequent geological disasters.

In addition, the arrangement should also consider the non-registered population living in the same area. Those who are willing should also be relocated. With this in mind, the actual number of planned people to be relocated has been more in each region.

4.4.2 Deciding Where to Relocate

Following the accurate identification about who to relocate, it is equally important to decide where to relocate and the construction of the relocation settlement. First of all, the relocation modes should be adopted in light of local conditions, with reasonable housing construction standards. Based on the principle of voluntary relocation and the preliminary investigation and survey on households in villages, the site selection for large-scale relocation would take into account the promotion of new urbanization with the analysis of the balance between water and soil resources and the appraisal of the carrying capacity of resources and environment.

Secondly, the relocation could be arranged in centralized places or in scattered sites, giving priority to the former. In selecting sites for centralized relocation, priorities have been given to livable places such as new villages, small towns, industrial parks, tourist attractions and rural scenic areas, with due attention to the construction of supporting facilities. The scattered relocation has taken many forms, such as moving to a particular place, working in cities, or joining relatives or friends to make a living. On the premise of being secured of housing and employment, monetary resettlement could also be an option.

Finally, the supporting infrastructure and public service facilities of the resettlement site may be constructed under overall planning and the principles of moderate sizes, reasonable functions, economic security, clean environment and good livability. They should be provided with water, electricity, roads, postal services, basic telecommunications networks and sewage and garbage treatment infrastructure, together with improved commercial outlets, convenience shops, markets and other amenities, in addition to necessary public service facilities concerning education, health, culture and sports.

4.4.3 Building Cost-Effective Resettlement Houses

The resettlement houses have been planned and built by adhering to the principle of ensuring basic needs, safety and affordability, with reasonable housing subsidy standards and relevant supporting policies formulated. Standards on the floor space of houses for the relocated poor have been strictly enforced to make sure that these people do not have to borrow money to build their houses. The structural design of newly-built ones should comply with relevant building codes and technical standards for housing quality and safety.

Housing construction in centralized relocation sites should be carried out under organized planning, and the construction undertaken by standardized bidding, or by migrants themselves or through agents. For resettlements built in small towns or industrial parks, local governments could buy back urban commercial housing that satisfies the area control standards, excluding public rental and low-rent housing as well as other housing that has been subsidized by the State. For those built in rural tourist areas, the resettlement plan and construction of housing, infrastructure, public service facilities and amenities should comply with local conditions, giving full consideration to the actual needs of tourism development, and promoting the agreement and unity of resettlements and the scenic areas.

4.4.4 Innovative Financing to Raise Funds

To achieve expected outcomes of relocation, channels of fund raising have to be expanded. The investment support from the central government has increased, together with innovations in investment and financing mechanisms to earmark special construction funds and local government bonds as capital for relocation projects, and issue special financial bonds to raise loan funds to support relocating.

It is important to establish or specify provincial-level investors and funders as well as entities at city or county levels in charge of the project implementation to undertake the operation of funds and housing construction. Local governments should coordinate their disposable financial resources and support provincial-level investors and funders in repaying loans by balanced use of the land for construction and for farming. Any surplus of funds for relocating the impoverished could be used to support the follow-up industrial development.

4.4.5 Differentiated Measures to Alleviate Poverty After Relocation

Relocating the impoverished from inhospitable areas has been an effective way for poverty alleviation, with the goal to help people gradually get out of poverty. This means that the requirement of relocation includes not only how to move, but also what to do after the relocation. In the follow-up efforts, the focus should be changed from how to move out to how to settle down and make a better living. With this in mind, industries and employment for poverty alleviation have been major approaches towards the goal.

In light of the actual conditions of the relocated people, the development of specialty agriculture and animal husbandry, labor economy and modern service industry as well as exploration of ways of poverty alleviation through assets income have been encouraged by coordinating and integrating government funds for poverty alleviation and rural development. All this has been done to ensure stable poverty alleviation through employment. The following five measures have been taken to promote the sustainability of production and life of the relocated.

First, boosting the development of agriculture and forestry industries to eliminate poverty. Relocated villagers have been encouraged to work out of poverty in response to market demands by developing specialty farming, efficient animal husbandry, underforest economy (planting, breeding, collecting of understory products, forest tourism and wellness industry), facility agriculture and leisure agriculture. All these have been supported by policy-backed government subsidies, technical services, information release and demonstrations of exemplary cases.

Second, boosting the development of labor economy to end poverty. Efforts have been made to develop labor economy as a major approach to continuously increase incomes of the poor labor, by providing job-specific training, expanding channels for employment and business start-ups and strengthening employment guidance and labor exports for relocated people.

Third, boosting the development of the modern service sector to eradicate poverty. Relocated people have been supported to increase their income through multiple channels in the service sector such as agricultural and sideline product marketing, catering, housekeeping, warehousing and delivery.

Fourth, alleviating poverty through assets income. This refers to trying out the approach to convert the assets of supporting facilities for relocation into shares and relocated people into share holders. With assets-generated dividends proportionately distributed to the impoverished, their incomes are increased.

Fifth, providing subsistence allowances for those unable to shake off poverty through their own efforts. Eligible relocated people have been covered and helped to get out of poverty.

4.5 Poverty Alleviation Through Ecological Conservation

China's poverty-stricken areas have highly correlated with national key ecological areas, and its destitute areas are mostly remote border and areas with large ethnic minority populations. For example, the mountainous areas in Southern Ningxia Hui Autonomous Region, which used to suffer from severe cold, is now still ecologically fragile; the mountainous areas in Yunnan, Guizhou and Sichuan provinces are rich in biodiversity, however, their per capita income has been below the national average. Ecologically sensitive areas are often accompanied by poverty, which has constituted a major part of China's basic national conditions at present.

There used to be a prominent conflict between ecological conservation and poverty alleviation for villagers in severely impoverished areas. Owing to lack of effective incentives for ecological protection practices, the value of ecological products could hardly be achieved effectively, resulting that the regional ecological advantage failed to be transformed into economic benefits. Therefore, it is of great significance to realize the integration of ecological conservation and poverty alleviation to enhance ethnic unity, stability in border areas, environmental protection, poverty alleviation and rural revitalization.

Since the 18th CPC National Congress in 2012, General Secretary Xi Jinping has prioritized ecological conservation. Many a time has he expounded on balancing the environment protection with development-driven poverty alleviation, strengthening the protection, governance and restoration of the eco-environment in poor areas and enhancing their capacity for sustainable development. At the National Conference on Ecological and Environmental Protection in 2018, Xi Jinping specified six key principles: first, ensuring harmony between human and nature; second, lucid waters and lush mountains as invaluable assets; third, good eco-environment as the most inclusive wellbeing for people; forth, mountains, rivers, forests, farmlands, lakes, and grasslands as an integrated community; fifth, protecting the environment on the basis of the strictest systems under the most vigorous rules of law; sixth, joining hands to promote global ecological conservation with other countries.[12]

These ideas have fully revealed Xi Jinping's priority on eco-conservation in his theory of poverty alleviation, and highlighted that we should revere and respect nature in the process of targeted poverty alleviation and elimination, keeping and leaving clear waters and green mountains for posterity, while lifting the present poor population out of poverty.

Eco-conservation is not in conflict with development-driven poverty alleviation. Measures such as carrying out major ecological projects, increasing compensation for eco-conservation, developing ecological industries, and consuming products and services from poor areas have been taken to coordinate the two for mutual benefits.

4.5.1 Implications of Poverty Alleviation Through Eco-environmental Conservation

This refers to a mode that integrates environmental protection with development-driven poverty alleviation. Staying true to the idea and practice that lucid waters and lush mountains are invaluable assets and taking poverty alleviation and elimination as the basic strategy, efforts have been made to lay equal emphasis on development-driven poverty alleviation and eco-conservation.

---

[12] Xi [11].

Effective measures have included: the construction of major eco-conservation projects, increased compensation for economic losses associated with reducing ecological damage, development of eco-friendly industries and innovation of measures for poverty alleviation through eco-environmental conservation. All these have given substantial support to impoverished areas and people by coordinating poverty alleviation with environmental protection so that poverty elimination and sustainable development could complement and promote each other with better overall results.

4.5.2 Major Principles and Targets of Poverty Alleviation Through Eco-environmental Conservation

These have been stipulated and clearly defined in documents from the central government, including Decision on Winning the Battle against Extreme Poverty and Plan on Poverty Alleviation during the 13th Five-Year Plan Period, putting emphasis on the awareness and practice of eco-conservation in targeted poverty alleviation and elimination. In accordance with the overall deployment of the State Council Leading Group of Poverty Alleviation and Development, Work Plan for Poverty Alleviation through Eco-Conservation has been jointly formulated by National Development and Reform Commission, the State Forestry Administration, Ministry of Finance, Ministry of Water Resources, Ministry of Agriculture and the State Council Poverty Alleviation Office, which specified major eco-conservation principles and targets in poverty alleviation.[13]

4.5.2.1 Major Principles

(1) A working mechanism with the central government acting as coordinator, provincial governments taking overall responsibility, and city and county governments overseeing implementation should be established. Relevant departments of the central government are responsible for formulating policies, specifying work plans and strengthening assessment and supervision. Provincial government departments are in charge of supplementing policies and measures as well as enhancing coordination and cooperation. The departments at the municipal and county levels should be responsible for all anti-poverty work within their respective administrative areas, to ensure that policies and measures are truly implemented.

(2) Institutional mechanisms should be innovated to mobilize all social sectors to participate in poverty alleviation through eco-environmental conservation to create a synergy. Efforts should be made to stimulate the enthusiasm, initiative, and creativity of the rural poor to protect and restore the eco-environment of

[13] See Work Plan for Poverty Alleviation through Eco-Conservation.

their hometowns by carrying forward the fine tradition of self-help and never faltering in pursuit of progress to shake off poverty by themselves.

(3) Unremitted efforts are required to put in to develop economic activities by taking advantages of local resources with eco-protection in mind, integrating respect for nature, adaptation to nature, and protection of nature into poverty alleviation through economic development. There should be better balance between the short-term poverty alleviation and long-term development by forward-looking planning based on the present reality. Factors of natural resource endowment, carrying capacity, local features and regional economic and social development should be taken into account to push forward the coordination of poverty alleviation and green development.

(4) Priority should be given to counties in the 14 contiguous destitute areas and designated counties outside these areas which are included in the national plan for development-driven poverty alleviation, identifying every registered individual and area in extreme poverty. Problem-oriented and goal-oriented, focus should be placed on poverty eradication and dovetailing of related policies by formulating and implementing more targeted policies and measures.

4.5.2.2 Specific Goals

(1) Increasing the income of the rural poor. Through 2020, the income of poor people would be significantly raised. And their working and living conditions would have been much improved by participating in eco-conservation and restoration projects as well as eco-friendly industries.

(2) Improving eco-environment. Through 2020, the natural environment in poor areas would be effectively improved, with the enhancement of supply capacity of ecological products. Compensations for economic losses associated with reducing ecological damage would keep up with economic and social development. The capacity for sustainable development would be further advanced.

(3) Specifically, through 2020, China would establish in its rural areas 12,000 specialized cooperatives of poverty alleviation through eco-conservation, including 10,000 afforestation cooperatives/teams and 2000 of grass-based animal husbandry, with 100,000 people participating in eco-projects. 400,000 new jobs would have been created for eco-work, including 300,000 for foresters and 100,000 for prairie keepers. It would have also increased the income of around 15 million impoverished people by putting emphasis on developing eco-friendly industries.

4.5.3 Major Approaches to Poverty Alleviation Through Eco-conservation

In order to break the vicious circle of both economic and ecological poverty, the fight should be carried out with the sound treatment of related ecological issues by exploring the sustainable realization of ecological resources to the value of poverty alleviation. Poverty alleviation through eco-conservation is not simple adding-up of several polices, but refers to a complex system constructed by multiple policies and measures, social players and individual targets, where the interplay between internal parts constitutes an internal cycling mechanism of poverty alleviation through eco-conservation.[14]

In practice, China has explored and shaped various approaches to poverty alleviation through eco-conservation, such as labor services, ecological relocation, employment placement, industrial development, and financial compensation. However, there is still a long way to go and more work has to be done given the fact that these approaches are yet satisfactory with limited coverage and less than ideal outcomes.[15]

4.5.3.1 Remuneration for Labor Services by Participating in Project Construction

Major ecological projects invested and implemented by the government are required to create jobs for a certain proportion of the rural poor who are able to work, with reasonable remuneration for their services to increase their incomes. This practice of earning remuneration from participating in project construction is commonly known as "jobs instead of grants". In terms of poverty alleviation through eco-conservation, afforestation cooperatives set up by specialists or by villagers themselves have been promoted to organize the rural poor to participate in ecological conservation projects by providing them jobs instead of grants. For the government-funded projects, a certain ratio of employment would be designated for registered poor people. For the enterprise-funded projects, there have been preferential policies such as special pair-up arrangements to recruit workers from poor areas in addition to government subsidies. Besides, poverty alleviation has been achieved through relocation. Those who agreed would be guided to move from alpine and outlying areas with complex geographical conditions and poor resources or areas with ecology to be protected or restored to places with better conditions. Targeted measures have been taken for each place and each household to ensure orderly and integral relocation including housing, employment, industries and culture to prevent hidden troubles and problems.

4.5.3.2 Steady Salary Incomes from Ecological Public Welfare Jobs

China has been expanding the provision of ecological jobs for poverty alleviation. The ecological conservator, a job on management and conservation of forests, grasslands, wetlands and desertificated lands, has been set up in poor counties for poor people capable of work to help them get out of poverty by themselves without having to leave their villages. Other similar jobs have been provided by taking advantages of

[14] Lei et al. [12].

[15] Yilan [13].

natural resources such as farmlands to be returned to forest and pasture, ecological protection areas, national parks and wetlands. These jobs have not only strengthened the ecological protection, but also brought to the poor people steady salary incomes to help them get rid of poverty.

4.5.3.3 Increased Operative and Property Incomes from Ecological Industries

Ecological industries, as an important form of ecological conservation for poverty alleviation, refer to a variety of activities such as "ecological + tourism", "ecological + characteristic planting" and "ecological + characteristic breeding".

On the premise of enhanced protection of the ecology in poor areas, ecological industries have taken full advantage of local ecological resources to accelerate the integrated growth of agriculture, industry and the tertiary sector for a healthy development of ecological industries such as eco-tourism, forestry, planting, breeding and processing of agricultural and forestry products. By means of land transfer, dividend benefit, cooperative operation, employment, entrepreneurship and so on, the interests of poor people have been closely tied up with the industries. This, in addition to the improvement of the distribution system and the increase of incomes from assets, has expanded the income resources for the rural poor.

4.5.3.4 Increased Transfer Income from the Policy of Compensating for Economic Losses Associated with Reducing Ecological Damage

The policy of compensating for economic losses associated with reducing ecological damage, as an important means of ecological conservation for poverty alleviation, has provided poor people substantial material support and played a key role in attaining and sustaining poverty elimination in ecologically fragile areas.[16] According to statistics, 95% of the poor population and most poor areas are distributed in places with fragile, sensitive ecological environment for priority protection, which function in ecology balancing, resource reserving and landscape projecting and are known for their awkward situation of "affluent poverty". The key of fighting against extreme poverty is to ensure that poor people in these areas keep pace with the progress of the country in building a moderately prosperous society. It would be wrong if the eco-protection only is stressed without considering solving the poverty problem. Compensation funds for ecological conservation and major national ecological projects and capital therefore have given priority to registered poor areas and poor people, particularly in allocating the funds for returning farmlands to forest and pasture and protecting grasslands. The registered poor have been given special attention to ensure that they get the financial compensation. This targeted and more

[16] Ren and Li [14].

sustained effort of financial compensation for ecological services has helped solve the dilemma of insufficient funds for ecological projects and low incomes of the local poor for ecological environment protection and ensure the stability of the ecological barrier function of these poor areas.[17]

4.5.4 Practices and Effects of Ecological Conservation for Poverty Alleviation

In recent years, China has continuously stepped up ecological projects and carried out three measures to alleviate poverty through financial compensation for environmental protection, afforestation and eco-industries, in an attempt to enhance, consolidate and sustain the overall results of poverty alleviation through ecological conservation. This has contributed to the final victory in the battle against poverty.

4.5.4.1 Stepping up Supports to Ecological Projects

To start with, the ecological conservation and restoration in impoverished areas have been strengthened and more priorities have been given to these areas in major ecological projects and funding arrangements. Poor people have been organized and encouraged to participate in major eco-projects to increase their income. For projects to return farmlands to forest and pasture, the government has adjusted the quota for basic farmland in poor areas with steep slopes above 25° to give more benefits to poor villagers. For the second-phase ecological protection and development projects for the source region of the Yangtze, Yellow and Lancang rivers in southern Qinghai Province, more efforts have been made to further promote the protection and development of the eco-system of forests, grasslands, deserts, wetlands and lakes in the source region of the three rivers and strengthen the restoration of the degenerative grasslands in black soil beaches and other places to effectively improve the productivity of the grasslands. For Beijing-Tianjin sandstorm source control projects, importance has been attached to the protection and restoration of vegetation and the treatment of disertificated lands in key regions. For natural forest protection projects, greater support has been given for forest protection in poor areas.

Better management and restoration against forest degradation have been reinforced for the shelterbelt system construction projects in the three regions of northwest, north and northeast China. For major water and soil conservation projects, the control of soil erosion in the upper and middle reaches of the Yangtze and Yellow rivers, Karst areas of southwest China, black soil areas of northeast China and other key areas have been strengthened. More preferential policies and projects have been introduced to poverty-stricken counties included in relevant plans for soil erosion control to harness sloping arable lands, erosive gulleys and small watershed systems.

[17] National Development and Reform Commission [15].

The comprehensive control project for rocky desertification has adhered to the principle of "integrating rocky desertification control with poverty alleviation". A variety of measures have been taken, including closing mountains for afforestation, artificial afforestation, forest tending and comprehensive treatment of small watershed systems, with greater supports given to rocky desertification control in impoverished areas such as desertificated regions in Yunnan, Guangxi and Guizhou, border mountainous regions in west Yunnan Province, and Wumeng and Wuling mountainous areas. The projects for restricted conservation zones of desertificated lands have been implemented in poor areas such as Inner Mongolia. There are also conservation and restoration projects carried out in wetlands of international fame and national wetland reserves in poor areas to improve their capacity of water conservation, flood storage and water purification. Poor counties have been supported for the implementation of projects concerning wetland protection and restoration, compensation for ecological benefits and pilot projects to return farmlands to wetlands for sustaining the wetland conservation system.

For integrated management projects of reclaimed grasslands in farming-pastoral ecotone, focus has been placed on poor areas. By increasing vegetation coverage through grass planting and establishing quality dryland forage bases, together with subsidies for forage sowing and purchases of agricultural processing machinery, poor areas have been provided with guidance and support for the development of herbivorous animal husbandry, so as to improve the quality and efficiency of the industry while restoring grassland ecology.[18]

In addition, cooperatives for ecological conservation to alleviate poverty have been established to provide jobs instead of grants for poor households to get remuneration from participating in the eco-environment protection projects. On November 13, 2018, the State Forestry and Grassland Administration, the National Development and Reform Commission and the State Council Leading Group Office jointly issued Notice on the Promotion of Poverty Alleviation Model of Afforestation (Grass Planting) Cooperatives, expounding the measures to promote poverty alleviation through cooperatives in seven aspects, namely, fully implementing the project tasks of the cooperatives, upgrading their mechanism of leading local poor people out of poverty, supporting diversified businesses, strengthening the management of funds, and improving the government procurement management system and member turnover mechanism. Since 2016, the central government has allocated more than RMB150 billion for poor areas to plant trees and grass, and 21,000 new cooperatives have been established in China, attracting 1.2 million poor people to participate in ecological protection.

4.5.4.2 Creating Ecological Welfare Jobs

Since 2016, the National Forestry and Grassland Administration, the Ministry of Finance and the State Council Leading Group Office have been carrying out the

[18] See Work Plan for Poverty Alleviation through Eco-Conservation.

employment of forest rangers from the poor population, updating Measures for the Management of Rangers Registered as below the Poverty Line to standardize the management of eco-jobs. An eco-ranger system has been formulated to cover the recruitment procedure, scope of work, responsibilities, rights and obligations, as well as team building, abilities and skills of eco-resource management, and pre-job training to raise the professional knowledge and safety awareness of foresters. There are now increasingly diversified types of eco-jobs in different areas, including forest protection posts, such as rangers for major non-commercial forests and for newly-added afforestation and forests, grasslands, wetlands and sandy lands; water protection posts, such as water resource managers, water and soil conservation supervisors and watercourse managers; rural eco-environment protection posts, such as rural highway maintenance worker, tourist toilet cleaner and village environment supervisor.

In recent years, eco-posts like ecological forest rangers have increased in number. In 2016, the former State Forestry Administration, together with Ministry of Finance and the State Council Poverty Alleviation Office, carried out the work by selecting registered poor people to serve as ecological foresters, and invested RMB2 billion in the same year. In 2017, the central government allocated RMB2.5 billion to help 370,000 registered poor people find jobs concerned. In January 2018, the Work Plan for Poverty Alleviation through Eco-Conservation was released, with focus on 22 provinces, autonomous regions and municipalities in central and western China. RMB3.5 billion was allocated for ecological foresters and more than 500,000 registered poor people were hired. According to the plan, an additional 200,000 ecological forest rangers and 100,000 grassland keepers would be hired in 2019. The extensive creation of eco-jobs has played an important part in targeted poverty alleviation through ecological conservation.[19]

4.5.4.3 Strengthening Poverty Alleviation Through Ecological Industries

The government has constantly reinforced the ecological conservation for poverty alleviation, giving special support to the development of eco-industries such as forest economy and forest tourism. Measures and policies have been explored for poverty reduction including organizational forms of ecological conservation, interest connection mechanisms and multiple-source income plans. In 2018, the total output of the forestry industry in 22 provinces, autonomous regions and municipalities in central and western China reached RMB4.4 trillion, a year-on-year increase of 12.8%. The plantation of oil-tea camellia has been expanded to 55 million Chinese mu, or about 3.667 million hectares. 370 forest economy demonstration bases have been built, and 350,000 poor households' incomes have increased through forest tourism with an average annual rise of RMB 3500. Business activities involving forestry and grasslands have been conducted for poverty alleviation with the sci-tech aid, introduced

[19] Yu et al. [10].

in the model of "technology + enterprises + poor households". 1316 demonstration bases of various types have been established and more than 7000 training sections held, with more than 800,000 local specialists and forestry farmers attending. 626 related programs have been launched. More officials from related government departments have joined in the campaign against poverty. For instance, the National Forestry and Grassland Administration appointed 156 officials to help the poverty elimination work in Tibet, Qinghai, Guangxi provinces and autonomous regions.[20]

In addition, shelterbelt projects in the three regions of northwest, north and northeast China have integrated ecological conservation with poverty alleviation by making full use of local resources of abundant sunshine and vast expanse of land. According to latest statistics from the National Forestry and Grassland Administration, 69.45 million Chinese mu, or about 4.63 million hectares of economic forest has been produced serving as major production bases for walnut, jujube, apple and other fresh and dry fruits. The annual output of fruits has been 48 million tons, over 30 times than that of 1978, with the annual production value of RMB120 billion. Fifteen million people have been lifted out of poverty through forest and fruit industries. The project-beneficial areas have also created a new pattern of eco-tourism, with forest parks as the primary attractions and wetland and desert parks as supplements, which have attracted 380 million tourists from home and abroad and contributed RMB48 billion to the annual direct income.[21]

4.5.4.4 Increasing Compensations for Eco-conservation

The government has constantly increased the benefits for poor areas and people by improving the transfer payment system and establishing diversified subsidy mechanisms to compensate for economic losses associated with reducing ecological damage. The following practices have been taken.

The first is to increase transfer payments in key ecological function areas, especially in the most impoverished "three regions and three prefectures" of Tibet Autonomous Region; Hotan Prefecture, Aksu Prefecture, Kashi Prefecture and Kizilsu Kirgiz Autonomous Prefecture in southern Xinjiang Uygur Autonomous Region; and Tibetan-inhabited areas in the provinces of Sichuan, Yunnan, Gansu and Qinghai; as well as the Liangshan Yi Autonomous Prefecture in Sichuan Province, the Nujiang Lisu Autonomous Prefecture in Yunnan Province, and the Linxia Hui Autonomous Prefecture in Gansu Province. The coverage of policy has been expanded and the ways of granting subsidies improved to gradually increase support for protecting and restoring major ecological function areas.

[20] National Conference on Ecological Conservation for Poverty Alleviation held in Luocheng, Guangxi [EB/OL]. (2019-09-30). http://www.forestry.gov.cn/main/4150/20190930/090835587464448.html [16].

[21] Shelterbelt Projects in the Three Regions of Northwest, North and Northeast China: Developing Ecological Industries to Increase Foresters' Incomes [EB/OL]. (2020-08-15). http://news.cctv.com/2020/08/15/ARTIUxEfmSKXR7sh5aybOeJv200815.shtml [17].

The second is to update the payment and subsidy mechanism and dynamic adjustment for forest ecological benefits to mobilize the initiative and motivation of relevant stakeholders to forest protection. Besides, payment policies have been improved to make them sounder and more reasonable. The supervision of subsidy funds has been carried out to protect the vital interests of the poor.

The third is to implement new subsidies and rewards for eco-protection of grasslands in pastoral and semi-pastoral counties in Inner Mongolia, Tibet, Xinjiang, Qinghai, Sichuan, Gansu, Yunnan, Ningxia, Heilongjiang, Jilin, Liaoning, Hebei, Shanxi and related areas, with due payments to herdsmen for their contributions in grazing prohibition and vegetation balance maintenance.

The fourth is to introduce trial practices for comprehensive ecological compensation. The government has integrated funds from many channels such as the transfer payment, horizontal compensation and compensation by means of the market to set up a comprehensive compensation system for ecological conservation in line with local conditions. Supported by effective supervision and evaluation systems, this practice has combined subsidy payments with protection outcomes to ensure that the villagers and herdsmen get due benefits from their participation in ecological conservation.

4.6 Poverty Alleviation Through Education

Winning the battle against poverty is a major decision and deployment by the CPC and the State Council. It is also an important indicator of achieving a moderate prosperous society for all. In this fight, education has been a major "battlefield" and an important means to win the victory. Since 2012 when the 18th CPC National Congress was convened, the Central Committee with Xi Jinping as the core has attached great importance to poverty alleviation through education. Xi has stressed for many times that the best way to help the poor is to raise their education level. To provide children in impoverished areas with access to good education is a top priority and an important means to prevent intergenerational transmission of poverty.[22] It is a fundamental task to ensure that they receive good education and get out of poverty.[23] To achieve this, the state has issued a series of policies and documents on poverty alleviation through education, including the Plan for Poverty Alleviation through Education during the 13th Five-Year Plan Period, Implementation for Poverty Alleviation through Education in Destitute Areas (2018–2020), and Suggestions on the Implementation of Poverty Alleviation through Education. Focusing on the key counties on the state's poverty alleviation work list and contiguous destitute areas (abbreviated as "poor counties") as well as registered poor population (including unregistered rural families with disabled members, rural recipients of subsistence allowance, and recipients of relief support for the extremely poor, same hereinafter), effective policies and

[22] Xi [18].

[23] Xi [3].

measures have been taken to accurately target the weakest areas of education and the poorest groups to ensure that "everyone has access to compulsory education and basic skills; every family has a better future to hope for, and every county gets assistance". Efforts have been made to achieve better development of people through receiving school education, acquiring skills and having access to employment so that all people may work together to win the battle against extreme poverty. We may well say that China has been determined to address targeted poverty alleviation through education, and the planning and deployment have been comprehensive and meticulous.[24]

4.6.1 Basic Principles and Major Objectives of Poverty Alleviation Through Education

To fully implement the guiding principles of the central government's conference on poverty alleviation and Decisions on Winning the Battle against Extreme Poverty issued by the CPC Central Committee and the State Council to accomplish the important tasks of developing education to eliminate poverty and prevent its inter-generational transmission, the Ministry of Education, the National Development and Reform Commission, the Ministry of Civil Affairs, the Ministry of Finance, the Ministry of Human Resources and Social Security and the State Council Poverty Alleviation Office jointly released in December 2016 the Plan of Poverty Alleviation through Education during the 13th Five-Year Plan Period, which clarified the basic principles and major objectives in this respect.

4.6.1.1 Basic Principles

First of all, accelerating development and taking the overarching goal of the country into account. Priority has been given to the development of education in poor areas by raising the overall educational level of the poor population, boosting the development of education-related industries and public services, and expanding the scope and capacity of education to serve the regional fight against poverty.

Second, adopting well-targeted measures. In line with the principle of trying best within capabilities and based on the education demand of different regions and groups, targeted measures and ways of implementation have been formulated and explored to ensure that policies and funds would be provided to right places and people.

Third, employment orientation with focuses on development of vocational skills. Efforts have been redoubled to develop vocational education and training, focusing on improving the basic knowledge and technical skills of the registered poor people, and enhancing their capabilities to get out of poverty, find jobs or start businesses of their own.

[24] Jin [19].

Fourth, government leadership with joint efforts from all sectors. While local governments assume primary responsibility, full play has been given to the advantages of the education sector in human resources strengths to mobilize social forces to participate in order to stimulate the internal driver of poor areas. A framework of poverty alleviation through education with participation and coordination of multiple players has been built.

4.6.1.2 Major Objectives

The first one is to develop preschool education, enhance compulsory education, and make senior high school education universal. Through 2020, the overall level of education development in poor areas would be significantly improved and basic public services such as registration for the impoverished population fully covered. The government has ensured that all children from poor families go to school and no students drop out because of poverty. Everyone has the opportunity to lift their families out of poverty through vocational education, higher education or vocational training. The education's capacity to serve regional economic and social development would have been greatly enhanced.

The second one has targeted the five groups of people registered as living below the poverty line. Preschool children should have access to preschool education; those of compulsory education age should receive fair and quality compulsory education; those of senior high school age should be provided senior high school education or secondary vocational education; those of higher education age are entitled to have more opportunities to go to universities or colleges; and those of post school age should be provided more vocational skill training to help them meet the needs of employment or entrepreneurship.

4.6.2 Measures for Poverty Alleviation Through Education

In terms of poverty alleviation through education, Xi Jinping points out that "only by educating the younger generations well, particularly those in poor and mountainous areas, can genuine outcomes be delivered in poverty elimination. A good education will also bring a better life and a brighter future for young people. The Chinese have a tradition of valuing education even when their families were financially challenged. Providing a good education will ensure that children in poor regions will not be losers before the race has begun, and will uproot poverty once and for all."[25] "To end poverty, the first step is to end ignorance and illiteracy."[26] He also puts forward the "Matthew effect" of education, that is, the poorer a place is, the more backward its education tends to be. It is a vicious circle in which "poverty" and "illiteracy"

[25] Institute of Party History and Literature of the CPC Central Committee [6].

[26] ibid.

cause each other, thus the implementation of poverty alleviation through education should be accelerated so that all children from poor families can receive fair and quality education to prevent intergenerational transmission of poverty." Guided by Xi Jinping's philosophy on education, poverty alleviation through education has greatly enhanced the awareness and capability of poor people to get out of the poverty, and achieve sustainable results. The following measures have been taken for education at preschool, compulsory, senior high school, vocational and college levels, as well as teacher training and education for special groups in poor areas.

4.6.2.1 Preschool Education in Poor Areas

Preschool education is of great significance to children's physical and mental health, habit forming and intelligence development and it should conform to the development of children's mind and body by resorting to nursing and education methods that may ensure their happy and healthy growth. To do this well, the preschool education funds should give priority to poor areas with each county working out its own detailed plans about its preschool system including nurseries and kindergartens to secure education for left-behind children. In addition, the plans will be based on the natural environment of the area, the distribution of school-age population and other conditions. Beneficiary kindergartens have been set up in towns and administrative villages with relatively large populations and volunteer teaching points, with full-time itinerant teachers provided for remote areas with scattered populations, to establish a preschool education network at the county, township and village levels. In 2019, 91.1% of the households in impoverished areas had access to local kindergartens, while in contiguous areas of extreme poverty, the percentage was 90.1% and for key poor counties, it was 89.4%.

4.6.2.2 Compulsory Education in Poor Areas

Compulsory education is the law-based education that every child and teenager of school age must receive. As its name suggests, it is compulsory, free and universal and is the top priority in China's education, while compulsory education in poor areas has played an even more important part in poverty alleviation. To consolidate and raise the quality of nine-year compulsory education, China has accelerated the improvement of the basic conditions of school running in poor areas, particularly in running the village schools and teaching points, establishing rural boarding schools to ensure that students can receive education nearby. It has also continued to implement the policy of "two exemptions and one subsidy" so that they are entitled to exemptions of tuition and textbook fees and are granted subsidies for boarding. The dropout prevention mechanism has been improved to ensure that students from registered poor households complete their compulsory education. In September 2017, the State Council issued Notice on Further Strengthening the Control of Dropout Rate and Guarantee of Schooling to Improve and Consolidate Compulsory Education, stressing that the dropout control mechanism should be law-based, systematic and well coordinated. The government has been required to fulfill its statutory duty in dropout control by improving the areas of weakness, completing its bottom-line tasks, updating the administrative mechanism for urging resumption of schooling, and establishing a working mechanism for joint control and guarantee of enrolment in compulsory education. Employers must not illegally recruit minors under the age of 16. Parents or other legal guardians shall send the school-age children or adolescents to school on time for them to receive and complete compulsory education according to law. Schools should establish and update relevant systems to work together with other parties to persuade dropout students to return to school, and further improve the quality of compulsory education.

4.6.2.3 Senior High School Education in Poor Areas

Senior high school education is an important part of basic education. Although it has been universal in China, problems still exist, such as unbalanced development, lack of teaching resources and shortage of funds, especially in poor areas. Therefore, China has put emphasis on supporting the development of senior high school education in poor rural areas.

Through plans and projects to build and upgrade regular senior high schools in counties with a weak educational foundation, there has been more support given to these schools to improve their operating conditions and ensure that students from registered poor families have access to more school education. Other efforts include consistent implementation of the policy of national grants which cover all students from registered poor families, who have been exempted from tuition and miscellaneous fees at regular public senior high schools. Since 2011, the central government has provided RMB 37.69 billion in support of poor areas in central and western China to improve the basic conditions of regular senior high schools, of which RMB24.8 billion, or 66%, was allocated during the 13th Five-Year Plan period.

4.6.2.4 Secondary Vocational Education in Poor Areas

The government has redoubled its efforts to boost secondary vocational education in poor areas to offer opportunities for the poor to acquire the knowledge and skills needed to get rid of poverty and become better off, and enhance their capability for employment and self-development. This has been an effective way to increase the attendance of high school education, and at the same time give play to the important role of vocational education in poverty alleviation, in order to block the intergenerational transmission of poverty. Priority therefore has been given to develop secondary vocational education by making it the major part of popularizing senior secondary education and constantly improving its distribution and structure. A number of secondary vocational schools have been built in poor areas where population is concentrated with needs in industrial development.

National aid programs have been launched and implemented, including the Vocational Education Action Plan, the Secondary Vocational Education Cooperation Program and Collegiate Collaboration Action Plan for the Development of Anti-Poverty Skills, coordinated selection of national demonstration and leading secondary vocational schools (including technical schools), targeted and separate enrollment of children from registered poor families to majors with good job prospects to ensure that they acquire at least one practical skill in work and business. The central government has continuously supported junior middle school graduates from needy families to receive secondary vocational education in economically developed areas outside their own provinces, autonomous regions and municipalities, granting them tuition exemption and state stipend, as well as necessary subsidies for accommodation and transportation to aid them to complete their studies and find jobs.

The state has given priority to enrolling children from registered poor families in vocational education jointly provided by schools and enterprises, such as requisition-based vocational education and apprenticeships. Secondary vocational education for such students is now free of tuition and fully covered by state grants. In addition, public welfare vocational training has been carried out extensively. Measures have been taken to step up the implementation of vocational skills upgrading programs and education and training programs for poor families to guide enterprises to integrate their poverty alleviation efforts with vocational education, and encourage vocational colleges to provide various forms of education and training.

4.6.2.5 Measures for Higher Education in Poor Areas

First, to boost the implementation of the preferential enrollment policy in colleges and universities. China has continued to accelerate the admission from classified examinations for vocational colleges, giving priority to students from registered poor families under the same conditions. Government-sponsored projects at national, local and college levels are implemented, undertaken respectively by universities and colleges affiliated to central and some local departments, or to particular provinces, autonomous regions and municipalities, and by colleges and universities directly under the Ministry of Education and pilot institutions of higher learning with independent admission programs for students from poor areas and the countryside, with priority granted to needy students from registered poor families under the same conditions. Other enrolment programs like ethnic preparatory classes and ethnic classes also give preference to eligible poor students. In recent years, colleges and universities have made clear their educational orientation of serving the economic and social development of poverty-stricken areas, focusing on the development of disciplines and specialties that support local industries.

Second, there has been continuous upgrading of school support and job-placement service system. Better subsidy policies have been introduced for needy students to have access to the national scholarships, national student loans, freshmen stipends, graduate student allowances, work-study programs, scholarships, financial aids, and tuition waivers, among others. In terms of job-placement services, the state has actively implemented policies to help impoverished college graduates find jobs or start their own businesses by setting up an information database for them with "one-to-one" dynamic management and services. The employment information service platform for college graduates is used to promote employment opportunities for needy graduates, organize employment probation and training of vocational skills and entrepreneurship, and provide subsidies according to related policies.

College graduates have been guided and encouraged to work in poverty-stricken rural areas through primary-level service programs, such as those in which college graduates work as village officials, or they work in the countryside to support agriculture, education and medicine or are engaged in poverty alleviation. There are also Agricultural Technology Specific Post Program, and the College Students Volunteer Service Program in the western region. While implementing these programs, priority has been given to the selection and recruitment of graduates with local household registration, with various preferential policies and measures offered to establish a long-term mechanism for graduates to be willing to "settle down, stay, do a good job and be mobile" in poverty-stricken areas.

4.6.2.6 Development of Teachers in Poor Areas

Due to the restriction of local conditions, there has been a big gap between the overall quality of teaching staff in less developed areas, especially in remote rural areas and ethnic areas, and in developed areas, which is mainly reflected in the following: ideas of education lagging behind the development of the times, low professional competence, and fewer opportunities to participate in teaching and research training. These constraints have affected not only their quality of teaching, but also the outcome of poverty alleviation through education.

Therefore, to improve the quality of teaching in China's poor areas, it is highly necessary to not only improve the construction of hardware facilities, but also train excellent teachers. To do this well, China has continuously implemented programs to support rural teachers. Among them, the Special Post Program gives priority to meeting the needs of poor counties, and the National Training Program focuses on training rural teachers and school principals.

A provincial-level mechanism for supplementing rural teachers has been established, monitored and improved, by which teachers' colleges have been entrusted to train rural teachers to become specialized and versatile. Special attention has been given to addressing the shortage of kindergarten teachers, and teachers of music, physical education, fine arts and foreign languages. Teacher training in areas with large ethnic minority populations has been strengthened. Special human resources and teacher support programs for remote and poverty-stricken areas, ethnic border areas and old revolutionary base areas have been implemented, with 30,000 volunteer teachers being selected to work in these areas every year. For example, in order to leverage the quality of teaching staff, the "three regions and three prefectures" in extreme poverty have made great efforts to improve the mechanism, tap the potential, and recruit primary and secondary school teachers through multiple channels. With the support of national policies, Kashgar in Xinjiang recruited teachers and graduates from public-funded normal universities for special posts and schools in remote and poor areas, with an increase of 26,799 teachers from 2011 to 2017. Qinghai Province has established a supplementary mechanism for rural teachers under provincial overall planning, with strict standards and targeted recruitment. The quality of newly recruited has been guaranteed from the very beginning through defined responsibilities and measures at different levels.[27]

4.6.2.7 Measures of Education for Left-Behind and Disabled Children in Poor Areas

Under the influence of the current mobile society, left-behind children have become a common phenomenon in rural areas, especially in poor areas. Bearing psychological pressure from their family, study, life and other aspects, these children often feel lonely, helpless and even miserable which have been too much for their age. To address the issue, the government has been paying more and more attention to improve the situation by upgrading the classrooms, dormitories, canteens and other learning and living facilities in primary and secondary schools in poor rural areas, keeping registrations of left-behind children from poor families for more assistance, and building a care and service network to help connect them with their families, schools, the government and social sectors.

Efforts have been made to boost the construction and rational distribution of rural boarding schools in areas where left-behind children are in great number, and raise the occupancy rate of these children. More and continuous attention has been paid to the mental health of the children by establishing and improving psychological care services, strengthening family awareness education and psychological guidance for their parents as migrant workers, and increasing investment in psychological training for social workers and teachers, so as to bring more sunshine and positive energy into the mind of these children. In addition, special education has been developed, particularly preschool education for children with disabilities, with substantial support to ordinary kindergartens in accepting such children. In accordance with categorized and targeted requirements, registered disabled kids and adolescents have been arranged in various forms for them to receive compulsory education.

4.6.2.8 Expansion of Resources for Poverty Alleviation Through Education

(1) Strengthening the role of think tanks in colleges and universities in providing advisory services for sound management and decision-making based on major

[27] Wu [20].

issues concerning economic and social development in poor areas. Taking the advantage of specialists from institutions of higher learning, training programs have been organized by inviting leading administrative officials, trade professionals, and technical personnel to help people in poor areas strengthen their competence in administration, management and professionalism.

(2) Organizing professional people such as experts and professors, agricultural sci-tech service corps and doctoral corps to have in-depth fact-finding tours in poor areas for local resources and geographical advantages that may be well integrated with their own research programs. Mobilizing and encouraging enterprises, alumni and other social forces to promote transformation and industrialization of academic research findings and achievements to create new economic growth points to help poor areas.

(3) Improving public health services and giving full play to the resource advantages of medical specialties and teaching hospitals in colleges and universities to help people in poor areas develop public health awareness. A healthy lifestyle has been advocated to prevent and reduce the occurrence of diseases.

(4) Promoting the progress of rural culture by mobilizing the Communist Youth League, student unions, volunteer service organizations, alumni associations and other forces in colleges and universities to carry forward the traditional Chinese virtue of helping the poor and work with needy people to develop modern ideas and lifestyles, and get rid of backward customs and habits.

4.6.3 Pooling Resources for Development-Driven Poverty Alleviation Through Education

(1) Increasing financial support. In allocating funds, higher priority has been given to increasing support for most impoverished areas and improve the mechanism for arranging and using funds in light of poverty alleviation tasks and changes in the poor population to ensure that the education funds is well-targeted for those really in need with effective outcomes. Taking anti-poverty education a priority of government spending, provincial-level financial and education departments have given full play to their overall planning role to update the mechanism for funding and allocate funds in order of priority and urgency with increased support for areas of difficulty and weakness. Special attention and substantial aids have been given to the most impoverished areas such as the most impoverished "three regions and three prefectures", and areas with toughest anti-poverty challenges to address, as well as areas with difficult conditions in running schools compatible with the comprehensive reform of the college entrance examination.

(2) One cannot build up self-belief through knowledge and skills to get rid of poverty without education. Education can produce not only economic benefits, but also power from within. To do this well, the principal role of the poor should be strengthened to fully mobilize their enthusiasm and creativity, arousing their

awareness of taking the initiative in lifting themselves out of poverty and causing changes to happen through hard work. The model of poverty alleviation has changed from mainly relying on external support like a blood transfusion to internal driver, a more sustained effort from self-motivation.

(3) A paired-up assistance action plan to help poverty alleviation through education has been implemented to help accurately identified and targeted kindergartens and compulsory education schools and needy students in poor rural areas at city, county and township levels. Eastern regions are encouraged to provide pair-up assistance for compulsory and higher education with schools, colleges and universities in contiguous poverty-stricken areas in western China.

(4) China has continued to increase the application of modern information technology by building the database of the poverty-stricken population as well as the schooling and financial assistance of school-age children, strengthening dynamic tracking and providing technical support to ensure that the poor school-age kids stay in school and are helped. There has been more investment in the construction of infrastructure in poor areas, with enhanced IT application in education in poor areas to speed up the provision of broadband network access for all schools, quality teaching resources for all classes and on-line learning for all students based on the building of public service platforms for education resources and education management.

(5) Extensive participation of social sectors has been encouraged to support public welfare organizations like China Foundation for Poverty Alleviation, China Education Development Foundation and others in their efforts to alleviate poverty through education. All social groups, enterprises and relevant international organizations are guided to make donations to help needy students get through their education. The roles of trade unions, the Communist Youth League organizations, women's federations and other public organizations are given full play to carry out public welfare or volunteer service projects such as the "Golden Autumn Education Aid Program", "Spring Buds Program", and "Postgraduates Voluntary Teaching Corps", and to organize volunteers to teach, offer training courses, and popularize modern science and culture in poor areas. Financial measures are also taken in helping poverty alleviation through education, with incentive policies for nongovernmental investment from all sectors.

4.7 Poverty Alleviation Through Health Programs

According to the Outline for Development-Driven Poverty Alleviation in Rural Areas (2011–2020), the overarching goal of China's poverty alleviation and development through 2020 is to ensure that the needy people are "secured with food and clothing, as well as access to compulsory education, basic medical care and housing". Therefore, it is a prerequisite for targeted poverty alleviation to ensure basic medical care and prevent people from falling into victims of poverty or returning to poverty because of illness.

Since the 18th CPC National Congress in 2012, the CPC Central Committee with Xi Jinping as its core has taken poverty alleviation through the health program an important and effective measure to win the battle against extreme poverty. A series of major decisions and plans have been made and implemented through health programs to upgrade medical and healthcare facilities and enhance related service capabilities in poor areas. This has been given a place of prominence in Xi Jinping's poverty alleviation theory.

In December 2014, Xi Jinping noted during his inspection tour to the health center in Shiye Town, Zhenjiang city of Jiangsu Province, "Without health for all, there will be no well-off society in all respects".[28] In August 2016, Xi delivered an important speech at the National Health and Wellness Conference, and put forward the strategic concept of "Healthy China".[29] The health program for poverty alleviation is a great practice of Xi Jinping's thought on development-driven poverty alleviation in the sector of medical and health care, which has fully demonstrated the "people-oriented" philosophy.

No one will be left behind on the journey to alleviate poverty and special attention has been paid to major regions, major groups of people and major types of diseases so as to prevent the vicious cycle of "illness-poverty-illness" among the poor. This constitutes part of Xi Jinping's theory of an all-encompassing campaign against poverty. To further strengthen overall coordination and pool strengths of all resources, effective measures have been taken to guarantee better health care security and enhance health service capacities in poor areas, with coordinated consideration of the parties involved in such aspects as raising public awareness, pooling resources and strengthening leadership to actively mobilize social forces to participate in the endeavor.

4.7.1 Goals and Tasks of the Health Program for Poverty Alleviation

The implementation of the health program for poverty alleviation is of great significance to ensuring that the rural poor enjoy basic medical and health services, preventing them from falling into victims of poverty or returning to poverty because of illness, promoting the building of a healthy China, and lifting the rural poor out of poverty through 2020. In June 2016, the National Health Commission and other departments worked out the Guidelines on Implementing the Health Program for Poverty Alleviation. The program echoed China's poverty alleviation goal and basic principles to prevent the poor from sinking back into poverty due to illness. Different policies have been applied to different places and each household and each person with poverty caused by diseases have been registered for targeted help. Priority has

[28] Xu and Shi [21].

[29] National Health and Wellness Conference held in Beijing from 19-20 [EB/OL]. (2016-08-20). http://www.gov.cn/xinwen/2016-08/20/content_5101024.htm [22].

been given to major regions, groups of people, and types of diseases to combine prevention with treatment to help fight poverty. To address key and difficult issues in the development of medical and health services in poor areas, and to increase the benefits of the poor rural population, existing resources have been integrated, such as medical security, financial projects, human resources and technology, to increase support for poor areas. More effective policies and measures in line with the local conditions have been adopted to ensure that the rural poor have access to basic medical and health services.

Through 2020, everyone in poor areas would have access to basic medical and health services, and receive timely and effective treatment for serious diseases. The burden of individual medical expenses would have been greatly reduced. Major infectious and endemic diseases will have been brought under effective control, and basic public health indicators would be close to the national average, with further rising of average life expectancy and significant dropping of maternal and infant mortality and the incidence of infectious diseases. At least one hospital (including one traditional Chinese medicine hospital) in each county of contiguous destitute areas and each of key counties on the state's poverty alleviation work list would have reached the status of second-tier medical institutions, with markedly improved service conditions, capacities and accessibility. Regional disparities in the allocation of medical and health resources and in the health of the people will have been further narrowed, and the problem of people falling into victims of poverty or returning to poverty due to illness effectively resolved.

4.7.2 Mechanism of the Health Program for Poverty Alleviation[30]

The health program for poverty alleviation has been launched to reduce the economic and health vulnerability of the poor population and to prevent the vicious circle of "disease-poverty-disease" so as to resolve the practical dilemma of "being trapped in or returning to poverty because of illness".[31] The following figure has illustrated the mechanism of the program mainly from two aspects: economic vulnerability and health vulnerability (see Fig. 4.1).

The health program can reduce the medical burden and economic vulnerability of families with members suffering from critical diseases. Many rural households became poor or returned to poverty because of illness, which was mainly reflected in the sharp increase of family expenditure beyond what they can cover within the range of their family accumulated income and resulted in their actual living standards deteriorating to a long-term absolute poverty. The health program may help in at least two aspects. Firstly, the direct economic burden of disease on families concerned

[30] Wang and Liu [23].

[31] Zhai and Yan [24].

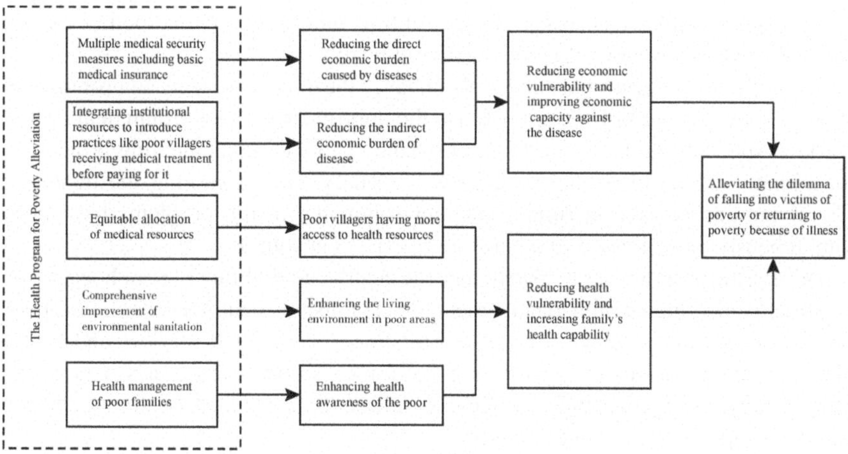

Fig. 4.1 Mechanism of the health program for poverty alleviation

could be reduced through basic medical insurance, medical assistance and commercial insurance, among others. For patients, the multiple medical security measures can help reduce medical expenses such as outpatient fees and fees for examinations, medicine and hospitalization. For family caregivers of the disabled, the program would provide them subsidies, easing their income loss caused by reduced working hours due to their routine and rehabilitation care of the disabled, and improving the economic capacity of the family against the impact of the disease. Secondly, the integration of institutional resources can also reduce the indirect economic burden of these families by introducing practices like poor villagers receiving diagnosis and treatment before paying for them and one-stop settlement, so that their economic capacity against the disease has been increased.

Generally speaking, the integration of multiple health care systems and resource has helped improve the economic capacity of poor families to cope with the disease risk, and prevent patients from delaying or giving up treatment due to inability to cover medical expenses which often causes a minor illness to turn into a critical or even incurable one. The probability of being trapped in poverty or returning to poverty has been significantly reduced.

The anti-poverty health program can improve the health capacity of poor households and reduce their health vulnerability. Equitable allocation of medical and health resources is not only the basis for improving medical and health services, but also an important guarantee for poor families to enhance health capacity.

Firstly, the health program reduces the health vulnerability of poor households by improving the medical services in poor areas. Through standardized construction of county hospitals, township health centers and village clinics, and the strengthening of basic medical and health personnel and capacity building, in addition to the promoting of paired-up assistance and remote medical treatment, equalization of health resources in stock, structure and distribution has been greatly advanced.

Poor villagers can have access to more health resources, timely and better- quality medical services for more effective treatment results.

Secondly, the program can effectively enhance the quality of living environment in poor areas by taking a holistic approach to the improvement of environmental health. Through speeding up the construction of sanitary toilets, implementing projects to consolidate and improve the drinking water safety, and promoting the treatment of garbage and sewage in rural areas, environmental health problems have been comprehensively addressed to control disease risks at source.

Thirdly, the program has helped reduce the health vulnerability of poor households by strengthening their health management. By establishing health records for the poor population and the practice of classified treatment, contracted services and health education, there has been a significant enhancement of health awareness among the poor population together with a change of ideas about medical treatment and the improved capacity to prevent diseases.

4.7.3 Policies and Measures in the Anti-poverty Health Program[32]

The program includes many policies, the core of which is that the rural poor can afford medical services and be healthier. Therefore, a holistic approach to implement the policies should be adopted to create a synergy and effectively prevent the poor people from falling into victims of or returning to poverty because of illness.

4.7.3.1 Improving Medical Security to Ensure Affordable Medical Care for the Poor

Continuous efforts have been made to raise medical security and lighten the burden of medical expenses on the rural poor.

Firstly, the new rural cooperative medical care system covers all poor rural people with preferential policies, with individual contributions being subsidized by the government in line with related stipulations. In impoverished areas, overall coordination of outpatient services has been implemented, and the reimbursement rate for hospitalization expenses based on the policy has been raised.

Secondly, there has been increased support for critical disease insurance to gradually lower the threshold for payment and raise the reimbursement rate of such insurance with more targeted payment policies so that poor people can get more benefits.

Thirdly, more medical assistance has been provided, including medical assistance for all rural poor people who are suffering from critical diseases. More temporary

[32] Guidelines on Implementing the Health Program for Poverty Alleviation [EB/OL]. (2016-06-21). http://www.gov.cn/xinwen/2016-06/21/content_5084195.htm [25].

and charity assistance is offered to those who are temporarily unable to obtain family support or who have difficulties in basic living due to sudden and serious diseases.

Fourthly, a dovetailing mechanism connecting the systems of basic medical insurance, critical disease insurance, disease emergency assistance and medical assistance has been established and is under constant improvement to let play a synergistic and complementary role by joining efforts. Medical rehabilitation programs for eligible disabled persons are covered by basic medical insurance, and medical security for poor disabled persons in rural areas has been improved.

Fifthly, there has been solid progress in the reform of payments to strengthen budgetary management of funds, and improve the compound payment method that combines payment by type of disease, payment by head, and payment by bed per day, so as to effectively control expenses.

4.7.3.2 Promoting Equal Access to Medical Services for the Poor

(1) Strengthening the medical and health service system in poor areas. There have been consistent efforts to advance the standardized construction of county hospitals, township health centers and village clinics in contiguous destitute areas and the key counties on the state's poverty alleviation work list, to achieve the goal of "Three Ones", namely, one state-owned hospital at the county level, one health center at the township level, and one clinic at the village level. Priority has been given to implement the program during the 13th Five-Year Plan period to improve primary-level TCM service capacity in poor areas, and TCM equipment and staffing have been strengthened. The government has speeded up the public health service network in the poor areas, with emphasis on the prevention and control of major infectious diseases, endemic diseases and chronic diseases, and provided greater support to capacity building of professional public health institutions such as those for disease control and maternal and child health care. Capacity building for telemedicine in poor areas has been strengthened to realize connectivity between county-level hospitals and medical and health service institutions at all levels and of various types within the county.

Paired-up assistance have been provided by sizable hospitals nationwide that are classified as falling into the category of "3-tier quality hospitals" (based on size and strength, the best being recognized as Tier-One hospitals) to county-level hospitals in contiguous destitute areas and designated impoverished counties by the state. 3-tier hospitals (including those of the People's Armed Forces and the armed police forces) with strengths have been selected from all over the country, and one-to-one assistance responsibility agreements defining the goals and tasks have been signed with hospitals of these counties. Medical teams have been regularly dispatched to provide centralized medical services for the poor in rural areas, together with technical support, personnel training and management guidance to improve the service capacity of assisted hospitals. Telemedicine platforms have been established for telemedicine services. Through 2020, the goal of "ensuring basic medical care for the poor population in rural areas, with the main indicators approaching the national average" set forth in the Outline of Development-Driven Poverty Alleviation in Rural Areas would be achieved. In 2016, 44% of people living in poverty, including ethnic groups, were poor because of illness. In 2019, the central government invested RMB 7.4 billion to support the construction of 200 county-level hospitals and trained a total of 12,000 medical and health professionals for poor areas. 1007 urban quality hospitals sent 6174 doctors to help county hospitals by regular rotation, and a total of 98,000 doctors and nurses have worked in rural areas at the township and village levels through various flexible approaches, such as "employment by counties to work in townships" and "employment by townships to work in villages", as well as selecting doctors from health centers on rounds of visits or as members of resident work teams. 16.2 million poor people have received medical treatment and contracted services for chronic diseases, and the program has proved to be effective.[33]

(2) Accelerating the coordinated reform of the medical and health care systems in poor areas. The practice that poor rural residents receive medical treatment before paying for it when they are hospitalized in their own counties has been introduced. In-depth comprehensive reform of public hospitals in poverty-stricken areas has been carried on together with the reform of medical service price adjustment, health insurance payment, cost control of medical institutions, and public hospital compensation mechanism to strengthen their cost management. Initiatives have been encouraged to innovate staffing administration of public hospitals at the county level and explore reasonable ways to verify the total amount of performance payroll in public hospitals and other medical and health institutions. This has aimed to figure out the proportion of incentive performance payroll in light of actual conditions to boost the enthusiasm of the medical staff. Continuous efforts have been made to regulate the mechanism for drug supply guarantee in poor areas, and coordinate drug supply and distribution management in county-level hospitals and primary-level medical and health centers. The practice of providing medical treatment before paying for it is introduced to the rural poor when they are hospitalized in local county hospitals. Designated medical institutions have set up comprehensive service windows, enabling one-stop information enquiry and instant settlement of basic medical insurance, critical disease insurance, disease emergency assistance and medical assistance. Poor patients only need to pay their own portion of medical expenses upon discharge from the hospital. For places where conditions permit, they are required to explore a settlement mechanism for poor rural people to receive medical treatment before paying for it when they are hospitalized at municipal or provincial hospitals. The establishment of a tiered diagnosis and treatment system has been promoted to boost the development of specialties and clinical specialties related to common and frequently-occurring diseases

[33] Health Program for Poverty Alleviation: Effective Outcome in Rural Medical Services and Staffing [EB/OL]. (2020-05-27). http://health.people.com.cn/n1/2020/0527/c14739-31726051.html [26].

in destitute areas at county level, and explore ways of county-township-village integrated medical consortium to upgrade grassroots services.

(3) Strengthening comprehensive development of human resources. The government has supported the development of medical institutions of higher education in poor areas, and guided medical colleges and specialties in the areas to make well-coordinated enrollment plans according to local needs. The development of medical and health professionals in poor areas have been boosted by offering standardized training for resident doctors, training for assistant general practitioners, job-specific free training, and special post programs for general practitioners and specialized doctors. New ways are being explored for the integrated management of human resources at county and township levels.

In response to local needs, technology programs have been organized and carried out. Demonstration bases relying on existing institutions have been established to conduct graded training and standardize the application of technologies. Primary-level medical and health personnel from poor areas, old revolutionary base areas, ethnic areas and border areas have been sent to pursue advanced studies and joint training in medical colleges and institutions. Appropriate TCM technologies have been popularized in targeted areas and a fuller play has been given to the role of national clinical medical research centers and collaborative research networks. Platforms for information sharing and training services have been built to enhance the technical skills of primary-level medical and health staff.

Many policies and measures have been worked out to encourage excellent health professionals to serve in poor areas; and incentive mechanisms have been introduced to boost the morale of grassroots health professionals, such as giving preference in the promotion of professional titles, more opportunities for advanced education and training, and better remuneration to medical staff who have been working at the grassroots level in poor areas for a long time. More realistic measures in line with local conditions have been taken to recruit and bring in new staff, and give medical and health institutions based in poor areas the right to choose their personnel. Efforts have been made to enhance team building of rural doctors, who have opportunities for regular training in rotation. They have also been given support and guidance in participating in the basic old-age insurance for employees or urban and rural residents as required, as well as other forms of subsidies, to raise their old-age benefits.

4.7.3.3 Further Optimizing Medical Services to Ensure Targeted and Good Treatment for Rural Poor

For rural poor people suffering from serious or chronic diseases, treatment by categories has been provided.

First, a dynamically managed electronic health record and a health card has been established for each of them to help grassroots medical and health institutions provide contracted services such as basic medical care, public health and health management for poor families in rural areas. Second, on a county-level basis and by relying on primary-level health and family planning service networks, the number of poverty-stricken families and sick people has been further identified, and patients with serious and chronic diseases that need treatment have been treated by category. Third, the Light Project, a love-outreach vision restoration program, has been introduced to provide treatment for impoverished rural cataract patients. The cost of treatment would be covered through the existing medical insurance system and other channels, together with the participation of charity organizations. Fourth, efforts to alleviate poverty for the rural disabled are doubled through the health program. Training sessions on rehabilitation knowledge have been provided to staff of medical institutions at the grass-roots level, and rehabilitation services centers at the county level have been set up to upgrade rehabilitation facilities. A working mechanism for effective connection and coordination between medical institutions and specialized rehabilitation centers for persons with disabilities has been in place to offer more targeted and better services. Fifth, effective ways have been adopted to intervene in specific diseases for particular regions. For example, strengthening the follow-up monitoring of registered tumor cases and the causes of death, expanding coverage of cancer screening as well as early detection and early treatment, and offering comprehensive prevention and control of endemic diseases such as Kaschin-Beck Disease and Keshan Disease. Technical guidance and support have been provided to places where tuberculosis (TB) is rampant, and in poor areas where AIDS occurs, there are prevention and control centers. Other diseases like severe mental disorders have been given more attention to tackle with effective measure such as screening, registration, treatment, assistance and other service to help prevent them from developing and spreading.

4.7.3.4 Launching Health Campaigns to Reduce Disease Incidence

(1) Making coordinated efforts to address environmental health problems and effectively raising the quality of the living environment in poor areas. Poverty alleviation initiatives to improve the living environment have been carried out and "Clean County/Township" campaigns regularly launched to keep the environment clean. Measures have been taken to integrate the toilet rebuilding program with that of the renovation of dilapidated rural houses to accelerate rural sanitary toilet construction. The monitoring of rural drinking water and environmental sanitation has been strengthened with regular survey and assessment, and the program of consolidation and upgrading of drinking water safety for rural residents has been implemented with improved sewage treatment. Efforts are being made to advance the comprehensive control of pollution of atmosphere, surface water and noise.

(2) Health promotion and education have been strengthened, with wide publicity of basic health knowledge and skills to enhance the health awareness of the poor rural so that they learn to develop good habits and healthy lifestyles. Free pre-pregnancy physical examinations, child nutrition improvement, and newborn disease screening programs have been implemented in poverty-stricken areas.

A rehabilitation and assistance system has been established for children with disabilities.

More attention has been given to raising the capacity to treat pregnant women and newborns in critical conditions, with more assistance to needy households in family planning. Free pre-pregnancy health check-ups, folic acid supplements to prevent neural tube defects, breast and cervical cancer screening, improved nutrition for children, and screening for newborn diseases have been provided to promote comprehensive early prevention and treatment of birth defects. A rehabilitation and assistance system for children with disabilities has been established to promote the gradual realization that children aged 0–6 with visual, hearing, speech, mental and physical disabilities and autistic children receive free operations, assistive equipment and rehabilitation training.

(3) More work has been done to strengthen capacity building in poor areas to treat pregnant women and newborns with acute and critical conditions, improve health care for rural women during pregnancy and childbirth, and ensure the safety of mothers and infants. We will increase support for family planning in poor areas, adhere to and improve the responsibility system for target-oriented management of family planning, and increase assistance to households with special difficulties in family planning.

4.8 Poverty Alleviation Through Social Security

This model is about social security, which is the bottom-line institutional arrangement for completing the building of a moderately prosperous society in all respects. It has a bearing on the achievement of the goals and tasks of poverty alleviation as scheduled and the quality of the better-off society. Since the 18th CPC National Congress, the Central Committee with Xi Jinping as its core has adhered to the basic strategy of targeted poverty alleviation and elimination, and made a series of major decisions and arrangements to ensure social security for those in need. In 2015, at the Central Conference on Poverty Alleviation and Development, Xi Jinping stressed the importance of "social security for those in need", requiring that subsistence allowances be provided to help those who have completely or partially lost their ability to work. He said, "In building a moderately prosperous society in all respects, we need to ensure that no one is left behind. No one should be left behind on the road to common prosperity." This has emphasized that the society of moderate prosperity China is to build must benefit all people, and no poor person should be left behind on the journey towards the goal.

For poor areas capable of independent development, measures should be adopted to give them the boost to eradicate poverty through development by themselves. For those who completely or partially lose their ability to work, they must be provided security measures such as rural subsistence allowance to maintain their basic living standards. Indeed, social security is a necessary and bottom-line measure to solve the problem of destitute poverty.[34] At present, the battle against poverty alleviation has entered a critical period, and lifting impoverished areas and people out of poverty has become the toughest task to cope with. As Xi jinping points out, people who are unable to shake off poverty through their own efforts alone are mostly the disabled, elderly with no family and people with chronic illness as well as some with little education and skills. For these special groups of poor people, poverty alleviation is the heaviest task and only through policy support such as subsistence allowances and charity aid measures can their special difficulties be addressed.[35]

Subsistence allowances and other social assistance are important parts of poverty alleviation. They are the basic institutional arrangements for winning the final battle against extreme poverty. They have a bearing on whether poverty alleviation can be accomplished on schedule and whether the building of a moderately prosperous society is completed with expected outcomes. President Xi Jinping has defined social security as one of China's five targeted measures employed for poverty alleviation, pointing out that the elderly, the weak, the sick, the disabled and other poor people who lack the ability to work will be provided with subsistence allowances and other social assistance to ensure that their basic living standards are guaranteed. On March 6, 2020, Xi Jinping stressed again the need to strengthen the social security system for the poor without the ability to work when he presided over a meeting on the decisive battle against poverty.[36]

4.8.1 Basic Principles and the Major Tasks of Social Security for Poverty Alleviation[37]

In order to implement the decisions and plans of the CPC Central Committee and the State Council on winning the battle against extreme poverty and effectively dovetail the rural subsistence allowances framework with poverty alleviation policies to ensure that all rural people living below the current poverty line can be lifted out of poverty through 2020, the Ministry of Civil Affairs and five other departments jointly issued Guidelines for Effective Dovetailing of the Rural Subsistence Allowances Framework with Poverty Alleviation Policies in 2016, in which the basic principles and the major task of social security were clearly defined.

[34] Literature Research Office of the CPC Central Committee [27].

[35] Huang [28].

[36] Xi [29].

[37] Ministry of Civil Affairs and Five Other Departments [30].

4.8.1.1 Basic Principles

(1) Full coverage of the eligible rural poor in need of help. The poor rural population should be accurately identified to cover all eligible recipients of subsistence allowances in the register, and provide policy support to help them lift themselves out of poverty and increase their incomes.
(2) Full coverage of the eligible rural poor in need of the allowances. The rural subsistence allowance system should be improved, so that the eligible recipients can be identified. The financial status of rural households receiving subsistence allowances should be checked, and all registered poor households are provided subsistence allowances to ensure their basic living standards.
(3) Dynamic management. Regular checks on rural recipients of subsistence allowances and the registered poor should be carried out, with updated records to see to it that all rural residents receive subsistence allowances when they are eligible, and are deregistered and have no more access to the allowances when they have emerged from poverty. Strict, standardized and transparent criteria, procedures and verifications should be established and improved for poverty registration and deregistration from subsistence allowances.
(4) Coordinated resources planning. All kinds of aid and poverty alleviation resources should be concentrated and better coordinated, with the government subsistence allowances framework being integrated with poverty alleviation policies to create a synergy and achieve comprehensive support for the poor rural population.

4.8.1.2 Major Objective

By effectively dovetailing the rural subsistence allowance framework with policies for poverty alleviation and development, a synergy has been created to provide policy-based subsistence allowances to eligible rural poor people and ensure that all poor rural people living below the current poverty alleviation standards would be lifted out of poverty through 2020.

4.8.2 Mechanism of Social Security

Government departments and social organizations are major players participating in social security for poverty alleviation, with the poor population to be helped. By strengthening the dovetailing and integration of social security and poverty alleviation, the participating players, led by the government, would raise funds needed for poverty alleviation through social security in poor areas from multiple channels. By accurately identifying the eligible targets, and making good use of the three major systems of social assistance, social insurance and social welfare, assistance in cash, kind or service are provide to poverty-stricken people or families in

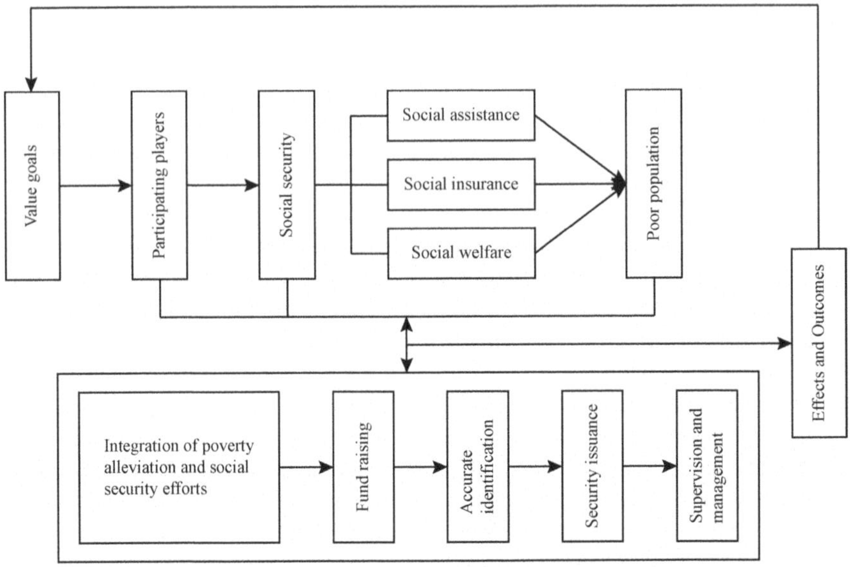

Fig. 4.2 Mechanism of social security for poverty alleviation

different ways to help them get rid of poverty and improve their subsistence and development capacity. In this process, the dynamic supervision and management mechanism gives constant feedback of the updates of social security provision for poverty alleviation, and timely adjustment is accordingly carried out to ensure that social security can have a greater part to play in poverty alleviation in poor areas through the integration of poverty alleviation and social security efforts such as fund raising, accurate identification, security issuance, and supervision and management, as shown in Fig. 4.2.[38]

4.8.3 Coverage of Social Security for Poverty Alleviation

The social security framework for poverty alleviation involves social assistance, social security and social welfare. Among them, social assistance is a bottom-line system in the social security framework and the government undertakes the basic living security responsibility of the poor population, such as the subsistence allowance program in poor areas, the assistance and support program for people in extreme poverty, the temporary assistance program, and special social assistance program. Social insurance is an intermediate system in the social security framework, which plays an effective role in sharing responsibility for poverty alleviation and development. The poor may enjoy insurance benefits after payment of some

[38] Gong and Gong [31].

premiums, and their life risks may be generally insured. Specifically, the social insurance system in poor areas includes the new rural cooperative medical system and the new rural endowment insurance system, which provides basic living security for the poor population. Social welfare has been an improvement system in the social security framework, which promotes the redistribution of social resources and improving the quality of life of the poor population, involving welfare systems for the elderly, the disabled, and women and children in poor areas.[39]

4.8.3.1 Improving the Social Assistance System to Ensure Bottom-Line Social Security[40]

Social assistance is the basic institutional arrangement for winning the battle against extreme poverty and the bottom line of social security. It is the political responsibility of civil affairs departments at all levels to ensure that every household and every single person of the most disadvantaged groups is lifted out of poverty and that they support the overarching goal of winning the battle and building a moderately prosperous society for all as scheduled. This has been carried out by the following efforts.

(1) Proactively improving the system of subsistence allowances for rural residents, which has covered: (a) impoverished people who have completely or partially lost their ability to work because of illness or disability and are unable to get rid of poverty through their own efforts; (b) all registered poor people who have not been lifted out of poverty or have returned to poverty, including the newly added eligible poor population. Severely disabled and critically ill people in registered poor households who have not emerged out of poverty would be no longer subject to checks of financial status, and their families would be managed dynamically in accordance with the "single-person household" scheme based on the subsistence allowance policy. In calculating the income of families involved, necessary employment costs would be deducted according to regulations. When the per capita income of a family exceeded the local subsistence allowance standard, the people concerned would be allowed a grace period to find jobs and make a living and sustain by themselves.

In addition, continuous efforts have been made to improve the integration of subsistence allowances for rural residents with the national poverty alleviation line. By the end of 2017, rural subsistence allowances in all counties, county-level cities and districts had met or exceeded the national poverty line. In December 2019, it averaged RMB5336 per person, with the 22 provinces with tougher poverty alleviation tasks hitting RMB4697 and the severely impoverished counties reaching RMB4199 per person on a yearly basis. And even the counties under the jurisdiction

[39] Zhu [32].

[40] Going All Out to Promote Social Assistance in Poverty Alleviation [EB/OL]. (2020-05-01). http://www.qstheory/cn/dukan/qs/2020-05/01/C_1125923915.htm [33].

of the most impoverished "three regions and three prefectures" had their per-capita subsistence allowances growing to RMB4068 per year. The standard of living for the poor included in the program was no less than 1.3 times that of the local subsistence allowance. By December 2019, a total of 18.57 million registered poor people and the most vulnerable groups in China had been provided with subsistence allowances, of whom 16.93 million had been lifted out of poverty. People covered by subsistence allowances have been guaranteed with adequate food and clothing.

(2) The policy of providing assistance and support to rural people in extreme poverty has been fully implemented, with the more standardized procedure of identifying people living in extreme poverty and more timely inclusion of eligible and registered ones. Priority has been given to providing care centers for the most vulnerable groups living in extreme poverty who were willing to have access to such support. The construction and renovation of care centers (nursing homes) for the elderly in destitute areas such as the "three regions and three prefectures" have been speeded up to improve their capacity to provide basic care and the quality of services. Those doing well have been encouraged to expand their services to offer low-fee or free centralized care to the elderly and the disabled from rural subsistence-allowance supported families, low-income families and registered poor families if they have spared capacity. By December 2019, there had been a total of 4.393 million rural people living in extreme poverty, of whom 752,000 were provided centralized care, including 1.073 million who were unable to take care of themselves. A total of RMB34.69 billion was spent for the help and support.

(3) Taking full advantage of the temporary assistance scheme. Local governments have simplified and optimized the examination and approval procedures and improved the efficiency of temporary assistance funds for townships and towns by raising the standards and making the assistance more responsive. The temporary assistance scheme has been effectively dovetailed with subsistence allowance policies to provide assistance in advance to those who return to poverty or newly emerging needy people. From January to December 2019, there were 9.177 million cases of temporary assistance nationwide, with a total expenditure of RMB12.8 billion and an average assistance of RMB1395 per person, including 3.04 million cases of registered poor people.

(4) Providing timely assistance to needy people affected by COVID-19. The sudden outbreak of COVID-19 has put people in need at risk of being trapped in poverty or returning to poverty, and brought about enormous pressure to social assistance. To secure the basic livelihood of poor people, civil affairs departments have implemented the decisions and arrangements of the central government, stepping up assistance to inflicted needy people, and providing temporary assistance to urban and rural low-income families, impoverished households, dependants in extreme poverty, left-behind children and children in need. A mechanism to increase social assistance and social security benefits when prices rise has been put in place. Since 2020, RMB 3.71 billion of temporary price allowances have been granted to social assistance recipients, benefiting 81.689

million people in need, in an effort to ensure that the basic living standards of poor people are not lowered due to rising prices.

4.8.3.2 Improving the Social Welfare System to Ensure Bottom-Line Social Security

Among the poor population, the severely ill, the disabled, the elderly and minors are major groups of people for whom civil affairs departments have provided services. Being the most vulnerable and the top priority in China's battle against poverty, they should be given special attention and care. In recent years, China has been improving the care system for left-behind children, women, elderly people and people with disabilities in rural areas, and implemented policies to ensure the livelihood of orphans and de facto orphans with no one to take care of them. All kinds of measures have been adopted to assist and take care of these needy groups.

Efforts have been made to establish and maintain a nationwide database of children, women and elderly left behind in rural areas with comprehensive and dynamic updates of information to provide strong support for targeted care and services. A special campaign of "Growing up with Joint Guardians" has been launched for concerted care and protection, with strengthened dynamic management of basic information on left-behind children and children in difficulties to improve the mechanism of rescue, protection, care and service. A series of practices have been introduced, such as the scheme of contact persons and regular visits, trial listing of care services, mutual assistance and volunteer services for the left-behind elderly to ensure that they receive basic living care. Rural women have been organized to receive vocational education and technical training, and they are provided equal employment opportunities, good medical and health services and maternity services so as to help built their own development capacity. Programs for persons with severe disabilities have been developed to raise their living and nursing allowances. More care services are provided for poor persons with disabilities, and ensure that subsidies are granted to the full extent and keep up to the standards.

Regular training in practical skills has been provided for the disabled to help them find jobs or start their own businesses; and priority has been given to support their families to develop production. There has been increased investment in public services for the disabled, particularly in improving rehabilitation services.

4.8.3.3 Improving the Social Insurance System to Ensure Bottom-Line Security

The social insurance system in poor areas involves the new rural cooperative medical system and the new rural endowment insurance system. With regard to the new rural endowment insurance system, the basic old-age insurance benefits for rural and non-working urban residents have been on gradual rise, with the government paying old-age insurance premiums for rural and non-working poor urban residents, recipients of subsistence allowances, and people living in extreme poverty.

In terms of the new rural cooperative medical care system, all poor people have been covered by basic medical insurance, serious disease insurance and medical assistance for rural and non-working urban residents. On the basis of strict cost control, diagnosis and treatment plans, fee rates for individual diseases, standardized referral and centralized designated treatment, more medical assistance and other support policies have been provided for rural and non-working urban residents who still find it difficulty to pay out-of-pocket expenses under the basic medical insurance and serious disease insurance. More possibilities have been explored for the establishment of supplementary commercial medical insurance to effectively cover the out-of-pocket medical expenses of poor people suffering from critical diseases.

4.8.4 Key Tasks in the Later Stage of Social Security for Poverty Alleviation

Social security is the last line of defense to win the battle against extreme poverty. It concerns whether or not the poor who have completely or partially lost their ability to work can be lifted out of poverty on schedule. The battle has now reached a crucial stage. In order to further improve the work for those in need, the Ministry of Civil Affairs and the State Council Poverty Alleviation Office released Action Plan for Poverty Alleviation through Social Security on February 20, 2020, which laid out key tasks for better social assistance as a major form of social security. (1) Improving the monitoring and early warning mechanism, paying close attention to the basic living conditions of people who have yet been lifted out of poverty or are at high risk of returning to poverty, as well as low-income groups with difficulties and potential aid recipients. (2) Implementing the policy of ensuring that all eligible people are covered by social security and social assistance. (3) Strengthening care and support for needed people by improving the system of care services for children, women, and elderly people left behind in rural areas. Policies to ensure living allowances for orphans and de facto orphans with no one to support them should be better delivered, and all possible measures should be taken to help and take care of groups with special difficulties. (4) Increasing preferential support for severely impoverished areas. Various poverty alleviation policies, programs, funds and human resources should prioritize the "three regions and three prefectures", and other deeply impoverished counties, townships and villages, providing social assistance to those in need.

Bibliography

1. The Proposal of the CPC Central Committee on Formulating the 13th Five-Year Plan for National Economic and Social Development. *People's Daily*, November 4, 2015.
2. The CPC Central Committee and the State Council. Strategic Plan for Rural Revitalization (2018–2022). *People's Daily*, September 27, 2018.
3. Xi, J. (2015). *Be a good county party secretary like Jiao Yulu* (24p). Central Party Literature Publishing House.
4. Xi, J. (2017). *The Governance of China* (II). Foreign Languages Press.
5. Wang, S., & Guo, Z. (2016). On China's targeted poverty alleviation. *Party and Government Vision, 7*, 44.
6. Institute of Party History and Literature of the CPC Central Committee. (2015). *Xi Jinping on poverty alleviation*. Central Party Literature Publishing House.
7. Wang, S., Yin, H., & Wang, Y. (2017). Practices, challenges and policy prospects of China's poverty alleviation and development [J]. *Journal of South China Normal University (Social Sciences Edition), 4*, 18–25, 189.
8. Wang, Q, & Wang, P. (2016). A sound approach to the three stages of targeted poverty alleviation: reflections on general secretary Xi Jinping's views on "Targeted Poverty Alleviation" [EB/OL], June 15, 2016. http://theory.people.com.cn/nl/2016/0615/c49154-28445645.html
9. Song, G. (2019). Poverty alleviation should focus on economic development. *Guangming Daily*, September 3, 2019.
10. Yu, H., & Wang, Y., et al. (2020). Win-win results on ecological conservation and targeted poverty alleviation through creating ecological public welfare posts. Rural Areas, Agriculture & Farmers, *2020*(1), 3(19–21).
11. Xi, J. (2019). Propelling china's ecological conservation forward. *Endeavor*, *2019*(3), 1–16.
12. Lei, M., Yao, X., & Yuan, X. (2020). Optimization of internal circulatory mechanism of local poverty alleviation through eco-conservation: based on the practice in Guizhou Province. *Journal of Nanjing Agricultural University (Social Sciences Edition), 20*(4), 152–162.
13. Yilan, O. (2019). Exploring the realization of poverty alleviation through eco-conservation. *People's Tribune, 21*, 70–71.
14. Ren, L., & Li, J. (2020). Review on poverty reduction through compensations for eco-conservation. *Issues in Agricultural Economy*, *2020*(7), 94–107.
15. National Development and Reform Commission: Compensations for Eco-Conservation Help Targeted Poverty Alleviation. [EB/OL], 25 May, 2016. http://wwwgov.cn//zhengce/2016-05/25/content-5076622.htm.
16. National Conference on Ecological Conservation for Poverty Alleviation held in Luocheng, Guangxi [EB/OL], September 30, 2019. http://www.forestry.gov.cn/main/4150/20190930/090835587464448.html
17. Shelterbelt Projects in the Three Regions of Northwest, North and Northeast China: Developing Ecological Industries to Increase Foresters' Incomes. [EB/OL], August 15, 2020. http://news.cctv.com/2020/08/15/ARTIUxEfmSKXR7sh5aybOeJv200815.shtml
18. Xi, J. (2015). Reply to teachers from Guizhou attending training courses by Beijing Normal University under the National Training Programs for Backbone Teachers in Midwest Rural Areas. *People's Daily*, September 10, 2015.
19. Jin, J. (2020). References and transformation of approaches in poverty alleviation through education. *Education and Economy, 36*(2), 10–18.
20. Wu, N. (2020). Poverty alleviation through education requires enhancement of the quality of teachers in poor areas. *China Education News*, June 3, 2020.
21. Xu, B., & Shi, W. (2020). There will be no all-round well-off without health for all. *Economic Daily*, May 13, 2020.
22. National Health and Wellness Conference Held in Beijing from 19–20 [EB/OL], August 20, 2016. http://www.gov.cn/xinwen/2016-08/20/content_5101024.htm

23. Wang, S., & Liu, M. (2019). Mechanism, implementation dilemma and policy choice of the health program for poverty alleviation. *Journal of Xinjiang Normal University (Philosophy and Social Sciences Edition), 40* (3), 82–91.
24. Shaoguo, Z., & Jinhang, Y. (2018). Management logic, realistic challenges and approach optimization of the health program for poverty alleviation. *Journal of Northwest University (Philosophy and Social Sciences Edition), 48*(3), 56–63.
25. Guidelines on Implementing the Health Program for Poverty Alleviation [EB/OL], June 21, 2016. http://www.gov.cn/xinwen/2016-06/21/content_5084195.htm
26. The Health Program for Poverty Alleviation: Effective Outcomes in Rural Medical Services and Staffing [EB/OL], May 27, 2020. http://health.people.com.cn/n1/2020/0527/c14739-31726051.html
27. Literature Research Office of the CPC Central Committee. (2018). *Selected literature since the 18th CPC National Congress (II)* (pp. 40–43). Central Party Literature Publishing House.
28. Huang, S. (2018). Giving full play to the role of civil affairs departments in the battle against extreme poverty. *People's Daily,* January 18, 2018.
29. Xi, J. (2020). Speech at the symposium on decisive battle and victory in poverty alleviation. *People's Daily*, March 7, 2020.
30. Ministry of Civil Affairs and Five Other Departments. (2016). Guidelines for effective dovetailing of the rural subsistence allowances framework with poverty alleviation policies [EB/OL], September 27, 2016. http://www.Xinhuanet.com/politics/2016-09-27/c_129302207.htm
31. Piming, G., & Pihong, G. (2017). Social security for targeted poverty alleviation. *Journal of Yunnan Minzu University (Philosophy and Social Sciences Edition), 34*(6), 89–96.
32. Wei, Z. (2019). Mechanism of social security for poverty alleviation. *People's Forum, 7*, 64–65.
33. Going All out to Promote Social Assistance in Poverty Alleviation [EB/OL], May 1, 2020. http://www.qstheory/cn/dukan/qs/2020-05/01/C_1125923915.htm
34. Xi, J. (2015). Notes on "The Proposal of the CPC Central Committee on Formulating the 13th Five-Year Plan for National Economic and Social Development" [N]. *People's Daily*, November 4, 2015.
35. Wang, S., & Liu, W. (2016). "Targeted efforts in six areas" as the essential requirement of targeted poverty alleviation: An analysis of Xi Jinping's Theory on Poverty Alleviation. *Studies on Mao Zedong and Deng Xiaoping Theories, 2016*(1), 40–43, 93.
36. Xi, J. (2012). Serving and delivering for Chinese People: speech made as Xi leads top leadership to meet press. *People's Forum, 33*, 6–7.
37. Xi Jinping's Speech at the Symposium on Poverty Alleviation in Destitute Areas (2017). *Party Building, 9*, 4–9.
38. Wang, Q., & Wang, P. (2016). On establishing a mechanism to accurately identify poverty. *Theoretical Guide, 6*, 62–63.
39. Xi, J. (2017). Secure a decisive victory in building a moderately prosperous society in all respects and strive for the great success of socialism with Chinese characteristics for a new era. *People's Daily*, October 28, 2017.
40. Xi, J. (2018). Speech at the symposium on deepening the development of the Yangtze River economic belt. *People's Daily*, June 4, 2018.
41. State Development and Investment Corporation (SDIC) Chuangyi Industry Fund Management Co. LTD., China Anti-Poverty Research Institute, Renmin University of China. (2019). Evaluation models of poverty alleviation and social benefits of fund investment enterprises.
42. The State Council. (2016). Circular on the plan on poverty alleviation during the 13th Five-Year Plan Period (EB/OL), December 2, 2016. http://www.gov.cn/zhengce/content/2016-12/02/content_5142197.htm
43. Qiu, X. (2016). Promoting employment transfer of poor rural people. *Administration Reform, 7*(7), 11–15.
44. *Circular on the Issuance of the Work Plan for Poverty Alleviation through Eco-Conservation* [EB/OL], January 26, 2018. http://www.cpad.gov.cn/art/2018/1/26/art_46_77286.html
45. Xi, J. (2015). *Be a rural CPC official like Jiao Yulu.* Central Party Literature Publishing House.

46. Ministry of Education and Five Other Departments. (2016). Circulation on the plan of poverty alleviation through education during the 13th Five-Year Plan Period [EB/OL], December 26, 2016. http://www.gov.cn/xinwen/2016-12/29/content_5154106.htm
47. Ministry of Civil Affairs and the State Council Poverty Alleviation Office. (2020). Circular on the issuance of action plan for poverty alleviation through social security [EB/OL], April 1, 2020. http://www.gov.cn/zhengce/zhengceku/2020-04/01/content_5497899.htm

Chapter 5
Outcomes of Poverty Alleviation and Targeted Measures

Targeted poverty alleviation is a milestone innovation in the world history of poverty alleviation. The practice has delivered successful outcomes in lifting the poor population and counties out of poverty, through policies for targeted individuals and households and mobilizing resources to accomplish major tasks. In the process, it has also had a positive impact on social development and administrative management. In addition, China has achieved the United Nations Sustainable Development Goals ten years ahead of schedule through its poverty alleviation efforts, providing Chinese approaches to address poverty for the world.

5.1 Remarkable Reduction of Poverty

5.1.1 Notable Poverty Reduction Results

Thanks to a number of poverty alleviation measures, China has achieved remarkable results in poverty reduction. The number of people living in poverty has been greatly reduced, with much lowered incidence of poverty and most of the poverty-stricken counties removing the "poverty" label that had been attached to them for a long time.

Measured by the current rural standard, the number of poor people decreased from 98.99 million at the end of 2012 to 5.51 million at the end of 2019, with more than 10 million people being lifted out of poverty for seven consecutive years. Only 3.23 million rural people remained poor in the western region,[1] 1.81 million in the

[1] The western region covers 12 provinces (autonomous regions and municipalities directly under the central government), including Inner Mongolia, Guangxi, Chongqing, Sichuan, Guizhou, Yunnan, Tibet, Shaanxi, Gansu, Qinghai, Ningxia and Xinjiang.

S. Wang, *Poverty Alleviation and Targeted Measures*,
https://doi.org/10.1007/978-981-96-1493-6_5

central region,[2] and 470,000 in the eastern region.[3] In terms of poverty incidence, by the end of 2019, the rate had dropped from 10.2 to 0.6%, and in the central and western China, it had dropped below 2.2%. Among them, the poverty incidence in 7 provinces (autonomous regions and municipalities directly under the central government) was between 1% and 2.2%, and that in 7 provinces (autonomous regions) was between 0.5% and 1%. With regard to impoverished counties, by the end of July 2020, China's 832 poor counties in 14 provinces (autonomous regions and municipalities) of Hebei, Anhui, Shanxi, Inner Mongolia, Jilin, Heilongjiang, Henan, Hunan, Hainan, Chongqing, Tibet, Shaanxi, Hubei and Qinghai had removed their "poverty" label, accounting for more than 93%. In the remaining seven provinces (autonomous regions), namely, Guangxi, Sichuan, Guizhou, Yunnan, Gansu, Ningxia and Xinjiang, 52 poverty-stricken counties would be lifted out of poverty through 2020.

5.1.2 Boosting the Economic and Social Development of Poor Areas

Poverty alleviation in poor areas has been oriented to the overall economic and social development, which has brought about a brand new look to them. Through creating new economic activities, offering employment support and other measures, local competitive industries have been cultivated and developed, and new forms of business have been emerging, such as e-commerce, projects integrating agriculture with Photovoltage (PV), and with tourism. New support measures such as asset returns and public welfare jobs for poverty alleviation are widely practiced, with a significant increase of operating income and wage income for the rural poor. The internal drivers of growth and the vitality of development grew markedly, with the improvement of the long-term mechanism for stable poverty elimination. The awareness and ability of the poor to participate in market competition have been greatly developed, with their capacity for sustainable development constantly enhancing. With upgraded infrastructure and public service facilities, people in poor areas have better working and living conditions, smoother information flow, better medical care and education. Their practical capacity has been significantly enhanced with better quality of life.

[2] The central region covers 8 provinces of Shanxi, Jilin, Heilongjiang, Anhui, Jiangxi, Henan, Hubei and Hunan.

[3] The eastern region covers 11 provinces (cities), including Beijing, Tianjin, Hebei, Liaoning, Shanghai, Jiangsu, Zhejiang, Fujian, Shandong, Guangdong and Hainan.

5.1.3 *Synergies Created by Joint Efforts from All Sectors of Society*

One of the notable achievements of poverty alleviation is the formation of an all-encompassing campaign against poverty, in which government-sponsored projects, sector-specific programs and corporate and societal assistance are integrated to create synergies. It has inspired and mobilized the government, social organizations and enterprises to participate and work together to fight against extreme poverty. Among them, the east–west collaboration in poverty alleviation, namely, the practice of pairing developed provinces and municipalities in the east with impoverished regions in the west, has been conducive to narrowing the regional gap of development. The flow of human and other resources and management ideas from the eastern region to the central and western regions has promoted their development. At the same time, the central and western regions also have provided the eastern region with labor forces, raw materials and other resources necessary for its economic development, greatly promoting coordinated regional development. The practice of paired-up assistance for poverty alleviation has unblocked channels between the CPC and government departments and poor areas, helping officials better aware of the actual situation at the grassroots level, and improving their work style and the way of selecting and promoting right people for leading posts. The central enterprises have been paired up with poor counties to provide assistance to the latter. By making good use of their own resources, these enterprises have introduced measures from different aspects to support poor areas to boost their development. The joint efforts from all sectors of society to eradicate poverty have carried forward the fine tradition of the Chinese nation of helping people in need and helping each other, which is one of the core socialist values.

5.1.4 *Generating Far-Reaching Political Impact*

There has been political impact on the county level. While the governments at all levels have invested huge funds to poverty alleviation, the central government has required that they should be earmarked for poverty alleviation projects, and the public must participate in their use and management, by being well informed, so that villagers can fully play their principal role. These have greatly enhanced the transparency of selection, implementation and supervision of poverty alleviation projects, which has upgraded the capacity of county-level governments to manage projects and funds more effectively.

The impact on governance capacity at the grassroots level has also been notable. Under the mechanism of resident work teams in poor villages, the CPC and the government have dispatched more than 3 million officials from different sectors to serve as first Party secretaries and resident work team members in poor villages. They lived and worked together with local people. Through identification of poor people, targeted assistance and poverty exit, they may have had better understanding of grassroots work and rural people as they were in a better position to learn about their life and needs. This has helped improve their work style and enhance their ability to work for the people and address complex problems. The experience may have even prepared them to become valuable human resources for the governance of their country. Through the "injection of fresh blood", the organizational cohesion and effectiveness of grassroots organizations in rural areas have been significantly enhanced, with the improvement of their governance capacity and management, and of the relationship between officials and rural residents.

5.2 Impacts on Regional Development

5.2.1 Impacts on Poor Areas

5.2.1.1 Significant Reduction of the Number of People Living in Poverty

Since the 18th CPC National Congress, the Central Committee with Xi Jinping as its core has mobilized the entire society to wage the final battle against extreme poverty, making decisive progress and achieving remarkable results. On the whole, according to the current poverty standard, the number of rural poor has decreased from 98.99 million at the end of 2012 to 5.51 million at the end of 2019, a cumulative reduction of 93.48 million, or an average annual decrease of 51%. For seven consecutive years, more than 10 million people have been lifted out of poverty every year, and the poverty incidence has dropped from 10.2 to 0.6%. This has changed the previous dilemma of smaller number of people being lifted out of poverty year by year after the implementation of the new standard. The bottleneck in the previous two rounds of poverty reduction was broken in which no more poor people emerged out of poverty when the number dropped to around 30 million. More than 93% of the country's 832 impoverished counties have announced their emergence from poverty, and the misconduct of keeping the label in order to continue accessing preferential treatment has been effectively prevented.

In terms of poor areas,[4] based on the current poverty standard, the number of rural people living in poverty was 3.62 million at the end of 2019, 56.73 million less than at the end of 2012, representing an annual decline of 21.44 percent. The incidence of poverty dropped from 24.4% at the end of 2012 to 1.4% at the end of 2019, a decrease of 23%. Among them, the number of people living in poverty dropped the most in 2013, reaching 9.69 million, with remarkable results in poverty reduction, which significantly alleviated overall regional poverty (see Table 5.1).

[4] Poverty-stricken areas cover contiguous poverty-stricken areas and key counties on the state's poverty alleviation work list. In 2017, seven cities and counties in Aksu Prefecture, Xinjiang Uygur Autonomous Region, which have enjoyed the preferential policy, were also included in the monitoring.

Table 5.1 Poverty population and incidence in poor rural areas, 2012 to end of 2019

Indicators	2012	2013	2014	2015	2016	2017	2018	2019
Population in poverty (10,000)	6039	5070	4317	3490	2654	1900	1115	362
Incidence of poverty (%)	24.4	20.0	17.1	13.9	10.5	7.4	4.2	1.4

Source Based on China Rural Poverty Monitoring Report 2019, The General Monitoring Report on Poverty Alleviation in Contiguous Destitute Areas (2019)

Table 5.2 Growth in per capita income and consumption of rural residents in poor areas, 2012–2019

Indicators	2013	2014	2015	2016	2017	2018	2019
Per capita income (RMB)	6079	6852	7653	8452	9377	10,371	11,567
Nominal growth (%)	16.6	12.7	11.7	10.4	10.5	10.6	11.5
Actual growth (%)	13.4	10.7	10.3	8.4	9.1	8.3	8.0
Per capita consumption expenditure (RMB)	5,404	6,007	6,656	7,331	7,998	8,956	10,011
Nominal growth (%)	14.9	11.2	10.8	10.1	9.2	12.0	11.8
Actual growth (%)	11.8	9.2	9.4	8.1	7.8	9.7	8.3

Source Based on China Rural Poverty Monitoring Report 2019, The General Monitoring Report on Poverty Alleviation in Contiguous Destitute Areas (2019)

5.2.1.2 Fast Growth of Per Capita Disposable Income and Consumption

The per capita disposable income of rural residents in poor areas was RMB 6079 in 2013 and increased to RMB 11,567 in 2019, 1.90 times that of 2013. The growth in 2013 was the fastest, with the actual rate reaching 13.4%. The living conditions of the rural poor have improved significantly and the per capita consumption expenditure of permanent rural residents was RMB 5404 in 2013 and increased to RMB 10,011 in 2019, 1.85 times that of 2013. The growth in 2013 was the fastest, with the actual rate reaching 11.8%. The living standard of people in poor areas has been significantly improved (see Table 5.2).

5.2.1.3 Marked Improvement in Infrastructure and Public Services

Poverty-stricken areas have seen significant increase of investment in infrastructure and public services, which has significantly enhanced their development capacity.

In terms of infrastructure, from 2013 to 2019, the proportion of rural households with access to highways and telephone connections in their natural villages increased respectively from 97.8% to 100% and from 98.3% to 100%. Cable TV signals, paved main roads and buses have been available to more households in their natural villages, with the proportions increasing respectively by 19.5 percentage points from 79.6% to 99.1%; 10.6 percentage points from 88.9% to 99.5%; and 20.4 percentage points from 56.1% to 76.5%. The significant improvement of rural infrastructure has laid a solid foundation for the industrial development of village collectives and poor people.

In terms of public services, the proportion of rural households with broadband access in their natural villages rose from 71.8% in 2015 to 97.3% in 2019, an increase of 25.5 percentage points. From 2013 to 2018, more rural households in their natural villages had access to central treatment of garbage, health stations, kindergartens and primary schools, with the proportions rising respectively from 29.9% to 86.4%, 84.4% to 96.1%, 71.4% to 89.8% and 79.8% to 91.9%, which were respectively an increase of 56.5 percentage points, 11.7 percentage points, 18.4 percentage points and 12.1 percentage points (see Table 5.3).

For healthcare, the number of ward beds in medical and health institutions increased from 860,000 to 1.21 million from 2013 to 2017. The number of social welfare organizations increased from 9372 to 10,169, with their number of ward beds rising from 690,000 to 800,000 (see Table 5.4). Notable progress has been made in communications, education, medical care and environmental protection in poor villages, which has basically guaranteed the conditions for poor people to participate in poverty alleviation projects, with their capacity effectively enhanced.

Table 5.3 rural infrastructure and public services in poor areas, 2013–2019 (Unit: %)

Indicators	2013	2014	2015	2016	2017	2018	2019
Proportion of households with access to highways to their villages	97.8	99.1	99.7	99.8	99.9	100	100
Proportion of households with access to telephone connections in their villages	98.3	99.2	99.7	99.9	99.8	99.9	100
Proportion of households with access to cable TV signals in their villages	79.6	88.7	92.2	94.2	96.9	98.3	99.1
Proportion of households with access to paved main roads to their villages	88.9	90.8	94.1	96.0	97.6	98.3	99.5
Proportion of households with access tp bus service in their villages	56.1	58.5	60.9	63.9	67.5	71.6	76.5
Proportion of households with access to broadband in their villages	–	–	71.8	79.8	87.4	94.4	97.3
Proportion of households with access to central treatment of garbage in their villages	29.9	35.2	43.3	50.9	61.4	78.9	86.4
Proportion of households with access to health stations in their villages	84.4	86.8	90.4	91.4	92.2	93.2	96.1
Proportion of households with access to kindergartens in their villages	71.4	74.5	76.1	79.7	84.7	87.1	89.8
Proportion of households with access to primary schools in their villages	79.8	81.2	81.7	84.9	88.0	89.8	91.9

Source Based on China Rural Poverty Monitoring Report 2019, The General Monitoring Report on Poverty Alleviation in Contiguous Destitute Areas (2019)

Table 5.4 Medical care in poor areas, 2013–2017

Indicators	2013	2014	2015	2016	2017
Number of ward beds in medical and health institutions (10,000)	86	96	104	111	121
Number of social welfare organizations	9372	10,202	10,421	10,314	10,169
Number of ward beds in various social welfare organizations (10,000)	69	78	81	82	80

Source Based on China Rural Poverty Monitoring Report 2019, The General Monitoring Report on Poverty Alleviation in Contiguous Destitute Areas (2019)

In terms of working and living conditions, the overall situation for the rural poor has been turning for the better. From 2013 to 2019, the proportion of rural households living in thatched huts decreased from 7.0 to 1.2%, a drop of 5.8 percentage points. More poor villagers have access to safe and adequate supply of cleaner piped water, purified tap water and drinking water, with the proportions rising respectively by 35.9 percentage points from 53.6% to 89.5%; 30.3 percentage points from 30.6% to 60.9%; and 14.9 percentage points from 81.0% to 95.9%. The proportion of rural households using private toilets increased from 92.7 to 96.6%, an increase of 3.9 percentage points. There had been fewer villagers using firewood for cooking, with the proportion dropping by 23.8 percentage points from 58.6 to 34.8% (see Table 5.5). Domestic pollution has been effectively controlled.

Table 5.5 Production and living conditions of rural households in poor areas, 2013–2019 (Unit: %)

Indicators	2013	2014	2015	2016	2017	2018	2019
Proportion of households living in thatched huts	7.0	6.6	5.7	4.5	4.1	1.9	1.2
Proportion of households with access to piped water	53.6	55.9	61.5	67.4	70.1	79.8	89.5
Proportion of households with access to purified tap water	30.6	33.1	36.4	40.8	43.7	56.4	60.9
Proportion of households with access to drinking water	81.0	82.3	85.3	87.9	89.2	93.6	95.9
Proportion of households with private toilets	92.7	93.1	93.6	94.2	94.5	95.9	96.6
Proportion of households that use firewood for cooking	58.6	57.8	54.9	51.4	49.7	39.2	34.8

Source Based on China Rural Poverty Monitoring Report 2019, The General Monitoring Report on Poverty Alleviation in Contiguous Destitute Areas (2019)

5.2.2 Impacts on Contiguous Destitute Areas

In December 2011, the CPC Central Committee and the State Council issued the Outline for Development-Driven Poverty Alleviation in Rural Areas (2011–2020), making it clear that contiguously poor areas would be the major targets for poverty alleviation, with all provinces (autonomous regions and municipalities directly under the Central Government) taking overall responsibility under their jurisdiction.

Under the guidance of the CPC and the government, plans for poverty alleviation and development programs have been formulated and implemented on a county-level basis. In line with the principle of "overall and coordinated planning on the national basis with focus on contiguous destitute and key areas" stipulated in the outline, and based on the indicators that are highly correlated with the level of poverty, such as per capita GDP, per capita general budget revenue of county finance and per capita net income of rural residents at the county level, and taking into account the requirements of increasing support to old revolutionary base areas, areas with large ethnic minority populations and border areas, fourteen contiguous poor areas were identified. They were Liupanshan Mountainous area, Qining-Daba Mountainous area, Wuling Mountainous area, Wumeng Mountainous area, Yunnan-Guangxi-Guizhou rocky desertification mountainous area, western Yunnan border mountainous area, southern foothill mountainous area of the Greater Hinggan Mountains, Yanshan-Taihang Mountainous area, Lyuliang Mountainous area, Dabie Mountainous area, Luoxiao Mountainous area, Tibet, areas with large Tibetan populations in Qinghai, Sichuan Yunnan and Gansu, and the four prefectures in southern Xinjiang,[5] involving a total of 680 counties. The progress of these contiguous destitute areas has well reflected the impact of poverty alleviation on regional development.

5.2.2.1 Significant Reduction of the Number of Rural Impoverished Residents

In general, according to the national standard of rural poverty (RMB 2,300 per person per year, at constant prices in 2010), the number of rural residents living in poverty in contiguous poor areas was 3.13 million in 2019, 47.54 million fewer than in 2012, or a decline of 93.66%. The incidence of poverty dropped from 24.4% in 2012 to 0.6% in 2019. This is a decrease of 23.8 percentage points, indicating a significant reduction in poverty (see Table 5.6 and Fig. 5.1).

In terms of the poverty population in the contiguous destitute areas, the reduction of poverty population from 2011 to 2019 varied by places, with an average decrease

[5] Three prefectures in southern Xinjiang Uygur Autonomous Region were mentioned in the Outline for Development-Driven Poverty Alleviation in Rural Areas (2011–2020). In 2017, seven counties in Aksu Prefecture, Xinjiang Uygur Autonomous Region, which have access to the preferential policy, were also included in the monitoring to become the fourth. In the following tables and figures, the data before 2017 is for the three prefectures in southern Xinjiang Uygur Autonomous Region, and the data in and after 2017 are for the four prefectures.

Table 5.6 Rural poor population and poverty incidence in all contiguous poor areas, 2012–2019

Indicators	2012	2013	2014	2015	2016	2017	2018	2019
Population in poverty (10,000)	5067	4141	3518	2875	2182	1540	935	313
Incidence of poverty (%)	24.4	20.0	17.1	13.9	10.5	7.4	4.5	0.6

Source Based on China Rural Poverty Monitoring Report 2019, The General Monitoring Report on Poverty Alleviation in Contiguous Destitute Areas (2019)

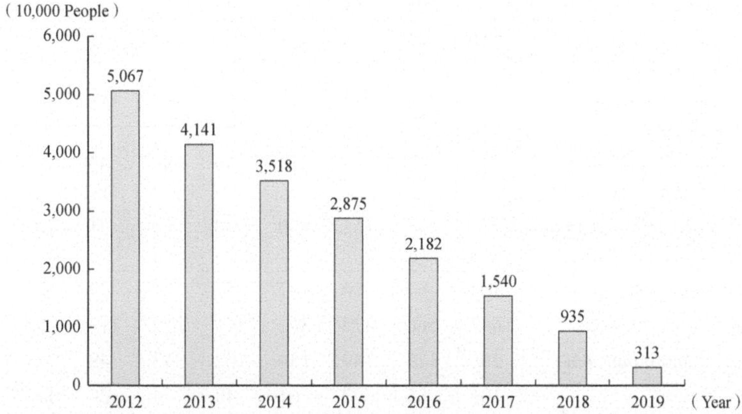

Fig. 5.1 Rural poor population in all contiguous poor areas

of 94. 81%. Among them, the reduction rate was the highest in the southern foothill area of the Greater Hinggan Mountains, up to 96.90%, and the lowest in the four prefectures of southern Xinjiang, which was 92.45%. Nine out of the 14 contiguous poor areas saw a greater reduction in poverty than the average, and they were Qinling-Daba mountainous area (96.69%), Yunnan-Guangxi-Guizhou rocky desertification area (95.59%), southern foothill area of the Greater Hinggan Mountains (96.90%), Yanshan-Taihang mountainous area (95.07%), Lyuliang mountainous area (95.19%), Dabie mountainous area (95.05%), Luoxiao mountainous area (95.63%), Tibet (96.23%), Tibetan-inhabited areas in Qinghai, Sichuan, Yunnan and Gansu (95.15%), in addition to Wumeng mountainous area (94.64%) which saw a decrease higher than the national average. With regard to the poverty incidence in these areas, Tibet had the highest decrease of 45.3 percentage points, while Dabie mountainous area had the lowest decrease of only 21.7 percentage points (see Tables 5.7 and 5.8).

5.2.2.2 Fast Growth of Per Capita Disposable Income and Consumption Expenditure of Permanent Rural Residents

On the whole, the per capita disposable income of rural residents grew rapidly, with the fastest growth rate reaching 15.4% in 2013, when the per capita disposable income

Table 5.7 Poverty population in different contiguous poor areas, 2011–2019 (Unit: 10,000 People)

Contiguous poor areas	2011	2012	2013	2014	2015	2016	2017	2018	2019
All contiguous poor areas	6035	5067	4141	3518	2875	2182	1540	935	313
Liupan mountainous poor area	642	532	439	349	280	215	152	96	45
Qinling-Daba mountainous area	815	684	559	444	346	256	172	101	27
Wuling mountainous area	793	671	543	475	379	285	188	111	49
Wumeng mountainous area	765	664	507	442	373	272	199	124	41
Yunnan-Guangxi-Guizhou rocky desertification area	816	685	574	488	398	312	221	140	36
Western Yunnan border mountainous area	424	335	274	240	192	152	115	72	28
Southern foothill area of the Greater Hinggan Mountains	129	108	85	74	59	46	35	19	4
Yanshan-Taihang mountainous area	223	192	165	150	122	99	71	40	11
Lyuliang mountainous area	104	87	76	67	57	47	29	16	5
Dabie mountainous area	647	566	477	392	341	252	173	99	32
Luoxiao mountainous area	206	175	149	134	102	73	49	31	9
Tibet	106	85	72	61	48	34	20	13	4
Tibetan-inhabited areas in Qinghai, Sichuan, Yunnan and Gansu	206	161	117	103	88	68	51	30	10
Four prefectures of southern Xinjiang	159	122	104	99	90	73	64	42	12

Source Based on China Rural Poverty Monitoring Report 2019, The General Monitoring Report on Poverty Alleviation in Contiguous Destitute Areas (2019)

of all rural residents in the contiguous destitute areas was RMB5956. It increased to RMB 11,443 in 2019, 1.72 times of that in 2013. With an annual growth rate of more than 10%, the income level has increased significantly (see Table 5.9).

In terms of different contiguous areas, the top three in per capita disposable income in 2019 were Dabie mountainous area, Tibet and four prefectures of southern Xinjiang, with RMB13,341, RMB12,951 and RMB12,009 respectively. The lowest per capita disposable income in 2019 was Liupan Mountainous area, with only RMB9370. The per capita disposable income exceeded the average level in seven contiguous areas out of the total, namely, Dabie Mountainous Area, Tibet, four prefectures of southern Xinjiang, Qinling-Daba Mountainous area, southern foothill area of the Great Hinggan Mountains, Luoxiao mountainous area and Wuling mountainous area.

Table 5.8 Incidence of rural poverty in different contiguous poor areas, 2011–2019 (Unit: %)

Contiguous poor areas	2011	2012	2013	2014	2015	2016	2017	2018	2019
Liupan mountainous area	35.0	28.9	24.1	19.2	16.2	12.4	8.8	5.6	1.5
Qinling-Daba mountainous area	27.6	23.1	19.5	16.4	12.3	9.1	6.1	3.6	2.6
Wuling mountainous area	26.3	22.3	18	16.9	12.9	9.7	6.4	3.8	1.0
Wumeng mountainous area	38.2	33.0	25.2	21.5	18.5	13.5	9.9	6.2	2.0
Yunnan-Guangxi-Guizhou rocky desertification area	31.5	26.3	21.9	18.5	15.1	11.9	8.4	5.3	1.4
Western Yunnan border mountainous area	31.6	24.8	20.5	19.1	15.5	12.2	9.3	5.8	2.3
Southern foothill area of the Greater Hinggan Mountains	24.1	21.1	16.6	14.0	11.1	8.7	6.6	3.5	0.7
Yanshan-Taihang mountainous area	24.3	20.9	17.9	16.8	13.5	11.0	7.9	4.5	1.2
Lyuliang mountainous area	30.5	24.9	21.7	19.5	16.4	13.4	8.6	4.6	1.4
Dabie mountainous area	20.7	18.2	15.2	12	10.4	7.6	5.3	3.0	1.0
Luoxiao mountainous area	22.0	18.8	15.6	14.3	10.4	7.6	5.3	3.2	1.0
Tibet	43.9	35.2	28.8	23.7	18.6	13.2	7.9	5.1	1.4
Tibetan-inhabited areas in Qinghai, Sichuan, Yunnan and Gansu	42.8	38.6	27.6	24.2	16.5	12.7	9.5	5.6	1.8
Four prefectures of southern Xinjiang	38.7	33.6	20.0	18.8	15.7	12.7	9.1	5.9	1.7

Source Based on China Rural Poverty Monitoring Report 2019, The General Monitoring Report on Poverty Alleviation in Contiguous Destitute Areas (2019)

Table 5.9 Per capita disposable income and growth rate of all contiguous poor areas, 2013–2019

Indicators	2013	2014	2015	2016	2017	2018	2019
Per capita disposable income (RMB)	5956	6742	7525	8348	9264	10,260	11,443
Growth rate (%)	15.4	12.9	11.9	10.9	10.5	10.7	11.5

Source Based on China Rural Poverty Monitoring Report 2019, The General Monitoring Report on Poverty Alleviation in Contiguous Destitute Areas (2019)

From 2013 to 2019, the per capita disposable income of all contiguous areas increased by 92.13%, with the highest growth rate of 110.98% in the four prefectures of southern Xinjiang and the lowest growth rate of 85.27% in Dabie mountainous area. The four prefectures in southern Xinjiang (110.98%), Tibetan-inhabited areas in Qinghai, Sichuan, Yunnan and Gansu (110.76%), Wumeng mountainous area (103.97%), Tibet (97.63%), Luoxiao mountainous area (96.19%) and Lyuliang mountainous area (94.50%) increased more than the average of all contiguous areas.

The fastest growth rate was in 2013 or 2014, and the specific growth rate varied greatly among different areas (see Tables 5.10 and 5.11).

In general, the per capita consumption expenditure of rural residents in all contiguous areas grew rapidly, with the fastest rate reaching 14.2% in 2013, when the per capita disposable income of rural residents in all the contiguous areas was RMB5327. It increased to RMB9898 in 2019, 1.86 times that in 2013, with an annual growth rate of around 10% and a significant improvement in consumption (see Table 5.12).

In terms of different contiguous areas, the top three in per capita consumption expenditure in 2019 were Dabie mountainous area, Wuling mountainous area and Qinling-Daba mountainous area, with RMB11,393, RMB11,079 and RMB10,568 respectively. The lowest per capita consumption expenditure in 2019 was only RMB8138 in the four prefectures of southern Xinjiang. There were five areas where the per capita consumption expenditure exceeded the average of all contiguous areas, namely, Dabie mountainous area, Wuling mountainous area, Qinling-Daba mountainous area, Luoxiao mountainous area and the southern foothill area of the Greater Hinggan Mountains. From 2013 to 2019, the per capita consumption expenditure in all contiguous areas increased by 85. 81%, with the highest growth rate of 105.22% in Tibet and the lowest growth rate of 51.72% in Lyuliang mountainous area. Eight out of all areas saw bigger increases than the average, including Tibet (105.22%), Tibetan-inhabited areas in Qinghai, Sichuan, Yunnan and Gansu (98.44%), western Yunnan border mountainous area (96.53%), southern foothill area of the Greater Hinggan Mountains (94.49%), Wuling mountainous area (94.33%), Wumeng mountainous area (90.48%), Dabie mountainous area (86.56%) and Yunnan-Guangxi-Guizhou rocky desertification mountainous area (86.21%). The fastest growth rate of per capita consumption expenditure in most contiguous areas was in 2013, and the specific growth rate varied greatly among areas (see Tables 5.13 and 5.14).

5.2.2.3 Steady Improvement and Growth of Production and Living Conditions and Consumption of Durable Goods

The working and living conditions in contiguous poverty-stricken areas have steadily improved. The proportion of rural households living in thatched huts dropped from 7.5% in 2013 to 1.3% in 2019, down 6.2 percentage points. More poor rural residents have access to safe and adequate supply of cleaner piped water, purified tap water and drinking water, with the proportions increasing respectively by 37.3 percentage points from 53.6% in 2013 to 90.9% in 2019; by 28.9 percentage points from 29.3% in 2013 to 58.2% in 2019; and by 16.1 percentage points from 80.0% in 2013 to 96.1% in 2019. The proportion of rural households using private toilets rose from 92.0% in 2013 to 96.5% in 2019, an increase of 4.5 percentage points. There had been fewer villagers using firewood for cooking, with the proportion dropping by 23.9 percentage points from 59.6% in 2013 to 35.7% in 2019.

The consumption of durable goods in contiguous poverty-stricken areas increased year by year, with the car ownerships per 100 households rising from 5.3 in 2013

Table 5.10 Per capita disposable income of contiguous poor areas, 2013–2019 (Unit: RMB)

Contiguous poor areas	2013	2014	2015	2016	2017	2018	2019
All contiguous poor areas	5956	6724	7525	8348	9264	10,260	11,443
Liupan mountainous poor area	4930	5616	6371	6915	7593	8429	9370
Qinling-Daba mountainous area	6219	7055	7967	8769	9721	10,751	11,934
Wuling mountainous area	6084	6743	7579	8504	9384	10,397	11,544
Wumeng mountainous area	5238	6114	6992	7994	8776	9650	10,684
Yunnan-Guangxi-Guizhou rocky desertification area	5907	6640	7485	8212	9109	10,073	11,262
Western Yunnan border mountainous area	5775	6471	6943	7754	8629	9560	10,931
Southern foothill area of the Greater Hinggan Mountains	6244	6801	7484	8399	9346	10,721	11,876
Yanshan-Taihang mountainous area	5680	6260	7164	7906	8593	9701	10,797
Lyuliang mountainous area	5259	5589	6317	6884	7782	8890	10,229
Dabie mountainous area	7201	8241	9029	9804	10,776	11,974	13,341
Luoxiao mountainous area	5987	6776	7700	8579	9598	10,637	11,746
Tibet	6553	7359	8244	9094	10,330	11,450	12,951
Tibetan-inhabited areas in Qinghai, Sichuan, Yunnan and Gansu	4962	5726	6457	7288	8018	9160	10,458
Four prefectures of southern Xinjiang	5692	6403	7053	7868	9845	10,762	12,009

Source Based on China Rural Poverty Monitoring Report 2019, The General Monitoring Report on Poverty Alleviation in Contiguous Destitute Areas (2019)

Table 5.11 Growth rate of per capita disposable income of each contiguous poor area, 2013–2019 (Unit: RMB)

Contiguous poor areas	2013	2014	2015	2016	2017	2018	2019
All contiguous poor areas	15.4	12.9	11.9	10.9	10.5	10.7	11.5
Liupan mountainous poor area	11.8	13.9	13.4	8.5	9.8	11.0	11.2
Qinling-Daba mountainous area	15.9	13.4	12.9	10.1	10.8	10.6	11.0
Wuling mountainous area	21.0	10.8	12.4	12.2	10.3	10.8	11.0
Wumeng mountainous area	13.5	16.7	14.4	14.3	9.8	10.0	10.7
Yunnan-Guangxi-Guizhou rocky desertification area	15.3	12.4	12.7	9.7	10.9	10.6	11.8
Western Yunnan border mountainous area	18.4	12.1	7.3	11.7	11.3	10.8	14.3
Southern foothill area of the Greater Hinggan Mountains	15.1	8.9	10.0	12.2	11.3	14.7	10.8
Yanshan-Taihang mountainous area	14.2	10.2	14.4	10.4	8.7	12.9	11.3
Lyuliang mountainous area	14.5	6.3	13.0	9.0	13.1	14.2	15.1
Dabie mountainous area	14.9	14.4	9.6	8.6	9.9	11.1	11.4
Luoxiao mountainous area	12.2	13.2	13.6	11.4	11.9	10.8	10.4
Tibet	15.0	12.3	12.0	10.3	13.6	10.8	13.1
Tibetan-inhabited areas in Qinghai, Sichuan, Yunnan and Gansu provinces	12.9	15.4	12.8	12.9	10.0	14.3	14.2
Four prefectures of southern Xinjiang	14.5	12.5	10.2	11.6	9.7	9.3	11.6

Sources Based on China Rural Poverty Monitoring Report 2019, The General Monitoring Report on Poverty Alleviation in Contiguous Destitute Areas (2019)

Table 5.12 Per capita consumption expenditure and growth rate in all contiguous areas, 2013–2019

Indicators	2013	2014	2015	2016	2017	2018	2019
Per capita consumption expenditure (RMB)	5327	5898	6573	7273	7915	8854	9898
Growth rate (%)	14.2	10.7	11.4	10.7	9.0	11.9	11.8

Source Based on China Rural Poverty Monitoring Report 2019, The General Monitoring Report on Poverty Alleviation in Contiguous Destitute Areas (2019)

to 19.6 in 2019, an increase of 14.3 percentage points. The number of washing machines, refrigerators, mobile phones and personal computers owned by every 100 households rose respectively by 25.7 from 65.1 in 2013 to 90.8 in 2019; by 39.2 from 52.3 in 2013 to 91.5 in 2019; by 96.7 from 175.3 in 2013 to 272 in 2019; and by 8.8 from 7.7 in 2013 to 16.5 in 2019 (see Table 5.15).

Table 5.13 Per capita consumption in contiguous poor areas, 2013–2019 (Unit: RMB)

Contiguous poor areas	2013	2014	2015	2016	2017	2018	2019
All contiguous poor areas	5,327	5,898	6,573	7,273	7,915	8,854	9,898
Liupan mountainous poor area	4,677	5,362	5,875	6,395	6,884	7,623	8,446
Qinling-Daba mountainous area	5,739	6,229	7,057	7,678	8,450	9,421	10,568
Wuling mountainous area	5,701	6,353	6,994	7,832	8,721	10,192	11,079
Wumeng mountainous area	4,718	5,298	6,077	6,795	7,659	8,053	8,987
Yunnan-Guangxi-Guizhou rocky desertification area	5,186	5,788	6,508	7,284	7,730	8,712	9,657
Western Yunnan border mountainous area	4,547	5,131	5,848	6,385	6,706	7,844	8,936
Southern foothill area of the Greater Hinggan Mountains	5,191	5,958	6,373	7,208	7,492	8,396	10,096
Yanshan-Taihang mountainous area	5,895	6,181	6,538	6,875	7,572	8,540	9,696
Lyuliang mountainous area	5,537	5,315	5,800	6,178	6,637	7,528	8,401
Dabie mountainous area	6,107	6,799	7,631	8,518	9,309	10,169	11,393
Luoxiao mountainous area	5,510	6,140	6,909	7,642	8,470	9,087	10,123
Tibet	4,102	4,822	5,580	6,070	6,691	7,452	8,418
Tibetan-inhabited areas in Qinghai, Sichuan, Yunnan and Gansu	4,691	5,010	5,437	6,186	6,586	8,246	9,309
Four prefectures of southern Xinjiang	4,803	5,033	5,207	5,512	5,999	6,942	8,138

Source Based on China Rural Poverty Monitoring Report 2019, The General Monitoring Report on Poverty Alleviation in Contiguous Destitute Areas (2019)

5.2.2.4 Steady Improvement of Rural Infrastructure and Public Services

Rural infrastructure in contiguous impoverished areas has been steadily improved. The proportion of rural households with access to highways in their villages rose from 98.0% in 2013 to 100% in 2019, an increase of 2.0 percentage points. Telephone connections, cable TV signals, paved main roads and buses have been available to more households, with the proportions increasing respectively by 1.9 percentage points from 98.1% in 2013 to 100% in 2019; by 22.2 percentage points from 76. 8% in 2013 to 99.0% in 2019; by 11 percentage points from 88.4% in 2013 to 99.4% in 2019; and by 22.2 percentage points from53.5% in 2013 to 75.7% in 2019.

Public services have also been under steady improvement. Among others, the proportion of rural households with broadband access in their villages rose from 70.0% in 2015 to 97.2% in 2019, an increase of 27.2 percentage points. More rural households have had access to central garbage treatment, health stations, kindergartens and primary schools, with the proportions rising respectively by 54.8 percentage points from 30.3% in 2013 to 85.1% in 2019; by 12.5 percentage points from 83.6% in 2013 to 96.1% in 2019; by 19.3 percentage points from 70.8% in

Table 5.14 Growth rate of per capita consumption expenditure in each contiguous pool area, 2013–2019 (Unit: %)

Contiguous poor areas	2013	2014	2015	2016	2017	2018	2019
All contiguous poor areas	14.2	10.7	11.4	10.7	9.0	11.9	11.8
Liupan mountainous poor area	8.7	14.6	9.6	8.9	7.6	10.7	10.8
Qinling-Daba mountainous area	12.4	8.5	13.3	8.8	10	11.5	12.2
Wuling mountainous area	14.6	11.4	10.1	12	11.3	16.9	8.7
Wumeng mountainous area	17.6	12.3	14.7	11.8	12.7	5.1	11.6
Yunnan-Guangxi-Guizhou rocky desertification area	20.8	11.6	12.4	11.9	6.1	12.7	10.8
Western Yunnan border mountainous area	15.5	12.8	14	9.2	5	17.0	13.9
Southern foothill area of the Greater Hinggan Mountains	7.7	14.8	7.0	13.1	3.9	12.1	20.2
Yanshan-Taihang mountainous area	9.0	4.9	5.8	5.2	10.1	12.8	13.5
Lyuliang mountainous area	30.6	– 4.0	9.1	6.5	7.4	13.4	11.6
Dabie mountainous area	14.9	11.3	12.2	11.6	9.3	9.2	12.0
Luoxiao mountainous area	14.5	11.4	12.5	10.6	10.8	7.3	11.4
Tibet	20.4	17.6	15.7	8.8	10.2	11.4	13.0
Tibetan-inhabited areas in Qinghai, Sichuan, Yunnan and Gansu	12.5	6.8	8.5	13.8	6.5	25.2	12.9
Four prefectures of southern Xinjiang	18.7	4.8	3.5	5.8	6.4	15.7	17.2

Source Based on China Rural Poverty Monitoring Report 2019, The General Monitoring Report on Poverty Alleviation in Contiguous Destitute Areas (2019)

2013 to 90.1% in 2019; and by 12.8 percentage points from 79.5% in 2013 to 92.3% in 2019(see Table 5.16).

5.3 Social Effects

In the fight against extreme poverty, the CPC Central Committee and the State Council have fully mobilized the initiative of people from all walks of life to establish a framework of social assistance in poverty eradication. The assistance is generally divided into three types: (1) paired-up assistance undertaken by the CPC and government departments at all levels; (2) collaboration between the east and the west; and (3) corporate involvement and assistance offered by non-profit social organizations and

Table 5.15 Production and living conditions and consumption of durable goods of villagers in contiguous poor areas, 2013–2019

Indicators	2013	2014	2015	2016	2017	2018	2019
Proportion of rural households living in thatched huts (%)	7.5	7.0	6.1	4.8	4.4	2.0	1.3
Proportion of rural households with access to piped water supply (%)	53.6	55.9	61.2	67.4	70.5	80.4	90.9
Proportion of rural households with access to purified tap water (%)	29.3	31.7	34.7	38.5	41.8	53.5	58.2
Proportion of rural households with access to drinking water (%)	80.0	80.9	84	86.9	88.6	93.6	96.1
Proportion of rural households using private toilets (%)	92.0	92.5	93	93.9	94.1	95.5	96.5
Proportion of rural households using firewood for cooking (%)	59.6	58.8	55.5	52.0	50.3	40.7	35.7
Number of cars owned by every 100 households	5.3	6.2	7.9	10.6	12.4	18.9	19.6
Number of washing machines owned by every 100 households	65.1	70.1	75.0	80.4	83.3	87.0	90.8
Number of refrigerators owned by every 100 households	52.3	58.5	65.8	73.8	77.6	86.2	91.5
Number of mobile phones owned by every 100 households	175.3	196.0	210.5	226.1	235.6	261.6	272.0
Number of personal computers owned by every 100 households	7.7	9.8	12.0	13.6	15.3	15.9	16.5

Source Based on China Rural Poverty Monitoring Report 2019, The General Monitoring Report on Poverty Alleviation in Contiguous Destitute Areas (2019)

individuals. Governments at all levels have pooled all possible forces to help impoverished areas develop economically and socially and the poor people get rid of poverty, which has generated a series of social effects.

Table 5.16 Rural infrastructure and public services in contiguous poverty-stricken areas, 2013–2019 (Unit: %)

Indicators	2013	2014	2015	2016	2017	2018	2019
Proportion of rural households with access to highways in their villages	98.0	98.9	99.7	99.8	99.9	100.0	100.0
Proportion of rural households with access to telephone connections in their villages	98.1	99.2	99.7	99.9	99.9	99.9	100.0
Proportion of rural households with access to cable TV signals	76.8	86.5	90.4	93.4	96.3	97.9	99.0
Proportion of rural households with access to paved main roads in their villages	88.4	90.1	93.7	95.6	97.3	98.0	99.4
Proportion of rural households with access to buses in their villages	53.5	55.4	58.3	61.2	65.7	70.9	75.7
Proportion of rural households with broadband access in their villages	—	—	70.0	77.4	85.6	93.8	97.2
Proportion of rural households with access to central garbage treatment in their villages	30.3	34.8	43.1	49.5	59.1	76.9	85.1
Proportion of rural households with access to health stations in their villages	83.6	86.2	89.2	90.6	91.3	92.7	96.1

(continued)

Table 5.16 (continued)

Indicators	2013	2014	2015	2016	2017	2018	2019
Proportion of rural households with access to kindergartens in their villages	70.8	74.2	75.3	79.6	84.7	86.9	90.1
Proportion of rural households with access to primary schools in their villages	79.5	81.2	81.2	85.2	88.0	90.1	92.3

Source Based on China Rural Poverty Monitoring Report 2019, The General Monitoring Report on Poverty Alleviation in Contiguous Destitute Areas (2019)

5.3.1 Narrowing the Gap Between the Rich and Poor to Maintain Social Stability

The all-encompassing poverty alleviation network has ensured that the government, society and the market work in coordination, with government-sponsored projects, sector-specific programs, and corporate and societal assistance supplementing each other. The joint efforts from all sides have created a synergy and greatly boosted the anti-poverty endeavor. Fully reflecting the CPC's aspiration to achieve common prosperity by encouraging those who become prosperous first helping those who lag behind towards a better life, these practices have helped narrow the gap of development between regions and facilitate social stability and good relationship between people. To take corporate participation for example. Companies and businesses have got themselves involved in poverty alleviation through the following four ways:

First, sizable state-owned enterprises have helped poor areas develop by undertaking paired-up assistance to designated poor areas.

Second, state-owned and private enterprises have made good use of their advantages in capital, technology, market, information and brand to absorb labor, raw materials and other resources from poor areas, and transfer human resources, capital and advanced management ideas to poor areas for a win–win growth. By providing technical services, job opportunities, orders and purchases and joint development of local resources, they have helped the poor population shake off poverty.

Third, enterprises and businesses have taken an active part in public welfare undertakings, investing, donating or subsidizing programs in science and technology, education, culture, medical and health care, ecological conservation and natural resource protection in poor areas.

Fourth, enterprises under the jurisdiction of the central government have jointly set up industrial development funds for poor areas, and worked by integrating the above three ways to help rural development.

Since the beginning of the targeted campaign against poverty, potentials of corporate participation have been greatly tapped, and they have played an important role in development-driven poverty alleviation. According to the economic theory of conditional convergence, only the regions with the same structural characteristics and similar initial conditions could eventually converge to the unified steady state. Poor areas are mostly old and poor mountainous areas, with a large population and less capital per capita. However, developed areas are just the opposite, with flat terrain and convenient transportation. Therefore, poor areas and developed areas tend to be in different stable states. By calling for social enterprises and organizations to join in the fight against poverty, the redistribution of social capital could effectively improve the per capita capital in poor areas and enhance their development motivation. It could provide favorable conditions for the poor areas to achieve transcendent development, reduces the gap of regional development, and create a synergy where the whole society works together to fight against extreme poverty, which is conducive to the binding of the Chinese nation and maintaining social stability.

Case 5.1 Industrial Funds for Poverty Alleviation in Poor Areas

In response to the unified deployment of the CPC Central Committee and the State Council, Ministry of Finance, the State Investment Group and China National Tobacco Corporation jointly invested RMB 2.8 billion in December 2014 to establish the Industrial Development Fund for Poor Areas, which was China's first government-backed, market-oriented, independently operated and self-financing industrial development fund for impoverished areas. On October 17, 2016, led by the State-owned Assets Supervision and Administration Commission of the State Council, together with Ministry of Finance, 51 enterprises directly under the central government including the State Investment Group and State Grid jointly initiated the establishment of the Industrial Investment Fund for Poor Areas. The two funds have taken into account both policy objectives and market principles, and have adopted market-oriented operation to support the industrial development of poor areas to enhance their capability for independent development to get themselves out of poverty and achieve sustainable development as scheduled.

As of September 2019, three rounds of fundraising have been completed, with a total amount of RMB 31.405 billion. Since its establishment, the fund has remained true to its founding mission of serving the national poverty alleviation endeavor, with investment in projects covering 26 provinces (autonomous regions and municipalities directly under the central government), 104 municipalities (regions, prefectures and league) and 203 counties (cities, districts and banner), covering all the 14 contiguous destitute areas, where a total of 61 projects worth RMB 11.545 billion were invested, among which 15 projects worth RMB 3.677 billion were invested in the most impoverished "three regions and three prefectures".

The funds have leveraged over RMB 150 billion of private capital by building seven platforms for modern agriculture, resource development, clean energy, medical and health care, integrating production and marketing, industrial finance and capital operation. Both direct models of poverty alleviation, such as production-driven, employment-driven, asset-driven, fixed-point assistance, and public donations, and indirect models such as paying taxes to local governments, helping local infrastructure construction, and promoting industrial development, have achieved remarkable results in helping impoverished areas develop and poor people lift themselves out of poverty. In August and October 2018, Wang Yang, then member of the Standing Committee of the Political Bureau of the CPC Central Committee and Chairman of the CPPCC National Committee, and Hu Chunhua, then member of the Political Bureau of the CPC Central Committee, Vice Premier of the State Council and head of the State Council Leading Group made important instructions respectively, fully recognizing the achievements made by the two funds in serving the national poverty alleviation efforts by integrating the advantages of state-owned enterprises, pooling social capital and supporting the rural industrial development. Their contributions to poverty alleviation have been widely applauded by all sectors of society.

5.3.2 Improving Public Supervision Mechanisms to Enhance Social Governance

Social institutions and non-governmental organizations have been encouraged to participate in community governance by improving oversight mechanisms. Social assistance in poverty alleviation with third-party evaluation has been introduced. With the increasing diversification of social players, the role of market and social mechanisms has become increasingly prominent. By entrusting some social affairs to enterprises and social organizations through purchasing services and bidding, the government has given fuller play to the synergistic effect of social governance and government management. The introduction of third-party evaluation in poverty alleviation is an important part of social governance, in which the "third party" refers to an institution that neither formulates nor implements policies and is independent from the process of policy formulation and operation. The third party evaluation is by nature a more objective social supervision. The practice is to bring in diverse players to participate in government management, so that social organizations have a more vital role to play in decision-making, policy implementation, effectiveness evaluation and open oversight. This has actually reflected and enhanced the credibility of the government.

Currently, the local government has to take evaluation and supervision in two issues: one is the evaluation of the effectiveness of poverty alleviation, including the work of provincial Party committees and governments, cooperation between eastern and western regions, and the work of central departments. The evaluation has been standardized in terms of deployment, training, implementation, assessment results, notification and feedback. The assessment has covered implementation of policies, responsibilities and actual outcomes, while the assessment methods have included third-party assessment, inter-provincial cross-examination and media visits without notice. The other is the evaluation of poverty exit of counties that have been lifted out of poverty. Since 2018, the provinces have been responsible for organizing and implementing the special evaluation, with the central government carrying out random inspections. The evaluation has mostly been undertaken by third parties.

The third-party evaluation mechanism is the most systematic and rigorously independent in government performance management since China officially established its first such professional institution to carry out independent evaluation in 2004. The use of third-party assessment has helped improve the social supervision mechanism and create an atmosphere for the whole society to work together to end poverty. As an external evaluation mechanism, "third-party evaluation" is independent of the stakeholders. It is not only an important evaluation mechanism in society, but also a major form of government performance management.

It is the requirement to improve not only the social participation, but also professionalism of social governance. It is also the need of poverty alleviation and of creating new models of governance. The third-party evaluation institutions have been mainly selected from domestic universities through public bidding, which have irreplaceable advantages over other organizations. First, they are independent and objective. As academic institutions, colleges and universities do not have administrative and interest relations with provincial and county governments, so they can maintain a neutral and objective attitude in evaluation. Second, they are professional and authoritative. Most of the heads of third-party evaluation agencies were professors or well-known specialists in particular fields in China, which can ensure the authority of the evaluation.

Most of the regional and local team leaders and surveyors have master's degrees or above in related majors, with professional background and theoretical foundation, which could ensure the professionalism of the evaluation. Institutions of higher learning as implementers of the third-party evaluation could help improve the social supervision mechanism, with social forces to participate in the process to ensure solid and authentic poverty alleviation outcomes that can survive the test of time. The practice has also enriched China's experience in the third-party evaluation. A number of third-party evaluation institutions with professional people have emerged to lay a foundation for future evaluation of rural revitalization with their specialized theories and practical skills.

5.3.3 Advancing Fine Traditional Culture and Practicing Core Socialist Values

In the fight against extreme poverty, four spirits have been developed, namely, self-reliance and pioneering; staying true to the original aspiration with the courage to take responsibility; loving and helping each other; innovation and dedication to practical actions and solving tough problems. These spirits have grown out of the fine traditional culture of the Chinese nation, and reflected the core socialist values.

The fine traditional Chinese culture is the spiritual lifeblood of the Chinese nation, embodying its deepest pursuit which has provided the cultural "gene" for the efforts of poverty relief. Among them, the hard work and the winning spirit of tackling tough issues head-on against poverty have been in line with the traditional values reflected in ancient sayings like "trials and tribulations can help one achieve great things". The heroic deeds in poverty alleviation can be traced back to stories like King Yu taming the flood and Yugong the Foolish Old Man removing the mountains. Loving and helping each other is the preservation and promotion of the traditional Chinese values of "the benevolent loving others" and "Loving your elders and the elders of others; fondling your children and the children of others". The innovation and enterprising spirit in poverty relief has been the carrying forward of the traditional values of encouraging go-ahead attitude as is expressed in the ancient saying "In spite that the State of Zhou is an old establishment, it has the mission to reform and innovate".

Prosperity, democracy, civilization, harmony, freedom, equality, justice, the rule of law, love of the country, dedication, integrity and friendship constitute the core values underpinning the socialist core value system. They reflect the fundamental nature and basic characteristics of the system, and are its highly encapsulated expression. Embodying the spirit of contemporary China, the core socialist values have been shared by all Chinese people. With all sectors participating to create a social atmosphere in which people work hard and live comfortably together towards a better life, targeted poverty alleviation has been an extensive practice of those core values.

Poverty alleviation with targeted efforts aims at achieving the goal of building a modern socialist country that is prosperous, democratic, civilized and harmonious. To be prosperous is to make the country and its people prosper. Only a prosperous country can ensure national stability and peace, protect the lives and property of its people, and provide good conditions for their development. The core of democracy is that the people are the masters of the country. This position is the essence and the very core of socialist democracy, a banner the CPC has always held high, and a political guarantee for creating a better and happier life for the people. Civilization is an important manifestation of the progress of human society, an accumulation of human spirit, public order and good customs, and an important support for the great rejuvenation of the Chinese nation. Harmony is the founding philosophy of Chinese traditional culture. The belief in "Harmony as the invaluable" and "harmonious development" is not only a fine tradition of the Chinese nation, but also a vital part of building socialism with Chinese characteristics.

By launching the "Ten major projects", targeted poverty alleviation has utilized new measures and models to help poor villagers, villages and counties lift themselves out of poverty and work towards happiness and well-being. In the process of accurately identifying needy people, "top-down" and "bottom-up" approaches[6]have been

---

[6] The "top-down" approach refers to the calculation by the National Bureau of Statistics based on sample survey data of rural households. In order to prevent local governments from exaggerating the poverty situation in order to obtain more preferential resources, local governments are strictly controlled to report the number of poor people, with an allowance up to 10 percent. "Bottom-up" means that due to the lack of reliable household income and consumption data, local governments have to adopt democratic evaluation method to identify poor people instead of identifying them based on income and consumption.

taken by referring to suggestions and proposals of all parties and applying democratic evaluation methods. In targeted poverty alleviation, the implementers have taken the responsibility to help poor areas and poor people develop modern, healthy and good living habits and concepts, promote sound practices of social etiquette and healthy ways of life, and create a culturally advanced local atmosphere together with fine traditions and customs, in addition to securing villagers of adequate food and clothing, and access to basic public welfare services.

In view of the "abyss consequence" in some places in recent years, namely, the unreasonable gap between poverty-stricken households and other villagers and between poor villages and non-poor villages, caused by intentionally or inadvertently raising poverty thresholds and setting irrational standards for poverty elimination, resident work teams went to villagers' homes to explain policies to them, patiently answering the questions of non-poor households and trying their best to placate their feelings to eliminate the negative consequence and helped build a stable and harmonious rural society.

The fight against extreme poverty has helped realize a better society of "freedom, equality, justice and rule of law". Freedom means that human beings have complete control of themselves, act according to their own will and be responsible for their own behavior. It is an important part of the better life that people aspire to and a necessary condition for people to fully realize their social functions. Equality refers to the equality of all citizens before the law, which requires the continuous realization of substantive equality, including the respect and protection of human rights and the right to equal development in society. Justice, namely social equity and justice, is the legitimate value orientation of a country and a society, and also the necessary presence of the development of human civilization to the advanced stage. The rule of law is an important symbol of human entry into modern civilization and an institutional guarantee for the realization of freedom, equality, fairness and justice as well as lasting peace and stability of a country.

Amartya Sen, a famous economist, believes that individual freedom is essentially a social product. According to him, freedom must be understood in a "substantial" sense and a person's poverty could be explained from the perspective of "capabilities". That is, a person's poverty is not only material poverty, but also the poverty of "capabilities", which refers to the combination of possible functional activities that a person can achieve. The capabilities that a person should have include political freedom, economic conditions, social opportunities, transparency guarantee and protective security.

Poverty alleviation not only concerns the income of poor households and the "Two Assurances and Three Guarantees", but also focuses on the development of poor households through industrial employment to improve their capabilities to participate in the market economy freely and equally, so as to promote social justice. The campaign against poverty also helps improve the legal system. Special poverty alleviation inspections, oversight and assessment mechanisms have been established and improved, which have promoted legislation on poverty alleviation and development. All this constitutes major components of socialist rule of law.

Taking the use of poverty alleviation funds for example. The central government has issued a series of rules to regulate the use of the funds, and dispatched inspection teams to monitor and supervise. Relevant personnel would be held accountable for any illegal use of funds and the case would be transferred to judicial organs according to law. The special supervision system has effectively protected the fundamental interests of poor households.

The poverty relief campaign has helped realize the basic civic ethics of "patriotism, commitment, honesty and amity". Patriotism is not only the primary requirement for citizens, but also a code of conduct to mediate the relationship between individuals and their motherland. It is the basic quality that every Chinese citizen should have. A good sense of commitment is the value evaluation of a citizen's professional code of conduct, as well as the ethical quality required in one's work, which is highly esteemed as professionalism in the socialist society. Honesty is an ethical tradition inherited from thousands of years of human society, with emphasis on honest work, keeping promises and treating people sincerely. Amity means that citizens should respect and help each other, and be friendly and amicable. It is the basic way of life and a fine tradition of the Chinese nation.

Targeted poverty alleviation is one of the three major campaigns in the new era (the other two being forestalling and defusing major risks, and preventing and controlling pollution). The CPC and Chinese government have mobilized and pooled human, material and financial resources from all sectors to raise all impoverished population and counties out of poverty, and eliminate poverty over entire regions for the completion of a moderately prosperous society in all respects. These efforts have been greatly appreciated by villagers, boosting their patriotic enthusiasm and consolidating the CPC's foundation of governance at the grassroots level.

By January 2018, a total of 2.778 million people had been dispatched to poor villages to help, with each resident work team consisting of at least three people for a period of at least two years. The leaders of the newly dispatched resident work teams were usually middle-level officials or their reserves of the CPC or government departments. During the period when they stayed in the village, they would not undertake the work of their original institutions, and the Party members' organizational relations were transferred to the poor village, so as to ensure they were fully committed to the assistance in the village. The resident work teams have helped change the working style of grassroots officials; strengthen their capability of governance and stimulate their enthusiasm and commitment to work.

The resident work teams have also helped in accurate identification and targeted assistance. The poor households have been required to provide accurate information about their relatives and financial status. A clear set of standards and procedures have been provided to help poor households develop the virtue of honesty and trustworthiness. In the poverty exit process when some villagers who had emerged out of poverty were not willing to be deregistered in order to continue accessing preferential treatment, the work teams would explain to them the policy that a "grace period" would be allowed for them, during which time poverty alleviation policies and government supervision would be continued until their status was secure. This has helped develop a closer affinity between officials and local people.

5.4 Political and Other Effects

5.4.1 Winning Public Approval and Strengthening the CPC's Governance Foundation

Eliminating poverty and improving people's livelihood is a solemn commitment of the Communist Party of China to the whole nation. By the end of the year 2012 when the 18th CPC National Congress was convened, there had still been 60.39 million people in rural areas living in poverty. If conventional approaches were taken, it would be unlikely for all these people to be lifted out of poverty through 2020 as scheduled. Adhering to the principle of putting people first, the CPC Central Committee with Xi Jinping as its core set a clear goal that: "We must win the battle against extreme poverty and ensure that through the year 2020, all rural residents living below the current poverty line have been lifted out of poverty, and poverty is eliminated in all poor counties and regions."[7]This is the best expression of the CPC's commitment to staying true to its original aspiration. Targeted poverty alleviation has boosted people's sense of happiness and gain, strengthened the foundation for the CPC's governance, and enhanced the people's recognition and approval.

5.4.1.1 Targeted Poverty Alleviation as a New Practice and Exploration of the Laws of the CPC Governance

To govern a country well, a political party must have a strong capability of governance, and the primary task to improve this is to grasp the laws of governance, which feature particularity and generality. Emphasizing only particularity and ignoring the generality may cause great limitations in understanding things and solving problems, while simply emphasizing generality and ignoring particularity may lead to mechanical copying governing experiences and modes of others. In leading the people in socialist building and reform, the CPC has constantly reviewed and explored its laws of governance, which mainly include the laws of theoretical innovation, of national rejuvenation, of governing for the people, of governing in accordance with the law, and of governing the Party with strict discipline. Targeted poverty reduction and alleviation practices since the 18th CPC National Congress have been manifestations of these laws of governance.

Firstly, the concept of targeted poverty alleviation has been a reflection of the law of theoretical innovation, which is vital for a political party to carry out self-revolution and keep up with the development of the times. A political party that has been in power for a long time is prone to slackness and following the old routine. Only by innovation and facing challenges head on, can it continuously deepen its understanding of new things and improve its capability to address new problems.

---

[7] Institute for Party History and Literature of the CPC Central Committee. *Xi Jinping on Poverty Alleviation* [M]. Beijing: CPC Central Committee Literature Publishing House, 2018.

Targeted poverty alleviation has been a specific approach proposed to boost the development of the poor population under the background that the role of economic growth in assisting and benefiting poverty relief was reduced and the remaining poor population was the poorest. The proposal has improved the theory of poverty governance with Chinese characteristics and enriched the theory of socialism with Chinese characteristics. It is the adherence and grasp of the CPC's theoretical innovation of its laws of governance.

Secondly, the concept of targeted poverty alleviation has been a reflection of the philosophy that development is the top priority of the CPC in governing and rejuvenating China. Development is always an issue for a country and a governing Party. "Without development, it is out of the question to preserve the Party's pioneering role and to give play to the strengths of the socialist system to realize the prosperity of the people and the country."

After more than 40 years of reform and opening up, the development of the eastern region has achieved initial progress, but that of the poor areas in the central and western regions has remained slow. Therefore, the development of the poor areas must be put on the agenda as the first of the "Two Centenary Goals" is due. The development emphasized by the law of rejuvenating the country by the Party is development for all and coordinated regional development. As Xi Jinping puts it, "Without moderate prosperity in the countryside, especially in poor areas, we will not be able to build a moderately prosperous society in all respects."[8] In this sense, only by modifying weaknesses in the development of poor areas can the country achieve all-round development.

Thirdly, the concept of targeted poverty alleviation embodies the CPC's principle of governing for the people. Serving the people is the aim of the CPC and governing for the people is its starting point and final goal. A well-off society with no one being left behind is a society of all-round prosperity. Following a people-centered philosophy of development, the CPC has mobilized and organized social resources to participate in poverty reduction by establishing an all-encompassing targeted poverty alleviation framework, with corporate and societal assistance, sector-specific programs and government-sponsored projects supplementing each other. The efforts have promoted the public participation in the governance of the country, and helped solve the problem of the subsistence and development of poor population, giving full play to people's principal roles.

Fourthly, poverty alleviation and targeted measures have also reflected strict self-governance over the CPC. Governing the country requires the CPC should govern itself with strict discipline. Targeted poverty alleviation has been a major decision and plan of the CPC Central Committee, and the special inspections, supervisions and assessments carried out to combat poverty have been important manifestations of the CPC's strict self-governance. Only by constantly strengthening intra-Party supervision and promoting the CPC's self-building can the CPC continuously improve and consolidate its capability and position of governance.

[8] Institute for Party History Studies and Literature of the CPC Central Committee. *Xi Jinping on Poverty Alleviation* [M]. Beijing: CPC Central Committee Literature Publishing House, 2018.

5.4.1.2 Targeted Poverty Alleviation as a Reinforce of the CPC's Leadership Through Strong Determination and a Complete Organizational System

Since the 18th CPC National Congress, the Central Committee has made development-driven poverty alleviation a key task in realizing the First Centenary Goal of building a moderately prosperous society in all respects. With an overall analysis of its significance, Xi jinping points out that anti-poverty is a major issue in all countries' governance. Eradicating poverty, improving people's livelihood and achieving common prosperity is the essential requirement of socialism and a mission of the CPC. To complete the building of a moderately prosperous society in all respects and achieve the First Centenary Goal, poverty alleviation is the most challenging task. It is a prominent area of weakness to modify and a defining target to reach. Redoubled poverty alleviation efforts should be made to ensure that all people have a greater sense of gain from joint contributions and shared development, and to promote universal individual development and common prosperity for all. Regarding it the great responsibility of Chinese Communists, Xi Jinping has always put poverty alleviation at the top of his work agenda and devoted much of his energy to it, with the determination to address the issue together with the central collective leadership. Governments at all levels have signed commitments to fight poverty and made a pledge to win the battle. This practice not only shows their determination to end extreme poverty and build a moderately prosperous society in all respects, but also helps them to achieve a clear division of responsibilities and ensure that the human, material and financial resources for poverty alleviation are effectively guaranteed.

Strong determination without action does not lead to any accomplishment. A complete organizational system is necessary. The anti-poverty campaign has a different organizational structure from previous campaigns. It is comprehensive, extensive, systematic, not only including the individual in the Chinese administrative system, but also social organizations, state-owned (private) enterprises and all kinds of institutions to form an all-encompassing framework led by the government, involving all governmental, industrial and social sectors joining forces for poverty alleviation. A wide range of financial, human and material resources are pooled to provide favorable external conditions to win the battle.

Governments at all levels have used special funds to meet the needs for poverty alleviation. Enterprises under the central government have carried out the campaign to support "one hundred counties and ten thousand villages" in poor old revolutionary base areas, and private enterprises have initiated the campaign of "1,000 enterprises helping 1,000 villages" to offer them targeted anti-poverty assistance. In implementing targeted poverty alleviation measures, the earmarked funds from the central government have increased by about RMB20 billion on a yearly basis, reaching RMB126 billion in 2019. By the end of 2017, China's 46,200 private enterprises had invested RMB52.7 billion in industrial assistance, helping and benefiting more than 6.2 million poor people in 51,200 villages. This system of coordinated policies and sufficient funds together with strengthened human resources has provided a strong institutional guarantee for winning the battle against poverty.

5.4.1.3 Targeted Poverty Alleviation as a Facilitator to Strengthen the CPC Conduct Through a Strict Assessment and Supervision System

The improvement of Party conduct is the eternal theme of Party building, which is an external manifestation of the Party's theories, organization and system. It has a bearing on the Party's image to the people and the public support, and is an important way to pool strengths. In improving Party conduct, the key point is to maintain a close tie with the people and ensure the Party's advanced nature and integrity to provide a guarantee for national building and development.

The CPC central collective leadership with Xi Jinping as its core has always put emphasis on the improvement of Party conduct. A system of supervision, inspection and evaluation has been established for major national drives such as poverty alleviation. On the one hand, it is to ensure that the outcomes of poverty relief stand the test of history and the people; on the other hand, it is an effective measure to improve Party conduct. By accomplishing the great cause of poverty elimination, the conduct of Party organizations at all levels, especially at primary levels, has been improved extensively and substantially.

Supervisions and inspections have been carried out to ensure the successful completion of various tasks and targets in poverty alleviation. The State Council Leading Group is responsible for the organization and leadership of the work for the Party Committees and governments in 22 provinces (autonomous regions and municipalities directly under the Central Government) in the central and western regions, as well as the central and the state departments. The inspection, focusing on the implementation of poverty alleviation responsibilities, special plans and major policies and measures, is mainly to find out misconducts such as dereliction of duty, inaction, being slack or perfunctory in work, as well as fraud and illegal practices and other violation of laws and disciplines. It is an exploration and innovation of intra-Party supervision and a re-supervision of the political responsibility of the Party organizations for poverty alleviation. The special inspection focuses on the "special" aspects by carrying out in-depth supervision and inspection of the implementation of the work in four aspects.[9]

The evaluation mechanism has mainly included the third-party evaluation of the poverty exit procedure of counties that have emerged from poverty and the effectiveness evaluation of poverty reduction. The former is to carry out spot checks on the counties that have withdrawn from the poverty list, while the latter is an annual assessment of the effectiveness of the anti-poverty work of Party committees and governments at all levels, the east–west collaboration and the paired-up assistance to designated areas for poverty alleviation of the central departments. Both have adopted

---

[9] The four aspects refer to implementation of the principles and policies of the CPC Central Committee for poverty alleviation; implementation of the responsibilities for poverty alleviation taken by Party committees (leading Party members' groups); implementation of the supervision responsibilities taken by discipline inspection and supervision commissions (discipline inspection and supervision groups) and relevant functional departments; and implementation of the rectification of problems in poverty alleviation discovered during supervisions and inspections.

third parties for evaluation to ensure the authority, impartiality and objectivity of the work.

5.4.2 *Improving Poverty Governance to Promote China's Building of Its Governance System and Capacity*

Since the start of the reform and opening up, great changes have taken place in China's poverty governance system. In terms of the development stage, poverty alleviation underwent several phases, from helping and benefiting poor population through rural economic reform, to putting focus on poor counties and villages, and now to the stage of poverty alleviation and development by targeting at both regional (contiguous destitute areas) and individual (poverty households) levels. The approach has changed from generalized broad-brush policies to targeted measures based on local conditions. Actually, China's approaches to poverty management at various stages have been adopted by fully considering factors concerning the economic and social development, features and conditions of poverty, and national resources at the given time.

In terms of the model of governance, the traditional one was dominated by the government with traditional departments as the core, while the governance system of targeted poverty alleviation, although still dominated by the government, has been a composite anti-poverty governance framework featuring multi-department and cross-department cooperation. At the same time, a governance system with multi-party participation has been established, encouraging the interplay of the government, businesses and social organizations.

More importantly, attention has been paid to encouraging poverty alleviation by participation of all parties, aiming at improving the development capacity of the poor through assistant projects and establishing a long-term anti-poverty mechanism. This change is a reflection of China's progress in the building of its system and capacity for governance, which has enriched and promoted the modernization of its capacity for governance in general.

5.4.2.1 Changing from Regional Poverty Eradication to Targeted Poverty Alleviation

Before the reform and opening up, the dominant anti-poverty goal for China was to ensure subsistence. Before the socialist system was established in 1957, land reform was the major approach to solve the problem of villagers' means of production while production efficiency was raised through mutual assistance and cooperation. From 1957 to 1978, China alleviated poverty by reforming the rural distribution system, setting up a social security system and developing rural public services.

After the reform and opening up, from 1979 to 1985, the CPC and Chinese government shifted the focus of work to economic growth. A series of rural structural reforms were carried out, including the household contract management system, relaxing the price of agricultural products, and vigorously developing township enterprises, which rapidly and effectively liberated and developed the productive forces and promoted the overall economic growth in rural areas. The increase in the income of the poor population at this stage was mainly the result of this effect.

In response to the poverty situation at the time, the state set up special funds and plans to support the work of poverty alleviation and development in some areas, such as the "Fund for the Development of Economically Underdeveloped Areas" established in 1980; special plan for poverty alleviation and agricultural development in the "Three Western Regions", referring to Hexi Region and Dingxi Region in Gansu Province and the mountainous area in southern Ningxia Hui Autonomous Region, the most impoverished contiguous areas in the country at the beginning of reform and opening up in 1983 (involving 47 counties, cities and districts, which expanded to 57 in 1992); and the work-relief fund established in 1984. This stage was China's trial practice of regional-based poverty alleviation and development policies, which to a certain extent promoted the economic development of extremely poor areas at that time and accumulated experience for the extensive development-driven poverty alleviation campaign later on.

In 1986, the Leading Group for Economic Development in Poor Areas of the State Council and its office, a special anti-poverty agency was set up, marking the beginning of a new stage in China's poverty alleviation endeavor, which lasted until 2000. From 1986 to 2000, the CPC and Chinese government established an anti-poverty working mechanism, introducing the practice that in places with challenging poverty elimination work, with the heads of provincial level Party committees and governments assuming overall responsibility. The approach to identify poor population was clarified, and the absolute poor without adequate food and clothing were taken as the main anti-poverty targets. With the increase of the input of poverty alleviation resources, and arrangement of special funds and mobilization of the whole society to participate, an all-encompassing framework of "government-led poverty alleviation with the participation of the whole society" was taking shape.

From 2001 to 2012, China's poverty situation changed again, with the poor population mainly distributed in the central and western regions. Following the principle of comprehensive and all-round development, the CPC and Chinese government improved the means of identifying poor population with new poverty standards, formulated the development plan for contiguous poverty-stricken areas, and introduced policies for strengthening agriculture and benefiting rural residents. Through these measures, the number of people living in poverty dropped to 98.99 million by the end of 2012. After 2012, changes in the macroeconomic environment and major social contradictions brought about new challenges to the anti-poverty work, resulting in weak effects of economic growth on poverty reduction, unbalanced regional development, and the omission of some poor individuals from the poverty list owing to the fact that more attention had been paid to regional poverty alleviation for a long time. All this called for new adjustments to poverty alleviation and development.

In 2013, President Xi Jinping proposed the idea of "targeted poverty alleviation", stressing that the poor population should be targeted and more targeted efforts should be made for identification, help, measures and exit so as to ensure that no one would be left behind in building a moderately prosperous society in all respects through 2020. China has since entered a new era of targeted poverty alleviation.

It is obvious that the shift of focus from poor regions to poor individuals, from generalized broad-brush policies to targeted measures based on specific conditions, and from focus on the overall regional development to the "Two Assurances and Three Guarantees" for individuals, China has updated its poverty governance system by keeping up with the times, constantly refining, deepening, improving and adjusting, and has developed good practices in poverty control with Chinese characteristics.

5.4.2.2 Transforming from Relief-Based Poverty Alleviation to Development-Driven Efforts

Development-driven poverty alleviation is the basic policy of China. Before the mid-1980s, the work mainly relied on relief, which was the traditional way of helping by cash and kind. Relief-based poverty eradication may alleviate the temporary living difficulties of the poor population, but it does not help their development capacity, and may instead encourage relying on and waiting for external assistance, which could be even more negative for the development of poor areas. In view of the conditions of poverty in China, it is not only necessary to increase the income of the poor population, but more importantly to change the backwardness of the poor areas by improving their production and living conditions and promoting their development.

Therefore, it is urgent to find a new way of poverty alleviation and development that could not only increase the income of the poor in the short term, but also promote the overall local development in the long term to boost their internal driver and build a stable poverty alleviation mechanism for the rural poor.

In December 1982, China launched a poverty alleviation campaign in the three Western regions of Hexi Region and Dingxi Region in Gansu Province and the mountainous region in southern Ningxia Hui Autonomous Region to boost their agricultural development, which was a groundbreaking event in China's poverty alleviation efforts. It generated a profound influence on the implementation of extensive poverty alleviation and development.

In September 1984, the CPC Central Committee and the State Council promulgated the Notice on Boosting Impoverished Areas to Take on a New Look, pointing out what was unsatisfactory about past practices of poverty relief, in which a lot of money was spent but little was achieved, and requiring that the relief-only conception and practice should be corrected, with the new focus on "enhancing the internal driver of poor areas by making full use of local resources and adjusting measures to develop commodity production in line with the local conditions". The release of the document was a milestone event marking the advance of the idea of development-oriented poverty alleviation.

The Ten-Year Plan for National Economic and Social Development and Outlines of the 8th Five-Year Plan adopted in April 1991 put forward the principle of "adhering to poverty alleviation mainly through economic development", which was the inception of development-driven poverty alleviation. In 1994, the central leadership held a National Conference on Poverty Alleviation and Development, and made arrangements for the implementation of The National Seven-Year Poverty Alleviation Program (1994–2000), clearly proposing the policy of development-oriented poverty alleviation which was defined: "Officials and people in poor areas are encouraged to foster the spirit of self-reliance and hard work and, with the support of the government, develop and utilize local resources for market-oriented commodity production by relying on modern technologies. This is a good way to secure themselves of food and clothing and get rid of poverty to achieve prosperity."

In 2001, the State Council issued The Outline for Development-Driven Poverty Alleviation in Rural Areas (2001–2010), in which the basic policy was improved, with emphasis on economic development as the central task to help poor people find a path of development that is practical and in line with local characteristics; and on improving the capacity of poor rural households for self-accumulation and self-development.

This was the first time that the anti-poverty policy explicitly emphasized the fostering of poor households' own development capacity. This supplement and improvement constitute the main goal of current strategy of development-oriented poverty alleviation—the establishment of a long-term poverty alleviation mechanism and the consolidation of anti-poverty achievements. In 2011, The Outline for Development-Driven Poverty Alleviation in Rural Areas (2011–2020) carried on the keynote of the policy.

In 2015, President Xi Jinping stressed at the Global Poverty Reduction and Development Forum that "We adhere to the policy of development-oriented poverty alleviation and take development as the fundamental way to overcome poverty, which not only helps poor people out of poverty but also build up their self-belief to give full play to their initiative and improve their development capacity." This is what China's poverty alleviation work has been adhering to till today.

Development-oriented poverty alleviation should have the following components: (1) It focuses on the development of not only local natural resources, but also human and social resources. This is conducive to promoting the development of agriculture, tourism, culture and other industries in poor areas, so as to facilitate the emergence of new forms of business and the integrated development of industries, extend the industrial development chain and increase the added value of industrial development for a coordinated development of industries in poor areas. (2) Development-oriented poverty alleviation is not about maximizing the development of natural resources, but placing equal emphasis on both ecological and economic benefits. We should never follow the old path of pollution first and treatment later, and fully respect the laws of nature and adhere to the principle that "lucid waters and lush mountains are invaluable assets". (3) Development-oriented poverty alleviation does not just mean to help the poor increase their incomes, but have equal access to basic public services. At present, compared with urban areas, basic public services such as education and medical care have been inadequate in rural areas. Therefore equal access to the services should be a part of the policy. (4) Equal importance has been attached to development-driven poverty alleviation and the social security system. At present, the poor population has been largely made up of the old, the weak, the sick and the disabled, who have a low capability to participate in industrial development and can only be helped through social security. Therefore, development-driven poverty alleviation should pay attention to "driving by two wheels", focusing on both development and security. Only in this way can the fight against poverty benefit more poor people who are either underprivileged or unable to work, so that no one is left behind on the journey towards moderate prosperity.

5.4.2.3 Promoting the Improvement of Local Management Capacity by Decentralization of Funding and Project Approval

As the campaign of poverty alleviation moved on, the goals and tasks became increasingly tougher. As an important tool of poverty eradication, the distribution of poverty funds and projects directly affected the outcomes. In 2016, the General Office of the State Council issued Suggestions on Supporting Poor Counties in Carrying out Coordinated and Integrated Use of Government Funds for Agriculture and Rural Areas on a Trial Basis, which made it clear that support would be given to poor counties by coordinating and integrating the use of government funds for rural development to address prominent problems. This should be done to ensure that funds are used with better accuracy and efficiency to contribute to accomplishment of poverty alleviation as scheduled. A new framework of using poverty alleviation funds came to its own, in which funds from multiple channels were integrated for targeted poverty alleviation.

It was also required in the document that poor counties, as the major implementers of the measure, coordinate and integrate the use of government funds in accordance with the poverty alleviation plan, and assume specific responsibilities for their safe, standardized and effective use. The funds included in overall planning and integration refers to those used by finance departments at all levels to arrange agricultural production development and agricultural infrastructure construction. There are as many as 19 such funds at the central level alone, and more than 10 at the provincial level.

Based on local poverty alleviation plans, poor counties have formulated plans for the utilization of funds for overall planning and integration, allowing them to be used across different categories.[10] In order to better coordinate, projects should be arranged in line with those in the county-level poverty alleviation project database. Under such constraints, the county-level government's capability to manage funds and build the project database complements and enhances each other.

There is no doubt that, in the process of poverty alleviation, compared with the central, provincial and municipal governments, the county-level government

[10] This refers to the practice that funds for the development of agricultural production and for the construction of rural infrastructure may be used in a coordinated way by mutual adjustment.

is the one with the easiest access to the most adequate local information and the best understanding of the local poverty alleviation plan. The policy of integration of government funds for rural development in poverty-stricken counties has given county-level governments full autonomy and stimulated their enthusiasm and initiative for poverty alleviation, which is conducive to solving problems of scattered use of funds lack of planning. An institutionalized and regular fund management mechanism for agriculture-related government funds could thus be established to ensure the effectiveness and quality of targeted poverty alleviation. Under the pressure of performance assessment in this aspect, all county-level departments must improve the project and fund management system, which may effectively improve their governance under the "project-oriented" model.

At the same time, the practice has adhered to the principle of public participation and public notice, with poor villagers involved in the design, implementation and acceptance of projects to ensure the transparency of project implementation. As a result, the rural poor may have an enhanced sense of gain and satisfaction, while the governance capacity of the primary-level government has been improved with better relationship between officials and the public.

5.4.2.4 Multidimensional Assessment Indicators Enriching Practices in Poverty Governance

The impoverished households are deregistered from poverty list by the criteria of personal incomes, and with reference to the "Two Assurances and Three Guarantees". The former requires that the annual average per capita income remains steady above China's current poverty line. The latter refers to assurances of adequate food and clothing, and guarantees of access to compulsory education, basic medical services, and safe housing for impoverished rural residents. In the criteria, rural poverty is understood beyond just low incomes by including access to safe drinking water, housing, education and other basic public services. These are what multidimensional poverty assessment theory is about. Based on Amartya Sen's theory of poverty, the two important elements of freedom of basic capabilities are economic conditions and social opportunities. Economic conditions refer to people's capabilities to possess and operate resources, while social opportunities stand for the right of individuals to public services, such as medical care and education, so as to promote individuals to have equal social opportunities. On the one hand, healthcare and education are public services that poor people should have access to. On the other hand, in terms of economic conditions, diseases and illiteracy lead to a weaker capacity of the poor to own and operate resources.

Research results of some scholars show that elite capture exists in different degrees in poverty alleviation programs and resources. The poor people had little participation in a considerable number of industrial programs for poverty alleviation, which resulted in the deprivation of poor people's industrial development capabilities and overall quality, while the inadequate participation was viciously caused by diseases and lack of capacities. The improvement of medical security conditions for the poor can effectively improve the human capital of the poor, enabling them to participate in industrial projects with capabilities and labor. Education can help interrupt the intergenerational transmission of poverty and enable poor people to participate in industrial programs or even develop their own industries in market competition. Medical care and education are important components of a long-term and stable poverty alleviation mechanism. Housing as shelter is a basic guarantee for human life and an important part of the bottom line of people's livelihood. Poverty alleviation and targeted measures have taken into consideration of multidimensional poverty assessment indicators to guarantee the basic conditions necessary for the development of the poor population.

For some rural poor who have fallen into poverty owing to irresistible external causes such as diseases, disability and lack of labor force and cannot get out of poverty by their own efforts, social security systems would be in place to provide them with basic security for medical care, elderly care and housing. At the same time, these have been supplemented by policies of subsistence allowances, special allowances for vulnerable groups and assistance to help the poor to better guarantee the income of those who are unable or have weak ability to work. During the process, China has gained in poverty management experience and the system has been improved.

5.4.2.5 Resident Work Teams Helping Enhance the Community-Level Governance

President Xi Jinping has pointed out that the primary level is the foundation for development-driven poverty alleviation. We should encourage and select outstanding young officials, veterans and college graduates who are reliable, professional and willing to serve the people to work in poor villages, and make destitute areas important platforms for training and selecting officials. By January 2018, a total of 2.778 million people had been dispatched to the countryside. In accordance with the requirements of the Guidelines on Strengthening the Selection and Management of Resident Work Teams in Poor Villages issued by the General Office of the CPC Central Committee and the State Council, the work teams have many roles to play, such as publicizing major policies of the CPC Central Committee and the State Council on poverty alleviation and elimination, taking part in working out poverty alleviation programs and plans, and participating in implementing various targeted measures in villages and households. Their tasks also include promoting the development of village collective economy and help manage and use well the village collective income, regulating government funds for poverty alleviation projects with the implementation of the publicity system. They should also make efforts to help poor rural residents to build up self-belief and have access to education so that they can create a better life through their own hard work, and update outmoded and undesirable habits and customs. Their work also covers promoting Mandarin Chinese and team building at the primary level, as well as cultivating and attracting all kinds of entrepreneurial individuals to start local businesses.[11]

Before the anti-poverty campaign, some of the village leaderships had problems such as lax organization, inadequate capacity and serious aging. The resident work teams have injected fresh blood into and effectively upgrade village management. The following part will analyze how the system can effectively improve the weaknesses of village management from the perspectives of "embedded" governance and political tournament.

The assistance system of resident work teams in poor villages is the entry point of re-embedding state authorities into rural areas to improve rural governance. Through rigid institutional requirements, the system has shaped the poverty management of poor villages by administrative means, which has not only realized poverty elimination of poor villages and households, but reconstructed the primary-level organizational structure and reshaped the rural governance system. In China's political system, the work team, which functions as a new intermediary mechanism between the central government and rural areas and an unconventional operation mechanism of the state power, is a complement that cannot be ignored in the process of national governance.

The resident work system has played an important role of connecting towns and villages, which by breaking from the bureaucracy and impersonal operation logic become a unique practice and model of operation for primary-level organizations in China. Under the embedded governance analysis framework proposed by Granovetter, the resident team has improved grassroots governance capacity through two embedding mechanisms, one structural and the other relational. Structural embedding refers to that of many actors in a broader social network, while relational embedding means that of economic actors in personal relationships. Structural embedding has to do with the structural reconstruction of the external actors in the macro-level system and management model in political, economic and social systems, as well as the integration of related element resources and functions related to the activities of multiple players. In contrast, relational embedding is concerned about the multiple organizational or individual players and other actors at the micro level, who, through learning, communicating and implementing policy rules, as well as identification and share of values and emotions, common aspirations and motivations, and exchange and reciprocity of interests, are embedded in the social relation network, which may turn into internal driver to cause a change in the original social structure and relations in a direction that helps achieve the intended goals.

In terms of the 10 tasks stipulated in the Guidelines on Strengthening the Selection and Management of Resident Work Teams in Poor Villages, 4 fell into structural embedding, namely, publicizing major policies on poverty alleviation and elimination, regulating government funds for poverty alleviation projects with the implementation of the publicity system, working together to draw up anti-poverty programs

[11] For details, see Guidelines on Strengthening the Selection and Management of Resident Work Teams in Poor Villages issued by the General Office of the CPC Central Committee and the State Council.

and plans and strengthening primary-level team building; while the other six, namely, participating in carrying out various targeted poverty alleviation measures in villages and households, promoting the development of village collective economy and helping manage and use well the collective income, helping poor rural residents build up self-belief and have access to education to stimulate their internal driver, updating outmoded and undesirable habits and customs by guiding the formulation of village rules and regulations, and promoting Mandarin Chinese, fell into the category of relational embedding. Through structural and relational embedding, the system of resident work teams has effectively intervened in the site of grassroots poverty alleviation by introducing a new way of village management to realize the delegation of the state power.

Political tournament has been a model of strong incentive pressure for local government officials under the current system, that is, the performance evaluation indicator system is taken as the main criterion for the promotion of local officials. The evaluation and incentive mechanism for resident work teams has been operated in the framework of the political tournament, so it is feasible to evaluate the improvement of local governance from the perspective of the political tournament. The Guidelines on Strengthening the Selection and Management of Resident Work Teams in Poor Villages have made it clear that the assessment and motivation of work teams should meet the requirements in three aspects:

First, strengthening the assessment. Party committees and governments at the county level would conduct annual assessment and inspection of the resident work teams in villages to ensure that their assistance has generated actual results.

Second, incentive recognition. The assessment results would serve as an important reference for comprehensive evaluation, excellence evaluation and promotion of officials. Those with outstanding performance records with approval from rural residents would be commended in accordance with relevant regulations or listed as reserve officials for promotion.

Third, accountability. Those who were proved incompetent would be recalled and replaced without delay and criticisms would be given to those who failed to deliver for the rural poor with unsatisfactory performance records. All cases of deception, dereliction of duty or other circumstances that have caused adverse effects would be dealt with seriously, and the responsible persons and the dispatched departments or institutions would be held accountable in line with relevant regulations.

Under the current promotion system, this mode combining strong positive and negative incentives would urge resident work teams to take positive measures to make their performance evaluation indicators meet the requirements of the superior department to get well prepared for future promotion. It is obvious that, under the action logic of political tournament, the resident team would work hard to carry out the tasks in all aspects.

5.4.3 *Motivating the Poor to Rely on Their Own Hard Work for Self-Development*

The internal motivation is the source of stable poverty alleviation for the rural poor. With the progress of targeted poverty alleviation, the issue of insufficient endogenous motivation of poor population has drawn more and more attention from scholars. Endogenous motivation refers to the driving force that has a positive role in promoting various aspects of self-growth, self-development, self-improvement and independent innovation. President Xi Jinping has proposed that the external support, which is often compared to a "blood transfusion", should always be combined with a more sustained effort from self-motivation, which is known as "blood production". We should always take ethnic groups and poor regions into consideration in our overall planning, with focus on fostering their capacity for self-development to achieve common growth. The development of poor areas depends on internal impetus. If a new village is created simply by external relief, or if a village only has its look changed without any internal life and vitality, without the return of labor and a sustainable source of economic resources, the future development of the place will still be a problem.

The core of China's development-oriented poverty alleviation is to stimulate the endogenous motivation of poor areas and people. On the one hand, it would promote the economic and social conditions in poor areas to gradually converge with those in developed places; on the other hand, by leading the poor to participate in industrial development, the poor could be enabled to fully develop in the market economy. According to the theory of endogenous growth, a region's economy can only achieve sustainable growth independently of external conditions, which is made possible by endogenous technological progress as an important factor. This has changed the law of diminishing marginal benefit of factors of production and challenged the conclusion of neoclassical economics that economic development stagnates as long as the accumulation of capital and labor force comes to a certain stage. Indeed, endogenous growth model has been a breakthrough of the neoclassical growth theory on the assumption of exogenous technology, which economists like Paul Michael Romer, Robert Emerson Lucas and others have held. They assumed that technology spillover effects would influence the whole range of economy and the existence of externalities make the aggregate production function show increasing returns to scale. Technology progress has been determined by the production of new knowledge capital accumulation and changes in the propensity to save would affect the economy's long-term growth. Lisa Barrow believes that the government is the decisive force to promote economic growth. Government services (such as infrastructure construction) enable production to show increasing returns to scale and realize endogenous economic growth.

Thinking in terms of the endogenous growth theory, poverty alleviation has not only brought advanced production technologies and management concepts from developed areas to poor areas through industries, employment and e-commerce, but directly promoted the development of poor areas. In addition, the scale effect of funds can play its role through the integration of policy-backed government funds for rural development. All these have improved the infrastructure construction, helped the logistics development, reduce information asymmetry, and indirectly improve the endogenous motivation of poverty-stricken areas and the poor.

Industrial development has boosted the internal driver of the rural poor for development. Most poor people in China have lived in rural areas, and poverty alleviation is actually aimed at these people. Agriculture is the leading industry in those areas and its development has been of paramount importance for the poor to get rid of poverty. Agriculture is also a solid foundation for regional development, which can directly help low-income rural families shake off poverty. The large-scale development has enabled agriculture to have a more significant and lasting effect on poverty reduction. For the rural poor, agriculture is the industry with the lowest threshold, and its economic development can benefit them most directly. By participating in the agricultural industrial chain, the impoverished population can effectively improve its agricultural production capacity, which is conducive to the sustainable growth of operating income. In addition, the development of secondary and tertiary industries also functions in poverty reduction.

In the great practice of relocating from inhospitable areas, many poor people moved to more livable nearby towns and counties. Follow-up employment assistance measures have been adopted to help them find jobs in local poverty alleviation workshops or factories. The "learning through work" effects have gradually showed up, helping poor people achieve sustainable growth in their wage income. Therefore, on the premise of practical participation in industrial development, the process itself is also a process of enhancing capabilities and endogenous motivation for the poor people.

Construction of infrastructure has stimulated the motivation for people development in poor areas, since the improvement of rural infrastructure and basic public services has been a key part of enhancing the sustainable development capacity of poverty-stricken areas and the viable capacity of the poor. The government's investment in infrastructure, with its multiplier effects, has driven the growth of related industries and the rural economy in general through the amplification of investment multiplier. This has been manifested in the following aspects:

Firstly, transportation conditions have been greatly improved with the increase of government investment in infrastructure, which is conducive to reducing agricultural production costs and improving production efficiency. Secondly, the improvement of infrastructure has effectively shortened the commuting distance and time between urban and rural areas, and increased the attraction of developed areas to rural labor, which has not only accelerated the integration of urban and rural areas, but also promoted the transfer of rural poor labor. Thirdly, the improvement of infrastructure can reduce all kinds of costs, such as the cost of labor transfer to increase the opportunities for rural labor to participate in non-agricultural employment; the cost caused by information asymmetry, so that villagers may choose the production of agricultural products that are more conducive to increasing their income; and the transport cost of agricultural products and the possible loss during the transport process. In addition, high-quality infrastructure may play a key role in rural poverty reduction by leading to sustained development.

Basic public services will inspire the rural poor to play their part to fight poverty for better development. Access to compulsory education and basic medical care has been an important part of improving the viability of the poor population. Educational development can bring positive personal and social returns to individuals and society, and improving individuals' education can realize rapid accumulation of human capital and provide a substantial guarantee and necessary means for increasing individual or family income. At the same time, development in education may also generate positive externalities, bringing positive social returns through improving health and increasing life expectancy. In terms of healthcare, people would be more willing to increase their investment in health security at the current stage of demographic dividend reduction in China, while the increase in medical expenses has brought about pressure and burden to some patients from poor families, which would easily fall into or back into poverty due to illness. Access to public services like health care can be effective in alleviating poverty by healing the physical and psychological trauma of diseases and enhancing the capability of people to generate income. Indeed, the improvement of basic public services has been effective to boost the internal impetus of the poor population.

5.4.4 Advanced Achievement of the UN Sustainable Development Goals with China's Approaches in Poverty Reduction

Sustainable Development Goals (SDGs) are the goals set by the United Nations following the UN Millennium Development Goals (MDGs) released in 2015. Aiming to guide the global development from 2015 to 2030, 17 Sustainable Development Goals have been set, covering poverty, hunger and food security, health and education, gender equality, water and sanitation, and modern energy. After winning the battle against extreme poverty, China would have lifted all the rural population out of extreme poverty and secured a decisive victory in building a moderately prosperous society in all respects. In other words, by that time China would have achieved the poverty alleviation goal set on the UN 2030 Agenda for Sustainable Development 10 years ahead of schedule, contributing China's approaches to global poverty governance.

5.4.4.1 Eradication of Extreme Poverty and Hunger

In the 17 Sustainable Development Goals set by the UN, Goal 1 and Goal 2 respectively read, "End poverty in all its forms everywhere" and "End hunger, achieve food security and improved nutrition and promote sustainable agriculture". China's poverty alleviation criteria mainly cover personal incomes and the household's situation with reference to the "Two Assurances and Three Guarantees", in which "Two

Assurances" refers to assurances of adequate food and clothing, and "adequate food" not only means security of safe and edible staple foods, but also requires that the poor have enough protein to take in. At the same time, there are corresponding requirements for safe and easily accessible drinking water, which is in line with the relevant goals of the UN Sustainable Development Goals on hunger eradication and clean drinking water.

5.4.4.2 Good Health and Well-Being

Good health and well-being are essential components of sustainable development. With the driving compass of the UN Millennium Development Goals, the people of the world have made great progress in life expectancy and in reducing newborn, child and maternal mortality, as well as in fighting diseases such as malaria, tuberculosis, polio and HIV/AIDS which constitute a major challenge for the world's sustainable development. However, redoubled efforts are still required for the whole world to zero in on the solutions in child and maternal health as well as HIV/AIDS and other communicable diseases and epidemics. In China's poverty alleviation criteria, one of the "Three Guarantees" is the access to basic medical services. The poverty-stricken population should have basic medical insurance and critical disease insurance, and receive timely treatment for chronic diseases. At the same time, medical institutions at the county, township and village levels have been required to ensure that the poor can afford medical services.

One of the cases in point was that of Weining County of Guizhou Province, which is located in the contiguous destitute areas featuring rocky desertification. With the largest number of poor population in the province, the county used to be perplexed by congenital heart diseases in local children and one of the reasons was the lack of the mechanism for prenatal and postnatal care. Women during pregnancy did not receive prenatal services and many even gave birth at home. In addition, nearly half of the county's 300 village clinics were not available because of their dilapidated conditions or other reasons, and some village doctors conducted treatment at home or rent houses, which were not standardized and had hidden safety risks. In response to the tough situation, the CPC Weining County Committee and government worked with China Merchants Group, an enterprise offering paired-up assistance to the county, in launching the "China Merchants Group·Village Health Clinics" project, with 300 village clinics listed in the construction plan. Meanwhile, they have also planned to invite World Vision and the China Population Welfare Foundation to provide medical training services for village doctors and poor people. At the same time, the clinics in each central village would be equipped with telemedicine equipment, which may realize remote consulting of villages with county and township hospitals to effectively address the problem of difficult access to medical services. According to the plan, the project would cover 50 administrative villages in 30 townships across the county, directly benefiting 160,500 people, including 18,504 registered poor people.

5.4.4.3 Ecology and Environment

Ecology and environment are also important elements of sustainable development. In UN's SDGs, cheap and clean energy, climate action, the protection of underwater and terrestrial life, sustainable production and consumption are all related to ecological conservation and environmental protection. China's implementation of green poverty reduction programs in its anti-poverty campaign is also an important measure to help poor areas achieve win–win ecological and economic benefits. Green poverty reduction, as a means of anti-poverty approach to promote the development of poor areas and lift the poor out of poverty through green industries and green industrialization, has helped promote the integration of the agricultural industry, shape models of poverty alleviation through tourism and agritourism, introduce new mechanisms of coupling interests to promote the internal impetus of poverty-stricken areas and poor people for sustainable development. This is in line with the ecological and environmental targets of the UN SDGs.

5.4.4.4 Education

Education is an important way to break the intergenerational transmission of poverty. Ensuring inclusive and equitable quality education and achieving universal access to education is an important part of improving people's lives and achieving sustainable development. Fifty-eight million children of primary school age are currently out of school in the developing countries, including more than half in sub-Saharan Africa. In the early stage of poverty alleviation, the education penetration rate of some deeply impoverished areas in China was also low, such as Liangshan Yi Autonomous Prefecture in Sichuan Province.

One of the "Three Guarantees" in China's poverty alleviation criteria is the guarantee of access to compulsory education. No students should drop out of school during the stage except for physical reasons, and vocational education can be carried out in advance for some of the population who are weary of studying. In addressing absolute poverty, China aims to ensure, first and foremost, that all children and adolescents in compulsory education can afford and must attend school. Achieving quality education is the next stage of addressing relative poverty. In addition, China has achieved remarkable results in promoting the equitability of education.

5.4.4.5 Coordinated Development of Urban and Rural Areas

Coordinated development between urban and rural areas has been an important part of China's sustainable urbanization and also a part of the UN SDGs. Specifically, building risk-resilient infrastructure, promoting inclusive sustainable industrial development and stimulating innovation are among the SDGs. An important goal of China's poverty alleviation campaign is to "bring the main indicators of basic public services to approach the national average". This includes both improving infrastructure and ensuring equal access to basic public services. Since the start of the targeted poverty alleviation campaign, the proportion of rural households in poor villages with access to highways increased from 99.7% in 2015 to 100% in 2019, and that with access to cable and electricity signals rose from 92.2% in 2015 to 99.1% in 2019. The proportion of rural households in poor villages with broadband access increased from 71.8% in 2015 to 97.3% in 2019, which was in line with the SDGs of the UN for infrastructure development such as transport and information technology.

Bibliography

1. Liu, Y. (2019). Winning the Battle against Extreme Poverty with the Driving Compass of Xi Jinping's Philosophy on Poverty Alleviation: Speech at the Policy Seminar on Poverty Alleviation Situation in Guizhou Province [EB/OL], August 26, 2019. http://www.sohu.com/a/336775493_120206205
2. Office of Household Surveys of National Bureau of Statistics. (2019). *Monitoring report on rural poverty in China 2019*. China Statistics Press.
3. Li, X. (2019). China's poverty alleviation practice enriched by innovation models [EB/OL], September 5, 2019. http://www.sohu.com/a/338988948_120043718
4. Amartya, S. (2013). *Development as freedom* [trans. R. Ze & Y. Zhen]. China Renmin University Press.
5. Hu, A. (2014). China's success in poverty reduction: Implications for the World [N]. *People's Daily (Overseas Edition)*, October 17, 2014.
6. Zhao, Q. (2014). Solving global poverty: A long way to go. *Chinese Social Sciences Today*, February 17, 2014.
7. Liu, Y, & Li, J. (2017). Geographical detection and optimization of county-level rural poverty differentiation mechanism in China [J]. *Acta Geographica Sinica, 2017*(1), 161–173.
8. Liu, Y., & Cao, Z. (2017). Supply-side structure of targeted poverty alleviation and its reform strategies. *Bulletin of Chinese Academy of Sciences, 10*, 1066–1073.
9. Liu, Y., Zhou, Y., & Liu, J. (2016). Regional differentiation and targeted poverty alleviation strategies of rural poverty in China. *Bulletin of Chinese Academy of Sciences, 3*, 269–278.
10. Wang, Y., & Wang, S. (2015). Analysis of rural poor population clustering and poverty reduction strategies. *Journal of China Agricultural University (Social Sciences Edition), 2015* (2), 98–109.
11. Yang, R., et al. (2015). Progress and prospect of rural transformation and reconstruction in China: Logic and framework. *Progress in Geography, 8*, 1019–1030.
12. Luo, Q., & Li, X. (2014). Progress in Overseas rural poverty geographic studies. *Economic Geography, 2014* (6), 1–8.
13. Liu, X., Su, S., Wang, Y., et al. (2014). Spatial poverty measurement index system of villages in contiguous destitute areas. *Scientia Geographica Sinica, 2014*(4), 447–453.
14. Pei, Y., Liu, X., Li, Y., et al. (2015). Survey and analysis of spatial poverty of villages in Liupan Mountain contiguous destitute areas: A case study of Xiji County, Ningxia Hui Autonomous Region. *Research of Agricultural Modernization, 2015*(5), 748–754.
15. Lu, C. (2016). Implementation of targeted poverty alleviation: Challenges and countermeasures. *Agricultural Economics, 2016*(7), 6–7.
16. Wang, S., & Guo, Z. (2015). On targeted poverty alleviation in China. *Guizhou Social Sciences, 5*, 147–150.
17. Liu, M. (2016). *Strategy of development-driven poverty alleviation in rural China*. Jilin University, Changchun.

18. Wang, S., Zhang, Y., Yang, L., et al. (2015). Household poverty alleviation projects in contiguous impoverished areas: Based on surveys of Wumeng Mountainous Area across three provinces and six counties. *Academic Journal of Zhongzhou, 3*, 68–72.
19. Si, L. (2011). Benefits of work-relief policies in rural poverty alleviation and development: Based on surveys of implementation in Gansu Province. *Gansu Social Sciences, 2011*(3), 237–239.
20. Ling, W., & Liu, X. (2016). Poverty alleviation with Chinese characteristics: The Concept, practice and implications for the world. *Socialism Studies, 4*, 69–75.
21. Zhang, Q., & Feng, D. (2016). China's poverty reduction practice and theoretical innovation: 1978–2016. *Reform, 4*, 27–42.
22. Li, X., Tang, L., & Xu, H. (2015). On poverty governance in China: An analysis based on the targeting and delivery of poverty alleviation resources. *Journal of Jilin University (Social Sciences Edition), 2015*(4), 90–98, 250–251.
23. Xu, H., & Li, X. (2016). operational dilemma of poverty alleviation projects from the perspective of targeted poverty alleviation: Explanations: A case study of competitive projects in County W, North China. *Journal of China Agricultural University (Social Sciences Edition), 2016*(4), 49–56.
24. Tan, X. (2017). On Improving current institutional mechanisms for targeted poverty alleviation. *Journal of China Agricultural University (Social Sciences Edition), 5*, 42–50.
25. He, Z., & Chen, Q. (2017). "Fragmentation" and integration of targeted poverty alleviation: A perspective of holistic governance. *Chinese Public Administration, 2017*(10), 87–91.
26. Wang, W., & Wang, A. (2016). Poverty alleviation in Gansu since 1982: Processes, reflections and prospects. *Journal of Lanzhou University (Social Sciences Edition), 1*, 112–118.
27. Zhou, D. (2017). Thirty years of poverty governance in China: Values, actions and dilemmas: An analysis based on policy texts. *Qinghai Social Sciences, 6*, 153–161.
28. Yi, L. (2018). The evolution and prospect of China's poverty alleviation policy in the past 40 years of reform and opening up: Based on an analysis of national policy texts. *Journal of Southwest Minzu University (Humanities and Social Sciences Edition), 2018*(4), 183–191.
29. Kong, F. (2018). Historical evolution and innovation of poverty alleviation policies since the reform and opening up: A review based on CPC Central Committee Document No.1. *Contemporary Chinese History Studies, 2018*(2), 111–120, 128.
30. Zhang, C., & Dang, X. (2007). *Public administration*. China Renmin University Press.
31. Elssφyen, & Zhang, D. (2000). Politics of poverty reduction. *International Journal of Social Sciences, 2000*(4), 43–48.
32. Yue, X., & Luo, C. (2010). Rural migrant workers and poverty alleviation. *World Economy, 11*, 84–98.
33. Li, B. (2004). Rural poverty, public finance and public properties in China. Agriculture Press.
34. Yao, Y. (2004). *A transitional China: A review of social justice and equality*. China Renmin University Press.
35. Cai, F., & Wan, G. (2006). *Income inequality and poverty in China's transition period*. Social Sciences Academic Press (China).
36. The World Bank. (2001). *World development report 2000/2001: Attacking poverty*. Oxford University Press.
37. Mo, G, & Lin, C. (2016). Framing of Performance improvement mechanism for targeted poverty alleviation from the perspective of government function transformation. *Studies on Party and Government, 2016*(5), 51–60.
38. Cai, K. (2014). Power models and promotion of poverty alleviation through cooperation between government and social organizations. *Chinese Public Administration, 9*, 55–65.
39. Guo, P. (2012). Obstacles for the government to purchase NGO poverty alleviation services and their solutions: Limits and orientation of public services. *Guizhou Social Sciences, 8*, 41–42.
40. The State Council Poverty Alleviation Office. Five Causes of Poverty [EB/OL], November 21, 2015. http://m.news.cntv.cn/2015/11/21ARTI1448082051328733.shtml
41. Poverty Alleviation Office Director Meets Press on the Battle against Targeted Poverty Alleviation [EB/OL]. http://www.china.com.cn/zhibo/content_50665654

42. The State Council Poverty Alleviation Office Notice on the Work Plan of Poverty Registration [EB/OL], April 11, 2014. http://www.cpad.gov.cn/art/2014/4/11/art_50_23761
43. Sen, A. (1981). *Poverty and famines: An essay on entitlement and deprivation*. Oxford University Press.
44. Bulletin No. 2 2018: Follow-Up Audit Results of the Implementation of Major National Policies and Measures in the Fourth Quarter of 2017. [EB/OL], April 18, 2018. http://www.audit.gov.cn/n5/n25/c121703/content.html
45. Du, Z., & Zhan, L. Implementing targeted poverty alleviation strategy: Challenges and solutions. *China Development Observation, 2015*(8), 23–26.
46. Tang, R. (2015). Interpretations of Xi Jinping thought on targeted poverty alleviation. *People's Forum, 10*, 28–30.
47. Zuo, T., Yang, Y., & Zhong, L. (2015). Targeted poverty alleviation: Technology orientation, theoretical analysis and practical challenges. *Guizhou Social Sciences, 8*, 6–162.
48. Tian, D., & Wang, D. (2014). Causes and solutions to the dilemma of "poverty in development": Surveys and analysis from the new stage of poverty alleviation in Chongqing. *West Forum, 6*, 81–89.
49. Mo, G. (2013). Rural entrepreneurship and poverty alleviation in areas with large ethnic minority populations: Based on empirical analysis of Tiandeng County, Guangxi. Wuhan University, Wuhan.
50. Hunag, C., & Shen, Y. (2013). Reflections on improving China's new rural poverty alleviation development strategy: On anti-poverty mechanism under the coordination of "three-dimensional capital." *Gansu Social Sciences, 3*, 139–142.
51. Liu, X., Huang, Z., & Cheng, W. (2007). Description and theoretical interpretation of upward moving of microfinance targets. *Chinese Rural Economy, 8*, 23–34.
52. Guo, X., & Zhou, Q. (2016). Perennial multidimensional poverty, inequality and poverty factors. *Economic Research Journal, 6*, 143–156.
53. Li, B., & Zuo, T. (2016). Implementation logic of policies concerning poverty alleviation industries from the perspective of targeted measures: A case study of Village Y Greenhouse Vegetable Industry. *Journal of Southwest University* (*Social Sciences Edition*), *2016*(7), 66–73.
54. Deng, W. (2014). Challenges, Countermeasures and approaches of targeted poverty alleviation. *Rural Economy, 6*, 78–81.
55. Yan, D., & Fu, H. (2016). An evolutionary game analysis of leading enterprises' participation in poverty alleviation. *Rural Economy, 2016*(2), 82–85.
56. Sun, Z. (2016). Poverty alleviation by disembedded industries: A case study of Guizhou. *Journal of Fujian Provincial Party School of CPC, 3*, 14–21.
57. Lu, Q., Sun, J., & Xiang, Y. (2016). Current situation, classification and comparison of member interests of property rights management of villager cooperatives: Why China lacks in effective villager cooperatives. *Economists, 2016*(9), 86–95.
58. Li, P., Chen, G., & Zhang, Y. (2015). *Social situation in China 2016: analysis and prediction*. Social Sciences Academic Press (China).
59. Luo, C. (2012). Economic growth, income gap and rural poverty. *Economic Research Journal, 2*, 15–27.
60. Zhang, R. (2015). new ideas and policies for regional poverty alleviation. *Guangming Daily*, September 30, 2015.
61. Zhang, Q. (2014). *China green poverty reduction index report 2014*. Economic Daily Press.
62. Liu, H. (2016). Problems, experience and strategy selection in the implemen-tation of targeted poverty alleviation: Based on the survey of Tongren City, Guizhou Province. *Rural Economy, 5*, 112–117.
63. Li, H. (2014). Multiple logic of poverty alleviation and public governance in specialized farmer cooperatives. *Guizhou Social Sciences, 2014*(7), 133–137.
64. Xue, Y., & Zhang, Y. (2016). Theoretical model construction of social entrepreneurship research and suggestions on key issues. *Journal of Tianjin University (Social Sciences Edition), 5*, 392–399.

65. Liu, Y. (2019). Average annual GDP growth rate of poverty-stricken counties: Over 2% higher than the national average [EB/OL], September 27, 2019. http://finance.sina.com.cn/china/gncj/2019-09-27/doc-iicezzrq8725110.shtml
66. General Office of the CPC Central Committee and the General Office of the State Council. Circular on Work Measures of Poverty Alleviation Supervision and Inspection [EB/OL], July 17, 2016. http://www.cpad.gov/art/2016/7/17/art_1742_45.html
67. Huang, C., & Qin, Z. (2015). Evolution of China's rural poverty governance system and targeted poverty alleviation. *Research on Development, 2*, 56–59.
68. Zuo, T., Jing, J., et al. (2017). Innovation dimension of anti-poverty governance system in China's campaign against poverty. *Journal of Hohai University (Philosophy and Social Sciences Edition), 19*(5), 6–12.
69. Wang, S., & Hu, J. (2020). From subsistence to development: Seventy years of anti-poverty practice since the founding of the PRC. *Issues in Agricultural Economy, 2020*(2), 4–14.
70. Xing, C., & Li, X. (2013). Elite capture and target deviation of government-funded poverty alleviation projects. *Chinese Public Administration, 2013*(9), 109–113.
71. General Office of the CPC Central Committee and the General Office of the State Council. Guidelines on Strengthening the Selection and Management of Resident Work Teams in Poor Villages [EB/OL], December 24, 2017. http://www.gov.cn/zhengce/2017-12/24/content_5250001.htm
72. Ding, Y. (2018). Flexible governance: the operation of the "work team" mechanism and the logic of governance. *Socialism Studies, 1*, 80–90.
73. Jing, O. (2012). Resident work team mechanism and changes in primary-level governance. *Journal of China Agricultural University (Social Sciences Edition), 1*, 111–115.
74. Zhu, Z., Tan, F., & Qin, H. (2020). How to embed resident work teams into village management? A case study of "getting closer to people" campaign. *Journal of Public Administration, 3*, 84–101.
75. Chen, T., & Liu, X. (2011). Tournament system, promotion game and local theater politics. *Journal of Public Management, 2*, 21–33.
76. Zhou, X. (2014). Deepening reform and promoting release and growth of internal impetus. *Journal of Fujian Provincial Party School of CPC, 8*, 52–58.
77. Jiang, H., & Liu, Z. (2016). Influencing factors of large-scale operation intention of specialty agriculture in poor areas: A micro analysis from the perspective of villagers. *Journal of South-Central Minzu University (Humanities and Social Sciences Edition), 36*(2), 106–111.
78. Guo, J. (2013). The impact of transportation infrastructure construction on rural poverty reduction. *Guizhou Agricultural Sciences, 41*(12), 213–217.
79. Li, G., Yin, C., & Wu, Q. (2015). Rural infrastructure construction and agricultural total factor productivity. *Journal of Zhongnan University of Economics and Law, 2015*(1), 141–147.
80. Zeng, F., & Cai, B. (2018). Rural infrastructure as the foundation of rural revitalization strategy. *Issues in Agricultural Economy, 7*, 88–95.
81. Gao, Y., & Li, S. (2006). Analysis of poverty reduction effects of infrastructure construction in China based on the CGE Model. *Journal of Quantitative & Technical Economics, 2006*(6), 14–24.
82. Liu, S., & Zhou, S. (2011). Access to infrastructure and income growth in Rural China: Regression results based on static and dynamic unbalanced panels. *Chinese Rural Economy, 1*, 27–36.
83. Kang, J., Guo, M., & Fu, Y. (2014). building roads and getting prosperous: An empirical study on the development of transportation infrastructure and poverty reduction. *Inquiry into Economic Issues, 2014*(9), 41–46.
84. Xie, S., Liu, S., & Li, Q. (2018). Access to Infrastructure and poverty reduction in rural areas: Empirical analysis from China's Micro-data. *Chinese Rural Economy, 2018*(5), 112–113.
85. Rothwell, R., & Zegveld, W. (1985). *Reindusdalization and technology*. Longman.
86. Amartya, S. (1979). Issues in the measurement of poverty. *Scandinavian Journal of Economics, 81*(2), 285–307.

87. Dorado, S., & Ventresca, M. J. (2013). Crescive entrepreneurship in complex social problems: Institutional conditions for entrepreneurial engagement. *Journal of Business Venturing, 1*, 69–82.
88. Amin, A. (2009). Extraordinarily ordinary: Working in the social economy. *Social Enterprise Journal, 2009*(1), 30.
89. Defourny, J., & Nyssens, M. (2009). Conceptions of social enterprise and social entrepreneurship in Europe and the United States: Convergences and divergences. *Journal of Social Entrepreneurship, 1*, 32–53.
90. Granovetter, M. (1985). Economic action and social structure: The problem of embeddedness. *American Journal of Sociology, 91*(3), 481–510.
91. Barrow, R. (1990). Government spending in a simple model of endogenous growth. *Journal of Political Economy, 98*(5), 103–125.
92. Ahmed, R. H. M. (1990). Developmental impact of rural infrastructure in Bangladesh, Research Report 83 (pp. 12–34). Washington D.C: International Food Policy Research Institute.
93. Gibson, J., & Olivia, S. (2010). The effect of infrastructure access and quality on non-farm enterprises in Rural Indonesia. *World Development, 38*(5), 717–726.
94. Gibson, J., & Rozelle, S. (2003). Poverty and access to roads in Papua New Guinea. *Economic Development and Cultural Change, 52*(1), 159–185.
95. Fan, S., & Zhang, V. (2009). Infrastructure and regional economic development in Rural China. *China Economic Review, 15*(2), 203–214.
96. Dale, S.B., & Krueger, A. B. (2002). Estimating the payoff to attending a more selective college: An application of selection on observables and unobservables. *Quarterly Journal of Economics, 117*(4), 1491–1527.
97. Jung, H.-S., & Thorbecke, E. (2003). The impact of public education expenditure on human capital, growth, and poverty in Tanzania and Zambia: A general equilibrium approach. *Journal of Policy Modeling, 25*(8), 701–725.
98. Lleras-Muney, A. (2005). The relationship between education and adult mortality in the United States. *Review of Economic Studies, 72*(1), 189–221.

Chapter 6
Winning the Battle Against Extreme Poverty: Practices and Theoretical Interpretations

Since the 18th CPC National Congress in 2012, under the strong leadership of the CPC Central Committee with Xi Jinping as its core, and with the driving compass of Xi Jinping Thought on Socialism with Chinese Characteristics for a New Era and his anti-poverty ideas and proposals, China has adhered to the basic strategy of targeted poverty alleviation and elimination, effectively implementing measures concerned. Through accurate identification of poor people, targeted management of the work and effective delivery of targeted measures, poor population and poor areas have been lifted out of poverty. The historic feat has been made possible thanks to the concerted efforts of the CPC and the people, and China has worked out an approach in poverty reduction with its own characteristics.

The most fundamental reason for China's remarkable achievements in poverty reduction is its adherence to the leadership of the CPC and the full play of institutional strengths of socialism with Chinese characteristics. Led by the CPC and Chinese government, China's poverty alleviation campaign has featured an all-encompassing framework to fully mobilize all social sectors and people and stimulate their anti-poverty enthusiasm to participate. In addition, there have been constant adjustment and improvement of strategies and policies with increasing input of all resources. These are what China has accumulated from its anti-poverty practice.

6.1 Giving Full Play to Institutional Strengths

Pooling resources to solve major problems is one of the strengths of socialism with Chinese characteristics, the biggest political strength in China, as President Xi Jinping puts it. The socialist system with Chinese characteristics includes the fundamental political system of people's congress, the system of multi-party cooperation and political consultation under the leadership of the CPC, basic political systems covering the system of regional autonomy for ethnic minorities and that of community-level

S. Wang, *Poverty Alleviation and Targeted Measures*,
https://doi.org/10.1007/978-981-96-1493-6_6

autonomy. There are also the legal system of socialism with Chinese characteristics, basic economic system with public ownership as the mainstay and various forms of ownership developing side by side, and the economic, political, cultural and social systems based on these systems.[1] To zero in on winning the battle against extreme poverty is a process of coordination of all systems. And the key is to adhere to the leadership of the CPC to constantly improve the basic economic system and fully develop the great spirit of the Chinese nation.

6.1.1 The CPC Leadership Providing Political Guarantee for Poverty Alleviation

The CPC is the core of leadership for the cause of socialism with Chinese characteristics and represents the fundamental interests of the overwhelming majority of the Chinese people. Upholding the CPC leadership has been of vital importance to do a good job in poverty alleviation and development so that poor people can be helped to shake off poverty towards a better life and share in the fruits of development. The leadership of the CPC is also the most essential feature of socialism with Chinese characteristics.

Firstly, the leadership of the CPC has provided the political guarantee for poverty alleviation. The fundamental purpose of the CPC is to serve the people wholeheartedly. Since the 18th CPC National Congress, the Party has placed poverty alleviation in a more prominent strategic position, making it the top priority of the government for a period of time. The implementation of the poverty alleviation strategy is not only an essential requirement of socialism itself and of completing the building of a moderately prosperous society in all respects, but also the responsibility and mission of the CPC as the representative of the interests of the Chinese people of all ethnic groups. Indeed, the CPC leadership has been a strong political guarantee and driving compass for the anti-poverty endeavor in China.

Secondly, the leadership of the CPC has provided institutional guarantee for poverty alleviation. Relying on its political and organizational strength, China has established a poverty eradication management network with the central government acting as coordinator, provincial, regional and municipal governments taking overall responsibility, and city and county governments overseeing implementation, prioritizing contiguous impoverished areas with emphasis on accurately identified counties, villages and households. Specifically, the CPC Central Party Committee and the State Council have assumed an overall coordinating role by launching over-arching planning, major policies and projects. The leading Party and government officials of provinces, autonomous regions and municipalities directly under the central government take charge of poverty eradication tasks by setting targets, issuing projects and placing funds, together with organization, mobilization, supervision and assessment. Party committees and governments at city or county levels are responsible for

[1] *Proceedings of the 18th CPC National Congress* [M]. Beijing: People's Publishing House, 2012.

coordination between the senior and junior levels within the region by supervision and inspection, and pooling resources to zero in on solutions to remove the poverty label as scheduled. Party committees and governments at the county level bear the responsibility of implementation, with Party secretaries and county governors as the first responsible persons who are to make progress arrangements, oversee project delivery, use of funds, human resources deployment and progress promotion. The leadership of the CPC has made it possible to establish such a complete responsibility system for poverty alleviation, and to clearly assign tasks to Party committees and governments at different levels and to specific individuals to ensure the smooth implementation of poverty alleviation.

Thirdly, the leadership of the CPC has provided theoretical guarantee for poverty alleviation, which involves many departments, dispersed targets and complex systems. It requires the guidance of systematic theories. To carry out a more extensive anti-poverty campaign, it is vital to adhere to the leadership of the CPC, Marxism-Leninism, Mao Zedong Thought, Deng Xiaoping Theory, the Important Thought of "Three Represents", the Scientific Outlook on Development, and Xi Jinping Thought on Socialism with Chinese Characteristics for a New Era. There has been a firm belief in and steady practice of the CPC's guiding principles of proceeding from reality, combining theory with practice, seeking, testing and developing truth from facts and experience by emancipating the mind, advancing with the times and being realistic and pragmatic. These have been the key to the success of China's campaign against poverty.

6.1.2 Basic Economic System as the Foundation for Poverty Alleviation

The drive of pooling resources to solve major problems has relied on the basic socialist economic system in China. At the Fourth Plenary Session of the 19th CPC Central Committee held in 2019, it was proposed that, "The basic socialist economic system is constituted by the socialist market economy and other economic systems, with public ownership and distribution according to work as the mainstay and various forms of ownership and distribution coexisting and developing. It has embodied the strength of the socialist system and conformed to the level of productive forces in the primary stage of socialism in China. It is a great creation of the Party and the people." The dominance of public ownership underlines China's socialist nature which is a vital guarantee not only for consolidating the CPC's governance, but also for poor areas and people to share in the fruits of reform and development, and an economic foundation for China to concentrate its efforts on poverty alleviation.

Xi Jinping has emphasized on several occasions the importance of holding on to China's basic economic system and the principle of "unswervingly consolidating and developing the public sector of the economy" and "unswervingly encouraging, supporting and guiding the development of the non-public sector." This can help better leverage the advantages of state-owned enterprises and guide all sectors of the economy, including the non-public sector, to participate and build an all-compassing framework of poverty alleviation.

With work-based distribution system as the mainstay and multiple modes of distribution coexisting, the government has been able to reasonably adjust the distribution relationship between urban and rural areas, as well as different regions and groups through the redistribution adjustment mechanism with taxation, social security and transfer payment as the major means, which has laid a solid foundation for resource mobilization and investment in poverty alleviation. At the same time, efforts have been made to encourage the development of charity and other public welfare programs by giving play to the role of the third distribution.

6.1.3 Chinese National Spirit Creating a Cultural Atmosphere for Targeted Poverty Alleviation

China has a long tradition of pooling resources to solve major problem. As Xi Jinping observes, "China has a fine traditional culture nurtured in the development of more than 5000 years of human civilization. This, together with a revolutionary culture and advanced socialist culture bred in the great endeavor by the Party and the people, has accumulated the deepest spiritual aspirations to represent the unique spiritual identity of the Chinese nation."[2] In the thousands of years of ups and downs, the Chinese people have stood firmly together as one through all the hardships to carry forward the spirit of solidarity, shaping a national character of working together to accomplish great things. Over decades of the great endeavor in the building of socialism, the Chinese people have firmly believed that unity is strength and the right way forward, giving rise to a national trait of governance that pools resources to solve major problems.

The fine traditional culture of the Chinese nation is in line with core socialist values, typically manifested in the traditional virtues of unremitting self-improvement and helping the poor. The cause of poverty alleviation has not only brought into play the hard-working spirit of officials, but also boosted the morale of the public in poor areas, strengthening their confidence and determination to change the situation of poverty and backwardness, and gathering a strong joint force of the whole Party and society.

6.2 Adherence to Government Leadership

Government leadership is a hallmark of poverty alleviation in China. Practice has proved that economic growth cannot automatically achieve poverty reduction. Although the market plays a fundamental role in endogenous poverty alleviation and

---

[2] Xi [1].

its mechanism is flexible, the market mostly focuses on profit-seeking investment projects with short return cycles and stable returns. Without guidance and support from the government, it is difficult for the market to enter the area of poverty alleviation with long return cycle, high risk and low profit, where the market usually fails.

6.2.1 Market Failure Necessitating Government Leadership

China's poor population was largely found in rural areas, with agriculture as the main source of income. According to the World Bank and the National Bureau of Statistics, 99% of the poor lived in rural areas[3] and 20% of the lowest income group had 54% of their income from agriculture.[4] The poor population used to be widely distributed in the vast central and western backward rural areas with poor living conditions, frequent natural disasters and poor public infrastructure, especially in old revolutionary base areas, areas with large ethnic minority populations and border areas.

The distinctive features of China's poor population and market failure have made it particularly necessary for the government to lead the cause of poverty alleviation in China. This is particularly felt in the following two aspects.

One is that the market mechanism cannot realize the balanced development of national economy. On the one hand, as a weak industry, agricultural production is under the double risk of natural and market factors, with generally a longer production cycle and low investment benefit. As a result, in the fierce competition, market players tend to opt for industries that are less risky with short cycle and high efficiency to invest resources in instead of agriculture in order to maximize the profit. This has led to the imbalance of agriculture in the national economy. On the other hand, market mechanisms follow free competition and trade to allocate resources. Due to the differences in regional resource endowment and location conditions, regions with congenital deficiency were in a weak position in market competition. The Matthew effect had been more and more felt as the economy developed, with the stronger becoming stronger and the weaker getting weaker, resulting in a wider gap between developed and underdeveloped regions and the rural areas in the central and western China were in a more unbalanced deteriorating position in the national economic development. This has required the government to play a leading role to consolidate the position of agriculture, optimize the industrial structure and balance regional development through the introduction of relevant regulation and control policies.

The other is that the market mechanism cannot realize the effective supply of public goods, which refer to the supply, consumption or use of non-competitive and

[3] The World Bank [2].

[4] Calculation based on household survey data 2006, National Bureau of Statistics.

non-exclusive products for all members of society, such as public service infrastructure, education, medical care, environmental protection, among others. Non-competitiveness means that the consumption or use of public goods by some people does not affect the consumption or use of the goods by others. Non-exclusiveness means that the consumption or use of some public goods by some people does not exclude the consumption or use of the goods by others. Due to the non-competitive and non-exclusive nature of public goods, the private sector has very low enthusiasm to provide them since most people would automatically take "free riding", benefiting from resources, goods, or services without contributing to them nor share the costs.

The targets of poverty alleviation, namely poor areas and poor people, are between pure public goods and private goods, which are quasi-public goods, non-competitive and non-exclusive to a certain extent, which determines that the private sector cannot automatically participate in poverty alleviation. It is therefore highly necessary for the government to lead, organize and guide the whole society to participate in poverty alleviation, and realize the effective supply of rural infrastructure, health care, education, culture and other quasi-public goods.

6.2.2 Government Leadership as the Fundamental Guarantee for Poverty Alleviation

From the government's point of view, the government has taken the lead in poverty alleviation and development by virtue of its powerful political mobilization and resource integration capabilities, and has invested a lot of human, material and financial resources. Poverty alleviation, as a top priority during the 13th Five-year Plan period, has always played a dominant role in promoting overall economic and social development. Without legal approval and guidance from the government, even the best projects cannot be possibly delivered.

It is inevitable for the government to play its central role in poverty control. On the one hand, the "people-oriented" development philosophy of socialism with Chinese characteristics and the development goal of "common prosperity" require China to fully play its role in the socialist market economy. The strengths of the CPC's political leadership and of the socialist system have made it possible to pool resources to alleviate poverty by integrating it into China's overall development strategy and giving full play to the role of the government in social security and the optimization of the top design of poverty alleviation policies to strengthen the establishment of various laws and regulations and the social security system to help the market mechanism play a role in the allocation of resources for poverty alleviation. On the other hand, the government can ensure the balance of economic aggregate by considering efficiency and fairness of economic development to promote the coordination of economic structure and the optimization of productivity layout. In addition, it can effectively connect social, market, individual and other resources to optimize the allocation of factors of production such as labor, capital, land and technology, and make macro-control of poverty alleviation resources more forward-looking, targeted and coordinated.

Severely impoverished areas have been the main targets for poverty reduction. These areas generally lack in internal poverty alleviation capacity and it is difficult for them to arrange suitable industries as economic support. Without the government's substantial support, it would be difficult to ensure that poverty alleviation is achieved on schedule. The government has given support in the following aspects.

Firstly, coordinating the interests of all parties to pursue fairness as well as market efficiency. The development of poverty-stricken areas involves various relations, including those between developed and poverty-stricken areas, different regions, the primary, secondary and tertiary industries in a given geographical area, as well as the relations between poverty-stricken households and between local officials and villagers. Underlying these relationships are the potential interests of different groups of people. Therefore, governments should coordinate their interests and ensure equity while achieving the objectives of market efficiency. This has been done through formulating corresponding economic policies, laws and regulations to effectively protect the interests of poor households.

Secondly, guiding players of all economic sectors to release their vitality in targeted poverty alleviation. This started with the stimulation of internal driver of the poor population to resume their principal role. To address the problem that some poor people were lacking in initiative and drive, efforts have been made to encourage them to rely on their own efforts rather than wait for external assistance, helping them build up self-belief and have access to education. This has been going hand in hand with the government's efforts to stimulate the participation enthusiasm of market players through preferential policies, industrial projects and local resources.

Poor areas were mostly found in mountainous and plateau areas with their landforms and climate conditions of a "tridimensional character", often harsh and extreme. This has led to the situation of "affluent poverty", a dilemma in which many poor areas were rich in resources like wild mountains and lands, waters, beaches and sandy lands, which are potentials for economic growth; however, they usually could not effectively develop and utilize them due to the lack of human capital. To address this issue, on the one hand, governments have attracted capital from developed areas through preferential policies and industrial projects to help develop their local resources and drive their development. On the other hand, they have given full play to the professional strengths of local organizations, research institutes and agricultural specialists to help cultivate competitive local industries, and promote the internal impetus for the development of poor areas.

Thirdly, the social security system has been brought into operation to help those in need. The system of subsistence allowances has covered poverty-stricken people who have completely or partially lost their ability to work and cannot be lifted out of poverty by industrial employment. Without the ability to use resources and lacking in the potential and sustainability for self-development, these people are largely from poor households with one or more disabled members, or with disabilities due to diseases or accidents. Through social security, the government has effectively helped them out of poverty.

Fourthly, overseeing the implementation of targeted poverty alleviation policies. Governments at all levels have been responsible for sound implementation of relevant policies and regulations through good mechanism design by setting up a hierarchical supervision system with dynamic management and performance assessment mechanisms to effectively monitor the enthusiasm and effectiveness of their poverty alleviation performances. Government leadership is the political prerequisite and guarantee for China to have achieved significant outcomes in poverty reduction. Since 1986, when the State Council Leading Group for Economic Development in Poor Areas (renamed The State Council Leading Group for Poverty Alleviation and Development in 1993) was established together with its corresponding organizations in governments at all levels, there have been special government agencies in charge of poverty reduction in China.

The government leadership has made it possible for China to launch the nationwide campaign against extreme poverty. Formulating well-conceived strategies and mobilizing various resources in line with the actual conditions, a network of poverty eradication management has been established, with the central government acting as coordinator, provincial governments taking overall responsibility, and city and county governments overseeing implementation. Top government officials at different levels signed written pledges to their seniors to strengthen the leadership responsibility system and have made good use of administrative power at all levels to ensure that relevant policies are implemented in every household. The strengths of the socialist system are also encapsulated in this government-led poverty alleviation approach.

6.3 An All-Encompassing Campaign Against Poverty

China's development-oriented poverty alleviation campaign had entered a new stage of targeted poverty alleviation and the approach had changed from generalized broad-brush policies for regional development to targeted measures for specific villages, households and individuals. With the changes in poverty alleviation practices and the macro economy as a whole, the vitality of market players and social organizations had been fully released, and a large-scale poverty alleviation framework had been established, with the government, society and the market working in coordination, mobilizing and integrating multiple players from different regions, sectors, departments and businesses to join in.

6.3.1 Multidimensional Nature of Poverty Determining the Participation of Multiple Parties

Market failure has provided the fundamental basis for government intervention, which, however, is not omnipotent since there is also the possibility of "government failure". With the progress of the anti-poverty efforts, the problem of "diminishing marginal benefit" emerged in terms of the outcome. To take government-sponsored projects for example. Owing to the government's insufficient knowledge of market laws, industrial projects may turn out to be homogenous in various regions and the subsequent development is likely to face greater market risks. At the same time, if the government works alone, there would be no chance for poor areas and poor people to develop market awareness which would impair their capability to effectively participate in market competition to fight poverty.

For a long time, because of the influence of poverty line and the limitation of the concept of poverty, people used to measure poverty by income. In fact, poverty is a wide-ranging social phenomenon. According to the World Bank, poverty is a clear-cut denial of well-being, for which there are also different interpretations. For instance, it can be measured by income or consumption for the wealth and resources possessed by a household, or by whether a household has access to all types of consumer goods, such as food, housing, healthcare and education, or by the concept of "viability". However, no matter how "well-being" is understood, poverty is a multidimensional concept that includes many non-monetary dimensions, such as access to public goods and services like education, healthcare and housing, in addition to income.

In 2011, Outlines for Development-Driven Poverty Alleviation in Rural Areas (2011–2020) was promulgated and implemented, setting out goals and tasks at this stage, namely, "Through 2020, the poverty-stricken people will have been assured security of food and clothing, and their access to compulsory education, basic medical care and housing guaranteed.[5] The per capita net income of rural residents in poor areas will have increased at a higher rate than the national average, and indicators in major areas of basic public services approached the national average, reversing the trend of a widening development gap." The requirement of "Two Assurances and Three Guarantees" has actually reflected a change in the major concern of China's poverty alleviation strategy and policy, which moved from mere assurance of adequate food and clothing in the past to the guarantee of a more dignified life for poor people. This is a multi-dimensional anti-poverty target, aiming not only to increase income, but also guarantee access to education, medical care and housing services, paying more attention to the development of people, a significant shift from poverty alleviation by economic development alone to a more extensive approach. The diversity of poverty alleviation targets has indicated that in the new stage, we should not only address the overall difficulties at the regional level, but also focus on specific poor people to ensure their subsistence and development capacity. This has put more emphasis on the necessity of mobilizing all social players to build an all-encompassing poverty alleviation network.

[5] Commonly known as "Two Assurances and Three Guarantees".

6.3.2 A Network Giving Full Play to the Strengths of All Players

The large-scale poverty alleviation network, or the all-encompassing campaign against poverty, is the system guarantee for winning the battle against extreme poverty, with government-sponsored projects, sector-specific programs, and corporate and societal assistance supplementing each other. The framework, by bringing in multiple social forces, has fully mobilized the initiative of the whole society, and encouraged market players in science, education, culture, health, environmental protection and other fields to participate in the great endeavor. The diversified development of the multiple players is conducive to giving full play to their various advantages and improving the accuracy of poverty alleviation measures.

The government has played a leading role through government-sponsored projects and sector-specific programs. The former focuses on measures such as relocating poor people from inhospitable areas, village-based poverty alleviation, providing jobs instead of grants, developing industries and promoting employment, piloting areas for poverty alleviation, and building old revolutionary base areas. The later puts emphasis on clarifying the responsibilities of various departments and industries to encourage them to offer assistance with their professional advantages by launching sector-specific programs, providing technological support, developing education, cultural undertakings and healthcare, as well as improving population service management, the social security system and paying attention to energy and ecological conservation. The market plays a complementary role through corporate and societal assistance, which includes paired-up assistance, east-west collaboration, giving full play to the role of the people's army and police forces, and mobilizing enterprises and all sectors of society to participate in poverty alleviation. In this process, market players can give full play to the role of the market mechanism and improve the income level and development capacity of poor areas and people. This is further illustrated in the following.

To start with, the market has improved the allocation efficiency of poverty alleviation resources. First of all, it is more professional and efficient. The arbitrary broad-brush approach failed to learn the specific needs and demands of individuals, resulting in a deviation of targeted assistance. At the same time, under the leadership of the hierarchical system, the quality of people in charge of poverty alleviation at the primary level also affects the use efficiency and the allocation of funds and resources. The market mechanism, through its own regulation, can improve the efficiency of resource allocation. Besides, the market could also achieve effective matching of various players and resources. Poverty alleviation involves a wide range of players, including government departments, enterprises, social organizations and poor households, as well as multi-dimensional resources that need to be allocated, such as healthcare, housing and education. This has determined that relying solely on the government will affect the optimal allocation of resources due to information deficiency. In contrast, the market may fully reflect all kinds of information through competition mechanism and supply and demand mechanism, and the multiple players can also accurately position themselves in the market and realize the optimal allocation of resources through their own adjustment.

In addition, the market has reduced the selectivity bias in the use of poverty alleviation funds. On the premise of "rational person" and maximization of profits, the market mechanism can automatically target through competition mechanism to reduce the occurrence of selective bias. Once there is a deviation in the targeting of the funds, it would be difficult for poor households to benefit. For example, the practice of village-based poverty alleviation projects may often lead to the unsatisfactory outcome that the villages in general have increased the income and consumption, but non-poor households instead of the poor got more benefits [3]. Differently, the "profit-seeking" nature of the market mechanism determines that the market-oriented poverty alleviation mechanism can achieve automatic targeting. As long as the interest guiding mechanism is reasonable, the mechanism would work to avoid selective bias, and all market players and resources can match each other and truly serve the poverty-alleviation households.

Finally, the market has given full play to the initiative of multiple players. Under the model of government-backed poverty alleviation, the government has at its disposal not only the resources, but also the supervision power. In the long run, villagers may get so used to "being helped" that they may grow to have a psychological dependence on the government, with diminishing self-belief and internal driver for development. This negative reliance on external assistance may even grow, obviously going against the ultimate goal of common prosperity.

Under the model of market-oriented poverty alleviation, the poor would directly participate in the assistance process and the market competition, and work together with the assisting players to build a cooperation mechanism of "sharing interests and risks", in which their own development potential would be stimulated. At the same time, the market players' own subjective initiative may also be stimulated to be willing to participate, which is conducive to avoiding the negative resistance under the administrative order alone and realizing the mutual growth of their own benefits and the effect of assistance.

6.4 Extensive Social Participation

Extensive social participation has been what drives China's remarkable achievements in poverty reduction. Although the government-led poverty alleviation campaign enjoys much strength, it also has some weaknesses, such as low efficiency of capital use, lack of close link with the market and insufficient flexibility of work. The coordinated participation of social forces can effectively make up for the deficiency of government-led endeavor against poverty.

Market players, social organizations and individuals have taken part in poverty alleviation through various forms, such as enterprises helping villages, paired-up assistance between businesses and counties, and poverty alleviation through public welfare, giving full play to their respective advantages. Indeed, they have played a significant role in the great endeavor through industries, education, health, relocation, and voluntary work.

Paired-up assistance and east-west collaboration systems have narrowed the distance between the poor areas and people and the designated departments, institutions and the developed eastern regions, and promoted their overall development. By social forces complementing and cooperating with the government in various anti-poverty efforts, a well-organized and well-coordinated network has been established in which the government plays a leading role and multiple players from the society participate to join forces and create a synergy in winning the battle against extreme poverty.

6.4.1 Participation of Social Organizations as a Major Complement

In China, non-governmental organizations are managed by the Civil Society Organization Administration. Therefore, it is also customarily referred to as "civil society organizations", for which "social organizations" is another term, including social groups, private non-enterprise organizations and foundations. Social participation here refers to the participation of social organizations and enterprises in poverty alleviation, not including paired-up assistance and east-west collaboration provided by government departments. Although the government leads the extensive poverty reduction in China, it has its own weaknesses such as low efficiency in the use of funds and lack of accuracy in identifying poor population. Social organizations can absorb idle funds from society and improve the efficiency of their use, in addition to filling in areas that the government cannot fully cover to speeding up the process. Specifically, they have played their complementary role in the following.

The first is that social participation has helped reduce the cost of poverty alleviation. To achieve targeted poverty alleviation, government departments need to invest a large amount of human and material resources, and the participation of social organizations has greatly improved the efficiency of the use of funds and reduced the cost in three aspects. Firstly, they have shared some of the government workload. It had been time-consuming and energy-consuming to identify and register poor households and to formulate relevant policies. With the help of social organizations, the heavy workload has been shared. Secondly, some of the staff members dispatched by the government to identify poor households and distribute project funds were temps who were not necessarily professional people and may be inefficient. In contrast, social organizations are usually specialized institutions with professional people, and can give full play to their own advantages and do the job efficiently. Thirdly, social organizations are capable to mobilize individuals, enterprises and other groups to invest in poverty alleviation and make up for the lack of government funds.

The second is that social participation has helped supplement poverty alleviation policies, which are an important institutional guarantee for the achievement of the set goals. However, there have been deficiencies at present, and some policies have yet been satisfactory. To make policies more workable to better protect the interests of poor households, opinions and suggestions from all sectors of society should be fully considered, especially the primary-level people, when formulating policies. Social organizations are usually where there is a splendid gathering of talented people and resources and they could speak for the public, especially the poor, and provide valuable suggestions. They may function as a bridge between the representatives of poor households and the government, so that the policy can be clearly targeted and workable. In the process of the promulgation of various measures, government departments have solicited opinions from social organizations and other social forces in various ways, such as policy consulting and public hearings, which have helped government departments make good policies and reduce errors and deviations.

The third is that social participation has helped prevent the abuse of poverty alleviation funds. China's poverty alleviation work has been led by the government, and without effective supervision, the funds may be misappropriated, embezzled or used for vanity projects. Especially in the implementation and supervision of relevant projects, if government departments within the same system supervise each other, rent-seeking or corruption may easily occur among some officials when they are driven by profits. According to investigations by the National Audit Office, funds earmarked for poverty alleviation in some counties were embezzled or wasted, and poor villagers were not benefited from preferential policies. Therefore, the introduction of social supervision to the anti-poverty campaign is one of the major functions of social organizations, which are usually more active and professional than the general public. The participation of social organizations in overseeing the government performance can better ensure the proper use of policies, projects and funds to reduce corruption and waste and promote the healthy development of the endeavor. Governments can entrust social organizations to participate in specific inspections of agricultural industry projects and reports about funding and work progress; as well as in performance evaluations concerning the use and management of government funds for poverty alleviation, so as to better prevent corruption and ensure better use of the funds.

The fourth is that social participation has helped the operation of poverty alleviation service brands to better meet the fundamental and common needs of the poor. By polling the strengths of social organizations in project design and implementation in a chain model, it has also greatly improved the professionalism of services in general. They may themselves lead as typical examples of government purchasing of poverty alleviation services and play the role model to arouse and enhance the responsibility and participation awareness of the whole society for targeted poverty alleviation. Their experiences and practices may effectively draw the attention from individuals, social organizations and social groups and stimulate more people to join in.

6.4.2 International Cooperation Promoting Innovative Poverty Reduction Mechanisms

In the process of international poverty alleviation cooperation, China has not only been a beneficiary of assistance funds from international communities, but more importantly, it has introduced a series of advanced international poverty reduction concepts, theories and methods which have been applied to China's poverty reduction practices and contributed a lot to China's anti-poverty efforts. The economic assistance provided by developed countries has been much more than just concessional loans and development aids. There have been well-developed concepts, systematic project operation capacities and efficient and flexible strategies. Among many international organizations providing assistance to China, the World Bank and the Asian Development Bank are representative.

Back in 1992, the World Bank and China's State Council Leading Group Office of Poverty Alleviation and Development jointly compiled a report to introduce new methods for strengthening poverty monitoring and a poverty reduction model involving multiple sectors with focus on labor mobility. The results of poverty assessment and demonstration projects were transformed into policy programs and a long-term strategy for development-oriented poverty reduction. In the gradual and steady implementation of poverty alleviation projects for the Southwest and the Qinling-Daba mountainous areas, which began in 1995, the World Bank demonstrated the effectiveness of a focused multisectoral rural development approach to poverty reduction, while introducing a new monitoring system to China to help strengthen poverty monitoring at the central and local levels. At present, the system has been adopted at the central level and extended to 592 poverty-stricken counties across the country, showing that China has acquired strong poverty assessment and mapping capabilities.

6.4.3 Participation in Poverty Alleviation Enhancing the Enthusiasm of the Poor

To stimulate the internal impetus of the poor by helping them build up self-belief and have access to education in the campaign against poverty has been an important part of Xi Jinping's ideas on poverty alleviation. While working in Ningde of eastern Fujian Province in 1988–1990, Xi Jinping stressed that "A weak hatchling bird can be the first to fly", and poor areas and people should first have the motivation of "flying" with the effort of "flying first". Relying only on external help from the government and society would not lead them anywhere. Without the internal driver, there would be no remedies to address the root cause of poverty of the rural poor, no matter how much help and aid they were granted.

The true outcomes of poverty alleviation can only be tested on the capacity and welfare of each poor individual in lifting themselves out of poverty. Therefore, it is inevitable that they should fully participate in the great endeavor by assuming their principal role. Instead of simply providing funds and projects to the poor, targeted poverty alleviation has focused more on enhancing the capacity of the poor by establishing effective mechanisms for long-term and stable poverty alleviation, and removing institutional obstacles for the poor to shake off poverty through their own efforts.

Only when poor people are deeply involved in the anti-poverty campaign and maintain the strong momentum of development with self motivation, can their enthusiasm for development be fully boosted. This combination of the internal impetus for development with the external help of relevant policies may create a synergy for poor people to get out of poverty.

6.5 Constant Adjustment and Improvement of Strategies and Policies

Constantly adjusted and improved poverty alleviation strategies and policies have been a strategic and policy guarantee for China to achieve effective outcomes in poverty reduction. The Communist Party of China adapted the Marxist thought on the comprehensive and free development of individuals to the Chinese conditions and established the fundamental mission of serving the people wholeheartedly. Since the founding of the People's Republic of China in 1949, especially since the reform and opening up in 1978, the CPC has always adhered to the people-centered philosophy and worked out a series of strategies and policies to alleviate poverty in line with China's national conditions and the latest progress, addressing phased targets by responsive measures. It has taken a path from relief to regional development and then to targeted poverty alleviation with poor households and individuals accurately identified to help. This shows the continuity and adaptability of China's poverty alleviation strategies and policies.

6.5.1 Past and Present

China's poverty alleviation can be divided into three major stages. The first stage was from 1949 to 1985, when the support measures were mainly material relief. The second stage was from 1986 to 2013, focused on regional poverty alleviation and development. The third stage was from 2014 to 2020, when targeted poverty alleviation became the basic strategy.

The first stage was based on the national macro strategy, and from the second stage, poverty alleviation became a special task. Our discussion will focus on the latter two stages, which feature significant differences in targets and objectives. Regional poverty alleviation targeted different regions, and the aim was to develop those areas faster so as to indirectly drive the poor people out of poverty. Targeted poverty alleviation has had poor households and individuals to help with the aim to directly lift them out of poverty.

Beginning from mid-1980s, anti-poverty programs tried to change the previous support policy of material relief to production assistance, supplemented by free relief. First, who to support was identified. According to China's financial situation and the distribution of poverty-stricken population at that time, it was decided that the support would be granted at the county level, with 332 national key poverty-stricken counties and 370 provincial poor counties identified. They were to be supported in infrastructure construction, building of basic farmland, implementation of work-relief, provision of credit funds and development of diversified operations, aiming to secure food and clothing in poor areas.

In 1984, the Central Government issued the Notice on Boosting Impoverished Areas to Take on a New Look, strengthening financial and material support to poverty-stricken areas,[6] mainly for the purpose of developing production, improving production conditions and enhancing regional economic vitality. It was essentially a policy for region-based poverty alleviation and development.

In 1994, the Seven-Year Plan for Poverty Alleviation was launched, aiming to solve the shortage of food and clothing for 80 million poor people in seven years. The general requirement was to "adhere to the policy of development-oriented poverty alleviation to improve the benefits of the endeavor and actively create basic conditions for food and clothing security" [4]. The number of poverty-stricken counties supported by the central government was increased to 592, and funds from the central government budget, credit, and work-relief programs were given priority to poverty-stricken counties. In terms of support funds, focus was adjusted to be placed on the central and western provinces, autonomous regions and municipalities, particularly on major projects for poor areas. In respect of the investment structure, the central government was responsible for the major part while provinces and cities were to increase their investment. At the same time, the responsibility system for poverty alleviation was emphasized by stressing centralized leadership and hierarchical responsibility, with provinces playing the principal role.

The major goal of poverty alleviation at the time was to ensure adequate food and clothing for poor households. Practice proved that planting, breeding and processing industries with agricultural products as raw materials were the most effective industries to eliminate poverty, with relatively high loan recovery rate. The approach was to raise the quality and efficiency of resource development by encouraging poverty-alleviation economic players to organize economic development which benefited households to ensure actual outcomes.

[6] From the early 1980s to the end of the 1980s, China set up seven special funds for poverty alleviation in order to help old revolutionary base areas, areas with large ethnic minority populations, border areas and poor areas change their backwardness. They were: funds for the development of underdeveloped areas, loans for the development of old revolutionary base areas, loans for the economic development of underdeveloped areas, special plan for agricultural development in the three western regions of Hexi and Dingxi in Gansu Province and the mountainous region in southern Ningxia Hui Autonomous Region, national special discount loans for poverty alleviation, special discount loans for pastoral areas and special loans for county-run enterprises.

By the early twenty-first century, widespread absolute poverty had been significantly reduced in China with the security of food and clothing for most impoverished rural population. A new round of development-oriented poverty alleviation was carried out against the backdrop of the initial establishment of a socialist market economy and a new stage of national economic and social development.

In 2001, the Outline for Development-Driven Poverty Alleviation in Rural Areas (2001–2010) was launched. The number of state-supported counties remained at 592, but all the quotas for the eastern region were given to the central and western regions, and 148,000 poor villages[7] were designated as individual targets for assistance. The basic goal was to "consolidate the achievements of food and clothing security and create conditions for a moderate prosperity". The approach was described as "one major task with two measures". "One major task" refers to the promotion of whole villages to improve the ecological conditions of production and living in 148,000 poor villages to enhance their development capacity. "Two measures" refers to labor transfer training and the industrialization of leading enterprises for poverty alleviation, with the main purpose of promoting the participation of poor people in the market. In addition to the approach, appropriate public transfer policies and numerous preferential policies for villagers were provided, which, together with the comprehensive implementation of the rural subsistence allowances system, contributed to the income growth of the poor population and alleviated the widening income gap in poor areas.

With the completion of the implementation of the first Ten-Year Program for Poverty Alleviation, the second Ten-Year Program (2011–2020) was launched in 2011, with a new poverty line[8] being set. 14 contiguous destitute areas were designated as targets for support, totaling 832 counties including those in contiguous destitute areas and on the state's poverty alleviation work list, with 128,000 poor villages designated for further assistance.

The overall goal of poverty alleviation in the new stage was to steadily achieve "Two Assurances and Three Guarantees", while requiring the per capita net income of villagers to grow faster than the national average and basic public services to reach the national average. "Two Assurances" was to ensure adequate food and clothing to eliminate extreme poverty and to consolidate the previous achievements of poverty alleviation. The "Three Guarantees" focused on human capital and development capacity, which were key issues to be addressed for the new stage. The emphasis on income growth and public services in poor areas was to further narrow the regional gap to eliminate overall poverty in the region.

Since the 18th CPC National Congress, the CPC Central Committee with Xi Jinping as its core, has attached greater importance to poverty alleviation and development and made the important decision to win the battle against extreme poverty in response to the changes in the macro situation, setting the goals that "Through 2020, we will ensure that all rural residents are lifted out of poverty as defined by the existing standard, raise all impoverished counties out of poverty, and eliminate poverty over

[7] The number increased to 150,000 later on.

[8] It was RMB 2300 per person per year at constant prices in 2010.

entire regions." In terms of supporting targets, the central government has adjusted the previous regional development-based anti-poverty model to the strategy of targeted poverty alleviation and eliminations by accurately identifying poor households and individuals to help and support. This strategy and policy adjustment was made based on the distribution of the poor population in China and the reality that they did not benefit equally from regional development, which exacerbated the income inequality within poor areas while reducing the regional gap [5]. Shifting from regional development to targeted poverty alleviation and adopting targeted measures for different poor households and individuals has been an inevitable and strategic move to achieve poverty alleviation, as well as a necessary measure to offset the reduction of poverty relief effect caused by the decline of economic growth rate and the inequality of income distribution [6].

6.5.2 Historical Experience

China's rapid economic growth over the decades has provided a material basis for sustainable poverty reduction, while the implementation of anti-poverty strategies and policies has ensured its good delivery. Practice has proved that China has chosen the right direction in its anti-poverty strategy and embarked on a path with Chinese characteristics. The strategies and policies have been phased, inherited and carried forward. Constant adjustment and improvement have been made on the basis of what has worked in the past, with valuable experience accumulated to make them play a more important role.

Firstly, steady progress has been made in the macro strategy. This has undergone a shift from focusing on economic construction to overall planning of economic and social development, and from the previous anti-poverty strategy of simply increasing the income of poor people through the "trickle-down effect" of economic growth supplemented by appropriate relief, to the implementation of the strategy of stable poverty reduction and elimination by promoting the improvement of self-development capacity of regions with relatively high concentration of poor people. Poverty alleviation policies have continued to develop and innovate on the basis of what has worked, with more targeted policies explored and introduced. Some policies were gradually transformed from being regional and local to become overall design and pilot implementation of targeted poverty alleviation at the national level.

Secondly, targeting policies have changed from being broad-brush to becoming more accurate. The targets for poverty alleviation in China used to be generalized, covering a wide region. Gradually they became counties and villages and are now accurately identified individual households. Based on a better understanding of the causes of poverty, targeting policies have been constantly changing. The current ones mostly feature the combination of regional and individual targeting, with a four-level mechanism of poor areas, counties, villages and households working together. The priority of targeted poverty alleviation efforts and resources has continued to be given to villages and individual households.

Thirdly, resources have been delivered more effectively. China's poverty alleviation resources used to be delivered equally and universally, ignoring the causes and group characteristics of poverty. Now the policies have focused on further subdividing the poor groups for more accurate targeting by introducing appropriate competition, through which limited poverty alleviation resources could be more effectively allocated to dynamically changing targets. More emphasis has been placed on making full use of market mechanisms or market players to achieve market-oriented allocation. The mechanism of mobilization, transmission and distribution of social poverty alleviation resources has been better designed, which is more stable, sustainable and regular in preventing and blocking poverty transmission, with more effective, targeted, practical and sustainable outcomes.

Fourthly, support policies have been diversified. In supporting the poor population, the Chinese government has paid more attention to the organic combination of targeted poverty alleviation policies for relief, development and prevention of poverty risks. The focus has shifted from providing material assistance alone to meet their subsistence needs to integrating policy-backed support and investment support with the self-reliance of the poor. Poverty alleviation policies have shifted from post-poverty intervention by assistance to pre-poverty intervention by reducing vulnerability and risks, and more attention has been paid to improving the capability of poor population to prevent and deal with poverty risks through investment in education, health and other aspects, rather than only providing support and assistance after they fall into poverty. The focus of the policies has shifted to ensuring equitable social distribution and giving those trapped in poverty a higher standard of living and a growing sense of happiness and gain.

Fifthly, there has been a more diversified approach to governance of poverty in China. It has developed from being policy-backed, mobilization-driven and campaign-based to long-term, institutional, standardized and abiding by the law, with significant changes from a sole government action to joint efforts led by the government. With social organizations joining in, and then an all-encompassing endeavor with government leadership and the participation of all social sectors and beneficiary groups, more attention has been paid to the agent role of all participants. There have been diversified and multi-department-led measures for poverty alleviation instead of rigid and simple management, showing the characteristics of market-based economic development and a state-led drive involving government leadership and participation of all players to jointly promote targeted poverty alleviation.

6.6 Extensive Mobilization of Resources and Investment

There is a Chinese saying that goes, "Even a clever housewife cannot cook a meal without rice", meaning that one cannot make something out of nothing. For a large country like China, massive mobilization of resources and investment has laid a solid material and human foundation for winning the battle against extreme poverty. This requires a rapid and long-term development of the national economy, which is also a major driving factor to win the battle. At the same time, the large-scale mobilization of human resources has vividly demonstrated the institutional strength of socialism with Chinese characteristics, which has made targeted poverty alleviation possible by pooling massive resources.

6.6.1 *Rapid Economic Growth as the Premise of Massive Resource Mobilization*

The effect of economic growth on poverty reduction is mainly reflected in two aspects: First, economic development provides more and better employment and income-generating opportunities for the poor population; Second, economic growth has increased the fiscal revenue of the government, making it more capable of helping the poor [7].

Economic growth plays a decisive role. It is impossible for a country to see a significant reduction in its poverty population without sustained economic growth. Globally, East Asia has witnessed the fastest poverty reduction and economic growth in recent years, while regions with slow economic growth have also experienced slow poverty reduction. Poverty is generally measured by economic welfare indicators, first of all by consumer spending and then by income levels. Only economic growth can raise income and consumer spending and thus reduce poverty. Some international studies show that economic growth can explain 70% of short-term poverty reduction, while in the long run, 95% is brought about by economic growth [8].

If a country does not focus on economic development, poverty alleviation alone will not be effective in the long run. Social mobilization of resources and investment is required, which is supported by economic growth and the increase of fiscal revenue, without which poverty alleviation is impossible. By comparing the changes in China's per capita GDP growth rate and its poverty incidence, we may see that there is a negative correlation between the two. The higher the GDP growth rate is, the faster the poverty incidence decreases. The elasticity of economic growth to poverty reduction is − 0.52%, that is, with every 1% increase in GDP, the poverty incidence will decrease by 0.52% [7].

In addition, agricultural development plays an important role in poverty reduction. Economic growth comes from three different sectors, namely primary, secondary and tertiary industries, and the growth in each sector has a different impact on poverty reduction. In China and many other developing countries, the primary sector, which is dominated by agriculture, has the highest impact on poverty reduction. First, China's poor population live mainly in rural areas, and the better those areas develop, the more the rural poor will benefit. The poverty reduction elasticity of the growth rate of the primary industry is − 1.13%, which is more than twice that of the overall economic growth [7]. Second, land and other major agricultural resources are distributed fairly in China, making it easy for the vast majority of rural households to benefit from agricultural growth. Third, the poverty reduction effect of agriculture is related to the income structure of the poor population. The poorer the family is, the more it depends on agriculture for a living. Agricultural growth has a profound impact on the income of the rural poor.

China's rapid and long-term economic growth has not only brought benefits to the poor through the "trickle-down effect", helping them to get out of poverty, but also enabled the country to have sufficient funds for poverty reduction. If the government lacks sufficient fiscal revenue due to the slowdown of economic growth, it would directly lead to insufficient investment in poverty alleviation funds. In China's current government-led poverty alleviation approach, this would directly lead to the stagnation of the endeavor. Therefore, economic growth is the first and foremost premise.

6.6.2 Scale Financial Input as the Material Foundation for Poverty Alleviation

Defects and failure of market regulation mechanism have provided the basis for government intervention. Market resources did not usually make active investment in poverty alleviation, and the amount was very limited even under the guidance of the government. This has called for the government to strengthen its leading role and fill the market vacancy by formulating fiscal and monetary policies to provide adequate financial guarantee for poverty alleviation.

With tight schedule and heavy tasks, massive financial input was highly necessary in order to win the battle against extreme poverty. Informed by statistics for the central government's investment in poverty alleviation, the annual funds increased from RMB800 million in 1980 to RMB139.636 billion in 2020, with remarkable growth especially since the start of the battle against extreme poverty. Over RMB100 billion was earmarked from the central government for three consecutive years (see Fig. 6.1). With a multi-dimensional investment system, the Chinese government had given strong support to poverty alleviation in financial funds, banking funds and land policies. More than RMB1 trillion of various funds are invested in poor counties and villages every year to help the poor people get rid of poverty.

6.6.3 Scale Mobilization of Human Resources as the Manpower Basis for Poverty Alleviation

Targeted poverty alleviation is the overarching strategy in the current stage and the goal is to lift all poor people and counties out of poverty through 2020 to ensure the smooth realization of the CPC's first centenary goal. It is basically about more accurately targeting poor villages and households, rather than staying at the regional level. It is very difficult to reduce poverty in terms of individual households, because

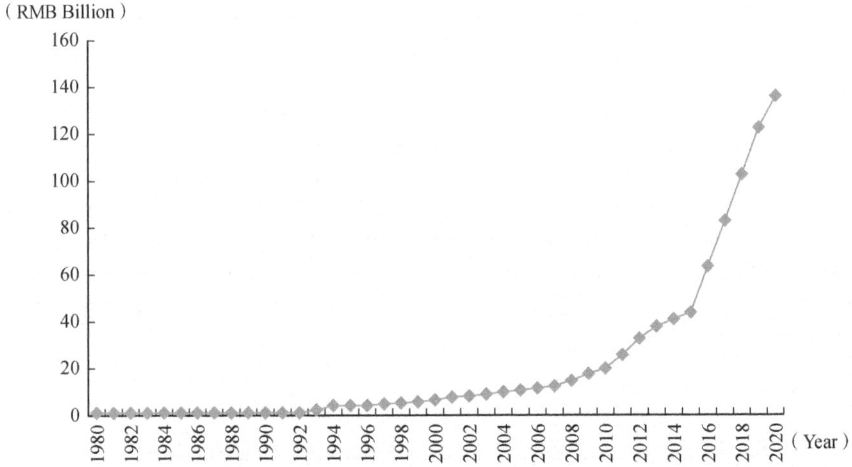

Fig. 6.1 Investment of special poverty alleviation funds from the central government over the years. *Note* In the special funds for poverty alleviation from the central government, the data before 2000 did not include poverty alleviation loans with discount interest, funds for poor state-owned farms and forest farms, which were included in the data after 2001. *Source* The data for 2014 and previous years are from China Poverty Alleviation and Development Yearbook 2015. The data for 2015 and later years are from the official website of the State Council: http://www.gov.cn/

there have been such a large number of people living in poverty with complicated situations. All this requires massive mobilization of human resources and painstaking efforts.

The first is to identify needy people. To help the poor, the first thing is to know who they are. In order to target, China has developed a set of standards and procedures to accurately identify the poor. The individuals and villages confirmed as poor are then registered. In 2014, 800,000 people were mobilized to spend time in villages for identification and registration. From 2015 to 2016, nearly 2 million people were organized in the review and examination to improve accuracy.[9]

The second is targeted assistance. On the basis of accurate identification, targeted measures have been applied for different households with different causes and types of poverty to eliminate major obstacles. An all-encompassing poverty alleviation network has been established, mobilizing all forces to take an active part. Nearly 30 million poor households, or about 90 million people,[10] were registered as targets for help. This called for mobilizing nearly 30 million officials from government departments and public institutions to implement the task. The CPC Central Committee and state departments and relevant institutions have provided paired-up assistance to major destitute counties, and officials were assigned to work in poor villages in charge of poverty alleviation, covering all listed poor counties since 2012. From 2002 to 2014, a total of 5229 officials took temporary posts in poor areas,

[9] Huang [9].

[10] Based on the data from the State Council Poverty Alleviation Office.

and more than 66,000 inspection tours were made to designated counties. By 2016, 260 counties and municipalities in the east had paired up with 287 counties and cities in the west to help. Provinces and municipalities in the east had provided a total of RMB13.27 billion in financial aid to 10 provinces, autonomous regions and municipalities in the west, and millions of officials had been sent to work in poor villages.[11]

The third is to conduct accurate assessment of the targeted poverty alleviation performance. This involves assessment and evaluation of the actual outcome for poor households, as well as of the performance of local governments to facilitate the work. To take China's third-party assessment for example. Since its introduction to assessing the effectiveness of poverty alleviation and the withdrawal of poor counties, more than 10,000 professional people from universities, research institutes, enterprises and think tanks have been involved to ensure that targeted poverty alleviation could survive the test of time.

6.7 Comprehensive Monitoring and Evaluation Mechanism

A well-designed monitoring and assessment mechanism has provided supervision and incentive guarantee for poverty reduction. To ensure that the targets are met on schedule with the veracity of results, China has established a sound mechanism.

Measures have been introduced to assess the performance of provincial Party committees and governments, as well as that of poor counties. At the same time, the assessment and evaluation of poverty withdrawal have been strengthened by increasing the weight of poverty reduction indicators in official appointment evaluation. At the top level, a complete oversight system has been in place, including special inspections by the central government, and those by governments, other political parties and the general public at all levels. This has been designed to ensure that CPC committees and governments at all levels take poverty alleviation as a major political task, supervise and evaluate the implementation and see to it that the outcomes are real and veritable.

Firstly, political oversight has been strengthened to have a clear division of political responsibilities for poverty alleviation. The leadership of the Communist Party of China is the distinctive feature of socialism with Chinese characteristics, as well as the fundamental source of China's institutional strength. In response to changes in the domestic and international economic situations and new developments in poverty alleviation, the CPC Central Committee with Xi Jinping as its core has formulated the great plan to win the battle against extreme poverty. Past practices have proved that if we were not firm and resolute in upholding the leadership of the CPC and implementing the blueprint of the Central leadership, it would inevitably lead to deviation in policy implementation and hinder the smooth progress of relevant undertakings. The primary task of oversight and evaluation is to implement the deployment by the

[11] Gu [10].

CPC Central Committee and President Xi Jinping's important ideas and proposals on poverty alleviation. The performance of Party committees and governments at all levels have been evaluated and supervised to see whether poverty alleviation has been given a prominent position, and to boost Party organizations and officials at all levels to earnestly shoulder their responsibilities and take actions to achieve expected results.

Secondly, problem-oriented efforts have been made to ensure the effective implementation of targeted policies. Poverty alleviation involves a large number of departments, with various policies, tight schedules and heavy tasks. After the introduction of major national policies and guidelines, it is inevitable that some policies to benefit the people may not be in place and there may be deviations. Targeted measures are therefore necessary to ensure poverty alleviation policies have been accurately carried out. Finding problems is the first step of solving them. Well-designed assessment and supervision should adhere to the problem-oriented approach and solve problems one by one. Through fund assessment and supervision, the key links of management were targeted and corruption could be prevented to ensure the effective use of poverty alleviation funds. Through the assessment and supervision of poverty alleviation projects such as industries, relocation, ecological conservation, education and social security, funds and projects have been under a closer public watch to ensure the smooth progress of the anti-poverty campaign.

Thirdly, work attitudes and styles have been improved to ensure satisfactory poverty elimination as scheduled. Tough and complicated as the task is, there will inevitably be various problems of formalities and red tapes that will affect the effectiveness of poverty alleviation. By inspections and supervisions, misconducts like administrative omission, reduced efficiency and slacking off after the removal from the poverty list can be effectively addressed. Accountability mechanisms have been established to tackle more serious problems such as manipulation or falsification of data, as well as formalities and red tapes. Efforts have been made to ensure that officials sent to work in poor villages are well informed, hard-working and are able to help people get out of poverty so that the truly poor are identified and helped to deliver genuine outcomes.

Fourthly, a realistic approach has been taken to seek both temporary and permanent solutions to promote innovation in poverty alleviation mechanisms. In January 2014, the General Offices of the CPC Central Committee and the State Council issued Guidelines on Promoting Rural Poverty Alleviation and Development through Innovative Mechanisms, setting the guideline of targeted poverty alleviation for the new era and requiring constant innovations in "six mechanisms", namely, improving the assessment mechanism, establishing the mechanism for more accurate identification, strengthening resident work team mechanism, reforming the mechanism for managing special government funds, improving the financial service system and innovating the mechanism of social participation. Among them, the assessment mechanism of poor counties has played a vital role. These mechanisms have integrated to create synergies to address bottlenecks and boost more innovative and effective practices.

"The people's aspiration for a better life is our goal." A sound assessment and supervision mechanism is to promote poverty alleviation more efficiently and ensure that the targets and tasks are achieved as scheduled. Through 2020, poor areas and poor people would join the rest of the country in entering a moderately prosperous society in all respects, which has been a common expectation of the CPC and the people. At the same time, combining the authority of intra-party supervision with the participation of the people, the assessment and supervision mechanism has adhered to the principle of "people's satisfaction as the ultimate standard for testing all the work of the Party committees and governments at all levels" to find, address and prevent problems, which has helped win people's trust and stimulate the enthusiasm of the entire society to participate in poverty alleviation.

Bibliography

1. Xi, J. (2016). *Speech marking the 95th founding anniversary of CPC*. People's Publishing House.
2. The World Bank. (2009). *From poor areas to poor people: The evolution of China's poverty alleviation agenda.*
3. Park, A., & Wang, S. (2010). Community-based development and poverty alleviation: An evaluation of China's poor village investment program. *Journal of Public Economics, 94*(9–10), 790–799.
4. Li, Q. (1994). State Councilor Chen Junsheng on the national seven-year poverty alleviation program. *Outlook Weekly, 1*, 4–6.
5. Li, X. (2013). Governance of China's rural poverty alleviation strategy implementation. *Guizhou Social Sciences, 7*, 101–106.
6. Wang, S., & Guo, Z. (2015). On targeted poverty alleviation in China. *Guizhou Social Sciences* (5), 147–150.
7. Wang, S. (2008). Overcoming poverty in development: Experience of extensive poverty reduction in China in the past 30 years. *Journal of Management World, 11*, 78–88.
8. Kraay, A. (2004). When is growth pro-poor? Cross-country evidence. *IMF Working Papers* (47).
9. Huang, C. (2017, August 23). *In-depth understanding of Xi Jinping's idea on targeted poverty alleviation to win the battle against extreme poverty.* http://dangjian.people.com.cn/n1/2017/0823/c412885-29489835.html
10. Gu, Z. (2016, July 20). *Joining hands to build a moderately prosperous society in all respects: A review of the 20 years of east-west collaboration in poverty alleviation.* http://finance.people.com.cn/n1/2016/0720/c1004-28567815.html
11. Chen, L., & Zhang, J. (2007). The dynamic relationship between economic growth, income distribution and poverty reduction: An empirical analysis from rural China. *Chinese Journal of Population Science* (1), 53–59, 96.
12. Chen, Z. (2018, May 24). *Addressing global challenges: China's initiative and commitment to the cause of global poverty reduction.* http://www.cpad.gov.cn/art/2018/5/24/art_61_84345.html
13. National Bureau of Statistics. (2015). *China statistical yearbook 2015*. China Statistics Press.
14. Rural Social and Economic Survey Division, National Bureau of Statistics. (2011). *China's rural poverty monitoring report 2010*. China Statistics Press.
15. Office of Household Surveys of National Bureau of Statistics. (2017). *Monitoring report on rural poverty in China 2016*. China Statistics Press.

16. Liu, J. (2009). *Poverty reduction in rural China.* China Financial & Economic Publishing House.
17. Liu, Y. (2017). Report of the State Council on poverty alleviation: Delivered at the 29th session of the standing committee of the 12th national people's congress on August 29, 2017. *Bulletin of the Standing Committee of the National People's Congress of the People's Republic of China* 750–755.
18. *A collection of documents of the 18th National Congress of the Communist Party of China.* (2012). People's Publishing House.
19. Wang, S., & Zeng, X. (2018). From regional efforts to targeted endeavor: Evolution of poverty alleviation policies in China in the past 40 years of reform together with challenges and countermeasures. *Issues in Agricultural Economy* (8), 40–50.
20. Wang, S. (2020). China's poverty alleviation performance and targeted poverty alleviation. *China Review of Political Economy, 11*(1), 130–148.
21. Wang, S. (2019). *Poverty alleviation in contemporary China.* China Renmin University Press.
22. Editorial Committee of China Poverty Alleviation and Development Yearbook. (2015). *China poverty alleviation and development yearbook 2015.* Unity Press.
23. Park, A., Wang, S., & Wu, G. (2002). Regional poverty targeting in China. *Journal of Public Economics* (86).

Chapter 7
Challenges and Countermeasures in the Battle Against Extreme Poverty

Since the implementation of targeted poverty alleviation, there has been a growing awareness of its importance, with more attention and financial investment than ever before from governments at all levels and participation from all sectors of society. In the battle against extreme poverty for the building of a moderately prosperous society in all respects, efforts have been made to take the assurance of food and clothing as well as the guarantee of access to education, medical care and housing together with upgraded public services and income standards as integral parts of the final goal to achieve advancement of both social security and income growth. This has overcome to some extent the long-standing defect of single-dimensional income indicators and relying mainly on economic development to drive poverty reduction. Through the effort, China has alleviated absolute poverty and curbed the widening income gap within rural areas, narrowing the development gap between urban and rural residents.

According to the current rural poverty standard, from 2013 to 2018, China lifted more than 10 million people out of poverty on a yearly basis, totaling 82.39 million, with a cumulative reduction rate of 83.2%. The incidence of rural poverty dropped to 1.7% at the end of 2018 [1]. This has created conditions for broadening the upward channel for low-income population and establishing an olive-type social pattern with middle-income groups as the majority. As a significant experiment in social intervention, poverty alleviation has mobilized abundant resources and attracted a great deal of attention from all sides, with more sophisticated governing expertise at the national level, which has had a profound impact on society.

We had written to look back the process of China's poverty alleviation efforts in the past 40 years of reform and opening up with an analysis of the challenges and countermeasures, putting forward that effective measures and innovative mechanisms should be introduced, together with the provision of short-term and long-term support. In the short term, the emphasis should be placed on addressing the poor people's livelihood, while in the long term, the lack of development motivation and capacity should be addressed, supplemented by social security [2]. This chapter will further analyze the

S. Wang, *Poverty Alleviation and Targeted Measures*,
https://doi.org/10.1007/978-981-96-1493-6_7

challenges and countermeasures in the battle against extreme poverty in response to the new situation and new problems, and based on the author's practical experience in participating in the third-party assessment (special assessment for the withdrawal of poor counties) in the past two years.

7.1 "Adverse Incentives" Under Extensive Poverty Alleviation

Although the new round of targeted poverty alleviation achieved remarkable results in poverty reduction, the challenge kept increasing, and the speed of poverty reduction slowed down obviously. Under the extensive investment, the "adverse incentive" phenomenon emerged, against the expectation of the policy design with unsatisfactory effects.

Most of China's poverty alleviation resources come from government input. With the help of a large number of government departments, the rural poor may have access, directly or indirectly, to resources such as the basic subsistence allowances for poverty alleviation (e.g., the basic living allowance, medical and pension insurance, among others), subsidies for basic production and living allowances (such as agricultural subsidies and those for renovating dilapidated houses, etc.) and investments that directly benefit the economic and social development of poor areas (such as planting and breeding subsidies and infrastructure construction, etc.), Basically, government funds have covered all aspects to achieve "Two Assurances and Three Guarantees" and income growth.

Many resource allocation mechanisms for poverty alleviation had their defects, manifested prominently in adverse incentives. Some of the root causes of the problem were to raise poverty thresholds or standards, make irrational promises to impoverished households, inaccurate identifying or simply giving dividends. What is implied by the targeted policy is that, basically, only targeted people identified as poor by the state (including poor counties, villages and households) could get or get more preferential resources. When the total amount was limited, those who pretended to be poor, or not that poor, but were more able to vie for resources, received more support. This indicated that there was the adverse incentive expectation behind the "poverty label".

It was not just some local governments and villages that had emerged from poverty were reluctant to be deregistered from the poverty list in order to continue accessing preferential treatment, quite a large number of rural "poor" did the same. Relying too much on the redistribution system of cash transfer and policy-backed poverty reduction, beneficiaries were likely to be misled to the addicted dependence of welfare, and adverse incentives emerged in competing for keeping the poverty label. Once the poor groups were registered as the target of assistance, benefits in housing, education, medical care and pension would usually come with it like bundled services. The likely message of the assistance to villagers may be that as long as they became poor, they may enjoy the "caretaking" of all kinds of policies. These possible economic benefits had disturbed the relatively simple life of rural residents they led before.

The "bundled" system provided a variety of welfare resources for the poor, which may accumulate to give rise to the "perfect storm" of superimposed welfare, leading poor households to weigh between the opportunity cost of withdrawing from the poverty list and the benefits of continuing to have access to the resources. There would develop a psychological and behavioral dependence on the policy-backed welfare, giving a chance for the illusion that "poverty alleviation is the political task of officials, which has nothing to do with me". In addition, some who were not eligible for registration or were in a marginal situation thus had the "expectation" to enjoy the limited poverty alleviation resources and vied for them. Tempted by the huge benefits, even some who were able to work were prone to take a negative attitude towards poverty alleviation. "Staying poor and not working" had been one of their means to game with the government [3].

A major reason for the above situation was that the current poverty alleviation system was distorted in some way. The state and society had borne too much responsibility and had been giving too much. What should be the issue to be addressed by poor individuals themselves became the sole responsibility of the government and society. This had misleadingly encouraged some rural poor to become or remain poor or strive for being registered. The more they "squeezed out" from the resources, the more likely they had a lazy mentality, with the less enthusiasm to get out of poverty and the more need for external assistance, greatly reducing the allocation efficiency of poverty alleviation resources.

In order to effectively curb the undesirable trend and improve the performance of poverty alleviation, efforts have been made to guide the expectations of rural poor and optimize the design of the incentive mechanism, so that adverse selection and moral hazards could be reduced to achieve "incentive compatibility". The central government has set a deadline of 2020 for all poverty-stricken counties and villages under the current standards to be lifted out of poverty, and for the registered poor population to reach "Two Assurances and Three Guarantees".

This would not make much difference for poor counties, villages and households, however, it would urge them to achieve high-quality poverty alleviation within a stipulated deadline, so that those who had emerged from poverty would have no more motivation to continue to "pretend to be poor" and would no longer appropriate the scarce resources. By improving the assessment mechanism of poor counties, shifting the focus from regional GDP to the outcomes of poverty alleviation, and abolishing the assessment of regional GDP in restricted development areas and ecologically fragile poorest counties, the undesirable trend of "competing for poverty" has been curbed.

In order to address adverse incentives from the root, the group of people with "no intention to get rid of poverty" should be re-examined to eliminate their "illusion" that the country and society could provide them with long-term, stable and high standards of social security and solve all their difficulties. To guard against adverse incentives, the central government has been adjusting its current policies. For example, the previous "profit-sharing" model of poverty alleviation through industries has been improved by creating public welfare posts, labor subsidies for registered households, home-based employment and other forms, so that registered poor households can earn wages and dividend incomes by providing labor services within their capacity.

Considering that the poverty status of many villagers is only periodic, and the assistance resources of the state and society can only help relief their poverty rather than make them rich, poverty can be regarded as a necessary rather than a sufficient condition for receiving assistance or support, and the beneficiary groups should be required to perform corresponding obligations to prevent adverse incentives and expectations. At the same time, it is necessary to improve employment willingness and ability through flexible subsidy and restraint mechanisms, such as conditional cash transfers (CCT) and welfare to work (WTW). By determining the benefit quota of every household, introducing conditional subsidies and management of restrictive use, as well as by developing workable conditional transfer payment programs, limited funds have been better transferred to the "developing poor" who are willing and able to lift themselves out of poverty, rather than simply helping the "poor" who are temporarily trapped in poverty [4].

Positive expectations and incentives should be established by emphasizing both rights and obligations, targeting by differentiation and introducing mechanisms for competitive and categorized assistance. A clear message has been conveyed that as long as one works hard and make efforts, he will be rewarded by both market return and government assistance [5].

7.2 Balancing the Cost and Benefit of Poverty Alleviation

Since the implementation of the new round of poverty alleviation policies, the central government has set binding targets with mandatory plans and timetables. The political agenda has been transformed into a moral action of the society, with the mobilization of the largest ever social resources and the input of most intensive human, material and financial resources. Targeted poverty alleviation has been more demanding for the rationality and accuracy of fiscal policy application. As policy instruments have become more sophisticated with more specific targets, a short-term policy performance is more reasonable. However, the conflict between short-term and long-term goals may lead to more obvious problems such as depletion of the long-term performance of policies [6]. The input and output of poverty alleviation resources have been disproportionate, and the inefficient allocation of resources has not been well tackled with.

Generally speaking, the resources or costs in poverty alleviation can be divided into the following categories: The first is the special funds from the central government, which are the main funding for poverty alleviation.[1] The second is public investment projects organized and delivered by relevant functional departments of

[1] Since 2016, central government subsidies for poverty alleviation in designated areas have grown at an average annual rate of more than 20%, reaching RMB 106.1 billion in 2018.

the central government, such as transportation, water conservancy, telecommunications, and health and education projects. The third is financial transfer between the eastern and western regions, such as exchanges of officials and professionals, partnership of industrial development and labor services, and collaboration in education, culture, health, science and technology. The fourth is enterprises' income transfer under administrative guidance, such as the poverty alleviation campaign by central enterprises and by private businesses, and enterprises' donations of funds and materials. The fifth is indirect financial expenditures, covering mainly administrative costs of implementing targeted poverty alleviation policies, such as accurate identification, dispatching resident work teams and first secretaries in poor villages, and organizing third-party evaluations[2] [7].

It is difficult to define accurately the benefits or effectiveness of poverty alleviation. If they were calculated simply by the number of people who have been lifted out of poverty, approximately tens of millions, the costs would be very high. For this, the Chinese government has its own logic. In spite of the fact that some short-term return on investment projects or industries as a whole is not high and some may even suffer losses and require government subsidies (such as photovoltage (PV) and assets income projects), the Chinese government still invests in them from a social cost-benefit principle, considering that the input can directly create opportunities for the poor and the country or region can obtain reasonable long-term returns [8]. Therefore, the benefits of poverty alleviation should be viewed from a multi-dimensional and long-term perspective, such as the long-term effects of massive investment in infrastructure and public services. At the same time, this round of poverty alleviation has been of great significance for officials to get closer to rural people and improve local governance system. These benefits are obviously precipitated fixed and intangible assets, which would play a long-term role.

Impossible as it is to accurately measure the cost and benefit of large-scale poverty alleviation, the effect of resource input has also been significant in terms of the number of poverty reduction. Assuming that the increment of other types of funds remained unchanged, for every RMB100 million of special poverty alleviation funds from the central government, the corresponding reduction of the poor population had decreased from 391,200 in 2012 to 69,300 in 2018, indicating that the marginal effect on poverty reduction calculated by the special poverty alleviation funds from the central government had significantly decreased (see Table 7.1). Because of the functioning of law of diminishing marginal returns, the remaining poor people are often the "hardest nuts to crack", and poverty reduction would becomes more difficult the further it is carried out.

As China's poverty alleviation financing shifted from poverty relief to development-oriented poverty reduction and from planned free disbursement to paid market-oriented financing to strengthen the capacity building of the rural poor, fund

[2] For example, in 2014, about 800,000 people were mobilized for identifying targets for assistance. From 2015 to 2016, the review and evaluation work involved about 2 million people nationwide, while during the same period, fewer than 40,000 people worked as permanent staff in poverty alleviation departments.

Table 7.1 Central governments' special funds for poverty alleviation and the rural poor population from 2010 to 2018

Year	Special poverty alleviation fund from the central government (RMB 100 million)	Poor population (10 thousand)	Poverty incidence (%)	Marginal effect of funds on poverty reduction (10 thousand/RMB 100 million)
2010	222.68	16,567	17.2	–
2011	272.00	12,238	12.7	87.77
2012	332.05	9889	10.2	39.12
2013	394.00	8249	8.5	26.47
2014	432.87	7017	7.2	31.70
2015	467.45	5575	5.7	41.70
2016	670.00	4335	4.5	6.12
2017	860.95	3046	3.1	6.75
2018	1060.95	1660	1.7	6.93

Note "Marginal effect of funds on poverty reduction" refers to the number (10 thousand people) of poverty reduction corresponding to each increase of RMB100 million of special poverty alleviation funds from the central government. The calculation method is (poor population last year—poor population the present year)/(government funds the present year—government funds last year), and the unit is 10 thousand people/RMB100 million. The poverty standard is the current one adjusted in 2011, namely, the net income of each person per year is RMB2300 (at constant prices in 2010)
Source Data on the central government's special poverty alleviation funds from 2010 to 2016 comes from the White Paper on China's Poverty Reduction Actions and Human Rights Progress, http://www.scio.gov.cn/zfbps/32832/Document/1494402/1494402.htm; Data on the number of poor population and the incidence of poverty from 2010 to 2016 are from China Statistical Yearbook 2017
Data on the central government's special poverty alleviation fund 2017 comes from The Central Government Appropriating RMB86.095 Billion as Special Poverty Alleviation Funds for 2017, http://www.gov.cn/xinwen/2017-06/08/content_5200771.htm; Data on the number of poor population and the incidence of poverty in 2017 is from China's Rural Poor Population Reduced to 30.46 Million by the End of 2017, http://www.gov.cn/xinwen/2018-02/01/content_5262917.htm
Data on the central government's special poverty alleviation funds 2018 comes from The Central Government Appropriating over RMB106 Billion as Special Poverty Alleviation Funds for 2018, http://www.gov.cn/xinwen/2018-05/04/content_5288150.htm; Data on Hull poverty incidence 2018 comes from National Bureau of Statistics: The Number of Rural Poor Reduced by 13.86 Million in 2018, http://www.gov.cn/xinwen/2019-02/15/content_5365982.htm

raising for poverty alleviation in China has been increasingly complementary to poverty alleviation policies. Targeted investment of the funds is more focused and leveraged, with more innovative use of the funds [9]. This indicates that China's input–output efficiency of poverty alleviation and development has been comparatively high, and the massive investment has lifted a large number of poor people out of poverty.

However, more input of funds and the declining poverty incidence does not necessarily mean the effectiveness of targeted poverty alleviation. On the surface, there are more and more financial funds for poverty alleviation, but the management has been decentralized. The funds have been under line management by different departments, which has led to low efficiency and inaccurate targeting of funds. Although more targeted measures have been taken in recent years to address these with enhanced accuracy of identification, reduced leakage of resources and better information sharing, some government departments continue to have institutional arrangements in allocating funds and projects based on sectoral functions. At the same time, the opportunity cost of poverty alleviation for help providers and those to be helped has also increased substantially. If the government puts too much pressure on the primary level to raise its authority and governance efficiency, it may also lead to the loss of efficiency caused by countermeasures such as "strategic implementations" or "quantity without quality".

A major manifestation of the low fund efficiency has been the disproportionate input and output of poverty alleviation resources and the mismatch between supply and demand. On the one hand, the investment may have been made on projects that were not in need. For example, some places have built plazas, libraries and clinics without fully considering their utilizations, which resulted in a serious waste of resources. Another case in point is that during the author's review visit to a central-China village when he was participating in a third-party assessment of targeted poverty alleviation outcomes (special assessment for the withdrawal of counties from poverty list), he found that the village had a new standardized clinic built without evaluating its utilization. Only a few minutes' walk from the township health center, the new clinic turned out to be almost useless with no permanent doctors, no patients and few drugs. It was more like window dressing for inspections than anything that could really help. On the other hand, there were cases when there was overinvestment in the demand. For example, some places that had already invested a lot of resources to pave roads from villager teams required further investment from individual households, without considering costs and benefits. Many poor villagers were widely scattered without many economic activities, and gravel or dirt roads could well satisfy their needs. The construction of cement roads may lead to serious waste of resources.

Generally speaking, there could be four main reasons for the low efficiency and inaccurate targeting of poverty alleviation funds.

Firstly, fragmented use of funds has made it difficult to generate economies of scale. China's rural poverty alleviation has shifted from putting focus on regional development in poor areas to targeted poverty alleviation of individual poor people and households. Although the policy of overall planning and integration of government funds for rural development at the county level has improved the situation to some extent, there were still localities where poverty alleviation efforts were generalized to regional development, and limited resources have been dispersed. This has resulted in fragmented management and use of funds which made it difficult for integration to generate economies of scale [10].

Secondly, the single means of assistance has reduced the efficiency of the funds. Some anti-poverty policies were reduced to project implementation, with the goal limited to directly raising incomes and welfare. The ways and models of assistance were reduced to giving cash and kind directly. More attention was paid to the grant of projects instead of capacity building of poor people. This result-oriented welfare system rarely took input costs into consideration and made it difficult to carry out comprehensive monitoring, which not only brought about growing financial burden but also contributed to the "welfare dependency" of the recipients.

Thirdly, power rent-seeking has led to inflated poverty alleviation costs. Poverty reduction programs are led by the government, and the funds are mostly allocated by the central government, supported by provinces and cities (prefectures) and counties, and used exclusively in the form of projects. However, the allocation of the funds by administrative means may deviate from the target, increase supervision difficulties and induce rent-seeking behaviors. The "resource leakage" caused by the misuse of funds or the deviation of the actual beneficiaries from the target population has led to the inflated cost. Things began to improve only after the introduction of active "poverty alleviation within a set schedule" under the backdrop of the project system coordinated with fund integration. A more sustained effort from self-motivation has been taking place of simply relying on external support.

Fourthly, formalism has increased the cost of poverty alleviation. Attention to details has been required for targeted poverty alleviation at grassroots level, which may be accompanied by different degrees of formalism. A lot of repetitive work caused by low efficiency of the administrative system has undoubtedly increased the cost of governance. For instance, frequent inspections, supervisions and assessments, as well as meetings and evaluations at various levels and of all kinds may also consume a lot of energy, crowding out the input of resources in other areas. Some substantive work went through formalities, resulting in superficial outcomes. At the same time, some frills took place of the central work, leading to deviation of the focus in poverty alleviation [11].

With the sharp drop in the growth rate of fiscal revenue, a stable and extensive investment in poverty alleviation resources may not sustain under the constraints of limited funds and budgets. One of the alternatives could be to improve the efficiency of the allocated funds through "low level and wide coverage". In line with different poverty situations, a comprehensive measure could be carried out about who are to be helped and who have emerged out of poverty, as well as the time and cost to ensure the balance between the inputs of different poverty alleviation projects.

Different roles of inclusive and preferential resources should be distinguished to guide the gradual transformation of the fund allocation from the generalized system of preferences (GSP) to the "GSP + ladder + preferential system", in order to reduce resource waste and improve the quality and efficiency of resource supply. This may prevent the opportunity cost of poverty alleviation from rising sharply. Attention should be paid to the following aspects.

The first is the identification of poor households. It is necessary to have a highly competent technical and professional team to reduce the management and operation costs and improve the work efficiency through technological and institutional innovation. Therefore, a more effective governance system requires encouraging the participation of social organizations [12] and shifting the identification of the poor population from the management of quota quantity to the more reasonable welfare certification [13].

The second is to help the poor. It is necessary to further boost the self-motivation of the poor households to get rid of poverty and protect their rights and interests. Considering the large external input of resources, if their agent role is not given full play, it will be difficult to activate their desire and capability to shake off poverty through their own efforts. Without internal driver, the risk of falling back into poverty will increase once the external resources are withdrawn.

The third is the management of poor households. It is necessary to build a targeted poverty alleviation information database and a big data platform to provide targeted management for the poor population, targeted allocation of resources, and targeted support for poor villagers. Inefficient management processes should be eliminated to reduce unnecessary formalities, and optimize the project operation system, so as to save financial resources and enhance the effectiveness of the use of funds.

The fourth is monitoring of poverty alleviation funds. This can be achieved by setting up a special fund management institution responsible for coordinating fund allocation, tracking project cash flow, overseeing the transmission cost of funds and identifying target groups. It may also see to it that the market plays the role of basic allocation of the resources, study and judge the possible duration of poverty and its dynamic transformation trend, promote the effective connection between the supply and demand to improve the efficiency of anti-poverty projects.

The fifth is to revitalize government funds. It is suggested that governments at all levels and financial departments should, in accordance with relevant national policies, increase the efforts to put the existing funds to good use, reduce their retention and modify the current situation of the coexistence of shortage and idleness of government funds. The funds that have been carried forward for several consecutive years can be used as surplus funds to be collected by the government and used for poverty alleviation by a certain proportion.

7.3 Conflicts Between Short-Term Poverty Alleviation and Sustainable Development

The new round of poverty alleviation has a clear timetable (2020) and a clear spatial division (the most impoverished contiguous areas, poor counties and villages). It is a political task that governments at all levels must complete on time and with good outcomes in order to achieve the expected goals ("Two Assurances and Three Guarantees" and income exceeding the poverty line) in a short period of time. However, there may be conflicts between short-term poverty alleviation and sustainable development in poor areas and the poor population, which may affect the effectiveness of targeted poverty alleviation.

First, in terms of objectives, there has been the conflict between the short-term evaluation goals for government performance with the long-term pursuit of stable poverty alleviation results. Under the current system, the central and provincial governments are responsible for strategic guidance of the poverty alleviation campaign; while primary-level governments see to it that the strategies are delivered. Targeted poverty alleviation is a political task of local governments under the constraints of multiple conditions. It is true that the campaign has in general boosted the enthusiasm of policy implementers and strengthened the efficiency priority logic of instrumental rationality, some local governments have been constrained by the pressure of assessment under the dual goals of pursuing efficiency and performance. The number of poor people getting out of absolute poverty in a short period of time has often been an important benchmark for assessing the performance of targeted poverty alleviation. Well-designed policies have been more often than not given simplified implementation due to the consideration of costs and other factors. Due to the discrepancies between the state's official system and local rules in distribution, layers of pressure have forced policy implementers to form their own set of logic, which may lead to regarding the development-oriented poverty alleviation as a phased work and responding to it with "strategic" approaches, typically reflected in the pursuit of short-term outcomes and explicit data such as the income level and the time it takes to shake off poverty. As a result, some policies were carried out off the track and the end became the means.

Second, in terms of measures, there has been the conflict between short-term benefits and long-term equity. Targeted poverty alleviation should prioritize the weak and the minority among the poor based on the principle of equity. In practice, however, implementers may tend to choose and apply effective or useful solutions to maximize the performance owing to the dual pressure of the tight schedule and demanding targets. As a result, the value pursuit for social fairness and justice may be replaced by the priority of efficiency, quick success and instant benefits [14]. At the same time, considering that the effective delivery of policies may affect the interests of implementers, for example, the introduction of projects may be accompanied by the risk of failure, and local governments may choose the action strategy of policy escape based on their own interests, leading to unsatisfactory outcomes of the policies [15]. Since the use of poverty alleviation funds is coupled with poverty registration and the outcome, most local governments tend to opt for selective support and easy projects that work quickly in resource allocation by making just an overall analysis and judgment on the development of poor households, previously impoverished people and other villagers out of the considerations of work efficiency and performance.

By pooling limited resources for poverty alleviation to give preferential policy allocation to poor areas with relatively good conditions and households with high capacity, conspicuous benefits and results could be seen in the short run, which is good for vanity report and increasing political capital of local governments. This has been a typical operation of using poverty alleviation resources to add to their "performance records". While these practices may seem to have made poverty alleviation efforts more efficient, they have failed to respond effectively to the real needs and aspirations of the poor, exacerbating the unfair distribution of resources. Some "Model villages" or "star households" are actually reflections of the "Matthew effect", a situation where the rich get richer while the poor get poorer, creating a widening gap between those who have more and those who have less, with more negative consequences in general.

Third, in terms of the outcome, there has been the conflict between the speed of poverty reduction and its quality. The two are dialectically unified. It is true that failure to ensure the speed would make it impossible to accomplish the arduous task of reducing the annual average of 10 million people as scheduled. However, poverty is not an absolutely static issue, but is dynamic and changing. This character has determined that poverty elimination is a long-term task. Therefore, targeted poverty alleviation is not an emergency task, which can never be solved once and for all. Under pressing demands, it may be necessary and understandable to adopt some effective policies and measures, but meeting deadlines and making progress to pass the assessment from the superior should never be at the cost of quality and safety. Otherwise, poverty alleviation would go against its original purpose and what has been striving for [16].

May cause a series of deviations. If too much emphasis was placed on speed instead of quality, resources may even be used to meet the targets at all costs, which may lead to serious and adverse consequences. Even if all poverty alleviation targets have been completed by 2020, the outcome will be greatly compromised and cannot stand the test of time if the poor population has not been on the right track of sustainable development.

Poverty is a long-term social problem in the period of social transformation. The purpose of targeted poverty alleviation is to more accurately and effectively address rural poverty and the imbalance in development. The central government has set a strategic goal of winning the battle against extreme poverty through 2020, making it clear that a "grace period" will be allowed for previously impoverished population, villages and counties, during which time poverty alleviation policies and government supervision are continued until their status is secure [17]. The message conveyed by the central government is that, before the building of a moderately prosperous society in all respects, we should vigorously guide poverty-stricken counties to adjust poverty management to the priority of their annual tasks, maximize the integration of internal and external resources, and shift the focus of governance from reducing the scale of poverty to improving the quality and consolidating the foundation for poverty alleviation. The parameters of poverty incidence, accuracy of identification and deregistration, satisfaction rate and the rate of returning to poverty are emphasized in evaluation rather than the one-sided pursuit of poverty reduction scale and quantity indicators. At this crucial period, poor areas should well address the conflict between short-term poverty alleviation and long-term sustainable development to prevent the negative impact caused by the rush for quick results.

From the macro point of view, to deal with the short-term and long-term issues, we need to balance between the short-term poverty reduction effect of relevant resources and the long-term mechanism of sustainable development of those that have emerged from poverty, and shift the focus from the speed to the quality. In recent years, the central government has intensified its assessment, supervision and evaluation of poverty alleviation. The Party committees and governments at all levels have established the performance appraisal system, adjusting the assessment parameters and strictly carrying out the corresponding accountability to guide local governments to focus on how to help people stay out of poverty and how to prevent them from sinking back to poverty. Efforts have been made to carefully examine and ensure that the implementation of each policy in "Two Assurances and Three Guarantees" is long-term and sustainable. By establishing a sustainable poverty alleviation mechanism, we can accelerate the transition from campaign-style management to institutionalized governance by exploring regular, long-term and standardized practice mechanisms to avoid remaining to be driven by policies and situations for too long a time. In terms of institutions, mechanisms should be set up to ensure that poor households can stay out of poverty, and effective institutional guarantees could be provided when people fall into or return to poverty [18]. In this way, their basic difficulties are addressed without developing over-dependence on external support. While receiving assistance, the poor people should be able to develop their own motivation and capabilities, so that the conflict can be better resolved.

From the micro point of view, to achieve sustainable development of poor households, especially those with the ability to work, it is important to develop their skills, build confidence in poverty alleviation and stabilize employment or industries, so that they can have stable income channels with access to steady income sources. On the one hand, poor villager can be helped to build an industry and trained into small specialized households. With the development of the industry, their capacity can be gradually improved and their business expanded. On the other hand, poor households can be helped to find stable full-time or part-time jobs, which may enable them to achieve long-term employment.

Therefore, the sustainability of poverty alleviation can be measured and relevant policies be improved from the following aspects: The first is to look at the income structure of multiple sources of poor households by observing whether it relies on industrial activity, employment, subsistence allowances, simple dividends or temporary subsidies, to judge whether the income is just a sum increased, or can achieve sustainable growth. The second is to look at different kinds of assistance measures by observing whether they are conducive to the development of industries or stable employment of poor households, with access to a stable source of income. The third is to see the accumulation of various types of assets of poor households by observing whether the accumulation for a period of time helps resist various shocks and risks caused by illness, disaster or accident. The fourth is to examine a variety of support policies by observing whether they can really help poor households to recover quickly from difficulties to get back to their normal standards of living.

7.4 "Abyss Consequence" Between Poor Households and Others

"Abyss consequence" refers to the characteristics and results of changes in the critical point (line), stage or range when quantitative changes break through the tolerable "degree" to cause qualitative changes. With the increasing investment in poverty alleviation resources, poor villages and households could have enjoyed funds and projects in excess of the standard due to fund integration and overlapping policies, which may lead to the situation in which what the poor have got are far better than the group with almost similar conditions, resulting in the unintended consequence of drastically different supporting policies for people with almost the same level of poverty, and unreasonable gap between poverty-stricken households and other villagers.

Such a gap between welfare for people above or below the critical point of poverty caused by the blurred boundary between people who have been supported and those who have not and the different standards of policy assistance is known as the "abyss consequence" of poverty alleviation policies [19]. When they only target certain groups, those who are close to the policy demarcation line but not enjoying the benefits may be in marginal poverty, resulting in a sense of relative deprivation and injustice when they compare themselves with the people with similar conditions who are being supported. After a period of time, the overall development between these two groups may even be fundamentally reversed. The "abyss consequence" has made the issue of the group of marginal poverty prominent, whose interests should be paid more attention in the new round of redoubled targeted poverty alleviation efforts.

In practice, it is often the (non-) poor villages and (non-) poor households that are on the edge of the "abyss consequence". On the one hand, being identified as a registered poor village is the main policy basis for accessing preferential funds and projects. In the process of project implementation, all kinds of dispersed and integrated funds tend to be invested in poor villages, resulting in their infrastructure construction, basic public services and industrial development exceeding the basic standards and that of the "Two Assurances and Three Guarantees".

In contrast, there are some villages that are not registered but have similar status of economic and social development and incidence of poverty, which are actually villages on "marginal poverty". Due to the lack of aiding funds, the development of these non-poor villages has slowed down, with stagnated or even regressed supply of infrastructure and the development of public services.

On the other hand, being accurately identified as registered poor households is a prerequisite for poor families to access poverty alleviation resources. At the present stage, a large number of assistance resources have been granted to the registered poor households and individuals, with only a small part spilling over to non-poor households and individuals. Some of the poor families that are not registered as poor are actually "borderline" or "marginal" poor households, whose production and living conditions are not much different from those of the registered and they may fall into the category this way or that. In the absence of supportive policies, these households have been highly vulnerable and at high risk of falling into poverty. This has been especially true in destitute areas, where people are generally poor with marginal differences between the poor households and other villagers. For the registered poor, the government would usually provide considerable assistance. If the beneficiaries are granted with full support of high standards without having to pay or by paying less, the "abyss consequence" may be more prominent. For example, in Liangshan, Sichuan Province, in order to improve housing safety, the registered poor households and those relocated from inhospitable areas were to raise no more than RMB10,000 by themselves, with other costs borne by the government, while for non-registered households, the general subsidies ranged from RMB30,000 to RMB50,000, with other expenses to be raised by the villagers themselves. In comparison, the subsidy for each household may vary by tens of thousands of yuan, and the divergence can be as much as about RMB100,000 [20].

In practice, the author found several cases of "abyss consequence". Taking for example the policy of the health program for poverty alleviation. During a third-party evaluation and inspection tour, it was found that the policy of a county-level city in Central China deviated from the target. First, households that were deregistered in 2014 and 2015 no longer enjoyed the basic medical insurance and critical illness insurance premiums paid by the government, nor the health program in general, which violated the "grace period" policy granted to previously impoverished population and caused the "abyss consequence" among households that had emerged out of poverty.

Second, there was over-coverage for serious illness. It is true that policy-backed measures have ensured that poverty-stricken populations have access to basic medical insurance, critical illness insurance, and medical assistance. They do have effectively solved the problem of sinking into or falling back into poverty because of critical illness. However, the high level of medical security may lead to the phenomenon that some registered households over-treat minor diseases by taking up excessive medical resources and increase the financial burden of the government.

Third, the assistance policy for chronic diseases has yet been satisfactory. Although relevant policies have been formulated, the list of outpatient drugs has not been stipulated, leading to the expansion of the chronic disease assistance policy. For example, during the inspection, it was also found that a county-level city in Northeast China used the guarantee of rural households' basic pension to make a bank loan to pay the basic old-age insurance premium in a lump sum for the registered poor population over 60 years old before the end of 2020, resulting in a net pension of at least RMB1540 each for the poor elderly. And that for the elderly over the age of 70 reached RMB3000, much higher than the basic pension for other villagers, which is about RMB1000. There was a big gap between them.

In anti-poverty practice, the long-term existence of "abyss consequence" may produce a series of unfavorable consequences. On the one hand, the sudden increase of welfare beyond standards would be likely to cause the psychological imbalance and a sense of loss among the group on the brink of poverty. They may feel somewhat deprived with growing resistance to the current policy, questioning its reasonableness and fairness. This may put great pressure on those who allocate resources for targeted poverty alleviation and affect the credibility of the government among this group of people. It may even lead to the accumulation of conflicts and the protest against poverty elimination, resulting in tension and distrust between poor and non-poor villages, between poor and non-poor households and between villagers and the village leadership, making it difficult for the effective governance of rural areas. On the other hand, when the welfare brought by the status of "poverty" far exceeds the psychological expectation of all parties and a considerable part of the benefits obtained are not the result of hard work but simply because of the label, undesirable consequences may occur. The mismatch between what one gets and what he gives may become one of the root causes of relying mainly on external support, or "vying for being a poor household" and reluctance to be deregistered after emergence from poverty. If the situation of low-income villages and households is not substantially improved in a long run, the under-expressed conflicts of interest between villagers of marginal poverty and those registered may be expressed through various forms. If we do not take effective measures to proactively address and resolve the consequence, the conflict may cause social instability in some areas once it spreads and intensifies, which will surely affect the overall poverty alleviation campaign.

Actually, once poverty alleviation is carried out and poverty standards are set, there will be groups on the brink. To prevent the "marginal effect" to become prominent, we must be pragmatic and should neither randomly lower nor irrationally raise the standards to avoid unfavorable consequences. Once poor households have steadily exceeded the current poverty alleviation standard, policies and measures should pay more attention to the gap of treatment between poor and other villagers without raising poverty thresholds or making irrational promises to impoverished households so as to ease the possible tension caused by unfavorable consequences and adverse incentives. Measures to address the issue can be summed up as the following.

The first is to pay due attention to critical poverty in identifying the targets for assistance. After determining the scale of poverty, there should be dynamic management of the people to be given support. Based on the registrations from the poverty alleviation department and the sampling data from the statistics department, the situation of critical poor villages and population should be well informed before estimating the number of people on the brink of poverty. In the opinion of the author, people whose per capita household income is within 5%–15% of the current poverty alleviation standard can be registered and managed by a unified classification and tiers.

In line with different factors such as income and family size, different types of multidimensional poverty line can be set up to screen out prospective poor households with different conditions for the overall support. Government funds for rural development can be integrated for use as a whole to solve specific problems in the practice and reduce the fuzzy part of the policy boundary. A proportion of the project funds or poverty alleviation assistance can be set aside to help and lead the rural residents on the brink of poverty.

A case in point is Wulong District of Chongqing, which carried out dynamic monitoring of "critical households" earlier and issued a relevant implementation plan in 2019. The plan stipulated that the following households would be listed as "critical", namely, those with per capita disposable income in the previous year within the range between the poverty line and 1.2 times of the line, and those not eligible for registration but with the per capita debt exceeding the previous year's per capita rural disposable income caused by rigidity expenditure such as medical care, compulsory education, necessary housing and major disasters. And these households would be provided assistance in medical insurance, medical care, industrial development, financial services and other aspects [21].

The second is to introduce new forms of support, with development and security assistance as the major forms supplemented by financial support. Anti-poverty policies in the new era should shift the focus from income growth to capacity building. On the basis of adhering to the standard of securing adequate food and clothing, and access to compulsory education, basic medical services, and safe housing, a system of assistance by category should be established, breaking down the family size and structural characteristics of the beneficiaries, such as age, gender, family structure, education level, and occupation. This shift from "targeting households" to "targeting different people" has been to achieve more accurate, equitable and efficient assistance to the poor, and prevent excessive supply of the resources. The policy gap between households lifted out of poverty in different time periods should be eliminated to coordinate support measures for poor people in poor villages and those in marginal areas, providing basic, timely and effective help and support to them and prevent the accumulation of the sense of relative deprivation.

The transfer income should avoid giving cash and goods directly to prevent enjoying only industrial dividends without participating in production or business operation. It is necessary to implement awards and subsidies for newly added industrial projects of poor households and prevent obtaining industry awards and subsidies by their own original industrial projects. The creation of public welfare posts should be based on practical use and sustainability, with focus on covering registered households with the ability to work so as to promote their long-term and stable income growth. The posts should not be granted to those who do not have the corresponding work ability, nor created under false names or with excessive number.

The third is to pay close attention to risk prevention and control, putting risk intervention in the first place. This can be done by decoupling all kinds of special assistance from the status of being poor households (subsistence allowance households) and providing support instead in the form of special assistance as needed to achieve full coverage of policies and reduce the gap caused by the resource allocation method that takes the status as the threshold for assistance and security. For example, the anti-poverty healthcare policy should not only target the registered poor population, but also extend to those with special types of diseases and chronic diseases, and improve the coverage of risk prevention policies. Considering the fact that many rural poor know little about or capable of making good use of security policies for risk prevention and control, the assistant agent system could be established by designating members of resident work teams or village officials in charge to handle the procedures for them, including things like registration for treatment of chronic diseases and outpatient reimbursement, by taking their advantage of being well-informed of the policies. This can effectively ensure the implementation of health programs for poverty alleviation, and reduce the medical burden of the poor population.

The fourth is to take the people on marginal poverty into consideration when building public infrastructure, providing public services and developing the collective economy. Considerations should be given to both the poor and people on marginal poverty in the distribution of public resources in light of national industrial policies and regional resources to create a relatively fair development environment. The labor potential of the poor should be fully tapped and the problems of insufficient and unbalanced assistance solved. In addition to the "preferential" policies for registered poor households and poor villages, there should also be the introduction of "inclusive" policies for "marginal poverty", so that all groups can equally enjoy the benefits of targeted poverty alleviation to enhance the capability of areas and the population with resource input to resist risks and share the results of poverty governance.

Bibliography

1. *Poverty alleviation and development moving ahead with historic achievements*, August 26, 2019. http://www.stats.gov.cn/tjsj/zxfb/201908/t20190812_1690526.html
2. Wang, S., & Zeng, X. (2018a). From regional efforts to targeted endeavor: Evolution of poverty alleviation policies in China in the past 40 years of reform together with challenges and countermeasures. *Issues in Agricultural Economy* (8), 40–50.
3. Zhan, G., & Zhang, X. (2017). "Helping the poor or the rich": Accurate identification and adaptive governance of poverty alleviation targets: Based on a field research of poverty alleviation in village X, county R, northern Jiangsu Province. *Modern Economic Research* (6), 95–103.
4. Wang, S., & Zeng, X. (2018b). On poverty after 2020. *Journal of Hohai University (Philosophy and Social Sciences Edition)* (2), 7–13.
5. Li, X. (2007). On adverse incentives and policy remedy in anti-poverty efforts. *Issues in Agricultural Economy, 2*, 88–93.
6. Huang, L., et al. (2019). On the performance of targeted poverty reduction by government financing policies. *Journal of Southwest University (Social Sciences Edition), 45*(5), 59–66, 198.
7. Zhu, L., & He, W. (2018). Forty years of rural poverty reduction in the process of industrialization and urbanization. *Studies in Labor Economics, 6*(4), 3–31.
8. Wu, G., et al. (2018). *Poverty reduction and development in China (1978–2018).* Social Sciences Academic Press (China).
9. United Nations Development Programme. (2016). *Report on sustainable financing for poverty alleviation in China.*
10. Xu, H., & Li, X. (2018). Targeted poverty alleviation: Theoretical basis, practical dilemma and path choice: Based on the investigation of two poor counties in Yunnan Province. *Exploration and Free Views* (2), 106–111, 143.
11. Chen, H., & Chen, X. (2019). Formality of substance and vice versa: Formation mechanism and deep root of formalism in targeted poverty alleviation. *China Rural Survey* (3), 52–63.
12. Zhou, M., & Tao, R. (2016). Market or government: Assessing rural poverty reduction policies in China. *International Economic Review* (6), 5–6, 63–76.
13. Qiu, Y. (2018). From quota to certification: Targeting deviation of rural poor population and system remedy. *Journal of Public Administration, 1*, 122–134.
14. Liu, K. (2019). Rational preference and execution distortion: A philosophical reflection on the practical dilemma of targeted poverty alleviation. *Journal of Hainan University (Humanities and Social Sciences Edition), 37*(2), 28–36.
15. Zhang, X. (2017). Policy escape in targeted poverty alleviation and solutions. *Theoretical Exploration, 4*, 86–92.
16. Wu, G. (2018). Prevention and control of latent risks in poverty alleviation. *China Institute for Rural Studies, Tsinghua University: Reference for Decision-Making on "Agriculture, Rural Areas and Rural People"* (14).
17. Xi, J. (2019, August 15). *Speech at the symposium on addressing pressing problems of "two assurances and three guarantees"*. http://www.qstheory.cn/dukan/qs/2019-08/15/c_1124874088.htm

18. Li, X., et al. (2018). Forty years of poverty reduction in China: A tentative interpretation based on history and sociology. *Sociological Studies, 33*(6), 35–61, 242–243.
19. Wang, Y. (2018). The abyss consequence and countermeasures in poverty alleviation. *Journal of China Executive Leadership Academy Yan'an, 11*(5), 122–127.
20. Peng, Q. (2019). Survey on poverty alleviation in Liangshan. *Qiushi, 16*, 59–65.
21. *Policies issued to help households on "marginal poverty" in Wulong of Chongqing*, May 24, 2019. http://www.xinhuanet.com/politics/2019-05/24/c_1124538605.htm

Chapter 8
Dovetailing Poverty Alleviation with Rural Revitalization

Winning the battle against extreme poverty and implementing the rural revitalization strategy was the major decision made at the 19th CPC National Congress to complete the building of a moderately prosperous society in all respects and achieve the Two Centenary Goals. It is also an effective way to address issues of unbalanced and inadequate development in a new era for China. The battle is now about to win and rural revitalization will follow as another important strategy for promoting agricultural and rural development in the next stage. Therefore, it is of vital practical significance to discuss the effective dovetailing between poverty alleviation and rural revitalization.

8.1 Poverty Alleviation Targets Under the Backdrop of Rural Revitalization

8.1.1 The Backdrop of Rural Revitalization Strategy

China is a large country not only in agriculture, but also in the number of rural people. They have played an extremely important role in China's economic and social development and have a far-reaching impact on the realization of socialist modernization. The unbalanced and inadequate development of urban and rural areas, as well as agriculture and rural people, has been the most prominent problem China encounters in its development at the present stage. To address these issues, the CPC Central Committee has made a major strategic decision to win the battle against poverty and carry out rural revitalization. Thanks to the joint efforts of the Party and the people, the fight against extreme poverty has yielded fruitful results. The number of people living in poverty in poor and contiguous destitute areas has been significantly reduced, and per capita disposable income and consumption have grown rapidly.

S. Wang, *Poverty Alleviation and Targeted Measures*,
https://doi.org/10.1007/978-981-96-1493-6_8

Infrastructure and public services have improved markedly, with better living environment, better education, better healthcare, and better culture. Rural communities in general have taken on a new look.[1]

However, we should not just stop at what we have achieved. Instead, we should soberly aware of the weak areas in the reality. As is pointed out in the Strategic Plan for Rural Revitalization (2018–2022), "The current situation of poor economic foundation and underdevelopment of rural areas in China has not been fundamentally changed. Agriculture, rural areas and rural people are still the weakest aspect in China's economic and social development and its modernization drive. This has been typically reflected in the following aspects: periodical coexistence of oversupply and undersupply of agricultural products; inadequate integrated development of primary, secondary and tertiary industries; unsatisfactory quality and efficiency of agricultural supply; limited capabilities of rural people to adapt to the development of productive forces and market competition; shortage of human resources; and backward rural infrastructure and insufficient awareness of environment and ecological conservation. In addition, the livelihood of the rural people is far from satisfactory, with wide gaps between urban and rural areas in terms of basic public services and income levels. The task of targeted eradication of extreme poverty remains arduous. The state support system for agriculture is not strong enough, with tough challenges in rural financial reform. There are still a lot to do to develop a sounder mechanism of efficient flow of factors between urban and rural areas and in the work at the primary level to enhance and update the rural system and capacity in administration and management. The overall rural development has called for immediate improvement."

To consolidate the achievements of poverty alleviation and to better prioritize agriculture, rural areas and rural people to facilitate the realization of rural modernization, the strategy of rural revitalization must be implemented. It is a necessary requirement for addressing the conflict between unbalanced and inadequate development and meeting the people's growing desire for a better life. It is a necessary requirement for delivering the Two Centenary Goals and achieving common prosperity for all. Rural revitalization is therefore of vital importance for China to become a country of industrial prosperity, beautiful environment, cultural and ethical progress, effective governance and a better life for its people.[2]

8.1.2 Inherent Coupling Between Poverty Alleviation and Rural Revitalization

Poverty alleviation and rural revitalization are both major strategic decisions put forward by the CPC Central Committee to deliver the Two Centenary Goals. They are the path we must take to make the Chinese dream of great national rejuvenation come true. The two are closely linked. Poverty alleviation mainly serves the first

[1] Wang and Feng [1].

[2] The CPC Central Committee and the State Council [2].

centenary goal, while rural revitalization would lay a foundation for the delivery of second goal [3]. Rural revitalization is an effective guarantee to consolidate the achievements of poverty alleviation, which is a prerequisite for implementing the rural revitalization strategy and plays a fundamental and key role in the framework of the task and the final victory of rural revitalization [4].

Poverty alleviation has been designed to dovetail with the goal of rural revitalization, carried out based on designated tasks for different stages. Both are centering on the Two Centenary Goals, which are in essence aimed at building China into a stronger modern socialist country and achieving common prosperity.

In terms of the development of rural people, targeted poverty alleviation has aimed at addressing their basic needs under the benchmark of "Two Assurances and Three Guarantees", such as food, clothing, housing, schooling and medical care, in order to remove obstacles in the follow-up development of rural poor and improve their quality of life by raising their per capita disposable income. Rural revitalization is the moving forward on the basis of poverty alleviation, in an attempt to achieve a "better-off life" and a "comprehensive development" of villagers. The purpose is to provide rural people with a stable source of income, a comfortable economy and a convenient life, to achieve the ultimate goal of common prosperity which seeks to achieve more equitable development and provision of public services.

In terms of regional development, the key to poverty alleviation is to address overall regional poverty, with focus on the weak areas in the development of poor villages, counties and contiguous destitute areas. Joint efforts should be made to improve their infrastructure and public services to narrow step by step the gap between poor areas and the average of rural areas in the country. On the basis of poverty alleviation efforts having solved overall regional poverty, rural revitalization drive is to promote industrial development, improve rural governance capacity and boost the equal access to infrastructure and public services between urban and rural areas so as to deliver the comprehensive upgrading of agriculture and development of rural areas [1].

At the same time, both the strategies are focusing on solving the issues of agriculture, rural areas and rural people and making institutional arrangements from the aspects of industrial development, relocation, infrastructure improvement, rural governance, security of people's livelihood and construction of institutional mechanisms [5]. From the logic of policy practice, rural revitalization is a test of the outcomes of targeted poverty alleviation, which is the priority and an indispensable part of rural revitalization [6].

8.1.3 Basic Poverty Alleviation Characteristics Under the Backdrop of Rural Revitalization

The year 2020 would be the final year scheduled for the fight against extreme poverty. China would soon step into the development stage of building a moderately prosperous society in an all-round way. The original approach of poverty alleviation and development also need to change in response to the development and changes of the times, which mainly includes the following three basic characteristics [7].

First, there will be a shift from eliminating extreme poverty to alleviating relative poverty. By 2020, absolute poverty would have been eradicated as all the poor people and villages would have been lifted out of poverty. However, the development between urban and rural areas and between villages, and the income level of different rural households are still unbalanced, and the relative poverty problem is still prominent. Poverty alleviation policies will be shifting from developing the economy to alleviating the uneven distributions of income.

Second, there will be a shift from focusing on solving income poverty to alleviating multidimensional poverty. With the elimination of absolute poverty, it is no longer comprehensive to measure the rural poverty situation from the perspective of income alone. Access to opportunities and personal development is equally important. At the stage of rural revitalization, addressing rural poverty is to improve personal development opportunities and the level of education, medical care, finance and other public services rather than ensuring subsistence. Therefore, after 2020, anti-poverty efforts will focus not just on improving the income of the people, but also on enhancing public services, personal development opportunities and social security, among others.

Third, the original focus on solving rural poverty will be shifted to solving both urban and rural poverty. During the targeted poverty alleviation campaign, the priority has been placed on addressing rural poverty through various measures such as developing industries, employment and social security. At the stage of rural revitalization, attention is to be paid to not only rural poverty, but also poverty issues in both urban and rural areas by standardizing support and improving mechanisms and measures for the integration of urban and rural areas.

8.1.4 Poverty Alleviation Objectives in Rural Revitalization

Strategies for rural revitalization and targeted poverty alleviation are closely related but different. We can never talk about poverty alleviation without rural revitalization, nor vice versa. With the change of development goals, goals and policies for poverty alleviation need to be adjusted to meet the requirements of the new era.

As a short-term poverty reduction campaign, poverty alleviation goals can be summarized as accomplishing "Targeted Efforts in Six Areas", namely, to identify the poor accurately, arrange targeted programs, utilize capital efficiently, take household-based measures, dispatch first Party secretaries based on village conditions, and achieve other set tasks; and taking "Five Measures for Poverty Eradication", which include: boosting the economy to provide more job opportunities, relocating poor people from inhospitable areas, compensating for economic losses associated with reducing ecological damage, improving education in impoverished areas, and providing subsistence allowances for those unable to shake off poverty through their own efforts alone. Together with emphasis on accurate identification, targeted help and management, poverty alleviation features targeted focus and operability.

As a long-term goal, rural revitalization aims at agricultural and rural modernization and the overall goal of achieving industrial prosperity, beautiful environment, cultural and ethical progress, effective governance and a better life for all people, which is characterized by comprehensive and systematic coverage [4]. The endeavor compasses the overall development of rural society, industrial economy and villager capability. Distinctively time-efficient and phased, the delivery of this goal can be divided into short-term and long-term dimensions. The former aims at implementation of targeted poverty alleviation to eliminate absolute poverty; while the latter is to address the problem of relative poverty on that basis to work towards the comprehensive revitalization of rural areas and socialist modernization.

8.1.4.1 Goals of Development for Rural Revitalization

A three-step strategic plan has been adopted for rural revitalization. The first is that by 2020 when absolute poverty has been eliminated with the completion of building a moderately prosperous society in all respects, relative poverty will still be there for a long time. By then, current measures aiming at eradication of absolute poverty should be gradually adjusted to routine support measures targeting relative poverty and integrated into the overall arrangement under the framework of the rural revitalization strategy.

The second is that from 2020 through 2035, there will be decisive progress on rural revitalization with agricultural and rural modernization taking shape. The agricultural structure will be fundamentally improved together with the enhanced quality of rural employment and further relief of relative poverty. The initiative of achieving common prosperity will yield more benefits for all. Equal access to basic public services will be guaranteed in urban and rural areas, with sounder systems and mechanisms for integrated urban and rural development. Further progress will also be made in cultural and ethical work in rural areas with improved governance system, better environment and living conditions.

And the third is that from 2035 through 2050, the rural areas will be fully rejuvenated with well-off farmers, a strong agriculture sector and beautiful rural areas.[3]

[3] Strategic Plan for Rural Revitalization (2018–2022) issued by the CPC Central Committee and the State Council [EB/OL]. (2018-09-26). http://www.gov.cn/zhengce/2018-09/26/content-5325534.htm.

8.1.4.2 Short-Term Poverty Alleviation Target in the Framework of Rural Revitalization

Opinions on the Implementation of Rural Revitalization Strategy issued by the central leadership in 2018 put forward that the eradication of poverty was a prerequisite for rural revitalization. Poverty alleviation and targeted measures should be given top priority to improve the quality. The standards shall neither be randomly lowered nor irrationally raised by taking more effective measures with more concentrated supports and more coordinated organization to win the decisive battle for building a moderately prosperous society in all respects. At the stage of rural revitalization, the short-term target is to win the battle against absolute poverty. Specifically, we will focus on the following.

First, there will be targeted assistance to the poor. Support for industries and employment should be given to those who are able to work, together with help in marketability and labor services, so that they may stay out of poverty. Relocations from inhospitable areas will be carries on to ensure smooth relocation and resettlement, and that those involved have the means to develop and better themselves. For the underprivileged people who are completely or partially incapacitated, a comprehensive poverty-alleviation policy will be implemented to ensure that the sick have access to medical care, the disabled to assistance, and their livelihoods are taken care of. More work should be done to ensure dynamic and precise management of subsistence allowances in rural areas to cover all eligible poor people.

Second, efforts will be focused on destitute areas. Their working and living conditions should be comprehensively improved and major indicators of basic public services approaching the national average. With the priority on solving major bottleneck issues, there should be more major projects and assistance for villages and households, with more preferential policies and the integrated funds to improve conditions in such areas and strengthen the development capacity of poor households to shake off poverty. There should be more financial support to destitute areas where the newly-added poverty alleviation funds should be allocated to. The quota of newly added construction land should give priority to the development needs of these areas.

Third, the internal driver of the poor population will be stimulated with both external support and internal motivation working together to create a synergy. They should be encouraged to work their way towards prosperity and provided with necessary education, so that they have the motivation to emerge from poverty and the skills to succeed and stay out of poverty. Poor people should be guided to overcome the mentality of relying mainly on external support and eliminate spiritual poverty. Efforts will be made to break poverty equilibrium and foster self-belief and self-reliance for poverty alleviation. Ways and means of assistance should be improved and mechanisms such as production awards and subsidies, labor subsidies, and work relief should be introduced to help poor people get out of poverty through their own hard work.

Fourth, mechanisms of responsibility and oversight will be strengthened. There should be close adherence to the poverty eradication management network with the central government acting as coordinator, provincial governments taking overall responsibility, and city and county governments overseeing implementation, strengthening the system in which heads of the Party committee and government take overall responsibility and the key role of county-level Party committees as the headquarters of the campaign. Party committee secretaries and county governors will be required to remain unchanged in their posts during the process. Special programs to combat corruption and misconducts should be launched to effectively strengthen the management of poverty alleviation funds and severely punish their misappropriation or embezzlement. Efforts should be made to well integrate the implementation of the rural revitalization strategy with the critical battle against extreme poverty by formulating three-year action guidelines to achieve sustained poverty reduction.

8.1.4.3 Long-Term Poverty Alleviation Target in the Framework of Rural Revitalization

The long-term target at the stage of rural revitalization is to alleviate relative poverty, which would inevitably arise in the process of development following the elimination of absolute poverty, and work towards fully-fledged rural revitalization and socialist modernization by 2050. The following are suggested to deliver the target.

First, we will continue to implement the policy of poverty alleviation through industries. More work should be done to encourage the development of new business players and establish a long-term benefit coupling mechanism to increase the industrial income of the low-income and poor population. Resolute efforts should be made to guard against the development of unsustainable industries for the sake of short-term gains in poverty alleviation [8].

Second, we will continue to implement the policy of poverty alleviation through employment. More work should be done to encourage low-income people to find jobs or start businesses in rural areas, and introduce poverty alleviation workshops through various channels. In addition, the creation of public welfare posts should take into account the improvement of the look of villages.

Third, we will continue to implement the policy of poverty alleviation through education. It is suggested that non-compulsory education be included in the education security system, covering kindergarten and senior high school education, to gradually increase the enrollment rate of preschool and senior high school education. At the same time, children from other families will be included in education security by giving them more support in this respect.

Fourth, we will advance rural revitalization step by step. There should be a scientific approach towards differences between rural areas in China, respect and give play to the initiative of the primary-level leadership and people. Good practices should be reviewed, introduced and drew on to boost the modernization drive of agriculture and rural areas in different regions and with different levels of development. We will give full play to the exemplary role of leading areas, such as the developed eastern coastal areas, the suburbs of cities with net population inflow, the rural areas with collective economic strengths and other better-off areas, to accelerate the development of key areas, such as those around small and medium-sized cities and towns as well as the countryside in the vast plains and hilly areas, which cover most of the villages in China and are the main battleground for rural revitalization. More efforts will focus on the development of impoverished areas, such as old revolutionary base areas, areas with large ethnic populations, border areas, and contiguous destitute areas.[4]

Fifth, we will establish a long-term mechanism to address relative poverty. It mainly includes: the relative poverty line set by the proportion in relation to the median income, with the proportion increasing with the development of economy; integration of urban and rural poverty alleviation systems to standardize the poverty benchmark and accelerate the integration of urban and rural social security systems; and establishment of the policy system for alleviating relative poverty [9].

8.2 Strategies for Alleviating Relative Poverty in Rural Revitalization

Eliminating poverty, improving people's livelihood and working towards common prosperity are the essential requirements of socialism and a major historical mission of the CPC. Winning the battle against poverty and eliminating absolute poverty are key measures to help all people share in the fruits of reform and development and lead a better life. However, the complete elimination of absolute poverty does not mean the end of poverty, and relative poverty will exist for a long time with the development of economic society. At the stage of rural revitalization, accelerating the establishment of a sound policy system and working mechanism for alleviating relative poverty so as to bring about better development conditions for people in underdeveloped areas are of great significance to achieving the phased goal of rural revitalization by 2035 and moving towards common prosperity.

8.2.1 Features of Relative Poverty in Rural Revitalization

China's No. 1 central document for 2020 was Guidelines on Agriculture, Rural Areas and Rural People as the Top Priority Work to Ensure a Moderately Prosperous Society in All Respects as Scheduled, which was issued by the CPC Central Committee and the State Council. It clearly stated that "Upon the completion of the task of targeted poverty alleviation, China's poverty situation will take on a major change, with the focus shifted to addressing relative poverty as a routine effort. We should explore and establish a long-term mechanism and promote the steady transformation of poverty reduction strategies and work systems. We will strengthen top-level planning for addressing relative poverty by incorporating it into the overall planning for implementing the rural revitalization strategy." At the stage of rural revitalization, relative

[4] The CPC Central Committee and the State Council [2].

poverty has replaced absolute poverty to become the major form of poverty in China, with the following obviously different features.

8.2.1.1 Greater Attention to Inequality in Economic and Social Development

For targeted poverty alleviation, the focus has been on meeting the basic development needs of the poor population and poor areas. To take poverty population for example, eradication of absolute poverty means they are secured in food and clothing and have access to improved drinking water supplies, compulsory education, basic healthcare and safe housing. In other words, it guarantees the basic living standards for subsistence of the poor.

At the stage of rural revitalization, on the basis of the comprehensive elimination of absolute poverty, alleviation of relative poverty will focus on poverty caused by social stratification and unequal income distribution in economic and social development. In addition to the basic subsistence needs of poor groups, more attention will be paid to the low income and the lack of education and medical resources caused by unequal distributions.

8.2.1.2 Wide Poverty Dimensions with Large Number of Poor People

Poverty is a comprehensive and complex social phenomenon, including not only the inability to maintain basic needs due to insufficient income, but also social exclusion caused by the inability to access basic resources such as education, healthcare and housing due to social predicament [10]. To begin with, the income standard for relative poverty is generally higher than that for absolute poverty, resulting in the larger number and proportion of relatively poor people. In terms of the distribution, the relative poverty people have a wider spatial coverage, including not only the rural poor, but also migrant workers in cities and urban low-income groups. In terms of measurement, relative poverty has to do with not only "Two Assurances and Three Guarantees", but also the degree of deprivation of resources and welfare such as education and medical care, with wide dimensions. All this has increased challenges and obstacles for alleviating relative poverty.

8.2.1.3 Scattering and High Mobility in Distribution

Since the targeted poverty eradication, there has been a continuous increase of support to the contiguous poor areas, which has significantly relieved regional poverty. Although poverty may still be relatively concentrated in some areas, the relatively poor groups are scattered across the country [9]. With the development of rural revitalization and urbanization, areas with rapid economic development will attract more and more rural labor, and some low-income groups are bound to move into cities with the transfer of rural people, leading to an increase in the number of urban mobility poor groups [9, 11]. At the stage of rural revitalization, the mobility of the relatively poor groups will make the identification, monitoring and assistance more complicated, which requires better coordination by integrating urban and rural development.

8.2.1.4 Vulnerable Groups as the Majority

At the stage of rural revitalization, groups prone to fall into relative poverty mainly include the following: marginal households that are not registered, people who have shaken off poverty by relying on the subsistence allowance policy, those who have just emerged from poverty but whose position is far from secure, low-income and weakly-secured rural migrant population, non-working urban residents with no source of livelihood and no legal provider, as well as the urban unemployed and groups falling into poverty caused by illness, disaster or accident. Based on the specific causes of poverty, these groups can be classified into vulnerable groups socially, naturally and physiologically [12].

Since the beginning of the poverty alleviation campaign, China has helped the vast majority of the working poor stay out of poverty through targeted measures such as industries and employment. Vulnerable groups, however, are more dependent on assistance policies since it is difficult for them to achieve poverty alleviation and income increase through their own efforts, which also makes it more challenging to build a long-term mechanism to alleviate relative poverty.

8.2.2 Key Areas and Challenges in Alleviating Relative Poverty in Rural Revitalization

In light of distinctive features of relative poverty, attention should be paid to the following key areas and challenges.

The first is to clarify the relative poverty standards. China has a large population base, and there is an obvious gap in the level of development between east and west. The change in the relative poverty standards may affect the welfare of millions of people. They should be adapted to China's national conditions and that is of great significance to the alleviation of relative poverty.

The second is urban and rural integration. The spatial distribution and mobility of relative poverty make it difficult to separate poverty reduction efforts between rural and urban areas. Coordinated arrangements should be made to ensure effectiveness.

The third is to stimulate the internal motivation of the poor. With the wide coverage and the large number of relative poverty population, there may be low efficiency by relying only on government support. At the stage of rural revitalization, it is necessary to give fuller play to the principal role of the relatively poor group, stimulate their internal driver and let more low-income groups with the ability to work participate in economic and social development and enjoy the benefits of economic development.

8.2.3 Measures to Alleviate Relative Poverty in Rural Revitalization

8.2.3.1 Greater Emphasis on Poverty Prevention

To address the issue of relative poverty at the stage of rural revitalization, it is necessary to highlight the importance of poverty prevention. In March 2020, the state leadership for poverty alleviation issued Guidelines on the Establishment of Monitoring and Assistance Mechanisms to Prevent Returning to Poverty, which clearly stated that "Prevention of the poor from sinking back into poverty must be given prominence." At the stage of rural revitalization, first, we need to combine pre-prevention with post-support by establishing a prevention-focused governance mechanism and policy system to avoid the situation where poor groups are left out due to inadequate anti-poverty work. Second, we need to implement dynamic monitoring and early warning mechanisms to prevent poverty.

8.2.3.2 Establishing Institutionalized Systems to Alleviate Relative Poverty

To address the issue of relative poverty at the stage of rural revitalization, it is necessary to establish institutionalized systems. The CPC Central Committee has adopted a series of bold measures to ensure the winning of the battle against extreme poverty and the delivery of the goal of building a moderately prosperous society in all respects as scheduled by 2020. For relative poverty, however, it is necessary to change from extensive social mobilization to routine and institutionalized management and incorporate it into the work of government departments to accelerate the establishment of an integrated urban and rural and multisectoral coordinated anti-poverty governance system [13].

8.2.3.3 Establishing a Long-Term Mechanism to Alleviate Relative Poverty

To address the issue of relative poverty at the stage of rural revitalization, it is necessary to establish a long-term working mechanism as soon as possible. First, we should make good industrial planning. We should actively explore the interest coupling mechanism to help poor groups alleviate relative poverty and well balance between industrial development for poverty alleviation and industrial prosperity while dovetailing the two.

Second, we should carry forward the practice of combining the external assistance with the principal role of the poor people to stimulate their internal impetus and self-belief. Various models can be introduced, like cultural undertakings, industrial development and employment, to boost the poor people's pursuit of a better life and increase their self-confidence and motivation for action by providing them with more development opportunities.

Third, continuous efforts should be made to boost government leadership and social participation, giving full play to the role of the government, the market and society to create a synergy in poverty prevention and reduction.

8.2.3.4 Establishing an Integrated Urban-Rural Governance System

To address the issue of relative poverty at the stage of rural revitalization, it is necessary to establish a poverty reduction management system for urban and rural areas. One is to build an integrated poverty monitoring mechanism. Considering the fact that the development varies greatly between eastern and western China, the mechanism should pay attention to the dovetailing not only between urban and rural areas, but also between different identifying standards for relative poverty. The other is to build an integrated urban-rural poverty reduction system to address the mobility poverty of rural migrant workers.

8.3 Institutionalized Mechanisms for Poverty Alleviation in Rural Revitalization

The remarkable results of poverty alleviation are closely related to effective institutionalized mechanisms. Drawing on the responsibility system established in poverty alleviation, a sound leadership system and mechanism has been established for rural revitalization.

First, a leadership responsibility system for the implementation of the strategy has been established, making it clear that the top Party and government officials are the primary persons responsible, with the Party secretaries at five levels taking charge of the implementation. Among them, the county Party secretary functions as the "front-line commander" of rural revitalization.

Second, the working mechanism of "the central government acting as coordinator, provincial governments taking overall responsibility, and city and county governments overseeing implementation" has been carried on and it is required that provincial-level Party committees and governments report to the central leadership on the progress on a yearly basis.[5]

Third, a performance assessment system will be established for municipal and county Party and government leaders in order to ensure that the responsibility and policies are fully implemented. The assessment results will be used as a major benchmark for the appointment and selection of officials. In addition, the successful experience accumulated by the third-party evaluation in the assessment of the effectiveness of poverty alleviation also provides important reference for the assessment of the effectiveness of rural revitalization, which is worthy of study for reference and application [8].

At the primary level, during the poverty alleviation campaign, local governments sent first secretaries and resident work teams to poor villages for long-term and paired-up assistance. These measures have worked remarkable effects on helping poor villages and households get rid of poverty and promoting village-level collective economic development, with reference value on how to enhance village-level governance capability for effective goals at the new stage. However, rural revitalization involves all villages and it is obvious that we cannot simply copy the method of resident assistance for poverty alleviation. For rural revitalization, the specific methods of residence, personnel requirements and the stay duration should be fully combined with the actual conditions of each place with corresponding adjustments, so that they can work together towards a harmonious society by enhancing the rule of law and virtue and autonomy of the village community as the fundamental goal [8].

8.4 Policies for Poverty Alleviation in Rural Revitalization

At present, the priority task of China's rural revitalization is to win the battle against poverty and promote the integration of the two to create a virtuous circle. Rural revitalization is an effective guarantee for poor households to get rid of poverty and prevent them from returning to poverty, while poverty alleviation is the basis and prerequisite for delivering the rural revitalization strategy [15]. Since the 19th CPC National Congress, rural revitalization and poverty alleviation have been more and more integrated. Its characteristics responsive of the times also inject new blood into poverty alleviation today, which brings new challenges and charts new courses for China's poverty alleviation.

In December 2018, the Central Rural Work Conference stressed that rural revitalization aims at the following: reshaping the relationship between urban and rural areas to promote their integration, improving the basic rural operating system to achieve common prosperity and deepening supply-side structural reforms to promote quality agriculture, adhering to the harmonious coexistence between human and nature to

---

[5] Key to Rural Revitalization Lies in the Party Leadership (Policy Interpretation: Focusing on No. 1 Central Document ④) [14].

propel the green rural development, carrying forward farming civilization to promote rural cultural progress and innovating approaches to improve the rural governance system to win the final victory of the anti-poverty battle.

In terms of combining the short-term and long-term poverty alleviation goals of rural revitalization, a clear division is necessary. Firstly, the short-term policy should focus on the completion of the final work of targeted poverty alleviation to eliminate absolute poverty and solve the remaining difficulties and bottleneck issues; secondly, in the long-term context, attention should be paid to address "relative poverty", and on this basis to promote agricultural modernization and the comprehensive cultural, ecological, economic, and organizational revitalization of rural areas.

8.4.1 Short-Term Plan of Poverty Alleviation Policies in Rural Revitalization

China's poverty alleviation policies have gone through the following four stages: from 1978 to 1985, when it was region-oriented for poverty relief; from 1986 to 2000, when poor counties were targeted for extensive development-oriented poverty alleviation; from 2001 to 2010, when it was comprehensive poverty alleviation aimed at entire villages, and since 2011, when needs of individuals and households have been addressed in continuous destitute areas. In general, China's poverty alleviation policies have presented a spiral development from "broad brush to centralized integration and to accurate identification" [16].

In the past 40 years of development, a large poverty alleviation network has been established, with the government, society and the market working in coordination, and government-sponsored projects, sector-specific programs,[6] and corporate and societal assistance supplementing each other. The approach has changed from generalized broad-brush policies to targeted measures based on specific conditions, and the framework has changed from one with the government as the only player to what we have now with the full participation of multiple players from the market and social sectors led by the government. The approaches have indeed enriched the institutional mechanisms and models of poverty alleviation.

The poverty alleviation policy under rural revitalization is the carrying forward of China's previous anti-poverty policies, which are consistent in the aim of targeted elimination of absolute poverty. The short-term goal is to win the battle and eliminate absolute poverty, which is also the main task of China at the present stage [15]. Therefore, the policies are consistent in the short-term goal, with the latter a continuous effort of the former. The poverty alleviation policies that have worked in the past can be used for reference and applied in the early stage of rural revitalization, and best

[6] Sector-specific programs for poverty alleviation refer to those of safe drinking water, relocation, dilapidated house renovation, education, healthcare, agricultural industry, employment, social security, technological support, transportation and other infrastructure construction, people training, culture, e-commerce, tourism, primary-level governance and ecological management.

practices should be carried on. In addition, current challenges and bottleneck issues should be addressed.

8.4.1.1 Promoting Targeted Poverty Alleviation to Solve Absolute Poverty

The in-depth implementation of the targeted poverty alleviation policy requires prioritized allocation of resources, more attention to extreme poverty, more effective measures to cope with the "abyss consequence", more targeted assistance to poor households and better stimulation of self-motivation of poor households [17, 18]. Specifically, the following aspects should be given prominence.

The first is to improve the system for targeted poverty alleviation. Measures should be taken in light of local conditions, individuals and situations, with pilot programs to develop multiple channels and paths to strengthen cooperation and support between the eastern and western regions, as well as regional industrial collaboration and industrial development. Paired-up assistance at the county level should be implemented to promote poverty alleviation and improve the system of resident work teams in villages.

The second is to focus on the issue of extreme poverty. More work should be done to cope with tough challenges, promote major projects and provide targeted assistance to individuals, households and villages. At the same time, there should be more preferential policies and financial support to optimize development conditions in destitute areas and increase the driving force for self-development of poor households.

The third is to address the "abyss consequence" in poverty alleviation. New imbalances may arise in the implementation of various policies, with the unreasonable distribution of poverty alleviation resources becoming prominent and the critical poor population not being helped by institutional mechanisms. Resources may have been over concentrated and increased on poor areas and poor households, which may even lead to excessive alleviation of poverty.

The fourth is to raise the accuracy of targeted poverty alleviation. Support should be provided to poor households who are able to work through industrial development, employment training and other means to improve their sustainable development ability based on sustained self-motivation. Various poverty-relief policies should be adopted to ensure that those who have lost the ability to work have access to medical care, and the disabled and elderly are taken good care of.

The fifth is to continue to stimulate the poor people's internal driver for poverty alleviation. Efforts should be redoubled to help those who have emerged from poverty build up self-belief and have access to education, so that they can create a better life through their own hard work. Subsistence relief should be provided together with the encouragement of self-motivation and the improvement of the quality and ability of poor households in agricultural production, work and business, so that their capacity for sustainable development is enhanced which can effectively prevent them from returning to poverty. Poor people should be guided to overcome too much reliance on external support and break the low-level equilibrium trap and vicious circle, developing self-reliance and confidence to get rid of poverty [19].

8.4.1.2 Improving Social Security Network in Multiple Dimensions

First, we will continue poverty alleviation through healthcare programs and improve the medical system. Efforts should be redoubled to boost the development of the basic medical and health system to prevent poor households from being trapped in or returning to poverty because of diseases. In particular, the basic medical insurance and medical assistance system, policy-backed major disease insurance system and commercial medical insurance system in China should be further improved to ensure that the poor can afford medical services. The full coverage of basic medical services should be achieved step by step to increase the reimbursement rate and ensure medical treatment to the impoverished with major illnesses, contracted healthcare to the impoverished with chronic diseases, and guaranteed medical services for the impoverished with critical illnesses. In addition, practices of treatment before payment and "one-stop" settlement should be introduced [20].

Second, poverty alleviation measures should be well dovetailed with low-income allowances and basic guarantees provided to the elderly, the disabled rural residents and minors who are unable to work, childless and infirm with no source of income or supporter. In the final stage of China's poverty alleviation, there has to be flexible and timely adjustment of policies to coordinate the relationship between different assistance and support. Balanced plans should be made in such areas as identification criteria, management models, and channels of support and assistance, with the focus shifted from poverty alleviation to a regular social security system and relief mechanism for rural revitalization.

8.4.1.3 Paying Attention to Multidimensional Critical Poverty of Marginalized Groups

First, prominence should be given to the groups in marginal and multidimensional poverty, exploring new ways of accurate identification and diversified support measures. The efficiency and intensity of policy assistance should be improved by strengthening follow-up supervision and early warning to improve the poverty prevention and alleviation system for these groups of people under rural revitalization.

Second, after the elimination of extreme poverty, the preferential policies of the poor and marginalized groups should be gradually shifted to relative poverty and low-income groups by comprehensive utilization of social resources and the establishment of early warning and help mechanisms for these groups.

8.4.1.4 Preventing Risks to Consolidate Poverty Alleviation Outcomes

At present, the population who has just emerged out of poverty is far from secure, with high risks of returning to poverty. Therefore, the first thing to do is to improve the long-term mechanism to prevent this to happen by drawing on experience to ensure that they stay out of poverty. The second is that attention should be paid to fostering their self-belief and self-help to get rid of the mentality of relying on external support. At the same time, an incentive system should be established to integrate poverty alleviation policies with the participation of poor households to cultivate and enhance their overall quality and practical skills.

8.4.1.5 Promoting Coordinated Development of Education, Finance and Technology

First of all, continued efforts should be made to vigorously develop poverty alleviation through education. Investment will be increased to prevent poverty by boosting the internal motivation of those targeted for poverty alleviation. Currently, great emphasis should be placed on developing preschool education, increasing compulsory education coverage and the popularity of senior high school education to complete the full coverage of the basic education system in poor areas as soon as possible.[7]

Second, more encouragement should be given to poverty alleviation through science and technology. More work should be done to improve the management system in this respect by reforming the local incentive mechanism and increasing the development and introduction of new agricultural varieties and technological achievements to enhance local innovation and entrepreneurial capacity. In addition, it is required that the technical upgrading of rural diversified industries be strengthened by giving full play to the advantages of institutions of higher learning and research institutes and establishing the mechanism for paired-up technical assistance to help the development of local specialty industries.

Third, a better job is required in poverty alleviation through financial programs. A financial poverty alleviation system is now taking shape in China in which the government leads and financial institutions participate. Efforts should be made to further financial reform for poverty alleviation and optimize approaches to and efficiency of poverty relief to promote rural industrial revitalization [22]. For example, innovative models of financial services such as micro loans and "finance + industry" have been adopted to meet the financial needs of production and life in poor areas for a more sustained effort from self-motivation and alleviate the financial pressure that have long plagued poor households.

[7] The State Council [21].

8.4.1.6 Strengthening Responsibility and Oversight for the Building of a Competent Anti-poverty Workforce

Firstly, we will improve the responsibility and oversight system. Poverty alleviation work should adhere to the practice with the central government acting as coordinator, provincial governments taking overall responsibility, and city and county governments overseeing implementation. The role of local Party and government leaders should be given full play, particularly the vanguard role of county Party committees. More work should be done to strengthen the supervision system against corruption and sloth work style by down-to-earth oversight and evaluation of the outcome [23].

Secondly, efforts should be made to better develop professional people. China's rural revitalization strategy and targeted poverty alleviation are in an urgent need of capable and experienced officials who understand the endeavor and are adept at communicating with villagers. It is highly necessary to improve the personnel system, expand the channels of recruitment and employment and actively recruit college graduates and young people who have returned to their hometowns to start businesses. Education and training of such people are also important for poverty alleviation team building at the primary level.

8.4.2 Long-Term Planning of Poverty Alleviation Policies in Rural Revitalization

The rural revitalization strategy should be implemented to alleviate relative poverty step by step on the basis of eliminating absolute poverty, with the ultimate goal of revitalization in all China's rural areas. Under this backdrop, the long-term poverty alleviation policy should not only be able to cope with problems remaining unsolved in short-term goals, but also dovetail with the rural revitalization strategy from a systematic and holistic perspective. In addressing "relative poverty", the modernization of agriculture and rural areas should be facilitated by improving the policy for employment and training and innovating mechanisms of eco-environmental conservation. A system of socialized agricultural services will be in full operation by speeding up the growth of primary-level organization and an efficient modern distribution system, as well as the development of new industries and new forms of business in agriculture and rural areas, including those led by supply and marketing cooperatives.

8.4.2.1 Carrying Out In-Depth Supply-Side Structural Reform for Quality Agriculture

In response to what is required by rural revitalization, it is necessary to develop rural industry by focusing on benefiting the majority of villagers and establish a long-term mechanism of rural revitalization to raise the capacity of sustainable self-development of agriculture and other industries. A sounder interest coupling mechanism should be explored and established to raise the economic income of poor households and achieve the organic unity of short-term assistance and long-term growth. In rural revitalization, the industrial development policy should take the supply-side structural reform of the agricultural industry as the priority, further the reform of supply and marketing cooperatives and promote the collaboration of various channels to practically improve the benefits of all parties in line with the reality.

(1) It is important to improve the agricultural and rural social service system. Agricultural modernization requires continuous upgrading of market innovation, brand competitiveness and industrial total factor productivity. Therefore, we should promote the development and prosperity of deep processing industry of agroproducts and promote the integration of agricultural industry chain. Advanced equipment should be introduced to extend the industrial chain, create local brands and increase the economic added value of pan-agricultural products. In addition, it is necessary to promote the establishment of a socialized modern agricultural service system by optimizing land trust services, linking the interests of villagers with modern agriculture and improving organization and marketability [24].
(2) Another important work is to upgrade the industrial structure for the development of multiple business forms. Efforts should be made to introduce new rural industrial forms and boost modern industries. Influenced by the human capital endowment of the poor population, poverty alleviation through industries mainly relies on the processing industry of primary agroproducts with low technology and other industries with intensive labor. In the Guideline on Deepening Supply-Side Structural Reform to Accelerate the Cultivation of New Growth Drivers for Agricultural and Rural Development issued by the central leadership, it is pointed out that rural areas should give full play to local resource advantages, create agricultural brands, develop leisure and e-commerce agriculture and rural tourism and promote the integration of agriculture with education, health, technology and other sectors. At the same time, new forms of business such as customized agroproducts, crowdfunding for agriculture and exhibition agriculture can be introduced on a trial basis. The following are some measures.

First, to boost the tourism industry to alleviate poverty. As an industrial resource calling for immediate development, the tourism industry may inject new vitality into the integration of the first, second and tertiary industries in poor areas, and it is also an important measure to connect it with the building of beautiful rural areas in China. Therefore, appropriate development of special leisure agriculture should be encouraged in light of local conditions to develop rural tourism and eco-tourism [25].

Second, the campaign of bringing e-commerce industry to the countryside can be launched to support the construction of modern logistics in rural areas. The state has encouraged e-commerce companies to open up online marketing platforms for special agricultural products, establish stable supply and marketing relationships with rural producing areas and accelerate the construction of rural logistics distribution system so that villagers have access to substantial benefits [26]. We will make full use of the demonstration role of the market in farm produce and guide rural households to produce on demand. In addition, we should develop a new Internet-based industrial system and optimize the industrial structure of agriculture, forestry, animal husbandry and fishery to promote the integrated development of agriculture, processing industry, leisure tourism and e-commerce.

Third, innovative measures should be introduced for income from assets to alleviate poverty. The central government should pool resources to advance the construction of agricultural infrastructure, environment conservation and projects of sizable new energy engineering such as photovoltaic, hydropower and wind power projects. Shares will be transferred to villagers or village collectives with priority given to poor households who have lost the ability to work [27]. This can go together with the compensation mechanism in poverty alleviation for economic losses associated with reducing ecological damage to introduce sound income distribution methods so that villagers may have more channels to increase their income.

8.4.2.2 Exploring New Management System for Good Rural Governance

(1) Establishing rural comprehensive service cooperatives and community service centers. They are supposed to provide information service, sports and entertainment, land management and trust, catering and accommodation services, senior centers and kindergartens, financial agency business, rural tourism planning, e-commerce logistics development, information technology training, community social security and medical services.
(2) Strengthening Party leadership. Primary-level Party organizations should be established in rural areas to train a large number of outstanding primary-level Party secretaries. The vanguard, exemplary and leading role of Party members should be given full play to encourage rural residents to participate in rural revitalization.
(3) Adjusting measures to local conditions with reasonable arrangement. In light of the different problems existing in different villages and the different levels of economic and cultural development, effective ways to realize rural governance according to local conditions should be explored and tried out.
(4) Building a system of good rural governance. We should adhere to the unity of rule of law and rule of virtue and promote rural autonomy at the primary level by improving its governance system and channels for all parties to participate. More support should be given for rural areas to accelerate the delivery of the goal of development of rural people, by rural people and for rural people [28].

8.4.2.3 Carrying Forward Farming Civilization to Revitalize Rural Culture

Emphasis should be placed on the following aspects:

(1) Inheriting the best of China's farming civilization and promoting the prosperity of rural culture. Good social etiquette in rural areas is the core link and carrier to sustain fine traditional Chinese culture. As an internal requirement for building beautiful countryside, cultural and ethical progress is highly necessary. We should carry forward farming civilization to enhance our confidence in rural culture, promoting the development of rural etiquette and village rules. The revitalization of farming culture is the way to revitalize rural areas in China, and it is also an important part of the strategy to realize the great rejuvenation of the Chinese nation.
(2) Breaking from path dependence and getting rid of the mentality of relying on external help. Poor households should be guided to shake off the inertia of dependence formed under the deadlock of poverty and to develop an attitude of self-help to get rid of poverty by their own hard work [29]. At the same time, necessary pre-conditions for applying for and receiving benefits should be set up to help increase the coverage of participation, together with the improved methods to combine them with production awards and subsidies, labor subsidies and work relief to guide villagers to become self-reliant.
(3) Promoting rural civilization. Cultural and ethical advancement is the key to rural revitalization. Fine traditional rural culture should be preserved and developed while outmoded and undesirable habits and customs updated. Good cultural practices are encouraged to bring a new look to local villages.

8.4.2.4 Encouraging Employment and Entrepreneurship to Raise Rural Residents' Income

This is carried out by paying attention to the following:

(1) Supporting employment and entrepreneurship in light of local conditions. This, together with helping the poor find employment locally, is one of the effective measures for poverty alleviation through industries. The poor can be guided to obtain employment through a variety of channels. By encouraging the development of rural characteristic agriculture, rural tourism, rural e-commerce and other industries, together with public welfare posts for poverty alleviation through ecological conservation, the participation and benefits of poor households can be improved and their employment can be facilitated through more channels [30].

Another effective measure is to create jobs through entrepreneurship. The construction of more rural business incubation bases should be accelerated, with better business environment and supporting facilities, more business training opportunities and better information services. There should be more encouragement for entrepreneurial individuals to start businesses and help and lead others out of poverty. Returned rural migrant workers, college graduates and retired soldiers should be given more support to start businesses in their hometowns [31].

(2) Boosting employment training to enhance the capability of human capital for sustainable development. Poverty alleviation by enhanced capability is an important measure to deepen the structural reform of the supply side and promote high-quality development and employment. It constitutes the major part of poverty alleviation through employment, and is most sustainable and fundamental. First of all, a sound system for employment skills training should be improved for revitalization of rural human resources. Vocational skills training should be better provided to enable the poor to find jobs. Local employment, industrial development and vocational skills training should be well coordinated to improve the pertinence of training. Another measure is to establish a multi-dimensional and multi-level training system, with intensive training by category for the rural poor based on their willingness to work and preference for the content of training. A systematic development of rural vocational training should be speeded up, with supportive training subsidies. In addition, education and training for rural development in various forms should be encouraged to facilitate agricultural modernization and the development of smart agriculture [32].

8.4.2.5 Adherence to the Harmonious Coexistence Between Man and Nature by Green Development

Good and livable environment is vital for rural revitalization, and greater importance should be attached to building a green ecological system in rural areas for better ecological conservation and more beautiful villages. Environmental protection and development-driven poverty alleviation are closely interrelated. Increasing support for rural poor households to eliminate poverty will be integrated with China's efforts for ecological conservation and sustainable development to ensure the coordinated development of the two.

Actions should be taken to build beautiful villages and improve the rural green ecological system. As President Xi Jinping points out, lucid waters and lush mountains are invaluable assets. We should adhere to the harmonious coexistence between man and nature and implement the sound philosophy on development by taking the path of sustainable development. Therefore, great efforts should be made to improve the rural environment, strengthen the treatment of nonpoint source pollution in rural areas and improve the urban and rural recycling and utilization system. There should be more effective measures for pesticide reduction, damage control, soil formulation tests and harmless fertilization. More work should be done to advocate the use of bio-organic fertilizer, low-toxicity and low-residue pesticides, and encourage the recycling of waste materials such as agricultural film, straw and pesticide packaging to promote the sorting, recycling and re-development of rural household waste. In addition, there should be more publicity and promotion to enhance the awareness of the importance of ecological conservation and environment protection so that rural people would develop good practices in their production and life of respecting the environment and saving resources.

A sound policy system for poverty alleviation through ecological conservation should be established. On this issue, China has developed a comprehensive model involving relocation for ecological conservation, compensation for economic losses associated with reducing ecological damage, employment placement and labor service provision [33]. On this basis, timely payment of salaries and wages should be guaranteed for poor households after their service. More ecological industries should be developed to raise their income and the compensation mechanism and transfer payment system should be explored on a national basis. The government should encourage more ecological conservation projects and innovation of management of resources and ecological posts to help implement the policy.

8.5 Models of Poverty Alleviation in Rural Revitalization

2020 is the final year scheduled for China to win its battle against extreme poverty, when all registered poor counties will get out of poverty. However, removing the label is not the end, but the beginning of a new journey towards rural revitalization. In this new context, poverty alleviation has been added with new implications in response to the changing times. The approaches will feature not only a continuance of what has worked in the past, but also an active exploration and innovation to open up new models of poverty alleviation. At the stage of targeted poverty alleviation, the models are mainly through industries, employment, relocation, ecological conservation, education, healthcare and social security. The remarkable results of targeted poverty alleviation are closely related to these effective models, which are also applicable to the alleviation of relative poverty at the new stage. However, this does not mean that measures should remain unchanged and past experience is blindly copied. On the contrary, innovative poverty alleviation models should be explored to meet the needs of the times.

8.5.1 Industrial Development for Poverty Alleviation in Rural Revitalization

On March 5, 2018, when attending the deliberation of the Inner Mongolia delegation at the 13th National People's Congress, Xi Jinping made the point that poverty alleviation should be organically integrated with the implementation of the rural revitalization strategy. For targeted poverty alleviation, industrial development is the first in the five key measures and the fundamental strategy to achieve sustained and stable outcomes, while industrial prosperity is at the top of the list of rural revitalization development goals and is the priority of the strategy, which provides the material basis and continuous driving force for delivering other development goals. Therefore, in order to achieve the organic integration of the two, the dovetailing between industrial activities for poverty alleviation and industrial prosperity should be explored.

Poverty alleviation and rural revitalization are characterized by similarity of tasks, interaction of functions and consistency of goals, targets and approaches [3]. Therefore, industrial development for poverty alleviation and industrial prosperity for rural revitalization feature internal consistency, which is mainly reflected in the following two aspects.

On the one hand, industrial development has laid the foundation for industrial prosperity. For one thing, it has advanced the growth of characteristic industries in poor areas. The central government has put forward the development of specialty industries to get rid of poverty in several polices. For example, the Decision of the CPC Central Committee and the State Council on Winning the Battle against Poverty defines the development of specialty industries to get rid of poverty and formulates requirements for the development plan. The Outline of the 13th Five-Year Plan for National Economic and Social Development of the People's Republic of China calls for the promotion of the "One Village, One Specialty" industrial campaign in poverty-stricken villages. The Guidelines on the Development of Specialty Industries in Poor Areas to Promote Targeted Poverty Alleviation makes comprehensive plans for the development of specialty industries in poor areas by a well-informed defining of the industries to promote the integrated development of primary, secondary and tertiary industries. According to the Plan for Poverty Alleviation during the 13th Five-Year Plan Period, each poor county should develop a number of local industries that may help poverty alleviation, and each township and village should try to develop competitive local products. These policy supports have created favorable environment and conditions for the development of local industries. They have driven impoverished areas to tap their advantageous local resources and promote the development of a number of distinctive industries. For the other, industrial development requires the incubation of new types of agricultural business players, which, with the support of government policies and funds, have grown and effectively driven the economic development of poor areas.

On the other hand, industrial prosperity can consolidate and improve the quality of industrial development for poverty alleviation. First, it can strengthen the anti-poverty achievements, promote the sustainable development and prevent villagers from returning to poverty. By the time when targeted poverty alleviation is completed, one of the important issues will be how to consolidate what we have achieved to ensure people stay out of poverty. Industrial development has helped tens of millions of poor people shake off poverty. However, due to the weak industrial foundation, low technological competitiveness and high dependence on government subsidies, the people who have just emerged from poverty but whose position is far from secure still face the risk of falling back into poverty due to the possible failure of industrial development. In the "post targeted poverty alleviation" era, industrial prosperity can bring policy, human resources and capital support to poor areas to consolidate the achievements. Second, industrial prosperity pursues the integrated development of primary, secondary and tertiary industries, which can promote the optimization and upgrading of industries to achieve poverty alleviation of a better quality.

In spite of the fact that industrial development and industrial prosperity are consistent by nature, there are still some issues to address in their organic connection. Firstly, under the constraint of pressing tasks, local governments may have been more inclined to choose projects with small investment and quick returns, without evaluating the market, which often led to serious homogeneity of industrial projects in various poor areas. These small-sized and homogeneous projects often failed to satisfy the diversification and sustainable development of rural industries.

Secondly, many of these industrial projects were low-tech and had focused on planting or farming, with short industrial chain and scarce integration of the primary, secondary and tertiary industries, bringing limited benefits to villagers. In contrast, industrial prosperity requires the integration of the first, second and third industries to develop and increase the added value of agricultural products. Therefore, the present concept of many industrial projects for poverty alleviation needs to be improved to gradually adapt to the new requirements.

Thirdly, the government has fostered a number of leading enterprises, farmer cooperatives and family farms as new agricultural operators to drive industrial development. However, some of the cooperatives were nothing but frills, and most enterprises helped poor households by means of dividends, which went against the original intention of giving them the capacity for independent development. In addition, the interest coupling mechanism between the new agricultural business operators and poor households was loose. These problems have made it difficult for modern agricultural entrepreneurs to play a leading role in industry prosperity.

Fourthly, projects of industrial development need to take into account both economic benefits and social responsibilities, which, side by side with the tight schedule and pressing tasks, were mostly promoted by the government. This was in conflict with the guideline that industrial prosperity should be "market-oriented and led by the government" [34, 35].

To address these problems, there should be appropriate adjustments of China's industrial development model for poverty alleviation to make it better align with industrial prosperity. First, we need to optimize top-level design and make overall, long-term planning. Compared with industrial development, industrial prosperity is a protracted war, and projects with little investment and short-term gains cannot bear the heavy responsibility of industrial prosperity. Therefore, poor areas need to fully evaluate the local resource endowment conditions and market trends to plan local industrial projects on a well-informed basis. Local governments should not blindly pursue the short-term income of poor households, but take a long-term view of sustainable development to help poor households stay out of poverty. Second, we will integrate the development of primary, secondary and tertiary industries and extend the industrial chain for poverty alleviation. In addition to developing traditional planting, farming and breeding industries, local cultural and natural landscape resources should be fully tapped to develop the tourism industry. Efforts should be made to actively develop e-commerce and expand the market for agricultural and sideline products through online channels. Third, the leading capacity of new business operators for rural development should be enhanced, together with the standardization of the operation of rural cooperatives and the improvement of the incentive mechanism for leading enterprises in poor areas to participate in industrial development, as well as a sound interest coupling mechanism between new business operators and poor households. Fourth, the government should give full play to the leading role of the market by transforming its own functions and the role from a promoter of industrial development into that of a leader and regulator.

8.5.2 Employment for Poverty Alleviation in Rural Revitalization

According to Guidelines on the Implementation of Rural Revitalization Strategy issued by the central leadership, a well-off life is fundamental to rural revitalization. Currently, hundreds of millions of Chinese migrant workers work in cities, and non-farm employment is their main source of income. Therefore, to solve the employment of villagers to improve their income and get better-off is the top priority in the present stage. In the process of targeted poverty alleviation, employment has been the key part of the whole strategy. Its positive effect on poverty eradication has also been supported by scholars in their studies. According to the World Bank, labor income for the poor is a more effective way to reduce poverty than cash [36]. Zhang and Zhou [37] found through their research on cases in China that providing employment to the urban poor could effectively increase their labor supply, thereby increasing their income and achieving the purpose of poverty alleviation and reduction. Therefore, under the backdrop of the rural revitalization strategy, targeted employment should still be carried out to eliminate poverty and improve people's livelihood [38]. Meanwhile, the models of employment should be adapted to the needs of rural revitalization.

This requires the combination of employment with the motivation of self-belief of the rural poor and support of education to stimulate the awareness of their own principal role in rural revitalization. The employment can be coupled with industrial development to not only increase villagers' income, but also accumulate material foundation for rural revitalization [39]. More work should be done to improve the employment quality of rural poor and to eliminate employment discrimination to prevent the occurrence of "working poverty" [40]. Poor people should be encouraged to find jobs locally or work as migrant labor in the rural labor service export program. Public welfare jobs should be created with the building of beautiful villages [8].

8.5.3 *Relocation for Poverty Alleviation in Rural Revitalization*

About 9.81 million people have been involved in the relocation program, which is an important part of China's poverty alleviation efforts. The work has not only helped rural poor from inhospitable areas shake off poverty but also provided valuable experience on how to plan the layout of the resettlement site, how to promote social integration of the relocated households, and how to help them find jobs after relocation. Many worthy attempts have been made for village-based relocation to draw on in rural revitalization [8].

However, there are still many areas to be improved in the relocation program in order to better connect poverty alleviation with rural revitalization.

First, advancing the industrial development level of the relocation areas. Industrial prosperity is the key to rural revitalization. However, in many resettlement sites, there are only single-structured, small-sized and low-tech industries which can absorb limited labor. Therefore, the government should pay attention to the industrial development of the relocation site before carrying out the relocation.

Second, turning former homes of the poor into farmland or woodland. Improvement of the eco-environment in these areas is a vital step for rural revitalization and an important measure to restore and improve the rural ecological environment. The reasons for relocation should be explained to the poor and the incentive mechanism should be improved for primary-level officials to carry out the reclamation and reforestation.

Third, strengthening education and training for relocated poor people. Cultural and ethical progress is the guarantee for rural revitalization. Affected by some outmoded customs for a long time, some relocated rural poor still stick to undesirable habits and backward mentality, resulting in their behaviors incompatible with modern community life. Therefore, the local government should place importance to both material and cultural progress by updating outmoded customs and guiding the relocated poor households with core values of socialism.

Fourth, improving community management services. Effective governance is the foundation of rural revitalization. The primary-level Party organizations and self-governing committees in centralized resettlement sites have been newly established and much work is still in the piloting stage. Poor populations in resettlement sites come from different villages, which increase the challenge of management, making it more difficult for the current community management service to meet their needs. Therefore, local governments should focus on improving the administration of resettlement sites to develop a governance system combining autonomy, rule by law and rule by virtue.

Fifth, stabilizing the income sources of relocated villagers. A better-off life is the guarantee of rural revitalization. In their former homes, the rural poor lived on their land. When they have relocated, they must rely on non-agricultural employment for a better living. Therefore, on the one hand local governments should promote labor exports, and fully develop local employment positions on the other hand to ensure the employment and income increase of relocated villagers.

8.5.4 Ecological Conservation for Poverty Alleviation in Rural Revitalization

Ecological conservation for poverty alleviation and ecological revitalization are inherently consistent, and they are both the expression of the unity of environmental protection and industrial development under the guidance of the thought that "lucid waters and lush mountains are invaluable assets" [41]. There are various practical poverty alleviation methods through ecological conservation in line with local conditions, such as ecological subsidies, ecotourism, fallow and rotation farming, among others, which have provided a lot of valuable experience for ecological revitalization [3].

Although poverty alleviation through ecological conservation and ecological revitalization are inherently consistent, they have different emphases. The former has the focus on poverty alleviation, while the latter puts emphasis on ecological conservation. Ecological conservation for poverty alleviation aims to improve the natural and geographical environment as well as local production and living conditions to increase the income of poor people by protecting the eco-environment. Ecological revitalization has its focus on good eco-environment, better living environment, rural pollution control and green agricultural development, with the major concern on the protection of natural environment rather than the increase of income.

Owing to the fact that there is a tight schedule for targeted poverty alleviation and the economic benefits from ecological conservation do not come quickly, this model does not account for a large proportion in the overall benefits of poverty alleviation. In contrast, rural revitalization is a foundation for the realization of China's second Centennial Goal and allows more prospects for development and historical patience [41]. In addition, the implementation of ecological revitalization will bring more opportunities and greater development for poverty alleviation through ecological conservation.

8.5.5 Education for Poverty Alleviation in Rural Revitalization

Human resources are indispensable for the implementation of strategies of poverty alleviation and rural revitalization, and boosting education is their common requirement. From the current situation, education can effectively block the intergenerational transmission of poverty and help poverty alleviation. In the long run, education helps reserve a large number of local human resources for rural revitalization [42]. In addition, poverty alleviation through education enriches the cultural life of the poor, improves their comprehensive quality and promotes rural culture in general [43]. It can be seen that there is a strong consistency and synergy between education for poverty alleviation and rural revitalization.

In order to further deepen the consistency and synergy between the two, education for poverty alleviation can be further adjusted and improved from the following aspects. Firstly, the non-compulsory education stage should be included in the education security system by focusing on increasing the penetration rate of preschool education and the enrollment rate of senior high school education [8]; secondly, local governments should invest more in building rural kindergartens and encourage social sectors to establish kindergartens by providing supervision and guidance [44]; thirdly, the team building of rural teaching staff should be strengthened by improving their salary, with preferential policies for rural teachers in their career development and professional promotion [45].

8.5.6 Healthcare for Poverty Alleviation in Rural Revitalization

One of the major concerns in the poverty alleviation campaign is the basic guarantee of medical services for the poor. The priority of the policy has been to make healthcare affordable and accessible to the poor. Measures have included the construction of a three-tier healthcare system at village, township and county levels, full coverage of basic medical insurance and policy-backed critical disease insurance, higher reimbursement rates, chronic disease subsidies and contracted healthcare for the impoverished, and preferential policies such as "treatment before payment" and "one-stop" settlement for inpatient treatment of serious diseases. The implementation of these policies and measures has played an important role in addressing the problem of poverty caused by illness.

In rural revitalization, most of the policies that worked in the past can be retained, and some will be extended to all rural residents. In particular, the establishment of a nationwide assistance system for major and chronic diseases will be accelerated based on the practice for poverty alleviation. However, in order to prevent the occurrence of excessive security and medical care for the poor in some areas, the level of security must be compatible with the local economic and social development and be financially sustainable. Medical and health departments should pay attention to the training of rural medical staff and general practitioners, promote the building of county-township-village medical communities and the popularization of telemedicine to substantially improve the primary-level medical services to enhance the health of the entire people [8].

8.5.7 *Social Security for Poverty Alleviation in Rural Revitalization*

Rural revitalization is a strategic measure to reduce the gap between urban and rural areas and promote social equality. Social security provides subsistence allowances for those who are completely or partially incapacitated and unable to shake off poverty through their own efforts alone, which fully embodies the principle of common prosperity under socialism and is a manifestation of keeping the promise of "leaving no one behind in shared and all-round prosperity". From this point of view, rural revitalization and poverty alleviation through social security is consistent.

The social security system has established a "safety net" of basic living security for poor areas and enhanced their capacity for further development. It has helped narrow the poverty gap, maintain social stability and provide a stable social environment for rural revitalization. To a certain extent, it releases the consumption power of poor areas and promotes the development of local economy [46]. Therefore, in the context of rural revitalization, attention should also be given to the vulnerable groups lacking independent development ability by strengthening social support based on accurate identification and dynamic monitoring and management. At the same time urban and rural social security support policies should be coordinated to achieve integrated management.

Bibliography

1. Wang, S., & Feng, Z. (2020). Logical relationship between poverty alleviation and rural revitalization. *Guizhou Social Sciences* (1), 4–6.
2. The CPC Central Committee and the State Council. (2018, September 26). *Strategic plan for rural revitalization (2018–2022).* http://www.gov.cn/zhengce/2018-09/26/content-5325534.htm
3. Dou, S., & Ye, J. (2019). Organic dovetailing and mechanism construction of rural revitalization and poverty alleviation. *Reform* (1), 19–29.
4. Lu, L., & Wu, X. (2020). Theoretical interpretation of the organic dovetailing between poverty alleviation and rural revitalization in the post-poverty alleviation period. *Contemporary World and Socialism* (2), 89–96.
5. Gao, Q. (2019). Logical relationship and policy arrangement of the organic dovetailing between poverty alleviation and rural revitalization. *Journal of Nanjing Agricultural University (Social Sciences Edition), 19*(5), 15–23, 154–155.
6. Chen, G., & Zhang, Y. (2019). On cross-regional collaboration for targeted poverty alleviation: Integration of urbanization and rural revitalization. *Chinese Public Administration* (4), 79–85.
7. Jiang, H., Zhang, Y., Ji, Y., et al. (2019). Transformation of poverty alleviation and development policy after 2020. *Review of Economic Research* (24), 104–112.
8. Wang, S., & Feng, Z. (2019). Organic dovetailing between poverty alleviation and rural revitalization: Logical relationship, implications and highlights. *Journal of Nanjing Agricultural University (Social Sciences Edition), 19*(5), 8–14, 154.
9. Ye, X., & Yin, H. (2019). From eliminating absolute poverty to alleviating relative poverty: China's poverty reduction process and its post-2020 poverty reduction strategy. *Reform* (12), 5–15.

10. Gao, Q., & Kong, X. (2020). On implications, characteristics and challenges of relative poverty and countermeasures. *Journal of Xinjiang Normal University (Philosophy and Social Sciences Edition), 41*(3), 120–128, 2.
11. Wang, X. (2020). Transformation of poverty management mechanism. *Journal of Nanjing Agricultural University (Social Sciences Edition), 20*(4), 144–151.
12. Zhang, Q., Yang, M., & Kong, M. (2020). Reflections on mechanism of relative poverty after 2020. *Expanding Horizons* (2), 26–32, 73.
13. Zuo, T., & Su, W. (2020). Strategic direction and policy choice of relative poverty management in china for rural revitalization. *Journal of Xinjiang Normal University (Philosophy and Social Sciences Edition), 41*(4), 88–96.
14. *Key to rural revitalization lies in the party leadership (policy interpretation: Focusing on No. 1 central document ④).* (2018, February 08). http://politics.people.com.cn/n1/2018/0208/c1001-29811947.html
15. Meng, T. (2020). Targeted poverty alleviation policy in rural revitalization. *Guangxi Quality Supervision Guide Periodical, 1*, 29.
16. Zhao, N. (2019). *Evolution and experience: Approaches to poverty alleviation led by the CPC since reform and opening up*. Qufu Normal University.
17. Chen, Z., Bi, J., Wu, G., et al. (2019). Current situation and evolution of poverty alleviation in China and the vision and strategic priorities after 2020. *Chinese Rural Economy* (1), 2–16.
18. Mo, G., & Yang, M. (2019). Prospects of poverty reduction in China after 2020: Turn of research and practice of targeted poverty alleviation. *Henan Social Sciences, 27*(6), 99–106.
19. Yu, Y. (2018). Issues on education for targeted poverty alleviation and management under the backdrop of rural revitalization. *Probe, 3*, 170–177.
20. Ren, Z., & Su, R. (2019). Transmission mechanism, current dilemma and innovation of countermeasures for rural medical security system against poverty. *Theoretical Exploration, 235*(1), 116–123.
21. The State Council. (2017, January 19). *Plan for the development of national education during the 13th five-year plan period*. http://www.gov.cn/zhengce/content/2017-01/19/content_5161341.htm
22. Meng, Y., Song, H., Huang, Y., et al. (2019). Performance of financial measures for targeted poverty alleviation in Jilin Province under the backdrop of rural revitalization. *Journal of Jilin Financial Research* (11), 34–39.
23. Li, S. (2016). Giving play to the supervisory role in helping targeted poverty alleviation. *CPPCC Fortnightly, 9*, 38.
24. Wang, Y., Li, Q., & Wang, W. (2019). Accelerating the building of social service system for agriculture to promote the priority development of agriculture and rural areas. *China Farmers' Cooperatives* (4), 62–63.
25. Qin, J., Zhang, P., & Chen, X. (2013). Poverty alleviation and development model of tourism industry and guarantee mechanism: A case study of Qinling-Daba mountainous area. *Journal of Southwest Minzu University (Humanities and Social Sciences Edition), 34*(7), 134–138.
26. Xu, T. (2019). *A field survey on the development of rural E-commerce service stations under the backdrop of rural revitalization strategy*. Zhejiang University of Technology.
27. Wang, S., & Liang, X. (2017). Practice and mechanism innovation of poverty alleviation by asset income. *Issues in Agricultural Economy, 38*(9), 28–37, 110.
28. Bai, J., & Wei, J. (2018). New rural governance system: Generation logic, governance function and practice path. *Xinjiang State Farming Economy* (11), 13–18.
29. Liu, J. (2020). Fostering self-belief and providing education to stimulate self-motivated development. *Co-Operative Economy & Science, 16*, 172–175.
30. Peng, Dejin, & Li, X. (2010). Industrial development programs help increase poor villagers' incomes. *New Chongqing* (2), 18–19.
31. Yu, H. (2003). More work on re-employment and promotion of the re-employment base construction through multiple channels. *Forestry of China, 14*, 42–43.
32. Liu, H. (2009). *Development ideas and countermeasures of education and training system for villagers*. Northwest A&F University.

33. Yi, Y. (2019). On industrial development for poverty alleviation and rural revitalization: Based on the concept of industrial ecology and ecological industrialization. *Food Science, Technology and Economy, 44*(2), 160–162.
34. Li, D., & Qiao, L. (2019). From industrial development for poverty alleviation to industrial prosperity: Dilemma and innovation trend in poor areas. *Truth Seeking* (6), 81–91, 109–110.
35. Liu, M., & Wang, S. (2020). Organic dovetailing between industrial development for poverty alleviation and industrial prosperity: Logical relationship, dilemma and realization path. *Journal of Northwest Normal University (Social Sciences Edition), 57*(4), 137–144.
36. The World Bank. (2012). *World development report 2013: Jobs.* World Bank.
37. Zhang, S., & Zhou, C. (2008). Labor supply effect of employment support policy for urban poor: A study based on natural experiment. *Economic Review* (6), 23–30.
38. Zhang, X., & Gao, F. (2019). Path and measures of targeted employment for poverty alleviation under the backdrop of rural revitalization strategy. *National Circulation Economy* (22), 115–116.
39. Wang, P. (2019). "To be well-educated to get prosperous": Reflections on rural revitalization assisted by employment for poverty alleviation in Xinhe County, Hebei Province. *Frontiers, 2*, 60–62.
40. Li, C. (2018). Mechanism and measures of poverty alleviation through employment under the backdrop of rural revitalization strategy. *Social Sciences in Chinese Higher Education Institutions* (6), 29–36, 154.
41. Hu, Y., Fu, R., & Jin, S. (2019). Ecological and environmental concerns in the organic dovetailing between poverty alleviation and rural revitalization. *Reform* (10), 141–148.
42. Kang, L., & Xue, W. (2019). An analysis of the strategy of promoting rural revitalization in mountainous areas of Northern Shaanxi by poverty alleviation through education: A case study of Qingjian County, Yulin City, Shaanxi Province. *Forestry Economics, 41*(2), 118–122.
43. Xiang, X. (2018). Coupling of targeted poverty alleviation and rural revitalization. *Journal of Shandong Academy of Governance, 6*, 94–98.
44. Sun, X. (2019). Implications, value and implementation path of targeted poverty alleviation through education in the context of rural revitalization strategy. *Teaching & Administration, 22*, 9–12.
45. Xu, Y., & Zhang, J. (2018). Policy prospects and implications of rural teacher support program. *Modern Primary and Secondary Education, 34*(1), 57–61.
46. Gong, P. (2017). Poverty alleviation through social security in targeted poverty alleviation and eradication. *Journal of Yunnan Minzu University (Philosophy and Social Sciences Edition), 34*(6), 89–96.
47. He, W., & Yang, Y. (2017). New explorations of financial measures for poverty alleviation: Ningxia Guyuan model. *Ningxia Social Sciences* (S1), 59–65.
48. The CPC Central Committee and the State Council. (2017, February 05). *Guidelines on deepening supply-side structural reform of agriculture and accelerating the incubation of new driving forces for agricultural and rural development.* http://www.gov.cn/Zhengce/2017-02/05/content_5165626.htm
49. The CPC Central Committee and the State Council. (2018, February 04). *Guidelines on implementing the rural revitalization strategy.* http://www.gov.cn/zhengce/2018-02/04/content_5263807.htm
50. Wang, H. (2016). Financial model for targeted poverty alleviation. *China Finance, 22*, 25–26.

The manufacturer's authorised representative in the EU is Springer Nature Customer Service Centre GmbH, Europaplatz 3, 69115 Heidelberg, Germany. If you have any concerns regarding our products, please contact ProductSafety@springernature.com

Printed and bound by CPI Group (UK) Ltd, Croydon, CR0 4YY

01/09/2026

02207166-0002